URBAN SP. ...N
AND WAYFARING
STRANGERS

Overlooked Innovators and
Eccentric Visionaries of '60s Rock

By Richie Unterberger

MF Miller
Freeman
Books

San Francisco

Published by Miller Freeman Books
600 Harrison Street, San Francisco, CA 94107
An imprint of Music Player Network
 www.MusicPlayer.com
 Publishers of Guitar Player, Bass Player, Keyboard,
   Gig, MC2, and EQ Magazines

Distributed to the book trade in the U.S and Canada by
Publisher's Group West, 1700 Fourth Street, Berkeley, CA 94710

Distributed to the music trade in the U.S. and Canada by
Hal Leonard Publishing, P.O. Box 13819, Milwaukee, WI 53213

Cover Design: Richard Leeds
Cover Photo of The Bonzo Dog Band: Michael Ochs Archives.com

Library of Congress Cataloging-in-Publication Data:

Unterberger, Richie, 1962–
    Urban spacemen and wayfaring strangers : overlooked innovators and
    eccentric visionaries of '60s rock / by Richie Unterberger.
        p. cm.
    Includes bibliographical references (p.) and indexes.
    ISBN 0-87930-616-5 (alk. paper)
    1. Rock musicians–Bibliography. 2. Rock music–1961–1970–History
    and criticism. I.
    Title.

    ML394.U66 2000
    781.66'092'2–dc21
    [B]
                                                                    00-057313

Printed in the United States of America

00 01 02 03 04 05   5 4 3 2 1

CONTENTS

Acknowledgments

An author who dives into the hidden corners of rock history needs the help of many fellow travelers to find the treasure. As with the inspiration for the music itself, help arrives from all directions, some unexpected or wholly unsuspected, and always deeply appreciated. Without such assistance, the trail to even locate many of the veteran musicians profiled in this book would have been hard and in some cases impossible to navigate. Thanks to all of the following writers, music professionals, and just plain fans who gave generously of their time and advice to help me establish contacts, set up interviews, and obtain valuable information and rare recordings: Gene Aguilera, Bill Allerton of Stand Out Records in London, Dave Blume, Cynthia Bowman, David Brown, David Carr, Irwin Chusid, Michael Clare, Alan Clayson, D. Cole, Jud Cost, Stan Denski, Raymond Dumont, Dawn Eden, Ben Edmonds, John Einarson, Shane Faubert, Bob Fisher, Tony Fitton, Ben Fong-Torres, Brett Freedman, Ken Freedman, Hector Gonzalez, Matt Greenwald, Jason Gross, Sam Hammond, Lenny Helsing, Chris Hill, Colin Hill, Brian Hogg, Jade Hubertz, Jan Hughes, Karl Ikola, Haydn Jones, Alan Korn, Harvey Kubernik, Cary E. Mansfield, Phil McMullen, Jon Mills, Alec Palao, John Platt, Susan Rabin, Andrew Sandoval, Mike Stax, Laurie Stevens, Denise Sullivan, Jeff Tamarkin, Bryan Thomas, Pat Thomas, John Tobler, Harry Viesel, and Chris Woodstra. Special thanks to Jeff Davis at Flat Plastic Sound in San Francisco for allowing me to borrow records from the store's large selection of rare and out-of-print LPs. Extra-special thanks to Pat Thomas for kindly providing access to so much rare archival material for the Richard & Mimi Fariña chapter, on such short notice.

As they did with my prior book *Unknown Legends of Rock 'n' Roll*, Miller Freeman Books gave their full support to a project that, once again, allowed me to shine a light on musical innovators that have remained out of the public eye for too long. Editors Dorothy Cox and Matt Kelsey are to be applauded for allowing so much freedom to investigate obscure and undervalued rock music, and for allowing the book to follow its own path as it developed into something rather different from, though still similar to, its predecessor. Production editor Nancy Tabor was essential to tracking down photos and songs for the accompanying CD, and for helping to design the volume, as was her colleague Gary Montalvo. Copy editor Ivy Jiggins and proofreader Roger Mensink did exemplary work on the manuscript. Sales manager Jay Kahn and marketing communications managers Corrina Cornejo and Nina Lesowitz have ensured that my Miller Freeman titles, and as a consequence the music it documents, receive maximum exposure. Paul Kantner is a well-known legend, but knows how to credit the unknown legends, and does so generously in the foreword he contributed.

Sound advice can take the shape of musical expertise, but also of friendship and emotional support as well. The counsel and feedback of Gordon Anderson, Stuart Kremsky, Susan Mallett, Dana Mayer, Janet Rosen, and Denise Sullivan are invaluable to both my writing and my well-being. Agent Robert Shepard delivered his habitual professional, knowledgeable, and sympathetic representation and recommendations. Susan Mallett and Curt Lamberth were infallibly cheerful and accommodating hosts for my five-week work/holiday stay in Oxford, England, allowing me to use their home as a base for setting up several of the interviews with British musicians. My parents Sue and Elliot were fully behind my efforts as always.

The biggest thanks of all go to the several dozen musicians, and various of their associates, who opened their hearts and minds for the interviews upon which this book is based. It wasn't always easy to find them, and it wasn't always easy for them to hash over the events of 30 to 35 years ago in fine detail. The pursuit, however, was more than amply rewarded by the results, certainly for me, and I hope for the artists themselves. And, we hope, for readers and listeners, about to enter undiscovered echoes in time that will reverberate forever.

About the Author

Richie Unterberger has been writing about little-known

and well-known rock and popular music of all kinds for nearly 20 years. His book *Unknown Legends of Rock 'n' Roll*, published by Miller Freeman in 1998, profiled 60 underappreciated cult rock artists of all styles and eras. He is also author of *The Rough Guide to Music USA*, a guidebook to the evolution of regional popular music styles throughout America in the twentieth century, and the travel guidebook *The Rough Guide to Seattle*. He is a senior editor for the All Music Guide, the largest on-line database of music biographies and album reviews. From 1985 to 1991, he was the editor of *Option*, a magazine devoted to coverage of all types of alternative and independently produced music. He is currently at work on *Turn! Turn! Turn!*, a history of the 1960s folk-rock movement. He lives in San Francisco. More information about the author, his books, and the music he documents can be found on his web site at www.richieunterberger.com. E-mail can be sent to Richie Unterberger at richieu@sirius.com.

Foreword by Paul Kantner

When I read some of my own words in the Fred Neil section of this book, a genuine tear came to my eye as I thought back to my own musical childhood and just what a force Fred was for us 1950s middle-class kids. A sweetly nostalgic tear, for the child I was, and for the paths that Freddie set me on.

As with many of the musicians chronicled in this book, Freddie set me, personally, on a path that was to be forever changed and from which there could be no retreat. That was Freddie's value to me and, I imagine, the value of the other strange creatures revealed here: their paths to heaven, hell, and everything in between.

The path less traveled…

The people in this book had their own particular place "beyond the pale." From Arthur Brown and the Pretty Things in Britain, to the Beau Brummels and Tim Buckley here in America, the world-absorbing nature of these eclectic artists and the turbulent times around them reflected a world exploding with possibility and impossible dreams. But they were dreams that often came true beyond the original intentions of any of us. Achieving some degree of success, as some of us did, my own Jefferson Airplane and the like made the path more confusing—though no less fascinating.

Freddie just led us to places that normal folksingers didn't go. His albums became as important to me as the albums of the Weavers, who were also part of my prime influence. Between the two of them, it set me off on a really good path.

The path less traveled…

This is invariably true about all the artists here, in relation to the people they eventually influenced.

Freddie imprinted me with a vital, genuine reality that served me well—the way the blues did for others of my kind. As Jorma absorbed the Reverend Gary Davis, and Jagger and Richards absorbed Howlin' Wolf, I absorbed Fred Neil. He was a tangible connection to the world of unconventional emotion. He set me on a trail, not to be like him, or to copy him, but to try to establish something as real to my own experience as Freddie's music was to his.

All of the urban spacemen and wayfaring strangers in this book contributed a certain "something" that was priceless as well as precious—then, and now. Like

Freddie, these musicians always existed beyond a certain pale…beyond beyond the pale, if you catch my drift. Their value is not necessarily so much in their individual works,

as it is in their very existence.
against all odds
into the wind

"the path less traveled"

Paul Kantner
April, 2000

Introduction

More great rock music was made in the 1960s than in any other decade. More than thirty years after that era drew to a close, its records continue to sell and get played on the radio, referenced by new generations of musicians, and, for better or for worse, licensed for lucrative commercials. There was no other time in which so many rock musicians made fabulous music *and* sold tons of records to a mainstream audience.

There was also no other time in which so many rock musicians made fabulous *unknown* music that did *not* sell tons of records, and remains virtually undiscovered by the general public. These artists crafted records that were almost as good as those of the period's prime icons. In many cases they actually influenced the sounds of the 1960s' biggest and best stars. Yet they have, to a large extent, been written out of the standard rock history available to the average listener through books, radio, the Rock and Roll Hall of Fame, and loudspeakers at major sporting events.

Urban Spacemen and Wayfaring Strangers profiles nineteen rock artists of the 1960s who did not receive (and still have not received) their full credit and acclaim. The assortment of personalities on these pages is diverse, from pop-rockers who would have liked nothing more than to be staples of AM radio, to avowedly uncommercial rebels whose very names ensured limited-to-nonexistent airplay. There are psychedelic daredevils, gentle folk-rockers, pre-worldbeat outfits, blue-eyed soul men, and even some non-musicians who made enormous contributions as producers and mentors. What links them together? The easy answer is that they are all joined by a disparity between the talent they exhibited and the lack of commercial and/or critical recognition they attained. The more complex explanation is that they are connected by an eclecticism, a willingness to take chances, and a search, conscious or unconscious, for artistic expression that led them down previously uncharted paths. These are the marks of almost any artist worthy of the name. Perhaps there were so many of them in 1960s rock in particular because so many paths in rock music had yet to be paved.

The 1960s, socially *and* musically, is probably the most analyzed (some would say overanalyzed) decade of the twentieth century. The rock giants that walked the earth—the Beatles, the Rolling Stones, Bob Dylan, Jimi Hendrix, the Beach Boys, even smaller giants like the Byrds and the odd cult giants like the Velvet Underground—have had their stories told and their work dissected many times over. This book is not an attempt to argue that the artists profiled within were better, or even as good. They *weren't* as good. They were *very* good, though. And their stories have rarely been told, or at least haven't been told often enough, or with the depth and respect they deserve.

I gave myself a similar task with my 1998 book *Unknown Legends of Rock 'n' Roll*, which profiled sixty unjustly underrated and overlooked cult rockers from the 1950s through the 1980s. *Urban Spaceman and Wayfaring Strangers* is a sequel of sorts, but is not exactly an *Unknown Legends of Rock 'n' Roll Vol. 2*. It started out that way. Books have a way of taking on a life of their own, however, and this one took me down a somewhat different path than its predecessor. Its ultimate direction had much to do with how I got involved with documenting obscure rock 'n' roll in the first place.

I don't remember the 1960s, because I wasn't there. At least, having been born in 1962, I wasn't old enough to experience the music *of* the time *at* the time. It was the rock of the 1960s, however, that moved and fascinated me the most as I became old enough to buy records. For me, the love of the music started with the most popular musicians on earth, the Beatles, just as it did and continues to do for so many rock fans. That love led me next to the other music of the era, starting, as it also did for so many, with the Rolling Stones, and then working down the ladder to the Who, the Kinks, the Yardbirds, the Jefferson Airplane, and others. It wasn't until 1979, at the age of seventeen, that I made my way to a 1960s band that could fairly be considered an obscure cult act. That was Love, whose 1967 *Forever Changes* album was the first record I bought by a band that no one I knew had ever heard. Its greatness was an indication that there was far more terrific music out there awaiting discovery than I even knew existed.

Throughout the 1980s and 1990s, I came into contact with a wealth of music that was impossible, or nearly impossible, to learn about through mainstream media channels. Working as a programmer at my college radio station, editing a magazine devoted to independent and alternative music of all sorts, and writing freelance reviews and articles for numerous books and publications, I heard an enormous amount of rock, soul, folk, jazz, and blues from throughout the twentieth century. Yet the rock of the 1960s, and particularly of the last half of the 1960s, continued to absorb me more than any other music did. These seemed more explosive years than any others for fueling unexpected innovations in rock music. There were so many directions to explore, so many nuggets to retrieve, and so many unpredictable sounds that had been conjured by musicians from all over the globe, influencing each other in obvious and subtle ways that were often unbeknownst even to themselves.

Some of these wonderful and (not necessarily) weird 1960s artists were profiled in *Unknown Legends of Rock 'n' Roll*, including Syd Barrett, Nick Drake, Skip Spence, the Misunderstood, and my old favorites Love. Even so, sixty chapters, only a portion of which were devoted to acts from the 1960s, were insufficient space to get to even half of the worthy underappreciated rockers from that epoch. When positive response to *Unknown Legends of Rock 'n' Roll* merited a follow-up, I determined that I'd focus entirely on overlooked performers that had emerged in the 1960s, repeating none of the selections from *Unknown Legends*. Again, I based these profiles around firsthand interviews with the artists themselves, or with close associates of theirs in cases where they were dead or inaccessible.

Furthermore, I decided to do far fewer chapters, allowing me far greater space to tell each story and far greater depths to plumb for each artist covered. This also allowed me latitude to cover artists whose multifaceted careers defied summarization in two or three thousand words, and also artists who were somewhat better known—though still not exactly *well* known—than the average ones documented in *Unknown Legends of Rock 'n' Roll*. In the introduction to that book, I lamented that space and balance considerations excluded chapters on some of my personal favorite cult rockers, specifically citing the Pretty Things, Tim Buckley, the Fugs, and the Bonzo Dog Band. To my enormous satisfaction, all four of those artists are included in this book.

There are those rock fans, both in the above-ground media and subterranean fanzines and indie record stores, who would claim that there has been enough written about 1960s rock already. Empty nostalgia, they decry. The 1960s are over, and they didn't change the world. Write about some new bands that really need the exposure, instead of retired or semiretired dinosaurs. Stop living in the past. Crank up that drum 'n' bass.

Such critics are missing a couple of essential points. First, writing about a bygone era of popular music in fine detail is not necessarily arguing that new music should not be covered as well, or that music of the past is better or more valid than that of the present. More important, when you go down the ladder of rock history, past the Beatles and then the Kinks and then even the Velvet Underground, to the Pretty Things and Fred Neil and even further to Randy Holden, there are certainly few grounds for calling it an exercise in nostalgia. You can't be nostalgic about music you didn't hear, or barely heard, until twenty or thirty years after it was made. That goes for those who were old enough to have experienced the 1960s directly but never had the opportunity to hear many great bands, or for those too young to even remember the 1960s at all, who first heard these artists long after their best records were issued. Young and old alike are not being drawn to 1960s cult rockers by nostalgia for the era. They're being drawn by the *music*, which has passed the test of great art and lasted. And they're discovering the records and the stories behind them with the same kind of excited enthusiasm that listeners feel when they discover current acts. Vault-combers at Ace, Rhino, Sundazed, Distortions, and other labels are continuing to unearth forgotten or even newly discovered recordings from the time—some great, some indifferent, some lousy—even as you read this. Why is it, though, that this era in particular continues to inspire so much fanaticism?

In a 1987 issue of the fanzine *Swellsville*, Dave Beltane opened his review of a forgotten 1969 gem of an album by Judy Henske and Jerry Yester (see the chapter in *Unknown Legends of Rock 'n' Roll* for further details) with an interesting observation: "Someday someone will have to do a case study on why the 1960s produced so many forgotten classic records, despite being the last era in which good music was constantly being created by those in the public eye." *Urban Spacemen and Wayfaring Strangers* is not that case study, nor are its nineteen chapters individual case studies. There are too many complex musical, social, and economic factors at work to answer that question in a few hundred pages, and the following profiles seek to celebrate the music rather than explicate its sociological context. There *are* some between-the-lines answers to those questions in these pages, and it might help to muse upon some possible forces at work before the journey begins.

The chief culprit—and I say this only half tongue-in-cheek—is our capitalistic economic system. Records are marketed, to a large degree, via radio airplay and other media exposure in television, videos, print reviews, and films. In the 1960s, regional radio charts and reports, as well as nationwide industry charts, could greatly affect how many radio stations, stores, and distributors broadcast or sold a certain artist's record. At any given time, not just the 1960s, there simply is not enough room on the airwaves, the charts, and the record racks to accommodate all of the records and artists making good music. Saturation airplay for masterpiece blockbusters by the Beatles, Stones, and the Who made it that much less likely you'd hear that album by the Fugs. It was not until the very end of the decade that FM radio took off and it became easier to hear album-oriented, more alternative-minded artists; in the United Kingdom, there were far fewer radio stations of any kind than there were in the United States. Moreover, as we all know, decisions on what records to play and push are not always, and perhaps not often, based on their musical quality. That is why, even if you were listening to rock voraciously in the 1960s, you may have barely or never heard Kaleidoscope, Dino Valenti, or the Bonzo Dog Band.

There were other forces at work that ensured you never heard some of the other records described in this volume. One is regionalism. Some great British bands like the Pretty Things, the Poets, and the Creation never made it to the U.S. and never enjoyed radio or label support here, if their records even got released on these shores. Groups like the Rationals and Thee Midniters were pretty big in their hometowns, at a time when radio airplay was less homogenous across the country, but couldn't get a national foothold due to weak distribution and other bad breaks. And at a time when the full-length album was just coming into its own as a vehicle for ambitious statements, it could be that all you heard of a group was its big hit single. This meant that numerous songs by great acts—such as the Left Banke, Bobby Fuller, the Beau Brummels, even a wild psychedelic artist like Arthur Brown who lucked into a fluke international hit—were barely known to most listeners. For those committed to hearing *only* nonmainstream stuff, college and noncommercial radio were in their infancy, and not nearly as much of a factor in the exposure of obscure music as they are today. Viewed from these angles, one is amazed not so much that so much fine music escaped notice, but that so much great music *did* achieve widespread notice on crassly commercial vehicles such as AM radio and prime-time variety shows.

The ultimate consequence of all this was that even the most dedicated listener could not possibly have heard all or most of the fine music being made at the time of its release. That's true of music at any time in history, of course, which is why it takes a lifetime to catch up on goodies you missed from the past. The narrower and perhaps more interesting question becomes: why such an abundance of unheralded treasures specifically from the 1960s? There is an overwhelming interest in excavating rock from 1964-1969. There is *not*, not yet anyway, a correspondingly overwhelming interest in excavating rock from 1972-1975, or rock from 1984-1988.

The answer lies, I believe, not so much in superior skills and imagination of the musicians, as in an especially fertile confluence of styles and elements specific to the era. In 1964 and 1965, there were not one but two major upheavals in rock that were totally unexpected: the British Invasion of bands from the U.K., and the combining of folk and rock music into folk-rock. Folk music and British rock had barely been considered as influences by rock musicians prior to this; the arrival of these styles sparked a myriad of untapped possibilities. At the same time, soul music was peaking at Motown, Atlantic, and Stax; studio and instrument technology was drastically increasing the diversity of sounds that could be coaxed from electric guitars and keyboards; and songwriting was breaking into new subject matter that strayed far beyond romantic love. Nonmusical movements infiltrated rock as well, with the drug culture influencing the course of psychedelia, and antiwar protests affecting the stances and songs of almost everyone who wanted to make a difference. Every juncture in time is surrounded by musical and social changes that affect the sounds of the era. In rock music, at no other time did such major and so many changes happen in such a short period of time as they did during the mid-to-late 1960s.

With the artists in *Urban Spacemen and Wayfaring Strangers*, this was reflected in an eclecticism that was willing to draw from almost anything. This was mirrored by the two songs honored by the title of this book. The Bonzo Dog Band had its one British hit with "I'm the Urban Spaceman," mixing daft comedy, English vaudevillian instrumentation, and psychedelic imagery on a single produced by a pseudonymous Paul McCartney. "Wayfaring Stranger" was a traditional folk standard done by no fewer than three different artists in this book, all in radically different fashions: Dino Valenti did an intense acoustic folk troubadour version, the Rationals made it a garage-surf rock instrumental, and Tim Buckley gave it a sensitive folk-jazz-rock interpretation. (Another group that could have well qualified for this book, H. P. Lovecraft, did a psychedelic-tinged hard rock rendition.) The different ways these musicians treated their material was indicative of the unlimited sense of possibility felt throughout rock in the 1960s. Too, the very names of the songs are revealing of a recklessly pioneering sensibility. So many of the musicians in the 1960s were urban spacemen (or spacewomen) of sorts, committed to exploring the furthest reaches of space and the psyche, but also grounded in the gritty realism of the street and the city. Everyone in this book was a wayfaring stranger, investigating strange new avenues of musical experimentation, in an open-minded fashion that allowed them to wander into different alleys as the tides of their environment shifted.

Documenting the courses of these wayfaring strangers leads to unsuspected detours and bypasses that might be similar to those undergone by the musicians way back when. Much of rock history, not to mention much history of all kinds, tends to retroactively classify performers into cubbyholes of genres and mini-genres, largely separate from each other's spheres of influence. Some would say, for instance, that the Pretty Things and Fugs were in this corner as pre-punks, Kaleidoscope and Arthur Brown in that corner as weird psychedelicists; Bobby Fuller and the Left Banke over there as pure pop people; Dino Valenti and Fred Neil over thataway as singer-songwriters; and so on. There are those mainstream outlets that view the era solely in terms of its major star performers—again, the Beatles, the Stones, and so on—and dismiss those who didn't get a wide audience as irrelevant or insignificant. In an equally misguided fashion, there are those who insist that only those performers who anticipated later punk and new wave sounds—usually the Velvet Underground, MC5, Stooges, Captain Beefheart, and some mid-1960s garage bands—are relevant in the modern age.

One of the rewards of doing a project such as this is that research exposes such stances for the artificial party lines they are. Yes, the Pretty Things were pre-punks; they also innovated the precise kind of psychedelic rock opera that many punks detest. Yes, Kaleidoscope did some weird psychedelic music, but it also did several varieties of folk-rock. Yes, the Pretty Things were scruffy rhythm and blues wildmen; they also gladly admit to being influenced by some performers, such as the Doors and the Fifth Dimension, that are trashed by many fanzines that exult the Pretty Things' gospel. Yes, the Fugs were rabid antiestablishment comedians. They also worked with Harry Belafonte's backup singers, recorded for Frank Sinatra's label, and employed guitarists who were later integral to the most popular recordings by James Taylor, Linda Ronstadt, Jackson Browne, and Carole King.

Similarly, innovations could be sparked by influences from the most unsuspected sources, sometimes transmitted from wavelengths totally outside of the rock 'n' roll arena. Thee Midniters played pounding garage punk on occasion, but also had horn arrangements inspired by the Jazz Crusaders. Giorgio Gomelsky remembers how his admiration of classical harpsichordist Wanda Landowska influenced his production of the Yardbirds' first hit, "For Your Love." The Fugs set poems by William Blake to song. Richard Fariña drew upon his literary background, as a published poet and novelist, for the songs he wrote to sing with his wife, Mimi Fariña. Tim Buckley wrote the melody to "Hallucinations" after listening to an album of Moroccan street music. History is more complex than a convenient division of the good guys versus the bad ones, the right stylistic choices versus the wrong ones, and if the 1960s was about anything, it was about keeping your mind open to anyone and anything.

In a less contentious fashion, digging into these artists' careers also reveals the relatively undocumented exchange of influences not only among themselves, but between them and much more famous acts. Arthur Brown believes the success of his first album helped fund the Who's much more widely known *Tommy*. The members of Kaleidoscope see the possible effect of their world music sandwich on the Grateful Dead and, much later, Camper Van Beethoven, and note how Jimmy Page—who named Kaleidoscope as one of his favorite bands—used a violin bow technique on his electric guitar similar to the one they had employed. Randy Holden speculates on how his volume-smashing technology aroused the interest of Jimi Hendrix. Giorgio Gomelsky recalls how, in 1963, he worked on a treatment of a film for the Beatles with ideas that resurfaced in *A Hard Day's Night*.

In addition, cult artists influenced each other, in ways they sometimes remain unaware of to this day. The Pretty Things, for instance, were virtually unknown in the United States, yet a couple of American musicians I interviewed could barely contain their enthusiasm for the group when its name came up in conversation. It also turned out that various people in the book knew and had even worked with others about whom I was writing. So it is that Arthur Brown talks about a collaboration on a "brain opera" with the Bonzo Dog Band; Larry Beckett, Tim Buckley's lyricist, remembers how he and Tim were inspired by watching Fred Neil record; Cyrus Faryar excitedly recalls his associations with both Neil *and* Dino Valenti; George Gallacher of the Poets remembers being bowled over by the savage power of the Pretty

Things at a London club gig, not suspecting that the Poets would be touring with the Pretty Things a year later. Such connections are not mere trivia, to be exclusively hoarded by record collectors who rarely venture into the sunlight. They are the connections that are the hidden lifeblood of rock history.

In doing a book such as this one, the writer becomes as much of a wayfaring stranger as the subjects in navigating the winding paths leading to interviews, and in conducting the interviews themselves. That began with the actual selection of who to include, which inevitably meant bypassing some worthy candidates and making extra-special efforts to include others. Even taken together with the 1960s artists profiled in *Unknown Legends of Rock 'n' Roll*, the musicians featured in this volume by no means represent all of the overlooked rockers of the time worthy of examination, or even all of the best of them. My goal was to present a cross section of many of the most interesting ones, varying in both style and level of recognition. Thus you'll find British Invasion bands, folk-rockers, psychedelic trailblazers, rock satirists, soul–rockers, pop-rockers, and producers. Some of them even had a huge hit single or two; some were briefly fairly successful album sellers; some are known mostly for the songs they wrote, covered with greater sales figures by others; some were big in their home cities, but not elsewhere; and some just weren't big anyway, anyhow, anywhere. They are grouped into seven sections in the book, but those are only meant as loose categories; the Fugs, Kaleidoscope, and the Beau Brummels could all fit into folk-rock almost as well as they fit into the areas to which they were assigned, for instance. Wherever they're placed, they're all underrated. I promise you.

As with *Unknown Legends of Rock 'n' Roll*, I also decided to only include acts that I was passionately curious about, regardless of the reputations of certain others among some critics and cultists. For that reason the Seeds, the Standells, the Silver Apples, Pearls Before Swine, Os Mutantes, the West Coast Pop Art Experimental Band, Roy Harper, Tim Hardin, and others—most of whom I quite like to some degree, some of whom I don't like much at all—did not make the cut, the slack to be taken up, perhaps, by some future book or other writer. Some bands that I like quite a bit had such brief careers (the C. A. Quintet, J. K. & Co., Blackburn & Snow) that it would have been difficult to give them a chapter of the length accorded to all the ones in these pages. A few artists I would have liked dearly to include—crucial folk-rockers Jackie DeShannon and P. F. Sloan, and Roy Wood of the Move—did not respond to interview requests. Regretfully I left these artists out, as I felt first-hand perspective and memories essential to the work. The one case I violated this rule (other than for the artists now dead, in which case I interviewed close associates) was for Fred Neil, who has not done an interview in more than thirty years, and whom I was determined to spotlight, which I did with the help of several people who knew him and played on his records.

As with *Unknown Legends of Rock 'n' Roll*, one of the most rewarding aspects of undertaking the project was the opportunity to gauge the reactions of artists to the belated acclaim for their achievements. As with *Unknown Legends of Rock 'n' Roll*, this varied widely, from near-shock to polite contentment to indifference. Things were nonetheless somewhat different this time around. As any journalist can tell you, the difficulty of arranging an interview is directly proportional to the fame of the subject. Similarly, the enthusiasm of the interview subject for participating is directly proportional to his or her obscurity. The artists profiled in *Urban Spacemen and Wayfaring Strangers* were, if not household names, certainly better known on the average than the ones in *Unknown Legends of Rock 'n' Roll*, and are not as easily flattered by the attention. All are well into middle age—a couple are senior citizens—and not necessarily interested in dwelling upon what happened thirty to forty years ago. Some, indeed, are not particularly flattered that someone wishes to put them in a book in the first place.

Our conversations veered between congenial ease and, less frequently, inhibited tension. One musician clearly would have rather been undergoing root canal work than talking to almost anyone at almost any time about almost anything, and divulged bits about the past in occasional paragraph-long spurts that made me pray the tape didn't need to be flipped over in the middle of a rare recollection. Others granted the interview with wary reluctance, but couldn't shut up once the memories gained momentum. One key talk took nine months of back-and-forth to set up. Others were ready to start as soon as I introduced myself over the phone.

Impressions from records and album sleeves meant nothing. Arthur Brown, for example, might have been expected to be a hard case, judging from his image as a god-of-hellfire singing about devils and spontaneous apple creations. Not so; he invited me to his house immediately over the phone and, on the eve of a flight to Spain to play at a rock festival, welcomed me as he would a dear friend, the perfect host as he prepared health food snacks and went over his career in fond, exacting detail. The Pretty Things made their name as riot-inciting punks in the mid-1960s; guitarist Dick Taylor made sure my tea was hot as he spoke with me for a couple of hours in the band's rehearsal space, although he had to drive back from London to the Isle of Wight that night. One interviewee was rumored to have earned millions from a particularly advantageous contractual settlement in the 1960s. Another was living on the dole in the United Kingdom, with an income of seventy-seven pounds a week. For those connected to the Internet—a much more common situation than it had been even three years previously, when I was researching *Unknown Legends of Rock 'n' Roll*—the E-mail messages flew fast and furious, especially when it came to correcting or elaborating upon small but significant points regarding their careers.

Despite some initial reservations, however, those interviewed were usually quite willing to speak about their experiences. They became more willing, in many cases, when it became evident that the conversations would focus mostly upon their music, and not solely upon their only famous songs. That would seem like a given with a book such as this, but one has to remember that when these musicians were first emerging, what press attention there was usually focused on their lifestyles, likes and dislikes, and celebrity gossip, not their creative process. Almost all of them have been interviewed at various points over the last few decades. However, they have not often, or sometimes ever, had the opportunity to speak in depth about their recordings, their songwriting, their inspirations, and their vision. In most cases, the opportunity—even if it arrives 35 years after their recording debut—is almost always welcomed, and sometimes deeply appreciated. On occasion, as with Chris Darrow of Kaleidoscope, they were not only eager to talk about themselves, but have also developed a sense of how important it is to help make the impossibly complex and thrilling mosaic of rock history clearer as a whole.

That is not to say that they, and I, didn't pass through some awkward moments as the scrutiny intensified. Careers in the music business, unfortunately, are rife with conflicts with record labels, managers, promoters, and, especially in band situations, other musicians. Accounts sometimes differed with those reported previously in other publications; sometimes accounts of key incidents even differed among members of the same group. Some memories were particularly painful to rake over, as when they involved the death of a band mate or collaborator who happened to have also been a brother or best friend. When controversial issues were raised, particularly regarding the exits of some musicians from bands, or who was responsible for certain songs or productions that had been contested, people's voices would sometimes trail off or they'd mumble into their shirts. Time does not entirely heal all wounds.

A disadvantage of compiling a book like this is that memories have inevitably faded to some degree over the decades. An advantage, on the other hand, is that time has healed *most* wounds and given the artists a perspective on their work that they might not have had when they were in the middle of creating it. With few exceptions, they're *still* creating it, whether performing live in bars and pubs, doing informal recording for small-label CDs, or even developing ideas and albums with hopes of making money and selling units. When I spoke to Willie Garcia of Thee Midniters, for example, he was finishing a CD, produced by David Hidalgo of Los Lobos, that will likely give him more nationwide attention than he's ever had. The Pretty Things find themselves more popular in the United States than they've ever been, and toured the country extensively in 1999—the first time their late-1960s lineup had made it over. Far from being embittered about not having been able to come over in the 1960s when the opportunity seemed obvious, they cheerfully figured it was better late than never.

Yet even when the musicians *are* embittered toward the music industry, those ill feelings rarely spill over to the fans who appreciate their work, even if it's taken nearly forever for the records to find their most devoted audience. These artists know that it's the music that counts from the 1960s, more than the psychedelic Fillmore posters that sell for absurdly high prices on the Internet, more than the tie-dye shirts or Beatle boots, more than the excessive drug-taking and passing fashion fads. The disappointments at not reaching more listeners, and in most cases not getting the chance to fulfill their maximum artistic potential, may never be alleviated. Great music endures indefinitely, however, no matter when it's finally heard. It is that music and its creators' voices that this book honors.

Richie Unterberger
San Francisco

Made in Britain, Lost in America

In a decade marked by rapid and unexpected musical change, nothing changed rock as quickly and decisively as the British Invasion did. The massive influence of the Beatles, the Rolling Stones, and other major British bands such as the Who, Kinks, and Yardbirds is well known. For all the boatloads of groups who crossed the water to the United States, however, many remained behind on the British Isles. Even some that had hits in the United Kingdom were known in America only on a cult level, in an era when few shops stocked import singles and LPs. The members of one such cult band, the Who—who were barely known in the U.S. before 1967—would eventually make it over, build a following, and become superstars there as well as at home. Most cult bands did not even make it over (in the 1960s, at least), and are still cult bands. At least their albums are easier to find now, in the import or even domestic bins, than they were when the bands were in their heyday.

The Pretty Things and the Poets are filed pretty close to each other in the album racks, but might seem at first glance to be opposites. The Pretties were known for both torrential Rolling Stones-styled R&B and psychedelic rock operas; the Poets specialized in delicate, almost folky ballads. The Pretty Things had a few big and small British hits; the Poets had one small British hit and nothing else chartwise. The Pretty Things are still going in 2000, and indeed might be better known in the United States now than they've ever been; the Poets only put out a half dozen singles, and by 1967 had changed personnel so many times as to become unrecognizable. The Pretty Things were from London; the Poets from Scotland. And so on.

Yet in some ways the Pretty Things and the Poets are a good match, and, as is so often the case among bands from a similar era, close inspection reveals unexpected close connections. The Pretty Things were founded by an early member of the Rolling Stones; the Poets were managed by the Rolling Stones' first manager. Poets lead singer George Gallacher is one of several musicians who recalls being blown away by the Pretty Things' live show; a year after he first saw them, the Pretty Things and the Poets toured with each other and sometimes even joined each other onstage. To some degree the bands explored opposite poles of the British Beat Boom, the Pretties the most raucous and bluesy one, the Poets the most melodic one. However, the Pretties could be subtle and melodic, and the Poets could unleash some ferocious rock 'n' roll, when the occasion warranted. The Pretty Things might have a dozen or so CDs available as of early 2000, and the Poets not a single legitimate one. But both groups are treasured on both sides of the Atlantic by 1960s aficionados for an originality and uncompromised vision that exceeded many a more famous British Invader.

The Pretty Things in the mid-1960s. Left to right: John Stax, Brian Pendleton, Phil May, Viv Prince, Dick Taylor. Credit: Courtesy Snapper Music.

The Pretty Things

It's **June 6, 1999,** and the Pretty Things have just finished a rehearsal, climaxing with "Rosalyn," the 1964 debut single that took the British blues-rock pioneered by the Rolling Stones to its punkiest extremes. In a few days, they'll play the 100 Club on Oxford Street, one of the dives where they built their following thirty-five years ago. That very weekend, the Rolling Stones are also playing in London. It's across town from the 100 Club, in a somewhat larger venue, Wembley Stadium.

Pretty Things guitarist Dick Taylor used to be in the Rolling Stones back in 1962. The band he founded after leaving—and the one he's still playing with—had a few hits in Britain, and provoked more than a few comparisons with the Rolling Stones, back in the mid-1960s. While the Rolling Stones conquered America, though, the Pretty Things stayed on the other side of the Atlantic, never touring the States in the 1960s, their music known to just a handful of U.S. record collectors.

"Now we're a cult band," says the still-gaunt Taylor as he sips tea. "As with all these decisions, we can't go to a parallel universe where you *do* go to America. And I can't go to a parallel universe where I'm still in the Rolling Stones," he laughs without bitterness. One senses that Taylor would much rather be playing to the true believers at the 100 Club than the sea of anonymity at Wembley in any case—and that he certainly has no regrets about ending up in the Pretty Things rather than the world's second-biggest rock 'n' roll band. "Commercial success was never particularly on our agenda," declares Taylor.

Taylor's pride in his lot is not perverse, but entirely justified. For the Pretty Things were unquestionably the finest British group of the 1960s not to have a hit in the United States. That inexplicable failure to tour the United States, causing them to be overlooked entirely in the tidal wave of British Invasion rock, provides the hook to most stories on the Pretty Things, but is hardly the whole tale. The Pretty Things were frontline pioneers of not just one, but two major styles of British rock, playing blues-R&B-rock with a savage power second to none in the mid-1960s, then taking experimental psychedelia into the stratosphere in the latter part of the decade.

Along the way were a number of firsts and mileposts, including the singer with the longest hair bar none among British mid-'60s rockers; the drummer who set the standards for modern rock looniness, predating even Keith Moon; the creation of the first rock opera, predating (and probably influencing) the Who's *Tommy*; and, in 1998, what was likely the first broadcast of a rock opera live on the Internet. In the 1960s, no group, American or British, made as much fine music that remains unknown to the mainstream, and almost entirely neglected by rock history books. The band members' explosive personalities and devotion to on-the-edge music making may have ensured that they did not become established stars. Those are the very qualities, however, that have enabled the Pretty Things' cult following to thrive over the last three decades, drawing new generations of listeners and—as the millennium comes to a close—according the Pretties a widespread critical respect denied many more famous bands of their age.

If there is one phrase overused to describe the Pretty Things' early sound, it's "a rawer version of the Rolling Stones." (Indeed, one of the musicians interviewed for this book—Scott Morgan, of the fine Michigan group the Rationals—described the Pretty Things to me, without any prompting, as "an even more raw version of the Rolling Stones.") The similarity did not arise from imitation, however, but from deeply shared musical and cultural roots. Dick Taylor attended the same grammar school as Mick Jagger in the London suburb of Dartford, and, in the early 1960s, began playing R&B with him for fun in a group called Little Boy Blue & the Blue Boys. At Sidcup Art School, Taylor made the acquaintance of fellow student and R&B enthusiast Keith Richards. When Jagger and Richards, childhood friends who had not been in contact with each other for years, ran into each other on a train, they discovered that they both knew Taylor, and it was natural for Richards to enter the Blue Boys' rehearsals.

Taylor continued to play with Richards and Jagger for a time as the group became more serious, changing its name to the Rolling Stones and adding other musicians, most notably yet another guitarist, Brian Jones. In hindsight, one group was not large enough to accommodate Jones, Richards, and Taylor, all guitarists with distinctive styles and musical visions. It was Taylor who got the squeeze, and although he might have been able to continue with the group if he'd been willing to accept the bass player position, he amicably drifted away from the ensemble, many months before they began recording. Although some would view this as a rotten turn of events, Taylor turned this to his advantage by helping to found a similar band that would allow him the lead guitar spot, and a much greater role in songwriting and musical direction than would have likely been possible in the Rolling Stones. The singer would be another Sidcup Art School student, Phil May, who happened to look a bit like Mick Jagger, with even longer (especially by 1963 standards) hair.

The British blues movement was taking off in the early 1960s under the guidance of "purist" older musicians, especially Alexis Korner, who were dedicated to preserving and recreating classical traditional blues forms. The Pretty Things, like the Rolling Stones and other younger bands, had something different in mind. "The Pretty Things found, in people like Jimmy Reed, Howlin' Wolf, and Muddy Waters, a kindred music we could identify with," says May more than thirty-five years later, over beer at his neighborhood London pub. "Where we stood, in society, being art students, was right on the fringe. The urgency where *we* were standing was overlaid on songs about being marginalized and fucked up by society. That's what was happening to us.

"But we weren't respectful in the fact we *didn't* copy it. We played it fast because we were seventeen, eighteen years old. We added some kind of thrash metal to it, put some urgency into it. And we played it at a speed, which early godfathers of British R&B said, 'Ah, disgraceful!' All the people like Korner, to them [playing the blues] was like a church. You couldn't be disrespectful. The harmonica was learned note-for-note. It was such bollocks. We just took what we wanted and made it our own. Everyone would dance faster, [at] the pace of our life."

May actually used Mick Jagger's songbook—which had lyrics of "every Chuck Berry, every Bo Diddley, every Jimmy Reed song"—to learn material. Yet the Pretty Things were also conscious of not trying to merely sound like the Rolling Stones, or any other of the numerous fine R&B bands starting in London around 1963, the Yardbirds being (other than the Rolling Stones) the best of them. "All the bands were very careful to play different things," May points out. "We had even a more irreverent attitude than the Stones did. The Stones *almost* copied stuff. They did quite a good rendition of the records, slightly faster. But we took that another step, and had to find our own identity in it."

"The Stones weren't a purist R&B band, but we were even less so than them," concurs Taylor. "We liked the same music, but we were maybe pointed a little bit more towards Bo Diddley." The Pretties, indeed, would take their name from a Bo Diddley song, "Pretty Thing," which they covered on their first album (which included no fewer than three other Diddley titles). It was a witty name given that to most of the public, the Pretty Things' appearance was not pretty, but downright shocking. When the average British band still played in matching suits (including the Rolling Stones at some 1963 appearances), the Pretty Things played in casual lounging-around-the-house wear. Phil May grew his hair past his shoulders at a time when only girls did that, with most of the other band members letting it down almost as far. With the addition of John Stax on bass and Brian Pendleton on rhythm guitar, they began playing art school and club gigs, within a few months attracting attention from Fontana Records. Before embarking upon a recording career, however, a final element would fall into place to elevate the already rowdy pack to a full-on threat to the status quo.

Drummer Vivian Prince, ironically, was drafted in by management and record label interests in the hopes of bringing some much-needed professionalism to the outfit. At a glance Prince's credentials, including sessions and work with Carter-

Lewis & the Southerners (during which he played alongside a young Jimmy Page), seemed sound. Prince would soon prove himself, however, to be the most out-of-control musician in the band by a long shot. In May's estimation, "We were sort of novice lunatics, but suddenly they hand us, like, the high priest of lunacy." As Taylor observes archly, "Viv was a very, very professional musician when he wasn't completely pissed."

But, Taylor quickly adds, "Even when he *was* completely pissed, he was a very professional musician." Prince was also a wholly overlooked influence upon Keith Moon, who would take a similar manic energy to the drum kit when he joined the Who. "I always remember Keith coming and standing in front of our set, watching the gig, right in front of the drums," says May. "Keith, later, would also say he idolized Viv. Before that, playing drums was quite sedentary. Boring. And through Viv, you'd suddenly realize you could be a drummer, but also an extrovert. You could be a star, and play your drums too. I think Keith realized he could be Keith, and didn't have to switch instruments. He could still play drums and let out all his lunacy through the drum kit. 'Cause Viv was amazing. He'd hit anything—mike stands, fire bucket, just anything he'd play. Drummed on the floor, on the guitars themselves."

Percussive madness was much in evidence on the Pretty Things' debut single, "Rosalyn," which in addition to Prince's nonstop hurricane of rhythm featured May's trademark hoarse wail of a vocal, pounding Bo Diddley chords, and keening slide guitar. Punk blues at its zenith (although the term "punk" was not in use then), it was hero Diddley's R&B-rock hybrid taken at a tempo accelerated just to the point of anarchy. Backed with a somewhat more refined version of Jimmy Reed's "Big Boss Man," it made the lowest reaches of the U.K. singles charts. The follow-up, "Don't Bring Me Down," was another prime slice of R&B-rock with garage raunchiness, infectious stop-start rhythms, and one of May's most salacious vocals. It made number ten in England, and the Pretty Things were British stars, for a while anyway, with Fontana granting them studio time for an album.

The Pretty Things largely replicated the band's stage set at the time, with songs by idols Bo Diddley, Chuck Berry, and Jimmy Reed standing alongside originals, or numbers supplied to the Pretties by management and other songwriters. Although the pace dragged at times, on the whole it was British R&B at its most raucous, punky but not so sloppy that the sheer energy of the group was undermined. "Big City" and "Judgement Day," though written by management, sounded like downright authentic Chicago blues covers, while "Mama, Keep Your Big Mouth Shut," "Roadrunner," "She's Fine, She's Mine," and "Pretty Thing" revealed the band as the finest white rock interpreters of Bo Diddley, particularly in May's half-shouted, half-sung vocals. "We did 'Roadrunner' and made it our own," proclaims May. "It's quite different from Bo's. Bo's is quite studied, quite nice, but quite controlled. [Ours is] a completely different speed, and much more rock."

The album made the British Top Ten, but the people at Fontana Records may have wished they didn't have to deal with the band at all, so unlike were the Pretties to the rest of the label's artist roster. "The guy who signed us was so straight it was untrue," recalls May. "He thought he was gonna produce the first album. And after twenty minutes, he ran out of the studio and told 'em to get Bobby Graham on the phone, and said, 'I'm not spending another minute with those animals.'" Graham, a session drummer who had played on the Kinks' "You Really Got Me" among many other records, would produce the Pretties' first two LPs.

"We'd never done a recording. So we were incredibly loud, and the mikes were getting blown up, and the engineers threatening to leave. They said we were very uncooperative. We didn't know what we were meant to be cooperating with, you know. In the end, basically, they put mikes in front of what we were doing, we set up in a line, and we played what we were doing on stage every night."

The album also included "Honey I Need," written by Dick Taylor and some friends, which gave the Pretty Things a number thirteen hit and expanded the R&B template a bit with the aggressive acoustic guitar that propels the song through its tricky rhythms. It would also be the group's last Top Twenty hit.

Throughout 1965 and early 1966, the Pretty Things generated classy singles that became small British hits, and deserved to do better. "Midnight to Six Man" was one of the best hits-that-never-were of the '60s, its slashing, descending riff, double-time chorus, and piano/organ embellishments (courtesy of Nicky Hopkins and Genya Ravan) tethering May's leering narrative of a swinger on the prowl for night action. "Come See Me" had another devastating riff (this time on John Stax's bass) and an effective mating of rock and soul grit; the B-sides "Can't Stand the Pain" (with its eerie pre-psychedelia aura of glissando slide guitar) and "L.S.D." (another riff-driven R&B stomper that referred to the old British abbreviation for pounds, shillings and pence, although there was an obvious double meaning) more than carried their weight. The group may have made a strategic blunder, however, in covering Solomon Burke's soul song "Cry to Me" on a single in mid-1965, as the Rolling Stones covered it as an album track at the same time. The Pretties always tried to avoid duplicating the Stones' territory, as previously noted (and they had previously abandoned "Walking the Dog" after the Stones recorded it), but did so here by chance. In any case, it was the single that started the band's commercial slide.

Those who summarize, or even dismiss, the Pretty Things as a junior Rolling Stones are overlooking the group's subtlety and diversity, which not only set them apart from the Stones, but also proved them capable of more than just growling R&B-rock (as magnificent as they were in that capacity). It's not often noted that Dick Taylor, in addition to playing raw-and-ready lead guitar somewhat in the manner of a more spontaneous Keith Richards, effectively varied his textures with acoustic guitars that sometimes even treaded towards folk-rock territory, as on "Honey I Need" and the much folkier "London Town." "We'd all been brought up on acoustic guitars, so it seemed like a completely natural thing to do on some things," says Taylor. "One of the drawbacks about recording electrics in those days was that studios got so uptight about you playing at any volume. They'd put you up against a wall, in a little booth, with a blanket over it, and say play quietly. At least you didn't have that argument with acoustics. You could thrash it out acoustic."

Also underrated were the group's sharp eye for material and interpretive abilities on songs that came from a variety of left-field sources. As noted earlier, the Pretties were conscious of not duplicating the cover choices of the Rolling Stones, Yardbirds, and others— not an easy feat considering how deeply the Chuck Berry and Bo Diddley catalogs in particular were getting plundered. Less noted is the group's knack for coming up with newly-penned tunes from the most obscure and off-the-wall places by outside songwriters, some of whom had no connection with the American R&B scene. "Rosalyn" and "Big City" were cowritten by comanager Jimmy Duncan; "Don't Bring Me Down" by little-known British singer Johnny Dee (who cowrote one of the best songs on their second album, "I Want Your Love"); "Honey I Need" by Taylor and some friends; "Judgement Day" by comanager Bryan Morrison; "You'll Never Do It Baby," another highlight from their second LP, by unknown British R&B band Cops & Robbers; "Come See Me" by American soul musician J. J. Jackson and others; and "You Don't Believe Me," the leadoff track of their second album, with the assistance of then-session musician Jimmy Page. And, Phil May emphasizes, the Pretty Things added a lot to such songs once they found them. "Don't Bring Me Down," he claims, "was pretty tame" when they first heard it, with a much slower tempo. "We hijacked it, and made the song."

The Pretty Things' musical force is still easy to appreciate on their early recordings, but the shock and outrage inspired by their live performances and very appearance is less easily grasped today. The Pretties' stage show was, according to Taylor, "louder and less controlled than even the singles. Nothing would ever be the same night after night. We used to sometimes let riffs go on for hours. Things like 'Hey Mama'—we could jam on that for *hours*." George Gallacher of the Scottish band the Poets saw the Pretties for the first time by chance on a wander down to the 100 Club, and corroborates: "They were the best live band I have ever heard, before or since; I was metaphorically and literally stunned. They did much the same set of blues standards as we did, but Jesus! The power and the playing was astonishing." The electricity sometimes spread through the audience as well, and May remembers riots at the band's appearance at Holland's Blokker Festival in 1965, where "it was like almost the Paris barricades. It's where the Dutch youth said, 'We're not going to be controlled. This is our music.' For the first time, the police couldn't control it, like they normally did. It was almost an establishment of the right to have a party, or the right to listen to music, and not let the church control youth."

Decent record sales and plenty of live work did not mean that the Pretty Things themselves avoided harassment, and it was a constant struggle for them to get served in pubs and taken in by hotels, merely due to the length of their hair. At times they were physically attacked because of the way they looked. "When you see the early pictures," muses May, "I guess we looked fairly radical, but it still doesn't equate, the effect it had on people. We used to get in a fight every night. If you had long hair in those days—I can't think of anything in comparison now. You could have your dick out—you'd have to be that far [today], to walk into a pub and get the kind of vibe we got."

The Pretty Things were among London's wildest ravers, and particularly renowned for the parties held at their abode at 13 Chester Street, where the Rolling Stones' Brian Jones also lived for a time, coming up from the basement to listen to records. One Pretty Thing proved too wild even for the rest of the band to accommodate. The group's 1965 tour of Australia and New Zealand aroused massive media indignation Down Under, particularly in New Zealand, where the Pretties earned a lifetime ban. This was particularly due to the antics of Viv Prince, who was alleged to have gotten wildly drunk at performances and set fires onstage. Prince was thrown off their flight back from New Zealand for disorderly behavior before it took off, and didn't show up in England for weeks. "We had to sack him because he was so bad in the end," laments May. "We couldn't finish a concert." To May's recollection, the capper was the time Prince refused to play a gig when the pub across the road refused to serve him a beer. "What he forgot was the night before, he'd gone there with a bunch of musicians and smashed the place up."

Now fondly recalled in the track "Vivian Prince" off the Pretties' 1999 *Rage for Beauty* album, Prince had, in his brief career, arguably set the benchmark for rock excess, only to be exceeded by the legendary Keith Moon. (Ironically, Prince would fill in for Moon in the Who for a couple of weeks in December 1965, when Moon was ill.) For the rest of the 1960s, Prince drifted through obscure bands (including one with ex-Moody Blues and future Wings guitarist Denny Laine), played with an early version of the Jeff Beck Group (which didn't last past the rehearsal stage), and did a flop solo single. In the early 1970s, he was said to have somehow managed the difficult feat of getting kicked *out* of the Hell's Angels for unruliness. Today he lives in an orange grove in Portugal, breeding Alsatians.

In the meantime, the rest of the band had recordings to do and live dates to fill. Their second album, *Get the Picture?*, came out in late 1965. While not as consistent as their debut, it showed the Pretties starting to stretch by absorbing soul and folk influences, as well as writing more of their own material. Much of the drums on *Get the Picture?* were handled by session players, particularly a pre-Jimi Hendrix Experience Mitch Mitchell and the seventeen-year-old Skip Alan. Both were considered for the permanent job, with the band opting for Alan, "an embryonic lunatic" (in May's words) whose personality was much more suited to the Pretty Things than the relatively straitlaced (at that time, anyway) Mitchell.

The Pretty Things were still a successful group in the U.K. and Europe. Holland in particular seemed to take the Pretty Things to heart as a major band, judging from the abundance of Dutch groups that made records saturated with the Pretty Things' influence (such as the Outsiders, one of the best rock bands ever to hail from a non-English-speaking country). Yet the Pretty Things were almost wholly unknown in the U.S., where they didn't tour and their records weren't played, or sometimes even released.

Since this was a time when the Stones, Yardbirds, Animals, and other tough British groups soaked in R&B were taking the States by storm, this has remained the big Pretty Things mystery over the decades: why such a fine band did not make a determined effort to invade America. You had to be a *very* dedicated fan to even find Pretty Things releases in the States. Somehow a few U.S. garage bands even released some Pretty Things covers, most notably the Montells from Florida, who had a regional hit with "Don't Bring Me Down." It didn't help that the Pretty Things' own version of "Don't Bring Me Down" was banned from many radio stations for the line "and then I laid her on the ground." (There were also the Brogues from California, featuring a pre-Quicksilver Messenger Service Gary Duncan on guitar, whose "Don't Shoot Me Down" was modeled on the Pretty Things' version of "Mama, Keep Your Big Mouth Shut"; Duncan named Phil May as his favorite singer in a Brogues bio, and even today feels the Pretty Things were "much better than the Rolling Stones.")

May concedes that the decision not to concentrate on the U.S. market "was a dumb move by [comanager] Bryan Morrison. But don't forget, the record we would have gone with was banned from all the radio stations within three weeks. It started off being bleeped, and then it got more and more bleeped. In the end, they wouldn't play it. So we'd have gone there, and a week later we wouldn't have had our record played on the air. It was banned [for the line 'laid her on the ground']; well, in some places, they were bleeping more than that. We were doing very well in Europe, and it seemed like, OK, we'll go with the next record, or the next record. But in some ways, it kept the band hungry. It left something to shoot at a bit later on. If we'd gotten to America and had the same effect in America we were having in Europe, I think we'd be dead, and it'd all been over in three or four years."

Taylor is less equivocal about the band's failure to tour America. "What decision could be more wrong than not doing that?" he laughs. "Obviously, it was a very big mistake. We all wanted to go. The decision really rested with the fact that we would have probably had to lose money for a couple of tours. Also, we were doing quite well in England and Europe. But really, we should have just bit the bullet and gone."

Late 1966 saw the Pretty Things in a bit of a crisis. Their last two singles, a cover of the Kinks' "A House in the Country" and the anonymous soul-pop "Progress," hadn't sold or been appropriate material. "We realized that unless we made a move, we couldn't exist with what we'd been doing," recounts May. "We had to write for ourselves, find our own voice as writers. We couldn't rely on people to bring us material. We wouldn't have survived. It wasn't something I wanted to do. I hate writing." But May and Taylor were already involved in writing most of the band's original material (most notably "Midnight to Six Man"), and their credits appeared on every track on *Emotions*, the band's third album. Other Pretty Things were not destined to stay the course, with Brian Pendleton simply getting off the train on the way to a gig and never returning, and John Stax leaving sometime during the recording of *Emotions*. They were replaced by multi-instrumentalist Wally Waller and keyboardist John Povey, both of the little-known harmony pop group the Fenmen; the new musicians would influence the band's turn away from R&B and toward psychedelia.

Emotions is still a source of great controversy among both the band members and their fans. May and Taylor (with some songwriting help from Waller) were, for the first time, going away from R&B and into a poppier direction, with intimations of folk and psychedelic music. Their songs were no longer rompers, but gentle, inquisitive, frequently third-person sketches with a British slant. Sometimes the ventures were quite effective, as on the hastily strummed acoustic guitar and dramatic story line of "Death of a Socialite"; the anthemic "My Time," with its jubilant Swinging London vibe; and the lovely "The Sun." Other songs were awkward, the group still ill at ease with its new territory, muting both the guitars and the rasp of May's voice. Most controversial, though, was the addition of overdubbed strings and brass by outside musicians, without full consent from or participation by the band members. Although these could sometimes enhance the mood of the songs when used sporadically, at other points their flatulence all but drowned the tracks.

Some takes of tracks without the overdubs appear on Snapper's CD reissue of *Emotions* (and also on the *Pure & Pretty* bootleg), but the damage was done, and even so the Pretties never got to record the compositions in the way they would have preferred. "It was something we were working on that got hijacked," states May flatly. "When they started fucking around with *Emotions*, putting orchestras on it, we could have said OK, cancel the whole album and we'll start again. But that would have meant another six months under contract."

Emotions ended the group's association with Fontana Records. Originally, summarizes Taylor diplomatically, "The people who saw us from Fontana did realize that where our merit lay wasn't in musicianship exactly. It was far more in the fact that we were rough, ready, and raw, had a lot of energy. That's why the first album and *Get the Picture?* work very well. Bobby Graham certainly realized the best way to go about recording us was to get as much immediacy as he could. I don't think [*Emotions* producer] Steve Rowland ever got to grips with who we really were. It was a pretty transitional thing; I actually quite like some of it very much. I'd have personally liked to put a load of electric guitars on and what have you. But we were starting to explore a bit, and it was something we had to do to get somewhere else."

That "somewhere else" would be EMI Records, where the Pretty Things would be able to, at the hallowed Abbey Road Studios, put down on tape what they were starting to hear in their heads. To help put food on the table at a time when their records weren't selling, they got work doing soundtrack recordings for De Wolfe. This allowed them an outlet for some material not deemed strong enough for their proper albums, as well as the ability to work out some ideas that would appear in modified form on their proper LPs. The best of these late-'60s De Wolfe tracks would eventually get wide release on an odd series of *Electric Banana* albums, the best of which is *Electric Banana in the Sixties*. In a more bizarre extracurricular activity, the band (minus May) also backed unknown French singer Phillipe DeBarges on unreleased recordings of original Pretty Things numbers in the late 1960s (now bootlegged on *Phillipe DeBarges*). Much of that decent, but not stunning, pop-psychedelic material was never officially released by the band with May on vocals; as May remembers, "Wally [Waller] and I just wrote a bunch of songs for this French millionaire. No kind of falseness about, 'he was a musician.' He just wanted to make a record with the Pretty Things, and he was prepared to pay."

For EMI, though, the Pretty Things had something more ambitious in mind, first realized in late 1967 with the single "Defecting Grey"/ "Mr. Evasion." "Defecting Grey," says May, is "about somebody who does a job. Grey suit, really. Somebody who suddenly realized that everything they'd lived for, and were brought up to believe in, possibly wasn't right."

"Defecting Grey" sounded like an entirely different band than the one that had blazed through "Come See Me" less than two years earlier; indeed, May sounded like a totally different singer, his grainy vocal textures abandoned for smoother tones that would fit better with the group's harmonies. A miniature suite of different song fragments molded into a whole, it was full-blown psychedelia, employing underwater-sounding vocals, smoldering effects-laden guitars, pretty vocal harmonies, gorgeous keyboard and percussion tinkles, sitar, and a booming bass-toned intro produced by letting the guitar fall to the floor. The multicolored arrangement and whimsical, dreamlike lyrics bore some resemblance to the classic psychedelic pop recorded by Pink Floyd in 1967, when that group was under the direction of its original mad genius leader, Syd Barrett. The similarity was not entirely coincidental, since both bands were produced by Norman Smith, who had engineered most of the Beatles' records through the end of 1965 before moving into production. "Norman went back to the heads of EMI and said, 'You can't cut this,'" says May. "It's something that grows and develops, and you can't cut bits out of it. Nothing lasts for more than a minute and a half."

Nevertheless, "Defecting Grey" had to be significantly shortened for single release. While the band and Smith continued to work in far-out vocal and instrumental effects on the next single, "Talkin' About the Good Times"/"Walking Through My Dreams," they were working towards a full-length piece that would not be constricted by the length of a 45 RPM single. This would be S.F. Sorrow, by most historians' reckoning the first rock opera, based on a short story by Phil May. By the time it was completed, yet another renowned looner, Twink Alder, had taken over from Skip Alan on drums.

S. F. Sorrow follows the life of protagonist S. F. Sorrow through birth, first love, induction into the army, loss of innocence and hope, old age, and death. The Pretty Things and Smith worked round-the-clock on occasions at Abbey Road. "We were so into what we were doing, we didn't want to be anywhere else," says May thirty years later. "We had unlimited studio time, which for us, at the time, was better than money." They really went to the limit on the multitextured acoustic and wah-wahing electric guitars, imaginative insertions of mellotron, dense Beatlesque vocal harmonies, dabs of sitar, and flowing segues between tracks. There had been some vague concept albums in rock before, from world-famous (the Beatles' Sgt. Pepper) to way-obscure (The Story of Simon Simopath, by British psych-popsters Nirvana). S. F. Sorrow was vague at points too, but was the first one to effectively follow a story from beginning to end, even if much of the operatic effect was derived from the eclectic continuity of the production rather than a standard libretto.

"I'd written this short story called 'Cutting Up Sergeant Time,' which was all based loosely about somebody in the First World War, in trenches," remembers May. "I started from where he was born and what would have happened to him on the way. It set us up for the next song, and the whole thing developed. We had like fourteen months to make this picture up.

"My only influence in terms of where I was looking for comparisons was in opera, where it starts off and they fall in love and she dies. I could never understand why an album had to be five A-sides, five B-sides. I thought, great; all the bits and pieces in that song, they can all be about one person's life. It's a forty-minute piece, something like having a film. It's meant to grow, and it's quiet bits and faster bits."

May enthusiastically credits Norman Smith as a sixth member of the band of sorts. "Norman spent as much time on the studio floor with one of us in the box as *he* spent in the box. He would be doing the fourth harmony, have this idea for a drum motif, and get up a boy's brigade drum and be playing that. Norman realized the best way to work with the Pretty Things was to be on the floor, to break down that [producer] job definition." May's praise for Smith seems at odds with comments uttered by some members of Pink Floyd, who thought that Smith was too straight for the producer's chair, and stopped working with him after their first few albums. "Roger [Waters, of Pink Floyd], he was such an egoist," speculates May. "The minute he could get rid of anybody who was doing anything in the Floyd, he would. Roger wanted the Floyd for himself. And he was a very powerful bloke. I've got a lot of respect for Roger, he did some great things. But it was control. And Norman wasn't part of that scenario."

Taylor points out that the transition from R&B to psychedelia wasn't nearly as sudden as it might appear from the recordings, as the group had always been into different kinds of music. The band members were being influenced from a lot of directions that party-line revisionists, eager to cast the Pretty Things as unreconstructed pre-punks, would not suspect. Taylor, for instance, mentions being impressed by the Doors, Sun Ra, John Coltrane, and Captain Beefheart, and notes that he was listening to the Fifth Dimension and Love's classic cult album *Forever Changes* as *S. F. Sorrow* was taking shape. He even admits to unconsciously nicking part of the riff of *S. F. Sorrow*'s "Balloon Burning" from Love's "A House Is Not a Motel."

"When we were in the first incarnation [of the band], we were playing stuff we *could* play," he emphasizes. "Stuff we liked as well. Then it became acceptable to play stranger sort of stuff, different sort of music. We discovered we had maybe acquired the technique to play other things than straight R&B. And even during our R&B phase, we used to do huge, long improvisation things. [On] 'Hey Mama' we used to get into some pretty odd stuff, doing huge solos, basically around one chord. Which wasn't reflected in a lot of recordings for Fontana, who wanted us to be a pop band." At EMI, "It was a bit like someone just opened up the doors, and let us out to play in the garden. We were probably hideously over-budget, but Norman just kept laying more and more time out."

S. F. Sorrow came out in Britain in late 1968. Another much more famous rock opera came out in mid-1969. Disputes over whether the Who was influenced by *S. F. Sorrow* in the construction of *Tommy* will probably not be resolved within the Pretty Things' lifetime, if ever. Complicating the comparison was the unfortunate delay of *S. F. Sorrow*'s release in the United States, which appeared (on, oddly, the Motown subsidiary Rare Earth) a few months after *Tommy* came out Stateside. *S. F. Sorrow* was dismissed by some American critics as a *Tommy* rip-off, even though it had plainly appeared about half a year before *Tommy* in the U.K. *S. F. Sorrow* was not as melodic, and boasted just as obtuse a story line as *Tommy*; it certainly was not as commercial. It was, however, indisputably first. Unfortunately it would not be performed live in the 1960s in its entirety, although the Pretties did a couple of mimes to excerpts from it in the late 1960s at the Roundhouse in London, with members of the band and some of their girlfriends taking the roles of various characters from the songs.

May evenhandedly notes his annoyance over Pete Townshend's recent claims never to have heard *S. F. Sorrow* in the 1960s—claims clouded by the extremely close resemblance between the opening acoustic guitar chords of *S. F. Sorrow*'s "Old Man Going" and the rapidly strummed acoustic guitar rhythms that usher in the Who's "Pinball Wizard." "In so many write-ups, he always said that *S. F. Sorrow* influenced *Tommy*. Just recently, Townshend's been apparently denying any knowledge. It almost sounded like a lawyer's statement—'we want to categorically deny we ever heard any copy of *S. F. Sorrow*.' You know, there's room for *Tommy* and *S. F. Sorrow*. It's never been a problem for me. I loved the Who, and [*Tommy*'s] great. It's not my idea that he's [admitted the influence in the past]. Journalists come to *me* and say, 'Pete Townshend, in so-and-so, says, this is a quote, *S. F. Sorrow*'s been the influence in *Tommy*.'" Taylor also remembers one of the Pretty Things' roadies, who was also a friend of the Who, taking a copy to a party attended by Townshend and later telling the Pretty Things how much it was played there. "If it isn't so, it's not so, but if it's not, I'd be rather surprised. It just seems a bit odd that someone should go, 'Hey, I took your album along and [Who comanager] Kit Lambert and Pete Townshend really loved it.'"

At the Pretty Things' creative apex, Taylor left after *S. F. Sorrow*—"since I'd left art school, I hadn't done anything else apart from being in the Pretty Things, [and thought] maybe I should try and see what else there is to do in the world." Through the previous five years, Taylor and May had been the principal songwriters and musical architects of the band (although Wally Waller joined their songwriting team starting with their psychedelic era, and other Pretty Things also shared in composer credits occasionally). His place could not be easily filled, and with their final album of the 1960s, *Parachute*, the Pretty Things began pushing in a more standard hard-progressive-rock direction. Twink Alder was replaced as Skip Alan rejoined the band, Victor Unitt took Taylor's place, and May was now the only original Pretty Thing.

Parachute took the *S. F. Sorrow* production sophistication and subtracted the operatic concept, although there was a subtle thread in that the LP was organized, as May puts it, into "an urban hymn on one side, and a sort of rural hymn on the other. So many people were leaving town and getting a farm, which I hated the idea of." Sounding at times like the Beatles' *Abbey Road* in its cannily thick guitars and harmonies (although the songs were not up to *Abbey Road*'s admittedly super-high standards), *Parachute* collected *Rolling Stone* magazine's album of the year award for 1970. Sales were not forthcoming, though, and the group even disbanded for a while in the early 1970s before reassembling, with guitarist Peter Tolson, and carrying on through the mid-1970s. In 1974, in fact, they were signed to Led Zeppelin's Swan Song label, and Led Zep's manager, Peter Grant, took over the Pretty Things' affairs. They even got to play in the United States, finally, as well as make the lower reaches of the American album charts with *Silk Torpedo* and *Savage Eye*.

However, by this time the Pretty Things were just an average 1970s hard rock band, albeit one with more history and depth of repertoire than most. Although May retains a lot of affection for this era, guitarist Peter Tolson's abilities, and this lineup's live shows, he admits "we got American slick. We were that sharp." It remains a strange circumstance of the Pretty Things' career that they are most known to many Americans for their least distinguished material, as albums from this time were the only ones to pick up significant U.S. airplay. May left the band in 1976, and the Pretty Things broke up a few months later.

Cultists all over the world continued to discover the band's vintage work, however, particularly since David Bowie had covered both "Rosalyn" and "Don't Bring Me Down" on his 1974 album of 1960s British rock covers, *Pin-Ups*. "I found out the other day," says May now, "that Johnny Rotten was taken from the age of twelve to see all the Pretty Things concerts. His mom was a big Pretty Things fan." With that kind of credibility, work was still there to be had, and the Pretty Things have been playing, off and on, at clubs and festivals throughout Europe (and, lately, the United States), for the last twenty years. May and Taylor, the latter of whom had done little in music in the decade after leaving the Pretty Things in the late 1960s (although he produced Hawkwind's first album), were always in the lineups, and there was even the sporadic live or studio release. They didn't push themselves as much as they could have because, as May notes, "In the Pretty Things, life's always been first. If people have been available, or wanted to do it, we've done it [played]."

In the late 1990s, however, the push became more intense. The 1967 lineup—May, Taylor, Waller, Povey, and Alan—is now back together again, with the addition of guitarist Frankie Holland. They have regained control of their vintage back catalog, and the Snapper label has executed a lengthy series of classy reissues of all of their 1960s albums and several from the 1970s, with historical liner notes and bonus tracks. The band's critical reputation, so long confined to cultists such as Mike Stax of the excellent 1960s-oriented rock magazine *Ugly Things* (which has run more than a dozen Pretty Things features and interviews), has begun to spread to the mainstream, with complimentary articles appearing in the *Village Voice* and the *New York Times*. Industrial music pioneer Genesis P-Orridge, rather to the surprise of critics, named *S.F. Sorrow* as one of his top five albums of all time. A new studio album that was almost twenty years in the making, *Rage Before Beauty*, finally saw the light in 1999. And on September 6, 1998, they assembled at Abbey Road to perform *S. F. Sorrow* in its entirety, live, for broadcast over the Internet, with Arthur Brown (famous for the 1960s hit "Fire") providing narration, and David Gilmour of Pink Floyd on guest guitar.

Gilmour knows how thin the line is between cult artist and international superstar. He was, after all, an unknown guitarist from Cambridge who had never played on a record, and who was tapped to replace Syd Barrett in Pink Floyd, at a time when both the Floyd and the Pretty Things were reaching the upper arcs of psychedelia at Abbey Road, with Norman Smith as producer. Gilmour, says May, is "somebody who appreciates other musicians who he knows, with a bit of luck, would be where he is." Like the Pretty Things.

Recommended Recordings:

The Pretty Things (1965, Snapper). The band's debut album is mid-1960s British R&B at its most exciting, especially on the galvanizing Bo Diddley covers "Pretty Thing" and "Mama, Keep Your Big Mouth Shut," as well as the management-supplied blues pastiches "Judgement Day" and "Big City," and the hit single "Honey, I Need." The CD bonus tracks include the essential singles "Rosalyn" and "Don't Bring Me Down," as well as the moody original "I Can Never Say" and the previously unreleased Diddleyesque shaker "Get Yourself Home."

Get the Picture? (1965, Snapper). A bit less exciting than its predecessor, but still plenty of stellar blues-soul-rock here, like the rowdy "Buzz the Jerk" and "Gonna Find Me a Substitute," and the first-rate pop-blues confections "I Want Your Love" and "You'll Never Do It Baby." "Can't Stand the Pain" and "London Town" hint at psychedelia and folk-rock; among the six CD bonus tracks are two of their best singles, "Midnight to Six Man" and "Come See Me."

Emotions (1967, Snapper). Their erratic transitional album actually has a number of outstanding songs, particularly "Death of a Socialite," "My Time," and "The Sun," all of which have a moody, yearning melodicism and a relative minimum of brass and strings. The rest of the album is patchier, but the addition of five overdubless versions amidst the bonus tracks gives some idea of how the album may have sounded had the orchestra not been involved.

Get a Buzz: The Best of the Fontana Years (1992, Fontana). With such outstanding secondary tracks as "You'll Never Do It Baby," "I Want Your Love," and "Mama, Keep Your Big Mouth Shut" missing, this is a less-than-perfect summary of their early work. It's the best single-disc compilation of that era available, though, and does include all the essential singles.

S. F. Sorrow (1968, Snapper). The rock opera is more impressive for its production wizardry and solid harmonies than for its lyrical content, but impressive nonetheless. The shift between a cornucopia of moods is always deft and sometimes breathtaking, as on the mellotrons announcing "S. F. Sorrow Is Born," the percussive footsteps of "Private Sorrow," the buzzing guitars of "Balloon Burning," the spooky vocals of "I See You," and the father-of-"Pinball Wizard" guitar riffs of "Old Man Going." The CD reissue adds four essential psychedelic tracks from their 1967-68 singles, including an expanded version of "Defecting Grey."

Parachute (1970, Snapper). Although not as groundbreaking or exhilarating as *S. F. Sorrow*, and suffering from the absence of Dick Taylor, this too boasts an ingenious blend of state-of-the-late-1960s production and instrumentation. As in *S. F. Sorrow*, the individual songs are not as important as the crafty flow and juxtaposition of quiet and intense passages. The CD reissue adds six less-vital tracks from early 1970s singles.

Electric Banana: The Sixties (1979, Butt, U.K.). This compilation of a dozen of the soundtrack recordings they did for De Wolfe in the late 1960s is not up to the level of *S. F. Sorrow*, but serves as something of a missing link between their Fontana and EMI years in its pop-psychedelia. You can hear some ideas that would surface on *S. F. Sorrow* here, particularly in the sparer version of "I See You" (which was redone on *S. F. Sorrow* itself) and the guitar riffs of "Alexander," which anticipate similar ones on *S. F. Sorrow*'s "Balloon Burning." Three of the songs also show up in different versions on the peculiar late 1960s demo LP done with Phillipe DeBarge on vocals; an acetate of that LP has been bootlegged, and is pretty fair psychedelic pop in the *Electric Banana* mold. Finally, a CD of mysterious origin, *The Electric Banana Blows Your Mind*, contains everything from *Electric Banana: The Sixties* and adds four more cuts from the De Wolfe records; three are taken from the first De Wolfe outing, and sound like mediocre *Emotions*-era outtakes.

The Poets

It's December 31, 1999 on the Internet, but George Gallacher isn't worrying about the (falsely anticipated, as it turns out) computer-generated end of the world. Trying to summarize what made the Poets stand out from the hordes of British Invasion bands of the mid-1960s, the ex-Poet seeks help from a Dead Poet. "There is a lovely little maxim from the nineteenth century art critic John Ruskin that says all about the Poets' stuff," he types in his E-mail message. "'It is far more difficult to be simple than to be complicated, far more difficult to sacrifice skill and cease exertion in the proper place, than to expand both indiscriminately.'" Gallacher also quotes a more recent source who puts things much more simply: "The much respected literary and music critic Brian Morton said on a recent documentary, 'Unlike all others of the 500 bands in Glasgow at the time, whom people went to dance to, one went to a Poets' gig to listen.'"

The ordinary British Invasion veteran does not summon quotes from past and present literary critics when his own words fail. The Poets, though, were never your ordinary British Invasion band. Mordant and introspective where most bands were cheerfully exuberant or raunchy with a pout, the group's hypnotic, eerie melodies evoked a brooding and beautiful landscape, not unlike the chilly, overcast, and luminous green vistas of their native Scotland. Spookily echoing twelve-string and acoustic guitars, rattling tambourines, and ghostly backup harmonies chased around each other with as much chilling effect as a wind whistling through a haunted

The Poets in 1965, rehearsing Fraser Watson, who had just joined the band. Left to right: Fraser Watson, Hume Paton, Jim Breakey, George Gallacher, John Dawson.
Credit: Courtesy George Gallacher.

house. They have sometimes been compared to the Zombies for their knack for original minor-keyed melodies, but the Poets' arrangements were far more guitar-based, their persona (not to mention their production) even more mysterious and ethereal. On the infrequent occasions on which they decided to rock hard, they did so with surprising crunching vengeance, marking them as one of the relatively few British bands of the time with an equal facility for ballads and raucous R&B.

The Poets seemed to have a lot going for them in 1964 and 1965: a recording deal with a major label, a huge fan base in their native Scotland, strong and even unique original material. Most important, they had one of the most powerful manager-producers in British rock, Andrew Loog Oldham, who also managed and produced the Rolling Stones. For whatever reason, though, it didn't happen for the Poets, who had just one small British hit, and remain totally unknown in the United States. It could have been behind-the-scenes management foul-ups, constant personnel changes, inadequate promotion, or records that were just a bit too out of the commercial mainstream for wide success. What's sad is that after just a half-dozen singles, the group that debuted with the single "Now We're Thru" in 1964 was indeed through. The best Scottish band of the 1960s never even got to record an album.

When the Poets began playing together in Glasgow in the early 1960s, they immediately set themselves aside from the other groups in the area by writing and performing original material. That hardly sounds like a radical statement today, but even in 1963 the Beatles were just starting to make an impact with their own songs, and most rock bands in the U.K. stuck virtually exclusively to covers. The Poets played blues, soul, and R&B covers live throughout their career, but their compositions were quite something else, both in their predilection for angst-ridden, almost folky ballads and their unusual twelve-string guitar sound. "Though we were limited in respect of playing technique—there were many brilliant players at the time in Scotland—we left them all standing in terms of playing discipline," claims George Gallacher, lead singer for the Poets, who wrote their original material at the outset with guitarists Hume Paton and Tony Myles. "We were the tightest band around, rehearsing every day, even though our playing schedule was hectic, sometimes playing three gigs a night at the weekends. This discipline, allied to imaginative versions of standard blues and rock stuff, was our strength."

Early primitive unreleased recordings survive in both the Merseybeat and raunchy R&B styles in which the group mimicked the sound of twelve-string guitars, which would only become common in rock with the advent of the Byrds and folk-rock. "The two guitars [had] the first and second strings tuned the same, thereby creating a semi-twelve-string effect," explains Gallacher. "Add this to the minor melodies, and there is the seminal Poets sound. A very distinctive sound, and potentially very commercial." Not commercial enough, though, for EMI and hit producer Mickie Most, who turned down the Poets about six months before the band met Andrew Oldham.

What initially grabbed the attention of Oldham, however, was not their sound but their look. In the same manner as the early Kinks, the Poets were long-haired mods dressed like dandies of an earlier century, with ruffled shirts, velvet-collared black suits, and high-heeled boots. On a quick trip to Scotland to marry his girlfriend (considered underage in his native England), Oldham spotted a newspaper photo of the Poets at the airport. He arranged for an audition at which, according to the band, he was as struck by their original repertoire as he was by their image. The group's live set, confesses Gallacher, "was in fact mainly a raucous affair, comprising largely of up-tempo rhythm and blues, although punctuated liberally with our own 'miserable' material. At the audition I remember poor Hume asking Andrew if he wanted to hear us do some Stones numbers, and me saying, 'Fuck the Stones, he wants to hear our stuff.' Of which 'Now We're Thru' was one." And such was the ease with which powerful managers could get things done in those times that within a few weeks, the Poets were being managed and produced by Oldham, and recording their "Now We're Thru" single for one of the biggest labels in the country, Decca.

"Now We're Thru" was an example par excellence of what Gallacher termed their "miserable" material, "miserable" referring to the emotional tenor rather than the actual worth of the tune. Oldham, like his role model Phil Spector, liked to embellish his productions with layers and layers of echo. However, the different British studios, Oldham's inexperience, and his clients' emphasis on guitar-oriented arrangements resulted in a brittler, more primitive Wall of Sound than Spector created with his orchestras. With the Poets he really went to town with the reverb. The blend of twelve-string acoustic guitars, bashing death-rattle tambourines, and the mournful backup vocals produced a cavernous effect quite unlike Phil Spector or the typical British Invasion record. It was a Wash of Sound, perhaps, rather than a Wall of Sound. With its dirge-like melody and wavering, doom-trumpeting tempos, "Now We're Thru" made number thirty on the British charts in late 1964, doing particularly well in Scotland. Although it wasn't their best record, it was by far their most commercially successful release.

"Now We're Thru" also inaugurated a run of singles which, arguably, constituted Andrew Oldham's most adventurous series of productions. This is not to claim that Oldham's records with the Poets were as good as the classic ones he made with the Rolling Stones, whom he produced until mid-1967. The Stones, however, were an act that lent themselves far less to the stamp of an idiosyncratic producer such as Oldham, as their sound (certainly before 1966) largely stayed within American rock, soul, and blues idioms. The Poets' gentler and wider sonic palette, by contrast, was open to quite a bit of refinement and experimentation in the studio.

Oldham was not an experienced record producer, and didn't even particularly know too much about R&B music, when he started handling the Stones in 1963, and members of that group (particularly Keith Richards) have sometimes disparaged his abilities behind the board. He has also been lampooned for his obvious idolization of Phil Spector, not only on forgettable records he produced with tons of echo, but also in his adoption of the same kind of sunglasses Spector was noted for wearing almost round-the-clock. On top of this was his apparent desire to be a Rolling Stone himself, acting boorishly in public with the group and writing *Clockwork Orange*-styled liner notes for their albums. Taking all of this into account, some historians have portrayed Oldham as a manic boy wonder (he was about the same age as the groups he managed) who might have had a talent for drawing publicity, but was a bit of a buffoon when it came to business and creative record production.

George Gallacher soundly refutes this characterization. When the Poets signed with Oldham, he points out, "My excitement was the chance to record in a professional studio with someone who knew what he was doing. Because all that was available in Scotland at the time was the BBC studios, manned by engineers and producers who hadn't a clue about what sound was about, and where experimentation was out of the question. Calvinism still reigned musically as well as culturally. So Andrew as the Antichrist suited me." Besides, he notes, "Andrew made it easier by buying two twelve-strings for us."

No Poets single better illustrates the polar opposites of the band's approach than the follow-up to "Now We're Thru," "That's the Way It's Got to Be"/"I'll Cry with the Moon." In total contrast to their debut, "That's the Way It's Got to Be" was a throbbing slice of mod rock, introduced by some of the fattest, most powerful bass lines ever heard on a rock record up to that point. According to Gallacher, the bass was "Andrew's idea, to give it more drive," and played on a six-string (as opposed to the standard four-string) bass by session musician John Paul Jones (yes, the future Led Zeppelin bassist) with a force that threatened to bounce the phonograph needle right off the turntable. It never did quite live up to the promise of those opening bass lines, but it did boast solid R&B-influenced riffs, given that characteristic Poets/Oldham touch by the twelve-string guitars and tambourines that hovered between the bass and the vocal throughout the track. "I'll Cry with the Moon" could not have been more different: an eloquent, acoustic ballad of almost suicidal despair, with no percussion save claves, delivered with such spare restraint that what would have been unbearably sappy in other hands was instead unbearably tense. "It's just as well we remained a minor group," quips Gallacher dryly. "Think of the kids that were saved from jumping off bridges."

Guitarist Fraser Watson, who would join the Poets later in 1965, still remembers the first time he heard "That's the Way It's Got to Be" on the radio. "I think I was out one night with a girlfriend, sitting in the car somewhere, trying to get it on and getting nowhere. The radio came on, and it was 'That's the Way It's Got to Be.' I could not believe it. That bass riff! I thought, this is fucking gonna be a monster hit. And it didn't get any airplay. Andrew didn't push it. A year later, Spencer Davis came out with 'Keep On Runnin'.'" A number one hit in Britain, "Keep On Runnin'," with Stevie Winwood on vocals, also led off with a pulsating bass riff, and although Gallacher doesn't think the Poets influenced the record, Watson contends "they only changed the key of the thing. It was basically the same vibe, the same riff."

For their third single, "I Am So Blue"/"I Love Her Still," the Poets chose to emphasize their misery to the max. Both sides were catchy and gloomy ballads, with the accent on the twelve-stringed acoustic guitars that figured in all of the Poets' early singles. "I Am So Blue" owed something to the Drifters' "On Broadway" in its chordal progression, the mood heightened by percussive strokes of hollow-block percussive instruments termed "skulls" to create effects akin to pebbles rippling through a pond. "I Love Her Still" was another tale of hopeless unrequited love, the prize touch this time around being the weird background wobbles, produced by running a rhythm guitar through a Leslie speaker cabinet. These and indeed all Poets ballads teetered on the edge of pathos, but never fell in, due in large part to the genuinely hurt and tremulous vocals of Gallacher, and the spell woven by the sumptuous melodies and spectral backup harmonies.

Gallacher is keen to stress that much of the unusual ambience on the Poets' singles is attributable to the extensive work put into the tracks in the studio itself, by both the band and Oldham. The Poets even did much of their actual composing in the studio, a luxury almost unheard of in Britain at the time, when sessions were usually run strictly by the clock and weirdness in general was discouraged. "Virtually all the songs after 'Now We're Thru' were done in the studio, I mean from start to finish, and Andrew relished this. It was a kind of 'tabula rasa' on which he could do his thing. The freshness, the immediacy fired him, and he had infinite patience with us. When I look back, the time he spent with us in the studio was incredible, and there was talk—perhaps exaggerated—that the Stones were none too pleased about this.

"The thing for Andrew was the fact that our stuff had no precedence. It wasn't blues- or rock 'n' roll-based. It came from nothing he had experience of, so it was a challenge to him every time. Although he produced fabulous stuff for the early Stones, the fact that their material was derivative, i.e. very blues-influenced, meant that there was a kind of predictability about the finished tracks. With us, there was no such thing, and he got off on that. Listening to the tracks today, notwithstanding the brilliant sound, there is a kind of cleanness of line, an unclutteredness about it that amazes me. For all that Spector fullness, every instrument is discrete; everything can be heard on its own. To me, this is Andrew. People saw him as a Spector clone, but whereas Phil built layer upon layer of multitracking for his Wall of Sound, Andrew recorded most of our stuff live." Oldham did get to use the sort of acoustic guitars, sluggish tempos, and droning textures the Poets favored on occasional classic early Stones tracks, such as "Tell Me" and "Heart of Stone." However, Gallacher believes that "where their productions sound cluttered, ours sound 'clean.' So I never made any comparisons.

"Most of the studio time was taken up with the writing and arrangements. Most of the time I would go to Hume—a clever guy who, like George Harrison, played within his limits—and Tony with a melody, and they would work the chords around it. Then we would modify it here and there, and once we were happy with that, we would play it to the others, who would add their bit and so on. The actual recordings were usually done in no more than two or three takes, no tricks. We could reproduce it easily on stage. All that distilled angst—I don't know how the punters put up with it."

Oldham did occasionally, as was common then, augment the group with session musicians to add parts like the six-string bass on "That's the Way It's Got to Be," and the exotic-yet-minimal percussion on "I'll Cry with the Moon" and "I Am So Blue." Hume Paton remembers Jimmy Page playing on an unreleased track called "Knowing You," which got as far as getting sheet music but somehow didn't get on record. And "There Are Some," the B-side of "Now We're Thru," was done with session drummer Andy White, who had played some takes on the Beatles' "Love Me Do" session in Ringo Starr's place. "Horrendous stuff, all those meaningless rolls on the snare," observes Gallacher, who dislikes "There Are Some. But then again, it's a meaningless song."

After a year there had been three Decca singles and just one small hit, but there was still reason for the Poets to be optimistic. Oldham was forming a new label, Immediate, that would be more open to creative ideas and projects than the big U.K. major labels were, and the Poets were to be on Immediate's roster. Yet this is the point at which personnel shuffles and management shenanigans would begin to eat away at the band's drive. Oldham had already played a hand in ousting drummer

Alan Weir, which Gallacher recalls with regret. "Although the same age as the rest of us, [Weir's] attitude was that of a man of forty, essentially a funless, lifeless kind of guy. For those in Andrew's office concerned with 'les belles images,' he also *looked* forty. We also convinced ourselves that he was not too good a drummer, and this element needs serious reviewing, because listening to the old tapes it is obvious that he was in fact a very good drummer indeed. I say this to right a grievous wrong done the man by us in this area. [Guitarist] Tony Myles was a friend of Alan, and it was inevitable that he would follow very quickly, and he was a real loss: an excellent rhythm guitarist with a great knowledge of chord structure."

Jim Breakey replaced Weir, and after the first three singles, Fraser Watson came in for Tony Myles on guitar. Subsequent Poets material, in Gallacher's remaining days with the band, would either be written by Gallacher and Paton, or by George with both Paton and Watson. Still, their Immediate debut in late 1965, "Call Again"/"Some Things I Can't Forget," was very much in the style of their Decca singles. Gallacher and Watson both think "Call Again" wasn't strong enough to be an A-side, and preferred a couple of unreleased songs, "It's So Different Now" and "I'll Keep My Pride," that have shown up (in rough sound) on the unauthorized *In Your Tower* compilation. These songs and "Call Again" did show a slight maturation in sound and songwriting, still keeping the haunt count and introspection level at the high end of the thermometer. The vibe was a tad more folky and placid, however, perhaps reflecting folk-rock's ascendancy in 1965, and a little less prone to self-pity.

For those who can't get enough of the Poets at their most morose, however, "Some Things I Can't Forget" is the group's buried treasure. Driven by urgent guitar strums and crisp tambourine so prominent in the mix that it skittered off the red end of the VU meter, this was the Poets, and particularly vocalist Gallacher, at their most tortured, navigating a host of compelling key changes in less than a minute and fifty seconds. Standing up to the very best of the Zombies' work as a minor-mood classic, it also served as a prime exhibit of the Poets' talent for building drama by effectively juxtaposing sad verses with far brighter, more uplifting melodies in the bridge—a talent shared by just a few top rock composers, such as the Zombies, Graham Gouldman (on the hits he wrote for the Yardbirds like "Heart Full of Soul" and "For Your Love"), and (though they used it with far lesser frequency) the Beatles.

For their second Immediate single, the Poets opted, for the first time, to do a cover that reflected their onstage repertoire. "Baby Don't You Do It" had been a small hit for Marvin Gaye in the States in late 1964, but had become a big favorite among British mod bands, including the Who and the Small Faces, both of whom would eventually record it. "Hume and I would track down what was then fairly arcane material, i.e. obscure blues and soul, and incorporate them into our set and rearrange them to suit our style and sound," says Gallacher. "This combination of original material and other exotica was what the critic I mentioned earlier would come to listen to; we had a reputation early on of being very different." So why were "That's the Way It's Got to Be" and "Baby Don't You Do It" the only tracks he did with the band that were dipped in an R&B sensibility? "Our hard rockin' side was a victim of the nature of the songs we wrote."

The Poets were also edging toward a harder sound with the arrival of Watson, who in Gallacher's estimation "was and still is a brilliant guitarist who was somewhat curtailed by the Poets' disciplined and relatively simple demands of their second guitarist. Hume recognized Fraser's talent immediately and deferred all the cover tracks on stage to him. Fraser's preference for heavier playing changed our original sound completely. Ironic, really, that such a gifted player should in the context of the original Poets' stuff be less effective than the lesser player, Hume. But such is the nature of this thing."

Although "Baby Don't You Do It," with another monstrous bass line and its unusual, jittery tempos, was an imaginative and powerful interpretation, Oldham was not on hand to guide them in the studio. The production chair was assumed by Paul Raven, a minor recording artist known to Gallacher as an audience applause coach on the set of the TV show *Ready Steady Go*. After a complete image makeover, he would reemerge in the early 1970s as glam rock star Gary Glitter. "Paul Raven blew the recording of 'Baby Don't You Do It,'" asserts Gallacher. "The band had essentially produced it themselves and done a fantastic mix, until the idiot child that was the future Gary G decided to remix the track after we left the studio. The result being the released version, which paled in comparison to the original mix. Fraser and I still have regrets about this interference, because our arrangement and playing is considered by many as the best ever done of this song."

"When we left the studio, the mix that we had was really solid, earthy bass drum, snare drum, the guitar was quite up and quite loud," affirms Watson. "A good solid, driving number. We were really pleased with it. And the next thing we heard was a finished thing that Paul Raven had remixed. [He] added echoes and did things with the vocals and bits of clinking in the background. There was a review in *Melody Maker* [by] a well-known keyboard player who was reviewing the singles that week. He said the Poets single sounded like the Lynton Girls Choir, recorded in the toilets of the Blue Boar Cafe halfway up the M-1 [motorway]."

"I think Paul Raven felt like he was gonna try and show Andrew [Oldham] what he could do. It just was an attempt to impress Andrew. And trying to be Andrew-style was like a few years, already, previous" [i.e. out of fashion]. The single did get a lot of airplay on Radio London and Radio Caroline, and got the band a lot of work, according to Watson. That was scant reward, however, considering that when they came down to London, they still had to live in their vans for weeks at a time, doing their washing up at Euston train station. "Andrew wasn't exactly spending money on us either, you know," adds Watson wryly.

Oldham's absence from the "Baby Don't You Do It" single was indicative of deeper troubles in the band's management. The Poets were undoubtedly the most talented artists, aside from the Rolling Stones, in Oldham's management/production stable, which also included (for a time) Marianne Faithfull (who was a long way off from realizing her full potential), expatriate American soul singer P. P. Arnold, British blue-eyed soul singer Chris Farlowe, and nonentities such as the Mighty Avengers. However, as was the case with Brian Epstein and the Beatles, his primary clients were so successful and placed so many demands on his time that the other acts on his roster inevitably suffered.

"Andrew was preoccupied with divorcing the Stones," says Gallacher, "and there was very serious money being played for. So ourselves, Marianne, Chris Farlowe, and P. P. Arnold were neglected during this time." Both Paton and bassist John

Dawson, he adds, "say that the [Mick] Jagger/Andrew rift was less significant [a factor] on the Poets' failure than the split between Andrew and his partner Tony Calder. Tony was the mover-shaker, the doer of deals, the puller of strings and the fixer. The split unfortunately happened 'round about the second release, when we were asked to choose between Tony and Andrew. Unhesitatingly we chose Andrew, a decision which, with hindsight, Hume and John feel was disastrous. However, I have no such doubts—I could never envisage us working with Tony. The partnership was resurrected with the formation of Immediate, but the impetus was lost by then."

So it was that some opportunities were lost, particularly in America, where the Poets made no impact. "So confident was Andrew in us that we actually cut a film here for the *Ed Sullivan Show*, but then those politics intervened. Bob Crewe, the producer of the Four Seasons, loved our stuff and offered to take us to the U.S., but we decided instead to go back to Glasgow for a rest. Christ, it sounds pathetic now!"

Like Gallacher, Watson, though cognizant of Oldham's shortcomings as a manager, defends Andrew's work in the studio. "Andrew was pretty far out compared to the standard. Recording in this country was still kind of BBC refined. You'd have a doorman, maybe a tea lady would come by with tea, and the engineers all had pinstripe suits. Andrew was a sympathetic producer. He had his own style and his own sound. I liked the kind of reverby sound that Andrew had. He was interested in the band, he liked the band, and he obviously knew the band had a bit of talent and was a bit different from most bands. A nice guy, he didn't treat you like shite or anything like that.

"I think he still had a lot of affection for the boys. But the band was not pushed the way it should have been pushed. I don't know where that came from. Sometimes it would be a bit of jealousy from the Stones. The Poets were writing songs before the Stones were writing their own material. The Poets already had a handful of songs when they came down [to record]. George told me that Andrew spoke to Jagger and Richards and said, 'Get yourself in the studio and start writing some songs.'"

Oldham's decreasing interest left an opening for more tensions that would cause Gallacher to leave. "There were rifts in the band developing about what direction we should be going in. My main reason, however, was that Hume's father, a millionaire businessman, started interfering in things, knowing nothing about the game and objecting to me objecting about his ignorance of music matters. His interference eventually drove Andrew and us apart, and by then I'd had enough. When I went, so did Andrew. After I left it was just another band, albeit a very good one, but honestly nothing original. A jump on the psychedelic bandwagon: heavy guitar, self-indulgence. Everyone was doing it, much as I did later on with the Dead Loss Band."

Andi Mulvey was asked by Watson to replace Gallacher, and for a brief time, as Andi was breaking in, Mulvey and Gallacher shared lead vocals. "Andi had a kind of soul-y voice," says Watson. "A nice guy, not a great singer. Quite a good front man. But George had something magic. George has that moody image. There was a nice wee period, a really nice wee week, [when] the two of them were singing. In fact, if we could have kept that band together, it would have been blowin'. With two singers complementing each other, the two had a nice vibe together, 'cause George was so relaxed," knowing that he was about to leave the band's problems behind in a few days.

With Gallacher gone, the Poets turned away from original material and toward soul covers. Although they still had a lot of fans in Scotland—their fan club had about

2,000 members, according to Watson, and would send four double-decker buses full of fans to gigs—"things were beginning to go downhill even when I joined them." And after Gallacher's departure, "Original material was getting to the stage, it wasn't very popular. The later version of the Poets was picking up stuff [to cover] that hadn't been heard before. A record shop on the south side of Glasgow, he'd bring you black imports he'd brought in, like maybe early Gladys Knight stuff; stuff that hadn't been released here, and was unheard of. We did a lot of Impressions, the Isley Brothers. [The Isleys'] 'This Old Heart of Mine' was our national anthem." In the mid-1960s the Poets' stature had been such that they could get away with doing a lot of original material live. In the absence of Gallacher and the surge of interest in soul dance music, the Poets needed to respond to the turn of the tide just to professionally survive.

Even though by 1967 there was not a single original member left from the group that had recorded "Now We're Thru," the Poets, against all the odds, managed to release one last fine 45 that saw them admirably progressing with the times. Now back on Decca, the band put out "Wooden Spoon" in early 1967, a marvelous midpoint between mod rock, soul music, and early psychedelia, with hurricane-like drumming and impeccably timed dive-bomb guitar riffs from Watson. The B-side, "In Your Tower," was an early foray into Indian-influenced psychedelia with more unusual distorted guitar, though somewhat sullied by overdubs of flute that sounded less like a snake charmer than they did a cuckoo clock.

Watson doesn't remember the single too fondly, in part because the A-side was a composition by their new manager, Eric Woolfson, "which we really didn't fancy very much. We thought it was a bit corny." Their new drummer, Stuart MacKenzie, missed the session as he'd gone on a drunken binge in London the night before and "gone berserk in Wardour Street and smashed 200 windows or something like that," getting arrested and held without bail for a couple of weeks. Perhaps it's a blessing in disguise; that wonderful drum part was supplied by an emergency fill-in, Raymond Duffy, from the Gaylords (and later of Marmalade). Watson admits that "it was actually not bad" after the band had arranged and recorded it, but expresses a lot of frustration with the limitations of the studio, as onstage he "got a nice loud sort of sustained, distorted, blues, pretty rocky guitar sound. You got in the studio, and everything was turned right down. So it sounds like fucking noodling, you know? That's what we were up against. If you played live with a rough, loud, maybe slightly distorted guitar sound, when you went in the studio, you played much quieter. The recording process was way behind what the bands were doing live."

Watson, perhaps, channeled a lot of his frustrations with the studio and the Poets' career into a few good laughs at his manager's expense during his final session with them. "Eric was a really nice guy, but it was getting quite uptight. You got at the stage where you'd start winding him up. The *engineers* would wind him up. When we did the B-side, he's walking about with leader tape sticking out the back of his pinstripe suits." For the "In Your Tower" session, "I put stink bombs under the bass drum pedal. We're rehearsing the number, and of course stink bombs are busting under the bass drum pedal, unknown to anybody. The whole studio's stinking. Eric walked out for an hour and left the session, refused to come back.

"We carried on doing 'In Your Tower,' and were quite happy with it. We didn't want the flutes on it; these kinds of cheap Indian flutes, bamboo flutes. He started saying, 'We've got to put this on.' And we went, 'No way.' He said, '*I'm* putting this on it.' I stuck a bit of chewing gum in the flutes. The track comes up, Eric starts blowing the flute, and nothing happens. [Eric] smashed the flute over [guitarist Ian McMillan's] head and walked out." Nonetheless, "When they had the finished demo, the flute was on it. We actually had more guitar." It was an odd, anticlimactic end to the career of Scotland's finest band. Not quite the end, actually; the group continued until 1971, although no more records were released. Mulvey and Watson, however, left in 1967, truly reducing the band to a Poets in name only.

Watson and Gallacher, now brothers-in-law as Gallacher had married Watson's sister, were to work with each other often over the next thirty years. Gallacher was briefly in a band with Scottish rock legend Alex Harvey, Palais, although Harvey wouldn't reach his biggest audience until the 1970s. After the Poets, Watson joined the Pathfinders, who recorded some demos of George Gallacher's songs, with George on vocals, in 1967. One of these, "Dawn," eventually saw the light of day as a track on the *Freak Beat Fantoms* compilation of British '60s rarities. A fine piece of restrained psychedelia, it retained Gallacher's characteristic aptitude for mysterious, teary melody, decorated by Ronnie Leahy's keening, fluid organ riffs. It also went beyond the standard boy-girl romantic themes of the Poets' compositions into more abstract lyricism in which the mood of the music is reflected by the elusive nature of the words. It was indicative, perhaps, of where the Poets' music would have headed had they managed to stay together longer.

Unfortunately, it remained an indication, as the Pathfinders sans Gallacher were signed to Apple Records, mutating into White Trash and then Trash. The Trash story is an epic in itself, with Watson and his band getting lost in the general chaos of Apple and the Beatles' breakup, issuing just two singles, including a cover of the Beatles' "Golden Slumbers." Still, it afforded them an opportunity for a close-up glimpse at some of the Apple infighting and madness (which, Watson says, cost them a chance to appear at Woodstock when the label wouldn't pay for Trash's airfare), and Watson got to play acoustic guitar on a couple of tracks on George Harrison's classic *All Things Must Pass*. Watson also got to visit John Lennon and Yoko Ono during their famous Bed-In campaign for peace in Amsterdam in 1969. He had to; the members of Trash were stranded in Amsterdam when their hotel wouldn't surrender their passports until the bill was paid, and they couldn't leave until Lennon had OK'd a request for Apple to cover it.

In the 1970s Gallacher and Watson formed the Dead Loss Band, in Gallacher's words "essentially a heavy rock band, very loud and self-indulgent and heavily aligned to far-left politics. We never sought a record deal, though there was some interest in us." To pay the bills they also formed the Dansettes, to play rock 'n' roll and 1960s classics. In the 1990s the nucleus of the Dead Loss Band, including Gallacher and Watson, formed the Blues Poets, who are still active today. Indeed, Gallacher's excited to report that they could be doing some soundtrack material for a Hollywood movie that might be made from a novel by Scottish author James Kelman, who is a Blues Poets fan. Given the Poets' gift for attracting literary fans such as Kelman and Brian Morton, it makes sense that Gallacher returned to university at the age of forty-five to take degrees in philosophy and literature. Currently he uses his postgraduate degree in teaching for his day job, working with Kosovar refugees in Glasgow.

At a time when many bands such as the Poets are being rediscovered and reevaluated, the Poets are still getting victimized to a degree by record company and management politics. Most of their singles have been reissued, in dribs and drabs, on obscure compilations of obscure 1960s British rock, some of which are already out of print. There has never been a Poets compilation album, the licensing for such an endeavor (which might include a considerable number of unreleased tracks) complicated by the split of their catalog between the Decca and Immediate labels. Gallacher also says "whoever owns the stuff shouts large bucks at anyone who has ever wanted to put one together." He's amused that "the plethora of psychedelic compilations that feature the Poets—and I mean when I was in them—do somehow credit us with being seminal to the genre. I guess it must be the fact that the music had no antecedent, that it was so different to what was going around. The greatest compliment that was ever offered was [John] Lennon's comment to Andrew that 'Now We're Thru' was 'weird.'

"I associate psychedelia with fun and swirling vivid colors. Yet the Poets—as any photo of the time will show—dressed in stark black and white, the complete and utter opposite. We looked like the old Calvinist preachers who still haunt the more extreme fringes of the Protestant churches here in Scotland. Miserable-looking bastards, who frown on anyone enjoying themselves. Historically, that's what happened during the Reformation: music and dance were considered sinful, evil, and were banned, and still are in parts of northwest Scotland. The Poets' image was cold and bleak, just like the music, and not what I would remotely consider psychedelia to be about."

What *was* distinctly Scottish about the Poets, he adds, "was that old Celtic self-pitying doom and gloom in our character and in the music. Those minor melodies: there is no irony or humor evident, only that unrelenting misery."

Gallacher is, of course, underselling the music here. The Poets' singles are a hell of a lot catchier than the doom-and-gloom goth rock of the 1980s and beyond, for instance (and not nearly as dark and depressing). Catchy tunes, however, are not always the tickets for pop success, and do not always come in sweet and easy-to-digest packages. That might ultimately be, Gallacher admits, why the Poets never became bigger than they did. Because in spite of those nice melodies, "Our stuff did not make for easy listening. I think it was as simple as that."

Recommended Recording:

In Your Tower (Strike). More than is the case for any other act in this book, the amount and availability of Poets' recordings is unjustly slim in proportion to the musicians' artistic worth. They never had the opportunity to make an album; their six singles have never been officially issued on one compilation, and some unreleased material remains tied up in the vaults. This unauthorized (but pretty legitimate-looking) compilation does include both sides of all six singles, plus the rough-sounding (in fidelity, not execution) outtakes "I'll Keep My Pride" and "It's So Different Now"; a longer version of "Baby Don't You Do It"; the late 1960s George Gallacher & Pathfinders demo "Dawn"; and two demos and a rare promo single of jingles, by post-Watson versions of the Poets. Until the official parties get their act together and give the Poets the aboveboard anthology they deserve, it's the only way to hear their legacy in one place.

Psychedelic Sailors

The psychedelic experience, in terms of drug-taking, might have meant exploring new dimensions of the mind and the senses. In terms of music, it meant exploring new dimensions of sound. Particularly in the last years of the 1960s, the psychedelic era allowed musicians to paint sonic pictures that were previously not even envisioned as possibilities. Though satirized or dismissed by some critics as excessive and naive, there was rarely as much risk-taking and border-smashing in rock as there was in psychedelia. Drugs might have played a part in the creation of psychedelic rock, but they wouldn't have done a thing if the musicians hadn't possessed fertile and creative imaginations in the first place. It's that sense of imagination and possibility, rather than eagerness for a soundtrack to LSD trips, that draws us back to the best of those reckless and exciting psychedelic records today.

Psychedelia is a loose assignation, and certainly half of the acts covered in other chapters—including such diverse artists as the Pretty Things, the Fugs, and Tim Buckley—immersed themselves in psychedelic rock at various points in their careers. The four acts selected for this section, however, were each in their way especially determined to burst into new sonic territory. Each achieved varying levels of recognition, and all are unified by the simultaneous singularity and underestimation of their achievements. Some would dispute the inclusion of Arthur Brown in a volume such as this, as he had a huge international hit and top-selling album. Perhaps due to the almost unparalleled speed of his commercial (not artistic) rise and fall, however, his stint as front man for the Crazy World of Arthur Brown has rarely been examined with the depth it deserves.

Brown was using his voice and lyrics to explore forbidden vistas of the mind. The Electric Prunes, both aided and restricted by input from their producer and outside songwriters, helped pioneer the use of the studio as a recording instrument with their ingenious, eerie guitar distortion and tape manipulation. Randy Holden, perhaps the most obscure performer examined in this book, used his guitar to smash the limits of volume and sound projection. Meanwhile, Kaleidoscope employed an arsenal of instruments to expand the palette of sounds generated by a rock band beyond what anyone had previously conceived. In the process the group paved the way for the harmonious co-existence of folk, rock, blues, and world music within the same band, a feat that has rarely been duplicated.

Arthur Brown, risking self-immolation in front of the Crazy World of Arthur Brown.
Credit: Michael Ochs Archives.com.

The Crazy World of Arthur Brown

"I am the god of hellfire and I bring you...FIRE!!!"* If there is one utterance that Arthur Brown is known for throughout the world, that demonic invocation—which kicked off his international chart-topper "Fire" in 1968—is certainly it. It's hard to reconcile the image of the "Fire"-shouter in death-mask makeup, complemented by flame-sprouting helmet, with the soft-spoken, wiry Englishman who greets me at the train station in his village an hour from London. As we leave the building, his eye catches a headline at the newsstand and he gasps softly, "Oh, *no.*" He's just learned that Screaming Lord Sutch, the man who introduced ghoulish theatrics into British rock 'n' roll, has hung himself.

"I was pretty saddened to see he'd popped off today," he says that evening, thinking back to when he first met Sutch in the late 1960s. "[Sutch] said, 'What I did was just a bit of a laugh and dressing up. What I like about what you've done, Arthur, is you've made it into real theater. It's not just gimmicks and a laugh.'"

Brown is serving me almond butter-covered rice cakes in his modest but pleasant basement flat in Lewes, a small and well-to-do town in the Sussex South Downs. The god of hellfire is hardly a threatening figure, or a cosseted rock star, on his home turf, talking animatedly with the college-age kids who call to him as we wind our way back to his house from the station, stopping at the health food store to pick up apricot cakes for tea. He knows when to turn his onstage persona on and off. At any rate, despite what you might think, "Fire" was just one element of his act, and just one face of a man adept at playing many roles as a rock 'n' roll front man. "Fire" might have been his only hit, but as he recounts his career while twilight descends on his living room, it's clear that the man and the music are far more complex than the stereotypical one-hit wonder.

The Crazy World of Arthur Brown album that contained "Fire" was a culmination of divergent energies and disciplines—R&B, jazz, opera, poetry, theater, and philosophical studies—which had engaged Brown for a decade before its release in 1968. Contrary to the perception of Brown as a one-song act, the album revealed multiple facets of a man determined to journey through hell and beyond, and could have been embraced as one of the first rock concept albums had he been allowed to construct it in accordance with his original vision. Only in 1968, perhaps, could such a strange single and album have made the Top Ten. Brown has in fact continued to explore numerous on-the-edge directions in his music and life in the ensuing thirty years, but it was just that once that his muse and the marketplace coincided. In retrospect, that success was something of an accident that Brown never particularly wanted, or regretted losing after the Crazy World of Arthur Brown group imploded in the late 1960s.

The Crazy World of Arthur Brown was the singer's first album, but Brown had been singing professionally almost from the beginning of the 1960s, usually in far more conventional groups. Listening to trad jazz bands in London around the turn of the decade, a few years before the Beatles kick-started British rock, first gave Brown the bug to make music. "When they went into the improvised thing, I went into another universe," reminisces Brown with pleasure, little of his enthusiasm dimmed by the subsequent forty years. "I'd sort of lost all my social inhibitions for a minute. When I came down I thought, 'God, that's what *I'll* do.'"

Brown's commitment to performance became serious when he was going to Reading University in the early 1960s, first in trad jazz bands as a bass player and singer, also in a folk duo, and then in a modern jazz quintet. Besotted by James Brown's classic 1962 recording *Live at the Apollo*, he got into R&B and soul music as part of the Southwest Five, covering Brown, Ray Charles, Little Johnny Taylor, and Bobby Bland numbers. If there was anything to set Brown off from the legions of other British R&B performers at this point, it was not repertoire, but his voice, with an operatic quality—dramatically resonant at the lower end, with a prickly shrillness in the upper register—that was rare among rock vocalists of that or any other time. An odd once-off single, "You Don't Know," was recorded in the mid-1960s as a charity giveaway with the Diamonds, and shows his rich voice, half-screams suggestive of madness, and taste for ominous R&B-derived chord progressions in place.

There was more hard apprenticeship to be done at a residency with the Arthur Brown Set in Paris, churning out the same music, seven nights a week, at the same club. Ennui with the soul covers expected of live bands in 1966 gave rise to a more original approach. "We'd get bored. It was a very wild club, very wild audience. So they encouraged us to do all sorts of adventurous improvisation. There was an air of freedom. It just allowed all of the theatrical stuff to come out—telling stories, doing mimes about General DeGaulle, anything that would put a different mood into [it].

"It was during that period that I started to want to do something that was theatrical, both musically and visually. The reason for doing it visually was because the imagery that I was using was not, in England at least, currently in rock. 'The Devil's Grip' [which would become his proper debut single] was not something that people put into music up till then. It needed something so that people would listen to the words, because if they were just listening as if it was normal music, they'd dismiss it. [With] the visual image, it became something else altogether."

By doing a backing track for a 1966 Roger Vadim film starring Jane Fonda (*La Curée*, titled *The Game Is Over* in the U.S.), Brown got enough money to return to England. There he met one of the most underrated keyboardists of the 1960s, Vincent Crane, whose background was a similar mishmash of the ordinary and the avant-garde. Although Crane had led his own R&B-stoked beat group, he too was attracted to merging rock with other forms. In 1966 he worked as musical director for the Word Engine, a mixed-media show of poetry, theater, and music, including the poet Pete Brown (soon to write lyrics with Jack Bruce for Cream classics like "White Room"). A *Melody Maker* ad brought in drummer Drachen Theaker, and the group decided to make a go of it as a guitarless trio, an unusual move at a time when guitar heroes were coming into vogue. A new sound began to take shape that, although grounded in R&B and rock, was more outrageous and eclectic in structure and execution.

"We could do semiclassical stuff, rock, R&B, soul, Indian-type progressions—anything," enthuses Brown. "Vincent was able to absorb various influences. He'd been to the Trinity School of Music, and could play classical music very beautifully. He could also play modern jazz, boogie-woogie, pop. He got, on one of the tours, twenty-one James Brown albums, and listened to them endlessly. He loved music hall, Gilbert and Sullivan, anything with wit in it. He occasionally would sit down with a guitar and sing some beautiful folk melody. And [he] could read music, compose it, write it, orchestrate it, conduct it.

"Because it was just the drums-keyboard, there was no need for any ESP between a guitar and keyboard to say, 'Which chord are we going to?' Because it was *just* keyboard. Vince would go somewhere, and I'd be there with him. So we were very elastic. We could go all over the place in the middle of one number, and then bring it back. So I learned how to do a lot of poetic improvisation, which was not really done [before then]. We'd do spoken poetry with just rhythms. It was all exploratory."

When the group, now named the Crazy World of Arthur Brown, began to perform, "We were singing all the songs that later became popular on the underground. But finding an outlet for it was well nigh impossible. It was a little too outrageous, and there wasn't an underground circuit." Brown even joined the pop-soul group the Foundations (well before their big hit "Baby, Now That I Found You") for a month in early 1967 to get some work. Then record producer and countercultural impresario Joe Boyd saw the Crazy World and "said, 'We'll give you one shot at the UFO Club.' And they loved it."

London's UFO Club, for which Boyd worked as musical director, was in operation for only about a year, but has attained mythic status as ground zero for the British psychedelic underground. A number of the best early U.K. psych bands built their following there, most notably Pink Floyd, but also the more cultish Soft Machine and Tomorrow, as well as the Crazy World of Arthur Brown. "The atmosphere was different from your normal pop atmosphere," explains Brown now. "The [lyrical] concerns were more poetic, more realistic. The music was exploring an inner landscape, not just the old—brilliant though it was—Chuck Berry landscape, which was more external imagery. The music broke out of the mold of pop up to that time, allowing what had only been present in modern jazz, which was improvisation, playing with electronics. Fifty percent of [our] act would be improvised."

A big part of their stage act grew in tandem with the Crazy World's songwriting, which was growing progressively more concerned with exploring extreme behavior and states of mind. "We had a light show which changed color with the mood of the music. I also had all these costumes on. The interior world of one person was mirrored in the costumes, because I wore different layers under each other, and took them off as I performed. There was, first, a guy with this huge Tibetan monk's robe and silver mask. That came off; underneath was a black cape, and it'd be 'I Put a Spell on You,' the magician. [For] 'Come and Buy,' we had lights and a sun god's outfit, a sort of huge sun with flames, rays of light coming out of it. There were huge costumes with these geometric patterns—orange, red, blue, not hellfire, but pure radiant fire. There was also the fire helmet. We would end the stage act with 'I've Got Money,' it'd be just shirt and trousers, I'd be a normal guy.

"And then stylized dances: a different dance for each of the characters. That, coupled with the lights, strobes, and costumes, produced something which was real theater. It wasn't just gimmicks. I think Peter Gabriel came pretty close, but I don't think anybody else has ever done it. *Proper* theater," he clarifies. "Alice Cooper did touch it."

The UFO performances won over an especially influential fan and set them on the course from the underground to the Top 10. "Pete Townshend came down to the UFO in his caftan. He liked it, and took me out in a Lincoln Continental American car. He said, 'Well, you know, my record company just missed the Bonzos [the Bonzo Dog Band, another theatrical, though more comic, group of the period]. We wanted to sign them, and screwed around so much that we lost them. So I want to make sure that we got you. I think we should put you on our label.'"

Through Townshend's influence the Crazy World of Arthur Brown was signed to Track, the label run by the Who's managers, Kit Lambert and Chris Stamp. With a roster including the Who and Jimi Hendrix, Track was in the always uncommon position of having commercially successful product *and* granting freedom for its acts to experiment. Lambert and Stamp also began managing the Crazy World, and in late 1967 the first single, "Devil's Grip"/"Give Him a Flower," appeared.

Although the single was not a hit, it served as fair warning that Brown was going to be dipping into the more disturbing undercurrents of the psychedelic experience. "The Devil's Grip" at last captured the Crazy World sound on disc, motored by Crane's creepy-yet-catchy black mass organ riffs, and put over by Brown's vocals, shakily gentle on the verses, rising into stentorian high-pitched yelps at the most dramatic crescendos. "Give Him a Flower," in utter contrast, was a pisstake on the flower-power movement, lighter and more comical than anything else the Crazy World recorded. The underground apparently didn't mind being targeted for vicious parody, as according to Brown, "It became the anthem for the hippies. They would all sing the chorus. There's a very limited version on the record. [Onstage] it would go on for like twelve, twenty minutes; there would be all those jokes, little skits." "Devil's Grip" was more indicative of Brown's intentions, particularly in its satanic references. "It was the record that introduced all that imagery to the rock field, in England at least," he claims.

"Devil's Grip" was child's play when set next to the roller-coaster suite of sounds and moods that comprised the Crazy World of Arthur Brown's debut album, released in 1968. Brown's vocals were not just those of a strange British R&B singer; there was a layer of psychedelic dementia, as interpreted by a man determined to explore the abyss separating good and evil, coherence and madness. Brown did not so much sing like a man possessed by demons, as easy as that cliché would be to apply, but like a philosopher privy to seduction by temptation and forbidden fruits, at the same time cognizant of their dangers. He may have been screaming about being trapped in nightmares on occasion, or intoning poems about the flames of hell, but one sensed he was savoring the experience as much as dreading it.

What set this apart from the subsequent innumerable inferior records (mostly by heavy metal bands) venturing into similar themes was the care taken to ensure musical and lyrical subtlety. Brown's voice was itself an instrument to marvel at, moving from alluring whispers and portentous spoken poetry to glass-smashing screams in an instant. "I couldn't do some of the things that other people could do," says Brown of his vocals, so often (and accurately) pegged as "operatic." "I remember talking to Lene Lovich"—another rock singer prone to high-pitched hysterics—"and that's how it sounds to her as well. She sang these other soul-y songs, and thought, 'Well, [I] can't do these very well. I want to do *this*, 'cause that's what *I* can do.'"

The arrangements also veered between meditative funereal passages and crazed psychedelic hyperdrive, accented by deft touches of orchestrated brass and strings. It is impossible to underestimate the contributions of Vincent Crane, possibly the most overlooked 1960s rock organist, in this regard. While playing in a manner similar to another British rock organist, Graham Bond, who fused jazz, blues, soul, rock, and classical motifs with sinister overtones, Crane took it to a yet more intense level. He complemented the mania of Brown's vocals with exhilaratingly vibrant and piercing riffs, devising unholy dissonant chords suitable for the devil's lair's doorbells. At times he spit out swirls of notes so rapidly that it sounded as if jazz organist Jimmy Smith had been kidnapped by the Merry Pranksters for an acid test.

"The thing with Vincent, you'd have to slow it down," chuckles Brown. "I couldn't sing at the speed he would play. Even on 'Come and Buy'...." He breaks off and sings a quick extract of that lyric at a hundred miles an hour: "'I can sell you suns from the morning, from suns to sell you for the morning for tea.' Well, he would play even faster! Nobody could dance, because he was so bloody fast.

"Vincent and I would thrash it out together. A lot of the chords would be ones that he would suggest, and I would then choose. Or sometimes, he would suggest the chord, and I would [say] 'Oh yeah, I can go to that.' Or we'd cut to the end of a particular place and I'd go, 'Listen.'" He breaks out into his trademark operatic trill. "And he'd go, 'Oh, *there*, you mean.'"

The Crazy World of Arthur Brown was a strange album, even by the standards of 1968 psychedelic rock, but it was not as unrelentingly weird as some remember. True, there were the foreboding scenes of nightmares, fire, and anxiety-riddled bewilderment that dominated the first side in particular. Yet the jazzy "Rest Cure" hinted at the possibility of a relaxing escape from the torture, while the heavy rock arrangements on the R&B covers "I Put a Spell on You" (originally by Screamin' Jay Hawkins) and "I've Got Money" (an obscure early-'60s James Brown single) introduced a bit of much-needed levity. "Spontaneous Apple Creation," its Dada poetry and special effects reminiscent of a 1950s science-fiction film computer gone haywire, was as crazy as the Crazy World of Arthur Brown got, but "Child of My Kingdom" ended the album on a more optimistic note. Like much of the record, it's an illustration of how adept the band was at playing different moods against each other, the melancholy Eastern strains of the verse segueing into the uplifting jazz-blues of the bridge, complete with jaunty whistling.

Though largely based on the group's stage act, the album and its songs of devils and deities, notes Brown, "was an internal journey inwards in somebody's psyche. It was through having immersed myself in Keats, Blake, Shelley, Shakespeare, all the great romantic poets that had dealt with the human interior landscape. I'd studied philosophy, I had connections with the Druids at that time. Because that was the background of the lyrics, the music had to mirror that. Instead of glossing over the darker area of the interior, it was like saying, OK, I want to have a look at it, using the language that had been developed by those other poets who'd looked at it. The imagery of the mind works through polarity. What are the poles? Well, you've got gods and devils. In the modern world, there was no other imagery."

The strings and brass that added to the classiness of the album very nearly did not make it onto the final product. "We had recorded the whole album with just bass, drums, keyboard, and myself. Kit [Lambert] took it over to America, and Atlantic Records said, 'Crazy stuff! But, uh, the drummer can't keep time.' So Kit came back and said, [here Brown adopts an exaggerated upper-class English accent] 'I don't know what to do about this! We've got to get it out over there, but they don't want to put the album....' And Kit had recorded it on four-track; he'd recorded the drums and the keyboard on the *same* track. I said, 'We can't possibly redo it all. It'd cost us a fortune.' 'Fire' was twenty-three takes, it wasn't just like one take and in. So it was a lot of money already invested. And he said, [he goes into his posh Lambert accent again] 'I know what we could do, Arthur. Dub some strings on it.' We found out Vincent could orchestrate it, and that's how it came about. And a good thing, too. I always felt that the strings and the brass, as far as the recording, took the place of the visuals for a live concert.

"I remember Kit took two weeks, probably fourteen hours a day to mix it. He said he would never again subject himself to such torture." Perhaps as a result of this mixing frenzy, the five songs on side one—the "Fire" side—also exist in mono versions that differ considerably from the more common stereo ones, especially in the addition of several entertaining orchestral intros and spoken sound bites linking some of the tracks.

One member of the trio was not so thrilled with the dressed-up tracks. "We were on tour in America when it came out. Kit had done the final mix. Chris Stamp came over to our hotel, handed us the acetate. He got about four minutes into the acetate, and Drachen leapt across the room, took it off the turntable, smashed it on the wall. Because his drums were buried. Kit not only did that, but on 'I Put a Spell on You' and 'Child of My Kingdom,' it was John Marshall, who later played in Soft Machine, who was the drummer." Brown also says that a different drummer, Jon Hiseman (who played with Graham Bond, John Mayall, and Colosseum), took Theaker's place on the pre-LP "Devil's Grip" track.

There was one song on the album that would overshadow all of the others, defining Brown's public image to such an extent that it gave him an unfairly one-dimensional image in some quarters. "Fire," built around an organ riff as insistent and memorable as the fuzz guitar riff that had anchored the Rolling Stones' "Satisfaction," was a classic that funneled the Crazy World of Arthur Brown's best traits into a tasty three-minute package. It was, again, structured to set off the hard rocking verses with serene, yet still uneasy, bridges in which Brown's vocals built from a lullaby to a cord-shredding yell, made all the more disquieting by his lunatic cackles. Television clips of Brown doing "Fire" in the late 1960s show a rail-thin man with black-and-white death-mask makeup writhing like a snake to the music before donning a fire-sprouting helmet and disappearing as clouds of smoke envelop the stage, the other musicians wearing skeleton masks and medieval robes. That might seem tame by Marilyn Manson standards, but in 1968 it was more than enough to shock Middle America.

"Fire" was the last song on the album to be written, says Brown and "I knew it needed something the other tunes didn't have. It needed to be really powerful, pushing. In the place that Vincent and I rehearsed, another couple of guys who used to come, Mike Finesilver and Peter Ker, had a song I quite liked. I said, 'I really like the melody. So do you mind if Vincent and I take hold of it and create something from it?' It's a bit like Bartok. He used to go around on the back of a wagon and listen to the peasants' songs, and when he came back, noted down what he liked of it, then orchestrated it, and it became his." (Finesilver and Ker, incidentally, would use their songwriting royalties from "Fire" to help start Pathway Studios, where seminal early new wave and pub rock tracks by Elvis Costello, Dave Edmunds, the Damned, Wreckless Eric, the Police, Siouxsie & the Banshees, Dire Straits, and Lene Lovich were recorded.)

Brown's gladiator-of-doom spoken "god of hellfire" opening should have been enough to keep the single from getting enough airplay to get a hit. Yet it rocketed up the charts in the summer of 1968, all the way to number one in England. Two months later it followed suit in the U.S., despite being banned on some stations, stopping at number two; only the Beatles' "Hey Jude," then in the midst of a nine-week reign at the top, kept it from going to number one. The Crazy World of Arthur Brown album, though people tend to have forgotten, was also a smash, making number two in the U.K. and number seven in the U.S. Brown had taken psychedelic pseudo-madness to the masses.

For all The Crazy World of Arthur Brown's impact, Brown feels that the record could have been a greater tour de force had he been allowed to sequence the album as he originally wished. "I had a big tussle with Kit Lambert. Kit had a very big eye for what would sell. So when I came up with the idea for this theme album, he said, 'Nobody's going to buy *that*.' I said, 'Well, Kit, you're *wrong*.' And he said, 'No, I'm not.' I was, 'Well, I'm *not* going to do all the bloody covers you want.' And he was, 'Well, I'll let you have control over one side of the album, and I want control over the other.' And I said [Brown assumes a disgusted tone of voice] *'Fine!'* Because if that's the only way we were going to get it out, I'll compromise to that extent. So he got the side with 'Spell on You' and stage numbers that went down well. And my side was the 'Fire' side."

This was back in the days, of course, when there were two-sided LPs instead of CDs, and Brown envisioned suites of songs for each LP side that would be linked thematically. "One side ended on a confused, almost violent note; it was more of a questioning. The other side was a peaceful ending, a resolution. It had gone through another progression. Neither of them was the A- or the B-side, so depending on what mood you were in, you would put one side on or the other. Then, depending which way you saw it, it might start where the first side ended with an uplift, or it might be the other way around. It was much more of a free think. Lambert wanted me to change side A, the 'Fire' side, and have it end with a nice gentle thing, so everybody'd feel happy. I said, 'That's not the point, Kit.' I'm thinking of redoing…doing the version with a complete A- and B-side."

Had Brown been allowed to make the album as he wished, it would have been something like an opera. The irony was that Lambert's other clients, the Who, would have a mammoth hit the following year with *Tommy*, which was very much a rock opera, in spite of Lambert's opposition to Brown's ideas along those lines. "Yeah, he was wrong [about my album]," laughs Brown. "But, you know, the nice thing about Kit was, he'd admit it in the end.

"I came back from an American tour to Lambert's flat, and he said to me, 'I'm going to do it, Arthur. You wait and see.' 'What are you talking about, Kit?' 'This thing that Peter's [Townshend] written—I'm going to call it an opera, which it jolly well is. But you just see. Those snobs will eat it up.' And he was right."

Although Brown has mixed memories of his association with Lambert, he still appreciates the good things of which Kit was capable. "Lambert and Stamp were masters of manipulating the media. Lambert was gay; he had all the gay friends. Stamp had all the young women, and Lambert had the *old* women. They loved Lambert's flamboyance.

"He went over to America, came back and said, 'Look, I don't know what to do. Because the FM stations, we're not quite what they want.' So what he did was, he eventually got a couple of AM stations to play the whole of one side of the album, whereupon they got such a response that the FM stations suddenly all started calling up and saying, 'We want it.' We had the unusual thing in those days of both AM and FM play, which wasn't normal.

"Hendrix, at the same time, had all the black stations. My makeup wouldn't let you know whether I was black or white, and I sounded black. So Hendrix said to all the guys, play *this* motherfucker. So we went on all the black stations, the AM *and* the FM stations. That is pretty incredible."

In the late 1960s, the Crazy World of Arthur Brown's popularity was such that the group was able to share bills with the Doors, Jimi Hendrix, the Mothers of Invention, the Who, the Small Faces, and Joe Cocker, among others. Brown found the American tours in particular simultaneously ecstatic and exhausting, with his frenetic, leaping stage presence resulting in accidents that were not part of the act, such as broken toes and a hand injury requiring fourteen stitches. The pace began to take its toll on the band even before "Fire" became a hit, when Crane and Theaker had to be replaced during a mid-1968 American tour due to nervous exhaustion. Soon Theaker was out of the band for good, as the timing problems that had necessitated overdubs and additional drummers in past recordings had become insurmountable.

"Drachen was very creative," says Brown. "A lot of the things that seemed to be Vincent's were actually Drachen's, because the rhythm [he breaks off to mimic one of Crane's high-octane organ riffs] well, Vincent copied Drachen. Vincent thought Drachen had good ideas, but his timing...Vincent found it intolerable. Finally it came to a point where Vincent said, 'Look, I can't do this anymore. Either he goes or I go. In a normal band, the drummer lays down a groove, and I solo around it. In *this* band, *I* have to spend all my time holding down the groove while he solos around it.' He later played with Love and Graham Bond; in 1970 he said, 'I've conquered my disability' [as a drummer]. He put on [a] Graham Bond track, and halfway through the first track, he slowed down, and then sped up. So it was a real problem he had." Theaker was replaced by Carl Palmer, who would play live with Brown for about a year, well in advance of rising to stardom as part of Emerson, Lake & Palmer. (Despite some written reports to the contrary, Brown says Palmer never played on any of the Crazy World of Arthur Brown studio releases.)

A greater problem was the band's onstage stagnation. At this point Brown had tired of the songs that comprised both the album and his stage act, and was ready to unveil an entirely new act and repertoire. The problem was that the songs that people were coming to see were the ones from the album, which were still new and exciting to listeners, if not the performers themselves, in late 1968 and early 1969. Brown realizes that the success of the "Fire" song in particular might have straitjacketed him into an image from which it was hard to escape. "While we were on tour, they took their 'Fire' track off the album and said, 'Right, here's the single. We want a heavy, hard image.' In a way, it became somewhat limiting. Because that's not what the band was about. It was much wider. There was the light side, there was the comic side, and there was the political side.

"See, we'd been doing that act for quite a while. We became top-drawer level with [soul singer and popular British live attraction] Geno Washington in England on the strength of the stage act before we put out any records. But then having done that, there was nowhere to go. We hadn't had a hit, we needed a new stage act, so we created the new stage act. Then 'Fire' was a hit, so what they wanted to see was not anything new. So we dropped the new one."

In fact, the Crazy World of Arthur Brown would end up releasing only that one album—an unbelievable state of affairs, on the surface, for a band that had made such a huge transatlantic commercial splash with both the LP and the "Fire" single. Brown had in fact worked on a second stage act that would have comprised different material, and gotten as far as making some demos of the tunes. As to what a second Crazy World album might have sounded like, he muses, "It would have broadened it, but have had the same basic root sound. It was a little more jazziness in some of the numbers, a little more *real* classical singing. There might have been one good single. There was one particular atonal number that was sung in very strange time, 10/8."

In 1969, when the band could have been consolidating stardom with a second album, it was collapsing. Brown was "strung out because I was dealing with all of that shit with America, and I got into drugs as well." A single, "Space Plexus," that took the weirdness of the band into yet more inscrutable realms, was prepared but not released (it can be heard as a demo on the *Track Record* bootleg, and was also recorded for *Galactic Zoo Dossier*, the 1971 album Brown would do with Kingdom Come). In mid-1969, Crane and Palmer left to form Atomic Rooster, a manic band bridging psychedelia with progressive rock and heavy metal. Despite Crane's presence and some hit albums and singles in Britain, they sounded like a cartoon version of the genuinely provocative music he had made as part of the Crazy World of Arthur Brown.

Brown, in the meantime, was making a 180-degree turn from the commercial success that seemed to be his for the taking. He rejected an offer for two-thirds of a million dollars to record for CBS. "At the last minute, I decided that because Kit and Chris had put me up there, I couldn't walk out just because I was dissatisfied. So I left the management, and stayed with the recording [for Lambert and Stamp] for a while. But then Kit was heavily into heroin, so I left altogether towards the end of '69.

"We had some new numbers we were working on. But when I rejected the CBS offer, we went back to the old tunes. We used to do about two new tunes in the act. In that time, I never felt that what we were doing actually represented what I was really feeling, so I didn't want to do it. By then I was very tired. You just don't have the energy to...it's boredom," he concludes.

This did not come as a surprise to a member of the UFO Club audience, Peter Brown (unrelated to the Pete Brown who wrote lyrics with Jack Bruce), who described Arthur Brown as follows in *Days in the Life: Voices from the English Underground, 1961-1971*: "The best dancer I've ever seen...if you see any character in the entertainment business who dedicates their whole being to make every night's performance like an opening night, then you know they'll never last. Well, Arthur was like that. It was obvious that he was going to burn out, because every performance was a total performance, the man literally burnt himself out every night."

Continues Brown: "My next band, Puddletown Express, just went out and improvised, and of course the audience was aghast. They wanted to hear our set tunes. We didn't play *any* of the old tunes. We were trying to persuade Polydor to let us put out an album a week, because we were an improvising band. We just wanted to do, like, small sales, and get it out to the fans. Do it like a comic, really. Of course they thought we were barmy." Around this time Brown started work on an aborted "Brain Opera," collaborating with Viv Stanshall of the Bonzo Dog Band (see the Bonzo Dog Band chapter for more details).

Brown was in one sense committing commercial suicide, and in another anticipating the more abrasive DIY, antiestablishment practices that would become widespread with the advent of punk, new wave, and alternative rock much later. "We had an alternative business structure. I decided that all this hierarchical, autocratic bullshit wasn't what I wanted to be involved [in]. We had a democratic band, a manager who got the same cut as everybody else, and we all lived together. It was a good experiment.

"I was more concerned with continuing to explore what meaning did life have. I wasn't concerned about hits, getting rich, and all that shit. I did music that reflected that, and all of the esoteric studying I was doing. The albums came out of those, they weren't mass-market type albums." That's quite an understatement, judging from the first of these. *Strange Lands*, actually billed to the Crazy World of Arthur Brown, was not released until the late 1980s, although it had been recorded almost twenty years earlier. Here it seemed as though the madness that Brown had dovetailed with on his first album was gaining the upper hand. Nominally arranged into a suite roaming through "The Country," "The City," "The Cosmos," and "The Afterlife," little in the way of R&B-grounded song structures remained. The sprawling set, sometimes dissonant to the point of atonality, owed more to free jazz in its conception and realization, while Brown upped the histrionic quotient in his vibrato vocals. Only "Planets of the Universe" sounded as if it could have fit on the first album, and even that was interrupted by an off-the-wall busk through "Dem Bones." "It was possibly the first freestyle rock," offers Brown, "because it was totally improvised lyrics."

Brown then formed a band, Kingdom Come, that was somewhat, but not terribly, more accessible than his improvised projects. (An intriguing, convoluted seventeen-minute untitled track, labeled as a 1970 EMI/Harvest audition tape, shows up on the *Track Record* bootleg and sounds like a missing link between the Crazy World's psychedelia and Brown's prog rock efforts, though Brown does not remember auditioning for EMI/Harvest.) Kingdom Come was part of the Continental drift from psychedelic rock to art rock, passing through several incarnations and finding mostly cult acceptance, doing concerts mostly in Germany. "The first [version] was quite heavy, exploring how far the body could go with drink and drugs and real aggressive music," puts forth Brown. "The second one was sort of whimsical. The third one was the electronic drum machine. They were all sort of explorations." Brown is particularly proud of "Sunrise," an opus that built in tortured intensity both vocally and instrumentally, and was chosen to represent Kingdom Come on Rhino's *Supernatural Fairy Tales: The Progressive Rock Era* box set.

Brown's use of an electronic drum machine on the third Kingdom Come album was considered something of a novelty in the mid-1970s, although it became common in rock by the 1980s and 1990s. "I used to play the drum machine. There was nobody doing it. I think Sly and the Family Stone, from what I've read now, worked with one in the studio. But there was no one using it as a live instrument instead of the drums. I remember doing interviews and saying, 'The advantage of this is you can learn it in two weeks. You've got to have a feel for music. This is a new direction for rock, because it's percussion-based rather than drum kit-based.'

"It had its limitations. We did a tour about a year and a quarter, and everybody thought it was stupid. But that part of Kingdom Come—with the drum machine, synthesizer, one-half hair short, one-half long—came out, what, ten years later as the whole New Romantic movement, with the same haircut, the same instruments. I know that Pete Shelley of the Buzzcocks said that particular incarnation of Kingdom Come had been a particular influence on him."

Also by the mid-1970s, Brown's influence, not often credited, was becoming apparent in shock-rock outfits that dumbed down the complexity of the Crazy World for the masses. Look at a clip of "Fire" from 1968, and then Alice Cooper in the early

1970s, and there's no mistaking the similarity of the singers' visuals, particularly in the black and white monster makeup Cooper used. Brown isn't bitter in the least. "He's never tried to say he originated it at all. When he came and did a gig with us at the Rainbow—we were doing the first Kingdom Come album and touring—he went back and created his own psychodrama and act. But he said, 'I got this from Arthur Brown.'"

As for other fellow travelers, "Peter [Gabriel] says he was influenced. The singing star with the high notes—you've got Bruce Dickinson of Iron Maiden and the Deep Purple band, who became the extension of the Crazy World sound. The high screaming vocals Robert Plant did were done in '69; mine was '67. With theatrical bands, Zappa had seen us down in the Marquee, which was where he got his idea of the Mothers of Invention wearing the grandmother's dress. Kiss took their image from my stuff. Kim Fowley was helping them out at the time, and said, 'You want an image? Take Arthur Brown's.' It's flattering."

Most mainstream rock fans last heard Brown when he played a priest in Ken Russell's film version of *Tommy*—the rock opera that Kit Lambert, says Brown, "used the money from the *Crazy World* album to do." Many assumed that Brown had vanished, but in fact he's kept pretty active in music and other arts for the past twenty-five years. He did several albums in the late 1970s with electronic musician Klaus Schulze (once of Tangerine Dream). An opportunity to record his own record for Schulze's label resulted in a short-lived reunion with Vincent Crane. "Because it was on Klaus' label, it was going to be a synthesizer album," relates Brown with some amusement. "And Vincent hadn't played synthesizer. So I arranged for him to go to classes: synthesizer school. Vincent went through the two weeks' arduous training, came out, and he was *not* going to play any synthesizer. So we got one electronic note on the album." He pauses to correct himself. "Two. *Two* notes. He plays the two synthesizer notes. That was *all* he would do. The rest of it was piano and some organ. So we lost out on what would have been quite a good album."

Unlike some rockers of the 1960s, Brown did try to keep pace with new electronic technology and marketing concepts, without getting a heavy sales payoff. One was "reviewed by *Musician* as being probably the best one I've done. We had a marketing campaign all worked out for it. We decided we'd sell it mail-order, not through the shop, and we were going to use the about-to-come-on-the-air MTV. At that time, their charter allowed advertising of particular products, with their price. Like, three days before we had the album out, their charter was changed. They no longer could advertise. So that put paid to that album," he laughs sadly. He hasn't given up on the overall concept, asking me during a break in our talk about whether I think he should sign with a proper record label or try to sell his albums through the Internet.

Brown is not bummed about his retreat from stardom to cultdom. The fact of the matter is that music has never been the sole focus of his intellectual and artistic pursuits. In 1977 he went to Burundi and became an adviser to Burundi orchestral musicians and drummers, as well as teaching music history in a local school. He spent the 1980s in Austin, Texas, running a house-painting company with ex-Mother of Invention drummer Jimmy Carl Black, raising a family. He also continued to be a sort of Renaissance man of alternative culture. He served as musical director and performer at a local restaurant, working on thematic events combining international food, dance, and music. He got his master's degree in counseling. He devised methods of sound healing utilizing gongs, maracas, choirs, and his own improvised songs. "It combined modern psychological methods with the old shamanistic [ones]," he says. "There was an article in *People*. They said, 'From god of hellfire to singing shrink.'"

Brown moved back to England in the mid-1990s, and is now rather more active a performer than he's been in some time, having done about forty concerts in the past five months when I spoke to him. In addition to rock festivals throughout Europe, there are lower-key local gigs; the setup can range from the costumed theater for which he is most known, to an acoustic tour with just Brown and two guitarists. He is in the process of reassembling some of his back catalog for reissue, planning future recordings, and trying to get paid royalties from Polydor for "Fire," which he says "they've consistently refused to do over the years." He served as the narrator for the first-ever live performance (and Internet simulcast) of the Pretty Things' 1968 rock opera *S. F. Sorrow* in September 1998. One item that is definitely not on the agenda is a reunion of the original Crazy World of Arthur Brown. Vincent Crane took his own life in 1983, and Drachen Theaker passed away in 1992.

"Any stuff I do on stage, I'm very careful about, because it's a magical event, not work," he reflects. "A magical event that draws things from unseen realms. To me, music was always a spiritual matter. It's always like alchemy.

"What was originally a spiritual quest [with music]—in the end, I've decided what was at the basis of that search was what was wrong. The actual desire to look for it was the problem. Now, I've arrived at a place probably back where I started, which is the intimacy and genuineness of singing, and of music. In a way, it's just as intimate as making love. Maybe even more."

Recommended Recordings:

The Crazy World of Arthur Brown (1968, Retroactive). The alpha and omega of the Crazy World of Arthur Brown, most famous for the inclusion of "Fire," but also an electrifying album as a whole. There is more diversity here than has been commonly cited, too, from the tense confusion of "Nightmare" and "Fire" and the lilting respite of "Rest Cure" and "Child of My Kingdom," to the brimstone-fueled R&B covers "I Put a Spell on You" and "I've Got Money," to the just plain bonkers "Spontaneous Apple Creation." The CD reissue has the pre-album "Devil's Grip"/"Give Him a Flower" single, and the non-LP B-side "What's Happening," as well as five mono versions of songs from the album. Those mono versions aren't extraneous, containing some ingenious linking orchestration and spoken bits that didn't survive into the stereo counterpart, although the musical tracks are thinner and weaker in mono.

Strange Lands (1988, Reckless). Brown's missing album of sorts, unreleased until the late 1980s. This is like hearing the original Crazy World of Arthur Brown without the qualities—Vincent Crane's brilliant organ, the catchy R&B-classical riffs, the tight songwriting, the tasteful orchestration—that put the first album over to millions of listeners. The wild-eyed improvisation remains admirable, if not always accessible, and "Planets of the Universe" sounds like the older Crazy World of Arthur Brown, with its gentle metaphysics and ethereal organ.

The Electric Prunes

"Backward sounds suspend reality for me, much like slow motion or time-lapse film tricks the eye/brain. I can't turn away from those images. Movement I can't perceive in real time, you know it can't be happening…but it is! Guitars yaw and groan with surprise crescendos, cymbals suuuuuuck, suuuk, suck…I love it."—James Lowe, lead singer, the Electric Prunes

From the opening bars of the Electric Prunes' first hit single, Lowe's manifesto to invert and subvert rock 'n' roll sonics was put into action. Wiggly backwards distorted guitar gradually swelled in volume, like the hum of a thousand-pound bee crashing through your windows and onto your turntable. It was the kickoff for "I Had Too Much to Dream (Last Night)," one of the first out-and-out psychedelic hit records. Peaking just outside of the Top Ten in early 1967, there have been few other rock records that were as simultaneously experimental and commercial.

Unfortunately, that single, and particularly that opening colossal bee-hum of a riff, is *all* that many people remember of the Electric Prunes. This despite another, smaller hit single, and several albums in which they continued to slake their thirst for combining garage rock, pop, blues, and avant-garde electronics in unusual fashions that stretched the boundaries of 1960s recording technology. Evil fuzztone, spaced-out guitar reverb, and extraterrestrial oscillation wove around varispeed tape effects, autoharps, raunchy blues-rock vocals, Bo Diddley beats, and compelling pop-rock melodies. The results were sometimes thrilling, sometimes dismal, and sometimes downright deranged.

One thing they weren't was boring, and at their best, the Electric Prunes devised arresting psychedelic rock with a sinister, otherworldly edge that walked a tightrope between innocence and madness. It was an odd confluence of idiosyncratic innovation, commercial pop, and outright exploitative business machinations. Sometimes these elements clicked in a serendipitous manner that yielded a brilliance greater than the sum of the parts. At others, they canceled each other out and produced musical disaster, as well as long-term damage to the group's career.

It is tempting to say that the band's story was as strange as its music. But the sad truth is that the forces that conspired to frustrate the full realization of their artistic visions in favor of half-baked short-term strategies are all too common in the music industry, now and in the 1960s. The Electric Prunes did seem to suffer the more extreme brunt of the stick in this regard, however. They were not permitted to record much of their own material. Their most ambitious project, an orchestral religious concept album, was devised without their input, written and arranged by someone else, and completed when members of another band were brought in to play some of the parts. And, in the unkindest cut of all, they didn't even own their own name. When the core of the original lineup disintegrated in 1968, other musicians were simply hired to record under the Electric Prunes billing, discharging two LPs that had nothing to do with the group's original sound and vision.

Due to the inclusion of "I Had Too Much to Dream (Last Night)" as the leadoff track of *Nuggets*, the premier compilation of 1960s garage rock, the Electric Prunes are now labeled by history as a one-shot garage-psychedelic group. That's not an en-

The Electric Prunes in 1967. Left to right: Ken Williams, James Lowe, Weasel Spagnola, Mark Tulin, Quint.
Credit: Courtesy James Lowe.

tirely accurate designation. First, the Electric Prunes did have another Top Thirty hit with their follow-up single, "Get Me to the World on Time," which was just as good as its predecessor. They were also considerably more inventive, sophisticated, and studio-savvy than most of the garage bands represented on *Nuggets* and hundreds of other compilations of 1960s American garage rock. For all that, it's rather amusing to find that the Electric Prunes—*unlike* most 1960s garage bands—*were* actually discovered in a garage.

By the mid-1960s, the nucleus of the Electric Prunes—lead singer Jim (later James) Lowe, bassist Mark Tulin, and lead guitarist Ken Williams—was playing together in the Sanctions. A raw 1965 acetate demo, "You Can Help Yourself," eventually showed up on a compilation CD given away with the *Ptolemaic Terrascope* fanzine, and shows them to be a sub-Rolling Stones-type blues-rock outfit, utterly indistinguishable from literally thousands of similar American garage acts of the time. Yet the band did have a latent interest in exploring more original textures, particularly on guitar. Lowe had been friendly with the best early surf music guitarist, Dick Dale, and was intrigued with Dale's use of delay, echo, and reverb, as well as the multitrack recording of Les Paul. The group, now called Jim and the Lords, got a chance to tinker with and refine its ideas in the studio when Barbara Harris walked by the garage where the band was rehearsing. Harris was in the neighborhood as a friend of a real estate saleswoman trying to sell a house down the street from the garage, and offered to introduce the group to someone in the record business.

In most times and places, that kind of offer would have come to nothing. Jim and the Lords, however, were in the right place—Los Angeles (or, to be precise, in the San Fernando Valley north of Hollywood)—and the right time, the mid-1960s. The man Harris hooked them up with was Dave Hassinger, an engineer at RCA Studios in Hollywood. The Rolling Stones, perhaps the biggest influence on the band that would become the Electric Prunes, had recorded often at RCA Hollywood in the mid-1960s with Hassinger as engineer. It was Hassinger who worked in that capacity on the Rolling Stones' first album of entirely original material, *Aftermath*. (He even wrote the liner notes, memorably concluding, "In this business of dubious standards, it's been great working with the Stones, who, contrary to the countless jibes of mediocre comedians all over the world, are real professionals, and a gas to work with.")

As he was looking to upgrade his status from engineer to producer, and for bands to help him do so, the Electric Prunes were signed to Hassinger's production company. And what of the origin of that name, chosen at a time when such quasi-Dadaist band monikers were rare, and now thought of as emblematic of the psychedelic weirdness of the era, along with such handles as the Strawberry Alarm Clock and the Peanut Butter Conspiracy? It grew out of the punch line to this joke: "What is purple and goes buzz?" According to Tulin, the decision was sealed when Hassinger showed a list of possible names to Mick Jagger, who supposedly gave the Electric Prunes option the thumbs-up. Like the joke that inspired it, the name was absurd. In some ways, however, it was appropriate for a group that would spend much of its time coaxing unlikely sounds from unlikely instruments—a process that might have been as difficult as trying to plug in a piece of fruit.

In addition to the support of Hassinger, the Electric Prunes had a crucial leg up on most similar garage bands in their situation: they wanted to play original material, instead of just playing other people's songs live, and were eager to explore the use of the studio itself as a noisemaker. "We rehearsed constantly, all types of sounds and music, and always with recording in mind," declares Tulin. "With no desire to play clubs we were freed from learning cover tunes. It was the freedom from having to be like someone else to get work that allowed us to move and change as we did."

Concurs Lowe, "We didn't want to play cover music, or win the battle of the bands. At a certain point we realized we needed to work only on recording technique and stop trying to play gigs. The record industry was where the money, acceptance, and chicks were. From the first day we got together we wanted to make records, so we just practiced all the time. We had a lot to learn, it was a crash course. Dave Hassinger was part of that. He prompted us to arrange things in different ways. That was his best contribution to the band, as I see it." Hassinger and the band holed up for some time recording demos in the home studio of future star recording artist Leon Russell, who was then primarily working as a session man and as an arranger for Gary Lewis & the Playboys.

Hassinger was also able to release Electric Prunes recordings through Reprise, with their debut single, "Ain't It Hard"/"Little Olive," appearing in 1966. This was no more than a fair garage-pop 45, the A-side a cover of a folk-rock song (originally done by the Cypsy Trips), the B-side a James Lowe original that matched a basic midtempo Stonesy rocker with a raga-rock-style instrumental guitar break. Following the single, drummer Michael Weakley, aka "Quint," was replaced (temporarily, as it turned out) by Preston Ritter, and guitarist James "Weasel" Spagnola came aboard to make the Prunes a quintet. All that woodshedding at Leon Russell's paid off, however, when an accident produced the opening hook for the Electric Prunes' next single, "I Had Too Much to Dream (Last Night)."

"We were recording at Leon Russell's house, and you couldn't see the studio from the control room," remembers Lowe. "We were recording on a four-track, and just flipping the tape over and rerecording when we got to the end. Dave cued up a tape and didn't hit 'record,' and the playback in the studio was way up: ear-shattering vibrating jet guitar. Ken had been shaking his Bigsby wiggle stick with some fuzztone and tremolo at the end of the tape. Forward it was cool. Backward it was amazing. I ran into the control room and said, 'What was that?' They didn't have the monitors on so they hadn't heard it. I made Dave cut if off and save it for later."

This was the massive fluttering bee-buzz that opened "I Had Too Much to Dream (Last Night)," written for the band by Annette Tucker and Nancie Mantz, two songwriters also signed to Hassinger's company. The single was the ideal collision of early psychedelia and catchy pop-rock. Lowe's alternately hushed and half-screamed vocals were backed by heavily textured guitar lines, which at various points produced massive tremolo, wavering fuzz, and snaky tones that sounded halfway between backwards guitar and violin. The ethereal verses—the blissful "dream" in which the narrator did all but make love to a beautiful girl—gave way to frightening moans and banging tambourines, announcing the intrusion of the cold reality of a womanless dawn, as lamented in the hard-rocking chorus. The shiveringly ominous descending chords of the fade were matched by Lowe's sharp intakes of breath, as the dreamer who had the wind knocked out of his sails. These were quite a lot of ideas to pack into a three-minute single, and quite an advanced production for late 1966, eventually rising to number eleven on the national charts early the following year.

"I Had Too Much to Dream (Last Night)" initiated an ongoing relationship between the Tucker-Mantz songwriting team and the group (although Annette Tucker sometimes wrote Prunes material with Jill Jones). The predominance of Tucker-Mantz compositions on their first two albums was in some ways a considerable frustration for the band members, as it allowed less space for original material. Yet at its best, the combination of Tucker-Mantz (or Tucker-Jones) with the Electric Prunes was a heavenly match, casting the musicians suitable skeletons upon which to wreak their off-the-wall raunch. And in no instance did they blend better than on Tucker-Jones' "Get Me to the World on Time," the follow-up to "I Had Too Much to Dream (Last Night)."

Every bit the equal of their first hit, "Get Me to the World on Time" featured another ear-catching intro of distortion, this time pulsating shockwaves of low-range tones that, like some of the sounds heard on "I Had Too Much to Dream," fall halfway between electric guitar and violin in timbre. Lowe put the track in psychedelic gear with his urges to go higher and higher, building from a whisper to a shout as the song exploded into a simmering rocker. Those violin-like pulses continued to hammer away as Lowe delivered a snarling lyric that, even by the exaggerated standards of 1960s garage rock, burst at the seams with sexual longing and desire. Best expressed by his repeated exclamations "here I go-go-go-go-go"—an onomatopoeic equivalent of orgasm if there ever was one, in 1960s pop-rock at any rate—these were made into something entirely more surreal than the usual '60s garage tune by the complementary exclamations to "Get Me to the World on Time."

If the title was surreal, it was nothing compared to the song's sudden shift, about two-thirds of the way through, into mesmerizing Bo Diddley-meets-Californian psychedelia. The pounding percussion thumped out Diddley's trademark pulverizing bomp, ba-bomp-bomp, bomp-bomp beat as fuzz guitar swoops fought it out in the background and Lowe's vocal verged on manic desperation, like Mick Jagger dangling from a broken fire escape. That wasn't all, of course: as Bo Diddley beats rode out the fade, high-pitched electronic tones ascended the scale until they ran out of room, like a spaceship taking the narrator (and the listener) to unimagined psychosexual heights.

"The beginning of that song," reveals Lowe, "is Dave Hassinger groaning through a mike, into the tremolo on a Fender amp. It creates pulse-like overtones that sound like strings." Adds Tulin: "The 'spaceship' at the end was created by riding the high E of a guitar up to the last fret, where we matched the note with an oscillator and had it take off from there. As far as the Bo Diddley beat, we were definitely aware of using it. That beat is an atavistic rhythm." For all its brilliance, Lowe says "Get Me to the World on Time" "always lacked something to me, a solo or something. We wanted to do some wild electronic effects and a tone generator is what we settled for."

While "Get Me to the World on Time" had enough going for it to make number twenty-seven on the charts, it's not nearly as well remembered as "I Had Too Much to Dream" (although the inclusion of both songs on the definitive four-CD, 1999 expanded box set version of *Nuggets* might help change that). The two hit singles formed the centerpieces of their 1967 debut LP, unimaginatively titled *I Had Too Much to Dream (Last Night)/Get Me to the World on Time*. The patchy but generally impressive album saw the band expanding its arsenal of inventive effects and instrumentation, even if it had a schizophrenic quality induced both by the juxtaposition of Tucker-Mantz tunes with band originals, and by the wildly versatile-to-the-point-of-mania Tucker-Mantz repertoire itself.

On the most positive side, Annette Tucker gave the group more saucy rockers, "Try Me on For Size" (written with Jill Jones, which came off like Paul Revere & the Raiders dipped in acid) and the wonderfully titled "Are You Lovin' Me More (But Enjoying It Less)" (by Tucker and Nancie Mantz). Tucker-Mantz also penned the fairly insane "Sold to the Highest Bidder," transformed by the band into a Greek-style rocker with a tempo resembling that of a 45 single sped up to 78.

It is unbelievable that Tucker and Mantz—the same team responsible for the inspired madness of "I Had Too Much to Dream (Last Night)" and "Sold to the Highest Bidder"—were the same writers behind the putrid, fruity mock-vaudeville of "Tunerville Trolley," and the effete, mediocre baroque-pop of "The King Is in the Counting House." Add their mousy teen-pop ballad "Onie" (which, like "Are You

Lovin' Me More," had lead vocals by Weasel), and the silly show-tune-styled "About a Quarter to Nine" (the latter of which was not written by Tucker-Mantz), and the album left the overall impression of a band spinning its wheels, trying all directions at once instead of concentrating solely on its strengths. As Lowe and Tulin take pains to point out, this half-baked eclecticism was not so much due to their own wishes as to the material that Hassinger imposed upon them. States Tulin, "We had nothing resembling freedom, let alone total freedom, in our selection of songs. Consequently there are definitely songs that I believe do not belong on the album and were, in fact, a waste of our time and energy." As for the self-conscious variety of Tucker-Mantz's output, Lowe notes, "They were trying to get hits. When you approached songwriting in a professional manner, you did whatever you had to to get your songs placed."

Although Tucker and Mantz wrote some of the group's finest songs, Lowe gives them mixed ratings. "Most of their material sounded like it was written for a female vocalist. I felt a bit uncomfortable with some of it, but at the time we couldn't write anything as 'commercial' so we just did it. That was the weakest part of the group, as I saw it; it always comes down to the songs. Melodically they were vague and this made it hard to take a strong position on how to sing them. Doubling all the vocals didn't help, either. That can take the personality out of things."

Tucker and Mantz were among the few female songwriters of the 1960s to write garage-pop songs heavy on aggressive sexuality (before writing for the Prunes they had done a minor classic of the sort, the Animals-styled "I Ain't No Miracle Worker," recorded by California bands the Brogues and the Chocolate Watch Band). That's an asset not lost on Lowe, whose own style, which could range from a crooning pant to a full-throated leer, was well-suited for such material. "I knew Annette, and she really enjoyed her craft. We always had a laugh at the variety and scope of the images …'placing lipstick kisses on the wall' [from "Antique Doll" on the Electric Prunes' second album]. They were lusty bitches!"

Because so many of the group's recordings were written by Tucker-Mantz, there's been speculation that they were no more than mouthpieces for the visions of others. It turns out, however, that the Electric Prunes were the ones responsible for the offbeat touches to make Tucker-Mantz's songs just a bit, or much more than a bit, off-kilter. It's especially surprising to hear from Tulin that "we worked up our arrangement of 'Too Much to Dream' from a demo that was slow with strings and had, I believe, [easy listening pop vocalist] Jerry Vale singing. Pure Vegas lounge act material. The other Tucker-Mantz songs were worked up following Annette performing them for us on a piano, most of the time in a spirited, but show tune/musical manner. She was at heart pure pop. It was always up to us to add whatever rock sensibilities were needed.

"Unfortunately, sometimes, try as we may, we couldn't overcome the inherent 'pop' in the material. With their songs, being 'clever' was more important than the actual song. For instance, "Get Me to the World on Time' was brought to us primarily because of the title. It was up to us to put musical credibility to their clever lyrics. I can guarantee there was no Bo Diddley beat when Annette played it on the piano."

Elsewhere the group helped make the Tucker-Mantz songbook into something that fell in the netherworld twixt pop and psych, with a marimba on "Try Me on For

Size," and the eerie spacey low notes in "Are You Lovin' Me More," produced by cello and Danelectro bass (Lowe: "Dave [Hassinger] kept asking what went in the 'holes'"). "Sold to the Highest Bidder" matched Bo Diddley-styled rhythm guitar shimmer with trills that could easily be mistaken for berserk balalaikas, although in fact these are super-sped-up-guitars. There was also an unclassifiable swooshing noise near the beginning of that track "that was spinning something on a drumhead for three-and-a-half hours, slowed down," says Lowe. "It was supposed to represent a coin or something. I fell asleep."

Undoubtedly Hassinger's experience engineering the Rolling Stones, particularly on the *Aftermath* sessions, filtered into the Electric Prunes' sound on occasion. The marimba on "Try Me on For Size" recalled the vibes that highlighted the Stones' "Under My Thumb," for instance, and the slide guitar and harmonica on "Luvin'" were quite similar to the slide heard on *Aftermath*'s "Doncha Bother Me" and the harmonica on *Aftermath*'s "Going Home." The raga-rock the Rolling Stones had tried with super-successful results on "Paint It Black" can be detected in the hyper-stiff drumbeats of "I Had Too Much to Dream (Last Night)." The Prunes even got to use some guitars and amps that the Stones had left behind in Los Angeles. Preston Ritter has recalled that the Gibson fuzztone used on "I Had Too Much to Dream," in fact, was the exact same one the Rolling Stones used on "Satisfaction."

"Luvin'" was one of only two group compositions allowed onto the debut album. The other was the more impressive "Train for Tomorrow," its insistent key-changes giving way to a vocal that dissolved in echo, followed by a jazzy coda with Wes Montgomery-inspired guitar. According to Tulin, there would have been more original material had it not been vetoed by Hassinger. "'Hideaway' was one of the first songs we recorded. Dave Hassinger thought it was 'too strange' for the first album. There were several other ideas we were working on, but [we] realized there was no use pursuing them because they too would have been 'too weird.'"

"Hideaway" would see the light, however, on the Electric Prunes' second LP, *Underground* (also in 1967). Like *I Had Too Much to Dream (Last Night)/Get Me to the World on Time*, it was uneven, and unlike the debut album, it lacked a hit single, or anything as immediately memorable as their pair of chart 45s. Although Tucker-Mantz were still supplying them with zanily wide-ranging concoctions, this time around, the band was able to write more than half of the material. As such, *Underground* is the most accurate representation of the group's vision, even if it found the members increasingly at odds with their producer and mentor, Dave Hassinger.

Corresponding with Tulin and Lowe today, it's obvious they are not acid casualties; they are in respected professions, answering questions about their past with lucid wit and insight. Listening to *Underground*, however, you could be forgiven for assuming that the band was made up of half-demented madmen, mixing normal California pop-rock, freak-out psychedelia, and unabashed lunacy with the delight of loony alchemists. (A lineup boasting members named "Quint" and "Weasel" did not exactly do much to counter that impression.) There was an opening track about "The Great Banana Hoax" that had nothing to do with bananas or hoaxes, followed by three subdued songs about antique dolls and windup toys that blurred the line between childhood paradise and nightmare. But just as you wondered if you had wandered into a concept album about lost childhood, there was a routine shit-kicking country tune, "It's Not Fair," that accelerated without warning into a brief parody of the spoken section of the old Neil Sedaka hit "Oh Carol," adding a spoken coda with spiraling-out-of-control-key changes, like a rural preacher whose brain has been fried by the midday sun. What could follow that, of course, but an obscure song by one of the top pop-songwriting teams of the 1960s, Gerry Goffin and Carole King? (That song, "I Happen to Love You," had originally been recorded in a rawer version by the obscure New York band the Myddle Class, with King's future husband Charles Larkey on bass, in 1966.)

Side two, if anything, got stranger, leading off with the most unhinged Tucker-Mantz creation of all, "Dr. Do-Good," gleefully delivered by Lowe in a voice suggesting the host of a children's television hour gone 'round the bend. "I," also by Tucker-Mantz, found the group wandering into moody San Francisco psychedelic territory, with sustained guitar riffs reminiscent of acid-rock bands such as Quicksilver Messenger Service, or the classic Country Joe & the Fish instrumental "Section 43." "Hideaway," the best song penned by the Prunes' principal songwriting team (Lowe-Tulin), was driven by a killer bass line and, says Tulin, "was our attempt to synthesize the Indian style with the rock sensibility," citing the Rolling Stones' "Paint It Black" and Indian sitar master Ravi Shankar as key inspirations. The momentum flagged with another unexpected cover of a straight pop-rock tune ("Big City") and the semiserious "Captain Glory." Yet the record came to a storming conclusion with "Long Day's Flight," the most straightforward garage psychedelia on *Underground*, with that Electric Prunes specialty: ferocious guitar sustain that quivered and curled like a violin. The overall effect of *Underground* was that of a psychedelic fun house that counterpointed the occasional optimistic romance ("I Happen to Love You") and headlong enthusiasm for the future ("Long Day's Flight") with devious undercurrents of paranoia, and dreamworlds where the lines between idyllic fantasy and hellish nightmare merged.

The Electric Prunes did not have *songs* to match the best psychedelic bands, but were second to few in their detonation of special effects and studio-heated noises to give their material an extra push. That weird sound near the beginning of "The Great Banana Hoax" that sounds like a motorcycle revving up? Lowe: "That is a 'growl' done vocally and slowed down some. I wanted to suggest moving furniture in heaven when we did it. It was just a device to make you take notice." Those percussive scrapes near the end of the same track that sound like a rock swirling around in a bucket? Tulin thinks that's "a kalimba, brought to us via Africa. Although, because we were trying anything and everything to see what it would sound like, it could actually be rocks being swirled around in a bucket." Those eerie squalls in Tucker-Mantz's "Antique Doll" (the best of the childhood-oriented songs that appear in sequence on side one)? Lowe: "Us crying at double speed. We played around with tape speed a lot...vso [variable speed oscillator] they called it." That spooky electronic keyboard solo in Goffin-King's "I Happen to Love You"? Lowe again: "A Vox electronic organ guitar solo. They brought a prototype in and took it back after they heard what we did with it." The chaotic burst of clatter getting sucked into a black hole that starts "Dr. Do-Good"? Lowe: "Ken Williams on a prototype slide guitar, kind of a steel guitar thing someone gave us. It was overdubbed numerous times and turned around, I think. I liked it, real noise." The evil Bugs Bunny laugh that sees

"Dr. Do-Good" out the door? Producer Dave Hassinger. "I told him I couldn't do it," admits Lowe, "and he kept showin' me how so we said, 'You do it.' It reminded me of Nervous Norvus"—the mid-1950s novelty singer who had a hit with "Transfusion," a queasy ditty about a guy who can't keep out of grisly auto crashes.

In addition to these one-off effects, there was imaginative fuzz and reverb by Ken Williams—an underrated pioneer of psychedelic guitar—throughout. Williams, in fact, would play the wah-wah guitar for a cheesy 1967 ad that the group recorded for Vox wah-wah pedals ("you can even make your guitar sound like a sitar!" exclaims the hyperventilating narrator). Lowe's autoharp added an exotic touch to some of the more normal pop tunes, such as "I Happen to Love You."

This fascination with conjuring a sorcerer's brew of undefinable sounds, agrees Lowe, was a vital factor in setting the Electric Prunes aside from most other so-called garage psychedelic bands, such as the ones that rub shoulders with them on *Nuggets*. "Though we didn't take it as far as we would have liked," he emphasizes. "A lot of groups worried about not being able to reproduce a recorded sound 'live.' Once you commit to tape or disc format you've changed the presentation, anyway. Why not take it as far as you can? Noise can be musical and beautiful. Vibrating a bunch of guitar strings is an effect, after all. Layering various textures puts a kind of depth to the record. I dig that.

"To me the best moments are when you're throwing licks back and forth and letting things happen that are outside song form. Feedback dogfighting guitars are a great release, and suggest a million things in their overtones. Even if it isn't 'music,' breaking glass gives me a strong sensory reaction. Voices don't have to sing understandable lyrics, or make recognizable sounds to be musical. You can create your own crazy world!"

Tulin was also conscious of pushing the limits of what could be conjured in 1967 studios. "Overall, I was pleased with the album, primarily because we were beginning to have more of a say in what we were doing. However, I was not pleased that a lot of the ideas we had did not/could not come off. We were still learning how to record and thus were at the mercy of our producer's studio 'expertise.' We would describe what we wanted to accomplish and were told how to do it, only to find when we were done that it wasn't close. Keep in mind those were the days when 'we'll fix it in the mix' was a byword of recording. And, in fact, the technology to do some of the things we wanted did not yet exist. Yet, had we known more about recording techniques, I think the album would have sounded even better. And, once again, although to a lesser extent, there were songs I didn't want to record. However, all things considered, I do believe *Underground* gives a good sense of who we were as a band and where we could have gone."

As for the music he was writing with Lowe, he goes on, "James and I have always had an affinity for working together musically. A big part of that is the willingness to try anything. James also has a great ability to take what would be a normal chord change, flip a chord or two, and make it something different; something I never would have thought of. Sometimes the song would be written from a desire to use a certain instrument or try a certain sound. Every Friday was set aside to present new material. We were open to hearing songs from any band member. With rare exception James and I would be the only ones with songs. The others didn't show much interest in writing. What we would occasionally do is give the whole band credit if there was an extended or special instrumental section, (i.e. 'Train for Tomorrow') even if they had nothing to do with writing the song."

"We just wanted to try something that would be electronic," chimes in Lowe. "That was always the basis. We tried to stimulate everyone to write, but it was like math class when they had to bring a song in. Nobody said 'the dog ate my song,' but that's about the only excuse that wasn't used. Mark and I have always had this connection with songwriting. I'm not afraid to show him an idea, thinking he will view it as stupid. He knows it will be stupid. So what!"

Underground, despite the musical progress, was not the easiest of times for the band. Original drummer Quint replaced Preston Ritter, who was given his choice of royalties or a credit on the sleeve; to his eternal regret, he chose royalties (which were not forthcoming). (Quint, incidentally, cowrote "Long Day's Flight" with, of all people, the son of Los Angeles mayor Sam Yorty.) Weasel Spagnola left after falling ill with hepatitis, taking with him a Magnitone amp that, remembers Lowe, "would make a guitar sound like an organ; had a unique tremolo too"; Mike Gannon replaced him to finish the album.

Plus the album didn't sell well, peaking at number 172. It didn't help that the first song from *Underground* released as a single, "Dr. Do-Good," was about the daftest choice imaginable, rising to a not-so-mighty number 128 as the third and last Electric Prunes 45 to chart. It's still a puzzle as to why "I Happen to Love You"—one of the best little-known songs by Gerry Goffin and Carole King, and one of the toughest, bluesiest items they ever wrote—was not selected. "We thought that song was cool," acknowledges Lowe. "I was surprised they didn't think it good enough for a 45." What this meant, particularly at a time when the market for rock music had barely begun to shift in focus from singles to albums, was dissatisfaction on the part of Dave Hassinger—and, in turn, severe limits on any opportunity the Prunes might have had to develop their studio experimentation.

"*Underground* was an issue between David and the band," asserts Lowe. "He thought it was unprofessional. He wore alpaca sweaters through the Cultural Revolution, for christ's sake. I don't think the management or David liked the music. They wanted teen stars, not guys experimenting with noises. I always felt like they were in another world, looking into something they didn't really understand, or want to. If you couldn't produce them a hit, out with your ass!

"I always thought he saw us as a threat after *Underground*. We refused to do the album he wanted to make and he saw we wouldn't back down. I had named the album. The band even went in and took the picture, found the girl's face in the trash bin at the photographer's studio for the background. This must have seemed like the inmates were taking over the asylum to Dave. I told him Reprise could do the back cover, so as not to offend Ed Thrasher, the art director for the label. They just made a negative image of the front cover on the back…very clever."

Because the Electric Prunes had hits with songs written by outside composers, and because their sound was colored so heavily by studio trickery, historians have often speculated that the group's sound was largely crafted by Hassinger, and not the musicians themselves. Lowe and Tulin calmly but firmly make it clear that this was not exactly the case. "Dave deserves all the credit in the world and has my eternal thanks for giving us a chance," stresses Tulin. "Dave made contributions to our records; initially more than later on. He encouraged us to try new sounds. He was just ill-prepared for where it would lead and alienated by our refusal to go along with his program. However, ultimately, a great portion of credit for the sounds of our recording should go to [engineers] Richie Podolor and Bill Cooper from American Recording. While Dave was sleeping, reading or otherwise occupied, they were working with us."

Lowe chips in, "Richie Podolor and Bill Cooper did most of the recording work, and, I think, resented being referred to as 'electricians' on the records. It must have been hell for them dealing with five Valley idiots trying to learn how to play, and an exploitative egomaniacal producer. If I wanted phasing or a delay effect, they were the ones I would ask how to do it, not Dave. He was old school single-phone military trained. I always had run-ins with him on sounds."

Tulin rejoins, "From the start I believe we were, for Dave Hassinger, a means to an end—that end being his becoming a staff producer for Reprise. Our single/album accomplished that for him. Having done that, I think he lost interest in us. He could move on to bigger names. The truth be told, the only one who had any vision of us whatsoever was us. With *Underground* we really came to a parting of the ways with Dave. We were definitely not what he wanted us to be, whatever the hell that was. I know he never understood what we were attempting to accomplish. His participation was limited and his enthusiasm muted." Though you have to give some credit, however grudging, to a man willing to groan through a mike into a Fender amp, or impersonate Bugs Bunny, to give his charges' records that little extra something.

As the Prunes' music was so riddled with studio-dependent effects, it's also been speculated that they must have had trouble playing the material live. Remarkably, evidence came to light thirty years later proving that the band members could approximate the sound of their records—even ones with pretty involved arrangements, such as "I Had Too Much to Dream (Last Night)" and "Get Me to the World on Time"—fairly well on stage. A December 1967 concert in Stockholm was recorded by Swedish radio and officially issued in 1997 as the *Stockholm 67* CD, capturing a powerful live set that included the two hits, some of their stronger LP tracks, and more. Although frills like backwards/varispeed tapes were impossible to fully reproduce in concert, there was plenty of killer guitar fuzz and distortion; even the bee-hum opening riff of "I Had Too Much to Dream" was credibly simulated.

Lowe is reserved in his assessment of the performance: "Strangely, that night in Stockholm we just jammed, and rather badly too. We went to Europe to blow them away and we got so many nights of people just looking, wondering what the fuck we were doing, that we decided to just play it straight that night." So what happened when they *didn't* play it straight? "We took steel slide guitars and some noisemakers and did 'The Great Banana Hoax' for twenty minutes with kalimbas and stuff. We were vibrating brats from the States, a production band. They probably thought we was poseurs, but wanted to play."

"The best part of that tour," feels Tulin, "was playing for an audience that seemed more musically aware than those we normally played for at home." Both "I Had Too Much to Dream" and "Get Me to the World on Time" had been small hits in Britain, and one wonders whether the Electric Prunes were overlooked, uncredited influences on some of the wildest psychedelia coming out of the U.K. in 1967. Certainly Pink Floyd's earliest records, when Syd Barrett was the band's leader, had guitar sounds reminiscent of those used on the first two Electric Prunes LPs. For instance, on the Floyd's first album (released in mid-1967), "Astronomy Domine" opened with a pulsating bass riff extremely similar to that which opens the Prunes' "Are You Loving Me More (But Enjoying It Less)"; also on that album, the Floyd's "Lucifer Sam" had eerie violinish guitars like those heard on the Prunes' "I Had Too Much to Dream." During that European tour the Prunes met Jimi Hendrix briefly, listening to a test pressing of Hendrix's *Axis Bold As Love* at his flat. They don't remember Hendrix commenting upon the group's music, but there's certainly a similarity between the slow-building, squiggly guitar on songs like "I Had Too Much to Dream" and the famous riff that opens Hendrix's "Foxy Lady." If you want to stretch the possibilities further, the Jefferson Airplane's "House at Pooneil Corners" (1968) had an ascending, crying sound quite similar to the ones heard on Electric Prunes tracks like "Antique Doll" and "Get Me to the World on Time" (Hassinger, as it happens, had engineered the Airplane's first two albums around the same time he was working with the Electric Prunes).

The Electric Prunes had some reason for beginning 1968 with optimism. They had just toured Europe for the first time, and new addition Mike Gannon, in Tulin's estimation, "brought a spirit of joy of playing to the band. He brought a more aggressive rhythm backing and was fully capable of playing leads with Ken or on his own. He gave us the ability live to have multiple leads going on at the same time." The year could have seen them scale new heights in the studio and in concert. Instead, they ended up right back in the trap they had partially escaped from with *Underground*, playing music and arrangements not of their own making on one of the goofiest early rock concept albums. And by the end of 1968, the band had been reduced to ashes, replaced by an entirely different group of musicians calling themselves the Electric Prunes.

Hassinger wanted to sell records. David Axelrod, who had produced discs by jazz great Cannonball Adderley, wanted to have his suite of quasi-religious songs recorded by a rock band. The group's manager, Lenny Poncher, thought it was a good idea (in fact Axelrod claimed, in a 1999 interview in the British magazine *Dazed and Confused*, that the idea originated with Poncher). So the three of them hatched *Mass in F Minor*, proposing that the Electric Prunes perform the material, arranged and wholly composed by Axelrod, combining rock instrumentation with Axelrod orchestration. And that's what the group did, with every word sung in Latin, no less. While the band members themselves played all the rock parts on side one, they weren't going fast enough for Axelrod's taste — we were slow, and only Mark read music" explains Lowe — and side two was completed with assistance from the Canadian group the Collectors. Essentially, the Electric Prunes had become session musicians on their own album.

"I like and respect Dave Axelrod," reflects Tulin. "I think he's a brilliant musician and he greatly helped expand my musical knowledge. However, he wasn't us. We were a 'known entity' plugged into an outside concept; a means to someone else's end. Trouble was, we were a band, not an inorganic artificial product that

Psychedelic Sailors   **63**

could be manipulated at will." To boot, the album didn't sell much better than *Underground* had, peaking at number 135.

Mass in F Minor was a traffic jam of musical apples and oranges, to say the least. The wildly distorted, reverbed guitars played off Axelrod's grandiose French horns and cellos, while Lowe's vocals were usually double-tracked to create a pseudo-Gregorian choral effect. For what it's worth, the album did contain some really freaky guitar sustain that wasn't too far removed from what Jorma Kaukonen of the Jefferson Airplane was playing in that group's *After Bathing from Baxter's* period. And no orchestration intruded on the best track, "Kyrie Eleison," with its tremoloed-to-infinity guitar chords. "Kyrie Eleison" got an unexpected second life in 1969 when it was used on the soundtrack to Dennis Hopper and Peter Fonda's classic counterculture road movie *Easy Rider*; it's heard in the scenes just after Fonda and Hopper arrive in New Orleans for Mardi Gras, including the one where they visit a local brothel. Either Fonda or Hopper must have owned the album, as Fonda remembers (in his autobiography) that the soundtrack was taken from their personal record collections. Which, as an aside, must have contained some pretty esoteric stuff; besides well-known tracks by Hendrix, Steppenwolf, the Band, and the Byrds, the soundtrack also had, in addition to "Kyrie Eleison," the damned obscure "If You Want to Be a Bird" (by the Holy Modal Rounders) and "Don't Bogart Me" (by the Fraternity of Man).

If the band's enthusiasm for the project was rather limp to begin with, it was wholly extinguished by the one and only live performance of *Mass in F Minor*. Tulin: "We were on tour when we were told we would be performing the mass almost immediately upon our return. Aside from the time spent recording it, this would be the first time we played the mass; the first time we played it straight through without the stops/starts facilitated by recording. There was one rehearsal, at the Musician's Union rehearsal hall. Four celli, four French horns, six vocalists (from the Smothers Brothers show), and the band. James took charge of the vocalists and I was put in charge of the musicians. I was told I was to play bass, play the organ and conduct. Didn't work, but I believe we managed to at least talk our way through the charts.

"That night, at the Santa Monica Civic Auditorium, we had the same complement of musicians/singers plus Richie Podolor (our recording engineer and a great guitarist in his own right) and Don Peake added on guitar. Don Randi was called in for the concert to play organ and conduct. Only problem was that prior to the last-minute call Don had spent the entire day on his boat. He was sunburned and burned out from the day. Everyone had to use music stands to read the charts because no one on stage knew the songs or arrangements.

"From the outset the performance was a disaster. We missed the intro on the first song and it never got any better. Amp speakers blew, charts fell off music stands and everyone was, in general, in a complete state of confusion. Ended up each song turned into one long jam. I think we were, at times, all in the same key. I made my way over to the four celli and four French horns and told them to 'jam in E.' Somehow we would hit a break and James would manage a vocal. Mercifully, this all ended and as we were leaving a few 'fans' said, 'We didn't know you guys were into avant-garde jazz.'" Lowe's memory is more laconic: "Ever heard a symphony orchestra out of whack? They thought we were making fun of Jesus or something."

The band did get the opportunity to record a final self-penned single with the

Tulin-Lowe-Williams lineup, which came out in early 1968. "Everybody Knows You're Not in Love" was an anomaly in the Electric Prunes catalog: a bouncy, California sunshine pop song, with a brittle scrape up and down the guitar in the instrumental break to remind you that this *was* the Electric Prunes, not the Grass Roots. It was outclassed by the B-side, "You Never Had It Better," a nasty blues-pop rocker with dual guitar lines and superb fierce distortion of Velvet Undergroundian intensity, particularly on the intro. The credit might read "P. Sangster-R. Schwartz-S. Poncher," but it was actually written by Tulin and Lowe, with partial credit granted to their manager's son, although Steve Poncher didn't actually contribute anything. In keeping with the generally curious business operations of the Electric Prunes, the band gave him a credit to help him through the aftermath of a bad acid trip. "He had had a rough time, we wanted to give him some confidence...prunthropy, I guess," shrugs Lowe.

Unfortunately, the single was also a final battleground between the Electric Prunes and Dave Hassinger. "Toward the end," says Tulin, "if we wanted to record a song we'd written we had to go into the studio on the sly, cut the track, then present it to him as if it were written by someone else. Then he wouldn't set about changing it. 'Everybody Knows You're Not in Love' was done that way. The demo we made was much better than what ended up being released, because by that time he knew the song was ours." What's more, one word on "You Never Had It Better" had to be beeped out, with an actual brief "beep" on the finished record: "We wanted to say 'shit' but knew that would never fly."

Continues Tulin, "I think the mass was David's way of distancing the actual band from him and vice versa. Who knows what might have happened if we could have worked with David Axelrod in creating the mass. To make matters worse, we were just starting to grow and [Hassinger], I guess, was as grown as he was going to be. He evidently decided to focus his attention on other Reprise acts he saw as having more 'commercial potential,' whatever that is. Ironic—I don't think he ever got another hit single. That alone speaks volumes."

One of the acts that Hassinger got to produce, incidentally, went on to become one of the biggest bands in the world, but only after they too had demanded more creative control and far-out experimentation than he could tolerate. Hassinger worked on the first two Grateful Dead albums, but threw up his hands and walked out in frustration partway through the second, 1968's *Anthem of the Sun*, after the band members told him they wanted to record the sound of "thick air." Recalls Lowe, "Dave told me about it, and I wrote an instrumental after the band broke up with that title because I thought it was a cool phrase. He told me they sat around for a couple of hours trying to capture it on tape...those were the Owsley days. Dave used to lay on the control room floor of American Studios and read the paper while we played tracks. That's not an inspiring production posture. Perhaps he was doing the same with the Dead?"

Frustrated both financially and artistically, and tired of touring, Lowe wore out and left the band in 1968. Although the Electric Prunes did another tour, "when James left he took the heart of the band with him," according to Tulin. "Without him we were a corpse on tour. Didn't do any of our old material. All in all it was depressing and degrading; a complete waste of time and energy." Joining as a new member of the band on this jaunt was the most unlikely participant of all in the Electric Prunes saga.

"The one positive aspect of the tour was playing with Kenny Loggins. I know where he's at now, but at that time he was a hard-core rocker and a pure joy to watch play. He went full bore, full-out every night. Then back in the hotel he'd play some great song he'd just written. He was one talented son of a bitch."

Were the Electric Prunes done when the group dissolved after the tour finished? Not quite. As the band was signed to Hassinger's company and not directly to Reprise, and as Hassinger owned the Electric Prunes name, entirely different musicians were recruited to become the Electric Prunes for two long-forgotten albums in the late 1960s that bore no relation to the Lowe-Tulin-Williams configuration. The first of those, *Release of an Oath*, was even a vague continuation of the *Mass in F Minor* concept; again composed and arranged by David Axelrod, it used the Kol Nidre prayer (recited on the night before the most important Jewish holiday, Yom Kippur) as the basis for another religious rock opus of sorts. The situation wherein the group was signed to Hassinger, rather than Reprise, had ultimately worked against the Prunes. "Had we been signed to Reprise when Dave/Prune relations started heading south, we could have gotten a new producer or possibly produced ourselves," muses Tulin. "As it was, Dave was in direct control of everything we did and, consequently, everything the label did for us."

The Electric Prunes' inability to mesh with the industry can be partially attributed to their greater interest in studio recording and experimentation than live performing, which was still an unusual attitude in 1967. Other than the Beatles, few bands of that time thrived by focusing mostly or exclusively upon studio work (and the Beatles themselves had only stopped touring in late 1966). "You need room to slink around a bit in the recording studio," offers Lowe. "That's the only way to capture a magic moment. We had some problems with playing proficiency; we were learning to play the instruments as we went along. Studio costs were always a factor, and we were not allowed into a session until we knew exactly what we were going to do on every track. We never jammed till 'Long Day's Flight.' We recorded on four-track, and that had some limitations. I always envied groups that 'took over' a studio for weeks; that's a luxury."

What might the Electric Prunes have done had they been given full support to pursue their own directions and generous allocations of studio time? Postulates Tulin: "Our third album, had it not been the mass, I believe would have, at the very least, had a true band feel and sound, one even more representative of who we were. In addition, we were just beginning to understand how to use the studio as its own instrument. Left to our own devices I think we would have expanded that knowledge. In addition, I think we would have stretched a little more in using vocal sounds as a complement to the band instruments. We were heading in a direction that would have allowed us to explore more intricate tonal ideas involving subtle manipulations of sound and song structure to create a more sensory and sensual experience."

Lowe would cross to the other side of the gate over the next few years, working as a recording engineer for artists such as Todd Rundgren, Randy Newman, Ry Cooder, Sparks, and Foghat. He then left the recording industry altogether to start his own production company—still operating today in Santa Ynez, California—for directing and producing television commercials. In the 1990s he began playing music again with Tulin, now a psychologist. Ken Williams and Quint were eventually located, and the quartet, along with guitarist Peter Lewis of Moby Grape, has done some recording in Lowe's home studio. In spring 2000, Lowe responds to my query as to how the Prunes' third album might have sounded if they could have maintained artistic control: "We have been doing THAT album for the last year. I forgot how much fun music is. Take away the profit motive and all that greed and you get back to trying to make a good record."

Which was all the Electric Prunes were trying to do in the first place back in 1968, before they got so rudely interrupted. It only took them thirty years, but at last they can make their music without the men in alpaca sweaters looking over their shoulder.

Recommended Recordings:

Long Day's Flight (1986, Edsel, U.K.). An eighteen-song compilation that pushes almost all the right buttons, containing almost all of their good tracks. Focusing on the first two albums, it also has their 1966 debut single and the non-LP standout "You Never Had It Better," although there's nothing from *Mass in F Minor.*

I Had Too Much to Dream (Last Night)/Get Me to the World on Time (1967, Collectors' Choice Music). Their debut album has more good stuff than bad stuff, though the bad parts—specifically the show-tune-like numbers—are very bad. Of course the best parts, particularly the two hits, are very good. Filling in the extremes are a half-dozen or so credible psych-pop and psych-garage tunes, sometimes nearly normal, and sometimes ("Sold to the Highest Bidder") as weird as can be. The CD reissue adds their non-LP 1966 "Ain't Hard"/"Little Olive" single as bonus tracks.

Underground (1967, Collectors' Choice Music). Another roller-coaster ride through admixtures of pop-rock, psychedelia, blues, and garage. Although nothing matches the hits featured on the debut, the insertions of wild and noisy effects and guitar are ever-surprising, and "I Happen to Love You," "Long Day's Flight," and "Hideaway" are all among their best songs. And "Dr. Do-Good" is more demented than Dr. Demento. The CD reissue adds their 1968 non-LP single "You Never Had It Better"/"Everybody Knows You're Not in Love."

Mass in F Minor (1968, Collectors' Choice Music). The group's religious concept album, composed and arranged by David Axelrod, is more ill-conceived than it is inspired. The sheer oddity of hearing fuzz guitars, Gregorian vocals, and orchestration battle it out has its value, though, and "Kyrie Eleison" has some of the coolest 1960s tremolo guitar you'll find anywhere. Each of the Collectors' Choice CD reissues of the first three Electric Prunes albums contains liner notes by this writer.

Stockholm 67 (1997, Heartbeat Productions, U.K.). Recorded by Swedish radio in December 1967, this decent live concert demonstrates that the group could perform even its more complex material well on stage. Besides "I Had Too Much to Dream (Last Night)" and "Get Me to the World on Time," there's an extended version of "Try Me on For Size," a rendition of "I Happen to Love You" that's rawer and better than the studio one on their second album, and raucous charges through "You Never Had It Better" and "Long Day's Flight."

Randy Holden

"I love the sound of a guitar playing, I love the way it makes me feel inside."—First lyrics sung by Randy Holden on his 1970 solo album, *Population II*

Randy Holden loved to play the guitar. No one who heard his records could doubt that. He's a good candidate for selection as the great unknown 1960s rock guitar hero. No other American guitarist was as skilled in creating the kind of sustain-heavy, snaky guitar lines pioneered by Jeff Beck in the Yardbirds. His recordings with the Fender IV, Sons of Adam, the Other Half, Blue Cheer, and as a solo artist don't only contain some feverishly inventive playing. They also chart the overall rainbow of the changes undergone by California 1960s rock guitar as a whole, from surf and pseudo-Merseybeat to psychedelia, hard rock, and heavy metal.

You haven't heard of him, however, both because he never got in the right band at the right time, and because of a series of shoddy breaks at the hand of an unsympathetic music industry. Brushes with the big time—a possible chance to join the Yardbirds was bypassed (at Holden's wishes), a stint with Blue Cheer only took in three recorded songs—were fleeting, and studio sessions never captured the sounds of Holden's guitar to his own satisfaction. At the very moment at which he was planning to unveil his most ambitious project, he found himself without money, without a record label, and, perhaps worst of all, without even his guitars and amps. The disappointment was so traumatic that it would be about twenty years before he even started to play guitar again.

Since beginning to play with Baltimore bands as a young teenager in the late 1950s, Holden wanted a BIG sound, perhaps bigger than the technology of his time could reproduce. "Most guitar players where I came from were more into rhythm and blues, where the guitar didn't play a major role," says Holden forty years later, speaking from his home in Laguna Beach, California. "But the guitar for me was a total, full-blast, full-on love affair. The louder and clearer that baby was, the more beautiful it was. Hitting that guitar string on a voluminous amp was just heaven, and people felt it.

"Basically, I went to school in the basement of a music store, instead of going to school. The guy [there] loved what I was doing. He'd extend me credit on anything I wanted. I had the first Bandmaster in Baltimore, the first Showman [amplifier], the first Dual Showman. I was in debt for years. Every time Fender would develop a new and bigger amp, I'd buy the thing on credit. [Leo] Fender, he was a brilliant man. He took military technology and turned it over into a use that was suitable for another purpose. Pretty amazing, when you think about it."

Another devotee of the Fender sound was Dick Dale, the first great surf rock guitarist, who actually road-tested Fender guitars and amps in his quest to create the most reverberant, aircraft hangar-filling sound possible. Holden was a big fan of Dale, who influenced Randy to adopt a staccato picking style and play the same kind of cavernously echoing, Middle Eastern-styled instrumentals when he moved to California himself. "Mar Gaya," the 1964 instrumental single by Holden's surf combo the Fender IV (reissued on the Rhino compilation *Guitar Player Presents Legends of Guitar: Surf, Vol. 1*), was a superb slab of surf grunge. Holden's rapid-fire, minor-key staccato attack wound itself through tortuous key changes until the tension became nearly unbearable, pacing one of the most ominous instrumental surf classics.

Randy Holden, great lost '60s guitar hero.
Credit: Michael Ochs Archives.com.

However, by the time "Mar Gaya" was released on Imperial in 1964, surf's wave was on the wane, eclipsed by music with vocals in general, and the British Invasion in particular. In order to survive, the Fender IV had to add Beatles songs to their set, and sing as well as play instrumentals. The schizophrenia they must have felt is evident on the B-side of "Mar Gaya," "You Better Tell Me Now" (written by Holden with Joe Kooken), which almost exactly bisected the Mersey sound and surf, its catchy verses and vocal harmonies bracketed by explosive surf guitar solos. "I wanted to do nothing but an instrumental thing," maintains Holden. "Kooken felt we should go vocal, and I really resisted, because the instrumentation was where I really got my joy. So I started writing vocally. We played with such volume and power, and with that surf guitar sound applied to the new kind of music, it made a really interesting character."

The Fender IV did try again with another surf instrumental single, "Malibu Run," a slow ballad that had some really far-out, ahead-of-its time echoing guitar effects from Holden. The reverb oozed out of the speakers like a giant sandworm slithering across the ocean floor, sometimes eschewing standard melodic notes for demonic, almost percussive scrapes that convincingly emulated the mood and mystery of the underwater. This foreshadowed some experiments of psychedelic rock, and the disquietingly minor chord configurations that dot "Mar Gaya," "Malibu

Run," and the outtake "Little Ollie" (now available on Holden's *Early Works '64-'66 CD*) prefigure Holden's knack for stormy-clouds-a-gatherin' motifs, which would culminate in his *Population II* album about five years later.

In 1965, however, instrumental surf music had already become an anachronism. Holden's next band, Sons of Adam, dispensed with surf altogether for Rolling Stones-styled rock and early Los Angeles psychedelia, although Holden is careful to note that the term psychedelic music wasn't really around during the Sons' brief life span. The Sons of Adam supported the Rolling Stones at one of their mid-'60s concerts in Southern California, and under their influence Holden moved away from surf reverb to a heavier sound. "They had state-of-the-art equipment that really blew me away. Bill Wyman had two big Voxes hooked in tandem. That's the first time I'd ever seen that, and it created such a big bottom end. Keith [Richards would] crank the Fender Showman up on ten, and that would create this warm tube distortion, whereas if you tried to do that with the reverb on, you would get a screechiness and sharpness that didn't work.

"From my own personal transition from the power level that I was using in surf music over to the feedback level, I had to get rid of the reverb to be able to accomplish getting the most out of the tubes, and find a way to preamp it. I started changing my concept of equipment and tone, and developing other ideas. Started playing with preamps, getting rid of the reverb, playing with feedback. I kept searching for other equipment to get more power, volume, and excitement. I started playing with feedback; that's where the psychedelia started to come."

Holden recorded just a couple of singles with the Sons of Adam, and complains that because record labels of the time were unaccustomed to a band of the Sons of Adam's volume, "People didn't know what to do in the studio with us. The engineer didn't know. They would freak out." Still, the solos on "Saturday's Son"—a garage-psychedelic number reminiscent of hard-rocking tracks by great 1960s L.A. psych-sters Love, such as "7 and 7 Is"—in particular unveiled Holden's talent for coaxing menacing, smoky sustain passages from his axe. In this respect he was exploring territory similar to that pioneered by Jeff Beck of the Yardbirds, whose "Mr. You're a Better Man Than I" was covered on "Saturday's Son"'s B-side. It is as a live band, however, that the Sons of Adam are primarily remembered, both in Los Angeles and in San Francisco, their names appearing on some of the highly-valued paisley posters advertising early psychedelic concerts in the Bay Area.

"The Sons of Adam was a unique band, because it was so powerful live that we could overthrow anything," boasts Holden. "It combined the power of surf with the power of blues at a really highly charged level. The club owners would—I mean, you could count on it say, 'Turn those damn things down!' Meanwhile they were making the money hand over fist. People would be lined up three deep around the block to come hear us. So every time that they would fire us for being too loud, the crowd would follow us and they would go broke again. The only band that was ever better than us onstage for a night was the Rolling Stones, and they put on such a great show that night I just went, 'Wow. Nobody's ever done that to *us*!' The weak point of the band was, it didn't come across on recordings, and the writing of the material was rather odd, in what written material there was."

It would be disagreements over original material that would lead Holden to leave the band around late 1966. "They wanted to do Byrds cover songs, or cover songs to play clubs, and I said, 'No, man, we gotta write. I want to play powerful, hard, and heavy-driving music. This is where we came from, and where it's going.' They were getting really frustrated with me, and it was a big division. I just said, 'I'm out of here. I can't do it anymore. I'm not gonna turn my amp down. I just don't *do* that.'"

Ironically, the one single recorded by the Sons of Adam after Holden's departure, "Feathered Fish"/"Baby Show the World," had sinewy distortion-speckled guitar solos that weren't too different from what Holden was playing at the time. "Feathered Fish" was an excellent, spaced-out crunchy psychedelic song written by Love leader Arthur Lee, although never recorded by Love. Holden remembers Lee giving him the song to do, and says he did record a version with Sons of Adam, although he doesn't know what happened to it; he would bring the song to his next band, the Other Half. (The Love-Sons of Adam connection wasn't limited to this one song; Sons of Adam drummer Michael Stuart joined Love after Love's first album.)

By the time he left the Sons of Adam, Holden's local reputation was such that when the Yardbirds needed a replacement for Jeff Beck for a show at the Santa Monica Civic Auditorium, he was tapped as a possible candidate. Like Beck, he recalls, "I played powerful, loud sustain and kind of out there on the edge, or over the edge. There was a rumor that Jeff was gonna leave the band. Somebody arranged a meeting between [Yardbirds singer] Keith Relf and I, and Keith wanted to get together and rehearse when the opportunity presented itself, so he took my name and number." Some Sons of Adam fans called Holden and "they said, 'Jeff refused to go on. They need somebody right now.' I was the only person anybody knew at the time that could do their music.

"But I hadn't rehearsed with them at all. I thought really hard about it, because I thought, 'Jesus, now that'd be a band I'd like to play with.' They were going more in the direction I was going. But I'm not going to get up there and not have even done at least a half-hour rehearsal to go through some material. I thought, 'Jeff is not gonna *not* play. He's *gotta* play! It would be stupid to go down there and make a fool out of myself if he's going to play.' But it turned out he didn't, and Jimmy Page took his place that night. Jimmy was well involved with the band, so he already knew that material, [and] was a perfect shoo-in."

After the Sons of Adam, laments Holden, "I just couldn't seem to find anybody to play with, and it was driving me nuts. I even went crippled in my arm for about six months. My arm locked up, and I thought it had been paralyzed [for] the rest of my life. It was a psychosomatic illness from not being able to play." The same Sons of Adam fans that had tried to get Holden to stand in for Beck, however, turned him on to a local band that did its own material. "So I went to hear the band and I sat in and plugged in. I turned everybody's volume up. I think I made 'em all mad right at the start." He laughs, the sound of a man who's always trying to up the wattage whether everyone's ready or not. "But they wanted to me to play right away."

With the Other Half, Holden would record a few singles and an album. Like the Sons of Adam, the Other Half is faintly remembered, if at all, for appearing in small type as a support act on posters for psychedelic San Francisco rock concerts. This has led to the group often getting erroneously referred to as a San Francisco band, although it was actually an L.A. group that frequently played San Francisco shows. And as with the Sons of Adam, the highlights of the Other Half's little-heard recordings were Holden's guitar parts, which growled with a ferocious roar at the low end and had a squiggly, Eastern-shaded tone in the upper register. Usually present were the swooping bent notes and phenomenal sustain that marked him as an American counterpoint of sorts to Jeff Beck.

Indeed, the Other Half themselves often sounded like the Yardbirds mixed with Californian psychedelic garage music, what with the frequent crossfire of guitar and harmonica riffs (between Holden and Other Half singer Jeff Nowlen) and blend of blues, hard rock, and Eastern melodic influences. Due to its inclusion on several anthologies of 1960s garage rock (including the best one, Rhino's *Nuggets* box set), their most famous track is the punky single "Mr. Pharmacist," which was covered by British punk band the Fall in the 1980s.

Yet for all its grinding appeal, culminating in a stinging solo that climaxes with a grating scrape down the strings, it's a rather misleading introduction to the Other Half, which usually took a middle ground between garage and psychedelia on its lone album and a handful of non-LP tracks. There was a raw version of "Feathered Fish," Holden alternating between speaker-melting fuzz guitar and corkscrewing notes on the high end of the scale. On the highway-to-doom-tempoed "Flight of the Dragon Lady," Holden uncorked some urgent squeals in the instrumental break's harmonica-guitar duel, ending with a dive-bombing blast of grumbling distortion that glided into high, humming sustain. For "Morning Fire," Holden concocted weirdly shimmering Asiatic-style lines; "I Need You," "It's Too Hard (Without You)," and "No Doubt About It" were effective matings of Haight-Ashbury-styled psychedelia with hard, bluesy garage rock.

Whatever the situation, Holden was adroit at working several octaves into his solos with grace, as on the waltzing "I Know," whose tormented guitar break made its way from the bottom to the top of the scale with eloquent despair, contrasting effectively with the subdued and sullen verses. On "I Need You" he moved from crunching 1960s punk to notes that vanish off the high end of the guitar neck as casually as if he was flicking a light switch off and on. The ballad "Wonderful Day" (written by Holden alone) revealed a more sensitive dimension to the guitarist, the lilting folky chords and bashing power chords contrasting effectively to drive home the hurt and angry lyrics.

Released on the small Acta label, the self-titled album by the Other Half hardly sold at all. And what does Holden himself think of this record, popular enough among collectors to have been bootlegged in editions that most likely heavily outsold the original pressing? "When I heard it I thought, 'What a piece of garbage!' I was amazed that it ever even got released." So much for historical revisionism.

Much of his dissatisfaction with the record, Holden elaborates, was sparked by his frustrations with the limitations of both the studio and the guitar he was using at the time. Judging from some of the sounds that somehow escaped onto the finished record—you can hear coughing on "Wonderful Day," for instance, and lame, distracted background chants on "I Need You"—the sessions were more rushed and incomplete than they should have been. "[The group members] didn't know what they were doing, the producers of the record didn't know what they were doing. I still didn't have a clue what I was doing in the studio. And I really wasn't very happy. I wasn't doing what I wanted to do, and I was trying to accommodate everybody else, at the expense of sacrificing my own soul and happiness. I didn't figure that out till a *long* time later.

"I liked a couple of the concepts, I liked 'Flight of the Dragon Lady' a little bit, except it didn't come off on recording at all. It was just dead and dull and dumb-sounding. It was not huge and magnificent and spectacular. I liked 'Morning Fire.' I was experimenting with this Indian double-tuning of the E string: I would tune the open high E string down to the same as the open B string, playing two strings at once in a simultaneous melody, and that was kind of an interesting thing. I wanted to take it further, but...." He sighs. "Limitations on the stupid guitar. I hate that guitar to this day. I got so angry with it one night at a concert we did in Denver, I smashed it. I couldn't stand it anymore. It was a piece of junk.

"I had a Jazzmaster; I had large hands, and I wanted this length that I could slide around on. But the thing had such an awful tone. I played the doggone thing for over a year and a half, and I just hated it. But I didn't have any more money to get another guitar," he laughs, "and it turns out the way it's built, it can't sustain. So it'll screech instead of sustain. It turned out more psychedelic than it was really intended."

The only times Holden remembers fondly from his stint with the Other Half did not involve actually *playing* with the Other Half, but jamming onstage with Steve Miller, and doing solo spots in which he would test the limits of the day's amplification. "We had a pile of Dual Showmans [amplifiers], and I would just link 'em all together and do about a twenty-minute psychedelic-type solo, everything cranked on ten. The band would take a break, and I would just go wild for a while and have fun, attempt to do something different and interesting. And the audience loved it."

It made sense that Holden's next band would be the San Francisco group that got physically dwarfed by the amount of amplifiers they would lug onstage. "Blue Cheer was a three-piece band using about eight Fender Dual Showmans; four on the bass, and four on the guitar. I used to use about six of them on the guitar when I'd do my thing. So everybody kept prodding me that I knew—'this is the band you should be with.'" It is odd that Holden is most known for his short stint in Blue Cheer (replacing Leigh Stephens), a young power trio already on the commercial decline after its one hit, 1968's proto-metal "Summertime Blues." Although Randy played with the band live for about a year, he ultimately recorded just three tracks with Blue Cheer, which appear on side two of the 1969 album *New! Improved!*

"For the first time, I was pretty much pleased with the sound that I was getting with my guitar," allows Holden of his Blue Cheer days. For him, the main problem with Blue Cheer was the insanity that went along with business interests pumping as much mileage out of the band as they could within a limited period of time. "When I joined the band, they had their songs, and I contributed some of my ones. We had four hours to rehearse all this before we went on tour. And I wrote several new songs on tour. But there wasn't once when [singer/bassist] Dickie [Peterson] and I would create together, or collaborate, because everybody was off doing something else. We could never get in the showplace where we were going to play, and have the whole day before to create or do whatever we wanted, invent music. When it came time to record the new album, the only new songs the band had were the ones that I showed them when I joined." Those songs are certainly the highlights of *New! Improved!*, Holden slapping his trademark sustain onto the elongated "Peace of Mind" and "Fruit and Icebergs."

Although Holden did not sell records like the Jimi Hendrixes and Eric Claptons did, he was certainly known to the competition. "Guitarists would always try to look to see what my amp settings were, and I would always wind them to zero to keep it undisclosed. I had a device that was a small silver box [with a] foot pedal button that increased the volume by 50 percent with no distortion. You wouldn't believe how many guitarists tried to heist that thing. I had to keep my eye on it like a hawk.

"Once in Boston on tour with Blue Cheer, I left the stage for a few minutes. As ordinary when closing the show, [I'd] return as soon as the lights went out to retrieve my silver box. It was gone. I freaked, as it was the only one of its kind, only a few ever made. I didn't even know who made it anymore; the name was worn off, and I'd had it for years, since Sons of Adam days. It was great for the extra edge on solo riffs. I was frantic to find whoever took it. I also just received my new Black SG Standard [guitar] right before that show backstage, and didn't even have time to tune it to use it. (It was the first Black SG.) When my silver box disappeared from stage, I went looking for our equipment guys to find it, only to find someone had stolen the brand new Black SG. The silver box was gone too, but I decided to look under the stage just for the heck of it, and bingo, there it was. Whoever had their sights on it grabbed it, threw it under the stage quick, like, planning to come back later to get it. It was an animal world out there."

Holden's report of his brief tour of duty with Blue Cheer makes life with a star act sound as joyless as boot camp. "I always had serious despondencies with the band, because it never rehearsed. It was never allowed to rehearse, never allowed to play together, except when we got onstage. There was no time to communicate musically, develop and create. There was never any money, even though we were making thousands and thousands of dollars. I'd be thrown some change that might be a shirt if I was lucky. There was a serious drug problem [elsewhere in the band], too, that just wouldn't resolve itself, and I think that was tied to the disappearance of the money, and why no one wanted to get a clear accounting.

"Then they wanted me to record a new album; I was never shown the contract. I'm just told I have to do all these things. And I wanted to know, where's the compensation for this? We're touring, now we're supposed to record, we've never even rehearsed—what the hell, is there some kind of accounting organization at all? And there wasn't. I didn't even have enough money to buy food, I was in the middle of recording this album, and I said to myself, 'Why am I doing this?' I just left."

Holden's next project would be even more reductionist than Blue Cheer's power trio setup—a power *duo*, Holden on guitar and Chris Lockheed playing drums and keyboards simultaneously. Lockheed had been the drummer with the obscure Northern California group Kak, which put out one album in the late 1960s; in fact, the lead singer, Gary Yoder, would join Blue Cheer after Holden split. Lockheed, remembers Holden, "heard I left the band and wanted to play. When he had a meeting with me, he said that he also played keyboards. And loving sensationalism as I do, I asked him, 'Can you play both at once, drums and keyboards?' He said, 'Yeah.' I thought, if this guy's got the confidence and nerve to do that, he's gotta be able to do it." There were very few two-man rock groups around at the time (and have actually been few at *any* time); the only such setup to achieve reasonable popularity in the late 1960s was employed by keyboardist Lee Michaels, whose sole accompanist on some of his records and concerts was his drummer, "Frosty."

Holden and Lockheed, claims Randy, made Blue Cheer sound "quiet, placid, and peaceful, what you listen to when you're eighty years old in your rocking chair. Live, it sounded like a huge band with a half-dozen members. We were ten times louder than Blue Cheer ever dreamt of being. *Population II* [the one album Holden and Lockheed recorded together] was nuclear.

"I had sponsorship from Sunn amplifiers. They were designing this new amp for me: 200 watts in every cabinet. They gave me all of them I wanted. I would cart these things on the airplane as excess baggage in those days. When I would show up at the airport, the guy would just freak out and see twenty huge cases coming out of this old black and white police bus."

Clearly Holden was thinking of sounds that were not just difficult to achieve with electric guitars and amps, but also beyond the range of what most people would conceive of as rock or even music. When he explains how he tuned his guitar a whole step lower than standard tuning, his tone becomes as metaphysical as musical. "There was a sound character to the wind and the sea that has a very distinctive but subtle thunder. I wanted to try to capture the essence of that otherwise silent thunder, deep growl. It's a pretty obvious sound if you've ever been in the presence of strong wind and waves. There's a howl and shriek that almost drowns out the other frequencies of the low end, but it's the low end that really has a deep roar, and can be very ominous.

"I once thought at some depth what a nuclear bomb would sound like in close proximity. I concluded it would be so overwhelming it wouldn't be heard, but simply be all-encompassing, beyond imaginable experience. I was so affected by the idea of what such sound would feel like that I wandered into the arena of attempting to produce a sound that would be so overwhelming, it would create a silence all its own. The sound I was after was way beyond things like decibel levels. It was off the Richter scale. The experience was one of hearing from the inside out, the reverse of the ordinary. With all those Sunn amps, that was exactly what it was like. Nothing quite like it on earth. Even a jet taking off doesn't have that effect."

It's possible that the most revered rock guitarist of all time may have been interested in experimenting with Holden's amplification. Although Randy only met Hendrix once (and briefly), a mutual acquaintance of both the guitarists mysteriously arranged with Jimi (for reasons still unclear to Holden) to borrow Jimi's Stratocaster to bring to Holden to try out. Hendrix's friend also let Holden know "how Jimi's road technician came up with the idea of placing a resistor in Jimi's guitars, in line between the pickups and the volume control that reduced the output, reducing the overdrive of the guitar, allowing the individual notes to come through, letting the overdriven amp produce the sustain. It made perfect sense. I never considered anything like that. But I plugged it in, and incredible, there was Jimi's exact sound, and everything he played was suddenly so easy to play it was magical, and effortless. It was totally beautiful.

"Why they did that was never clear to me on its face value, since it wasn't like Jimi and I were best buds hanging out, and it wasn't customary to give your trade secrets to anyone. What I had were the new Sunn amps that were secret, no one had or could get. I know for a fact that had I been able to keep his guitar I would have wreaked literal havoc on the rock guitar scene in conjunction with my Sunns. That would have been seriously damaging. It would have been a completely different sound than I was getting, but also would have been very different from Hendrix because of the amps. I also know that had Jimi been able to get hold of my Sunns, and use his guitar through them, he would have cleaned my clock before I had the chance, and I would have stood to be accused of mimicking him.

"In retrospect, if he wanted to give me Jimi's guitar and sound secret to check out, and then set it up to bring Jimi around to check out my Sunn amps set up secret, he'd be doing something for both of us. My feeling tells me Jimi didn't have any idea what this guy was doing, and this guy was just working both ends, doing favors for both of us, with an objective of something in return for him down the line somewhere. As irony would have it, a few weeks later Jimi died, and I hadn't thought about the incident again."

Population II (so-named after the total population of the group: two), billed to Holden as a solo artist, was the link between the psychedelia-cum-metal of Blue Cheer and early hard rock-heavy metal. It was more sinister and experimental than most early metal recordings, though, at times sounding like sub-Jimi Hendrix jams in a dark mood. Holden tossed off some passages of ingenious intensity, the bee-stinging licks of "Guitar Song" suggesting perpetual wide-eyed surprise, and the superamped wobble of "Fruits and Icebergs" sounding like a science fiction soundtrack, sometimes sustaining notes as if he was trying to use his guitar strings to bounce lasers off the stratosphere. It's one of the relatively few tracks from his 1960s repertoire that Holden speaks of fondly: "It had these beautiful atomic chords that were just so dark, deep and painful. But beautiful, at the same time."

The lurching tempos and sludgy rhythm arrangements were a distant ancestor of grunge, and as Holden explains were a consequence of Lockheed needing to play drums and keyboards at the same time, which ruled out anything faster than a crawl most of the time. "It was really laborious for him to try to do that," observes Holden. "It was very numerical, mathematical, and calculated. I realized that the job he faced sucked. To me, it would have been no fun at all. Because you're totally restricted. On one side you have to have this soft touch on keyboards, and the other, you have to be slamming. It's amazing he didn't overdose on schizophrenia, just trying to do that.

"Chris wasn't—to no fault of his own, I don't think anybody could have done it—able to play the rhythms of both the bass and the drum at the same time. It was slow because Chris *had* to go slow. Chris was into country music, he was wearing cowboy boots with spurs, a cowboy hat and a plaid shirt. And he's up there trying to play this extreme heavy metal dark music.... I mean, it must have been so bizarre for him to even conceive of that. He was probably more of a mathematical robot than anything else.

"We rehearsed and rehearsed, ten hours a day, every day, just to be able to accomplish it. I rented this opera house; it would seat about 1,200 people, and it had a huge stage. It was the only place we could rehearse that would carry all the amplification. But whenever I would invite people to a rehearsal, they would sit there and stare like they did not have a clue what was going on! I think I probably scared everybody with what I was doing. Nobody really understood it. But I thought it would move people once it happened, once we got the album released. If the thing would have been released and we would have toured, that thing would have been so big it would have scared you to death. Because it was so much fun, and ahead of what was happening. But the record companies—they can keep things from happening. And that's what happened."

According to Holden, *Population II*, recorded for the small Hobbit label, never came out. Some promo pressings and/or tapes must have escaped, however, as the record has been issued in unauthorized and bootleg editions on several occasions. Its nonappearance caused Holden's musical and personal life to enter a free-falling spiral. "I was up at the office trying to get some release date information on the album, and [an executive] said to me, 'You know, you young kids just amaze me, how you can spend all your time at the beach just having fun.' He blew me away so bad, how clueless he was. I worked my butt off for twenty hours a day rehearsing, writing, just total devotion, seven days a week, and this clown is sitting there with some illusion that I'm going to the beach. I went into a state of deep intense shock."

On top of that, an equipment manager sold all of Holden's gear to a Hollywood music store, and "basically I went bankrupt after *Population II* didn't get released. I found myself on the street with no money, no amplifiers, all my equipment stolen, no friends, and I said, 'This sucks! This doesn't work at all. I'm not doing this anymore.'" Around the end of 1970, Holden abandoned music entirely, moving to Hawaii, sailing around the world, buying boats and developing a fishing business, going through a couple of divorces.

In 1989, Holden was falsely accused of stealing a boat by the lawyer from whom he bought it. The accusation was thrown out of court before going to trial because there was no probable cause for the warrant being issued in the first place. Randy successfully sued for damages, but not without suffering financial and emotional devastation for seven years. The lawyer was found guilty of fraud, malice, and oppression in a jury trial whose verdict also found that the lawyer knew at all times his criminal accusation was false, and there was no probable cause ever present for him to pursue a criminal complaint. The brutal experience will form the subject of an entire book, presently being coauthored by Holden and his attorney. Music, and the cult reputation Holden was accumulating among 1960s psychedelic collectors, was not on his mind. His extensive encounters with the legal world, he notes, did eventually allow him to resolve an issue of royalties that he contended had been unpaid for years, after he learned that his music was being sold all over the world without his knowledge.

In 1990, however, someone gave Holden a tape of *Population II*, "and I listened to it. I really didn't want to. It depressed me to think about it. But I permitted it. When I heard it, I went, 'Wow. That's pretty fascinating.' It has its own kind of thing that draws you into it. It's almost like quicksand, in a sense. It's like it almost pulls you into it. And when you get pulled into it, it's very enjoyable." Holden had played guitar on only one occasion since 1970, but "after not playing all that time, when I was finally seduced into taking a guitar and doing it again, it finally showed itself to me as a beautiful woman again. It was like something magical happened. It was brand new, refreshing, and alive. And I kind of blew myself away, because I can play things like I was in another world, that I could not have even come close to trying to accomplish at the height of my playing before I quit." With the encouragement of Randy Pratt, a fan who had tracked Holden down in the early 1990s, Holden made the album *Guitar God* with ex-Blue Cheer drummer Paul Whaley (whom Holden had not seen for about a quarter of a century). Holden's still playing a metal-hard rock hybrid at times, but the record is also sometimes reminiscent of Neil Young's hard rock outings, both vocally and instrumentally.

Now back in Southern California, and happily married to painter Ruth Mayer, Holden's personal life—after bouts of anxiety in the early 1990s that made him feel like "I was utterly destroyed, I really wasn't sure if I was going to be alive the next minute, it was so bad"—has completely turned around. Much of his time these days is devoted to working on painting and publishing art prints, but in 1999 he was full of enthusiasm for the latest guitar technology, talking excitedly about the guitar his wife had custom-built for him as a present. "I probably have four or five albums in the works," he enthuses. "I just can't stop creating. I know what I want, and I don't do what somebody else wants me to do now. I get in the studio and I turn into something else. People start passing out cold on their instruments, and after twenty-four hours, the engineer's passed out, and I'm still raring to go."

For Holden, the opportunity to make music again and the realization that he had a cult of devoted fans around the world is both a blessing and a cautionary tale. "I thought nobody liked what I did," he confesses. "People in the business have this way of taking an emotionally vulnerable musician, who's young, and making them feel like they're garbage and worthless. When you're that emotionally vulnerable, you believe. Even though you know it's not true. Especially when you're doing something on the cutting edge that nobody's really done."

Recommended Recordings:

By Randy Holden:

Early Works '64-'66 (1997, Captain Trip, Japan). It contains the two 1964-65 singles that Holden did with the Fender IV, and the two 1965-66 singles he did with the Sons of Adam, along with some previously unreleased material by each group. It's a comprehensive view of his pre-Other Half recordings that follows his journey from surf music to early psychedelic rock, with some real standout guitar solos on the Fender IV's "Mar Gaya" and "Malibu Run," and the Sons of Adam's "Saturday's Son."

Population II (circa 1970, Hobbit). Holden is more of a guitarist than a singer-songwriter, and the elongated heavy psych-metal cuts on this coveted collector's item bear this out. He does unleash some ferocious sustain throughout, and the exploration of two-man power-duo arrangements has been seldom duplicated in rock to this day.

By the Other Half:

The Other Half (1968, Acta). Although Holden makes it clear he doesn't think much of this album, it's a good if underproduced slab of garage psychedelia with a dab of Haight-Ashbury melodicism, marred by some half-assed songwriting and jamming here and there. An unauthorized reissue on the French Eva label, *Mr. Pharmacist*, adds non-LP cuts, including "Mr. Pharmacist," which also appears on *Nuggets* (Rhino), a four-CD box set of 1960s garage rock.

Kaleidoscope, in David Lindley's house in Pasadena, ready to play anything at any time. Left to right: Chris Darrow (with mandolin), Solomon Feldthouse (with oud), David Lindley (with harp guitar), John Vidican (drummer, though kitless in photo), Chester Crill (with bass). Credit: Photo by Steve Cahill. Courtesy Chris Darrow Archives.

Kaleidoscope

Eclecticism—far more than the vaunted simulation of the drug experience—was the primary shared characteristic of the many 1960s bands now described as psychedelic. No bands, psychedelic or otherwise, were more eclectic than Kaleidoscope, whose very name served as a calling card for the group's hunger for investigating and fusing all forms of popular music. Old-time folk, British folk, folk-rock, jug band, R&B, blues, jazz, Middle Eastern, Cajun, Appalachian, comedy, flamenco, and yes, feedback-riddled psychedelic jams: all were fair game for Kaleidoscope's sonic pinwheel, sometimes within the same track. As a cult band, the group was a natural, not only to record collectors, but also to fellow musicians. Jimmy Page is but the most famous of these, calling Kaleidoscope his favorite band in one interview, and perhaps drawing inspiration from the group for his own violin-bowing guitar techniques and occasional African-Eastern-rock cocktails.

Their commanding ambition sacrificed consistency and was, perhaps, too demanding a palette for the pop audience to embrace, even as the group anticipated the worldbeat blends of the 1980s and 1990s. The wide scope of Kaleidoscope's tastes and virtuosic talents fueled some groundbreaking experimentation on the group's late-1960s albums. At the same time, it may well have contributed to the tenuous stability of a band that changed personnel with almost every album, as members were sacrificed and shuffled in a tangle of competing interests. The act that could, apparently, play anything at any time, on almost any instrument, could not manage to survive into the 1970s, despite a couple of reunion albums in subsequent years. More than thirty years after their heyday, their approach has seldom been duplicated within the framework of rock music. "There were very few people trying that kind of thing," declares one of Kaleidoscope's multi-instrumentalists, Chester Crill, "and to this day, I don't understand why."

As with so many Californian psychedelic groups of the 1960s, Kaleidoscope's roots were not so much in rock or R&B as in traditional folk music. (Incidentally, an entirely separate British group called Kaleidoscope also recorded some albums in the late 1960s, accumulating a small cult following with whimsical pop-psychedelia that was dissimilar to, and not to be confused with, that of the Kaleidoscope from Southern California.) Chris Darrow and David Lindley, both of whom were proficient on several stringed instruments, had played traditional folk in the Mad Mountain Ramblers and the Dry City Scat Band in the mid-1960s, though Darrow was out of the Dry City Scat Band by the time they did a scarce EP and two tracks on Elektra's *String Band Project* compilation. Another future member, Solomon Feldthouse, was playing flamenco guitar in folk clubs, mixing in a little Leadbelly-styled music.

As Chester Crill remembers, "I was staying at a place in Berkeley, and [Lindley] and Solomon were upstairs practicing. They appeared locally up there as David and Solomon, the Kings of Israel. I'm not kidding. I went and played with him [David], just to show them how to do it right, because neither of them could play violin as well as I could. And [Lindley] instantly said, 'You should be the bass player in this rock group I'm doing.'" Another piece of the puzzle arrived with John Vidican, a drummer who, according to Darrow, "was an eighteen-year-old hippie who looked pretty good, kind of the high school marching band drummer. Judging what I can gather, he was just sort of picked because he was cute."

If this sounds like a motley configuration for a fledgling rock band, it should be remembered that many of the best folk-rock groups were assembled from similarly disparate and illogical parts. None of the musicians in the very best folk-rock band, the Byrds, had extensive experience playing rock or electric instruments. As it happened it would be the Byrds' label, Columbia, that signed Kaleidoscope (on its Epic subsidiary) on the basis of a demo written by Lindley, "Why Try," with session musician Billy Mundi (later in the Mothers of Invention) filling the drum chair. The band might not have progressed past the demo stage had Lindley's old band mate (and present brother-in-law), Chris Darrow, not been recruited.

"I was married and had a kid," says Darrow. "I was going to graduate school, working in the graduate school art gallery, hanging up a show. I got a call from Lindley about eleven o'clock at night saying, 'Looks like we've got a record deal. You want to join our band?' And I said, 'What's it about?' He [told me], and it took me like two seconds to say yes. My ex-wife still would have loved for me to become an art professor.

"Chester tells me that the band could have broken up if I hadn't showed up and tied it together, because there wasn't enough of a focus. There was Solomon's Middle Eastern and flamenco. There was David's country and his overlap into the flamenco/Middle Eastern stuff. There was Chester's jazz-meets-rock 'n' roll kind of thing, and the drummer, who basically was just a rock 'n' roll drummer, so he kind of had to learn everything. I think it was a band looking for a sense of something. I had been in a band already, and had for a couple of years been playing electric music; I could play electric guitar and bass. As it turned out, I was the major writer; I was writing original material, and other guys weren't. They really didn't have a band when the [Epic] deal was [made], they just sort of had a concept. The one song [the "Why Try" demo] was enough to represent the concept."

And what exactly *was* the concept? "The idea was that it was a myriad of possibilities. Once we got together and started talking about this stuff, it became evident that we wanted to have original material that reflected somewhat the psychedelic/Middle Eastern/metaphysical kind of area that seemed so important at that time. Even when we did interpretive stuff, our rule was to always make it our own. When I was brought in, I was told that this was going to be a leaderless band; everybody had their own strength, and each one of these guys could lead their own band their own way. But when it was my song or my turn to do it, I'd be the one to be able to tell everybody what to do, or instruct. If Solomon was doing the Middle Eastern stuff, he could say, 'Well, this is how you play 9/8 time, this is how you play 7/8.'"

Echoes Crill: "Each of us would have our own [area] there was no question that we were the authority in. Then we would teach the other people how to play in that style. That's what we did, Chris in particular. He was the only one that had any rock 'n' roll knowledge at all.

"We did work out a thing where we would sit down and say, 'Now you get one-fifth of the piece, you get one-fifth of the pie, how are you gonna spend that?' Solomon would say, 'We're gonna do one flamenco tune, and we're gonna do one Arabic tune,' and David would say, 'We're gonna do one country and western tune, and we're gonna do one Appalachian tune.' And I'd say, 'We're going to do one jazz tune, and we're going to do one R&B tune.' That always worked out real well.

"We ended up trying real early stabs at fusion. We'd play Eastern beats with Western instruments, jazz on Eastern instruments, throw it every direction we could. The major reason it ended up that way was because we were all multi-instrumentalists. There wasn't anybody who didn't play [at least] three instruments."

Kaleidoscope might have nominally been trying to be a rock 'n' roll band, more or less. However, the instruments they used—and the ability of everyone save Vidican to play several of them—ensured that they did not sound much like any normal rock 'n' roll band. Lindley could play guitar, banjo, harp guitar, and violin; Darrow guitar, bass, violin, Dobro, and mandolin; Crill organ, bass, harmonica, piano, violin, harmonium, viola, and harpsichord; and Feldthouse guitar, bass, oud, saz, and clarinet. "It was a wonderful experience, because none of us had been involved in anything quite like this," says Darrow. "At the time, you couldn't get an electric violin anywhere; you couldn't get an electric almost anything. So we were taping on contact mikes and all kinds of things, trying to make stuff work in this electric world."

The ten tracks on their debut LP, *Side Trips*, lasted a mere twenty-six minutes, yet within that limited space they covered so much ground that some listeners must have wondered whether it was the work of one band or several. The opening cut, Feldthouse's "Egyptian Gardens," went into the Middle Eastern-rock mating dance with gusto. The sly R&B-influenced vocal (not too different from what Dr. John sang in his early days) alternated with tight violin-led instrumental breaks that could have been mistaken for an authentic Turkish folk ensemble, ending with an accelerated rave-up. If songs like "If the Night" and "Please" approached yearning and tuneful Byrdsian guitar-based California folk-rock—Darrow's "Pulsating Dream," indeed, was one of the closer mimics of the Byrds circa 1966 ever recorded—there were darker and more mysterious cuts that tempered the pop sensibilities with Eastern exoticism. Darrow's "Keep Your Mind Open" was a subtle anti-Vietnam protest, decorated by tinkling percussion, hypnotic modal guitar runs, and bursts of gunfire that were nearly buried until the very end of the track. Slightly ragaish trills could also be heard on "Why Try," the song that had gotten Kaleidoscope onto Epic in the first place.

If the early Kaleidoscope had an Achilles' heel, it was the jug band updates of old-time folk and jazz material. Passes at "Hesitation Blues" and "Minnie the Moocher" were comic interludes that fell flat, and now sound corny and dated. In retrospect the band might have been better advised to include the non-LP B-side "Elevator Man," a Feldthouse original that demonstrated the group's aptitude for straight-ahead R&B, tinged with a bit of trippy weirdness in the lyrics and haphazard organ. Yet not all of their covers were failures by any means. "Oh Death" was an effective reworking of a mordant folk standard, colored by the band's knack for humming fiddle lines and rattling percussion, adding an atmospheric texture missing from straight acoustic revivals of the much-covered tune.

Darrow on the first album: "The reason it's so tight and short is that we were well-rehearsed. We recorded seven songs in like eight hours. I think had we been a little more unsure of ourselves in that regard, we might have even done a better first album, because we might have spent more time in the studio working out stuff. 'Cause none of us really had any studio experience."

For a major label, Columbia signed a hell of a lot of adventurous cult rockers that never moved big units nationally in the 1960s, including Kaleidoscope, the United States of America, Skip Spence, Dino Valenti, the Remains, and the Rising Sons. Kaleidoscope may have been on one of the biggest labels in the world, but being on Columbia was no guarantee of commercial success. According to Darrow, *Side Trips* only sold about 5,000 copies. Columbia's promotional budget for *Side Trips* did not even extend to a color cover, the front illustration getting printed in newspaper black-and-white. It was as a live act that Kaleidoscope really began to make some noise in 1967, both in folk festivals (which were in reality beginning to include some definite rock bands by 1967) and on rock bills as the audience for underground music began to expand.

Kaleidoscope immediately stood out in this company not just for how it sounded, but for the sheer entertainment of watching musicians playing so many different instruments, switching to several different ones over the course of a single performance. Photos from the period show the band posing with so many different instruments that the unwary might well figure the pictures to be mere poses, rather than the real thing. The instruments were not props, though; they were actually played, often and well. "We were all ethnomusicologist kind of guys by the time we were twenty, eighteen years old," explains Darrow. "We were always multi-instrumental guys, [going] back to our Mad Mountain Ramblers and Dry City Scat

Band days. Mike Seeger in the New Lost City Ramblers was our idol. He, Tom Paley, and John Cohen, who were also in the [Ramblers], played banjo, fiddle, mandolin, and guitar. They could all sing, and they'd just trade instruments back and forth. So it was no big deal for us to pick up a fiddle, then a Dobro, then a banjo. We were all learning the instruments simultaneously, because we wanted to be like our idols. I would say if you asked Ry Cooder, Taj Mahal, David Lindley, me, you would get, 'I wanted to be Mike Seeger.'

"I have a picture when we were in the Mad Mountain Ramblers, of all our instruments; it was like twenty instruments. We would always trade things back and forth and play two fiddles on one thing, or two mandolins, or two banjos, or one guy playing Dobro. It goes back farther conceptually than just [Kaleidoscope]. It became part of our selling point. When people came to see us, we'd have things laid all over the stage, and it looked very impressive."

"The only reason we existed was because of our success as a live band," elaborates Crill. "Our recordings didn't sell doodle. We never had a bad response, anywhere. Even if it was just opening for seven other bands. You could put us on any bill, and you weren't going to go to sleep while we were on, because we changed it up like crazy. It was very entertaining to watch, because it wasn't just five hippies who looked alike. It was five very *ugly*-looking hippies who had entirely different ways of approaching things. A lot of our early live concerts, the only problem was the timing of throwing the instruments around the stage."

Kaleidoscope compensated for the absence of conventional poster-ready mugs with a certain oddball charisma, particularly from the man who would qualify as the onstage front man of the supposedly leaderless band, Solomon Feldthouse. Feldthouse's gypsy wardrobe, weird (by 1967 standards) Middle Eastern stringed instruments like the oud, and evasiveness about his background gave rise to speculation that he was a genuine Turkish fellow, although he actually grew up in Idaho, according to Darrow. "He also was interested in playing clarinet, which was never my favorite instrument," laughs Chris. "But he'd always end up staying up all night, playing it in the other room while we were trying to sleep. It was annoying, but nonetheless, he was actually not too bad of a sort of Middle Eastern clarinet player.

"I've always had a little trouble with him and his disposition, because he was kind of an asshole, most of the time. You'd have to just put up with his shenanigans. Everybody worked it out, because everybody thought he was good." As for Feldthouse's raspy vocals, which did convey a sardonic kind of charm, Crill observes wryly, "Only that particular period of time would have even tolerated somebody who sang like that."

Crill himself was the band's comedian, with a taste for bizarre multiple identities that foreshadowed his later success as a comic book author. Each Kaleidoscope album saw him assume a different, preposterous pseudonym: Fenrus Epp, Max Buda, Templeton Parcely, Crill's female alter ego Connie Crill, anything but Chester Crill. On some records, the noms de plume subdivided into multiple identities; the third LP, *Incredible!*, credited Parcely with violin, organ, and vocal and Buda as a "guest artist" on harmonica, while the album was dedicated to the memory of Epp. "I made fun of participating in show business all the time, 'cause we really were *not* in show business," comments Crill. "They'd go out and do lip syncs on local TV shows and stuff. I would never do that. I'd always send a sub. And I would always send the most ridiculous sub I could find. A sumo wrestler or a big fat chick, something like that. But never anybody who looked remotely like me, or even looked like they knew what they were doing." A picture of "Connie Crill," dressed to kill the average passing truck driver, appears on the sleeve of Kaleidoscope's fourth album, *Bernice*. "Chester would come up on stage with a dress on, cowboy boots, cowboy hat, and big hair, and you didn't know whether he was a boy or a girl," says Darrow.

For their second album, *A Beacon from Mars*—recorded during 1967, and released around the beginning of 1968—Kaleidoscope maintained, indeed exceeded, the high standard of versatility set by *Side Trips*. There was the slightly spacey folk-rock of "I Found Out," perhaps the most "normal" cut of the lot; the Appalachian accents thrown into the folk-rock brew on Darrow's "Life Will Pass You By"; the blues of "You Don't Love Me"; the Cajun cover of Doug Kershaw's "Louisiana Man"; and the buzzing Celtic folk-rock of "Greenwood Sidee," which anticipated the approach Fairport Convention would bring to similar material a year or two later. The album ran a generous (in comparison to *Side Trips*) forty-three minutes, yet even so it is a shame there was no room for "Rampé Rampé," a captivating Greek-Turkish-spiced instrumental that wound itself into a progressively faster rhythm; it was used as the B-side when "I Found Out" was issued as a single. (There were yet more off-the-wall covers that the band played around this time that never made it to the Epic releases, such as "Midnight in Moscow," the Coasters' "I'm a Hog for You Baby," and the blues instrumental "Steppin' Out," popularized by Eric Clapton in his stints with John Mayall and Cream.)

The two jams that hovered around the twelve-minute mark, however, were the real highlights of the album, and the tracks that represented the furthest advancements from *Side Trips*. Darrow lifted a lick from Howlin' Wolf's "Smokestack Lightning" for the root riff of "Beacon From Mars," which evolved into a psychedelic improvisation with harmonica wails from Crill and eerie Hendrixish feedback, squeals, scrapes, and sustain on guitar. "Taxim" was almost the same length but completely different, showcasing the band's facility for Middle Eastern-rock fusion on an instrumental that, as in most of their efforts along those lines, built in intensity and speed over a long period, underpinned by mesmerizing melodic lines. "We weren't trying to play phony Middle Eastern stuff," notes Darrow with pride. "We were integrating Middle Eastern stuff into our particular viewpoint of the world, which is something different than Paul Simon hiring a bunch of African guys to play on his record."

For the second album, "we insisted on having some live recording time," emphasizes Darrow. "When 'Beacon from Mars' was recorded, we wanted to take some time and really record it the way we sounded live. It wasn't like the Buffalo Springfield, where they spent the whole week on a fucking banjo part or something. We weren't allowed the luxury of that kind of recording at that time. It was in and out; we were the low-budget end of the scale."

Darrow believes that the methods he and Lindley were using, particularly on the title track of *Beacon from Mars*, may have influenced Jimmy Page to apply the violin bow to the electric guitar in the Yardbirds and Led Zeppelin. "During 'Beacon

From Mars,' David and I both played with violin bows. I played the bass, and used it to get overtones and those long notes. [Lindley] was using it to do what he did on the guitar; there were two of us playing violin bows at the same time. It never even occurred to us that we were doing anything particularly unique or far out. A lot of the stuff we were doing was a lot more far out than using the violin bow on a guitar. But it was a good show business technique, and something that people remembered.

"I was always under the impression that there was this bad blood between Lindley and Page because David thought that Page had ripped him off. I saw the Led Zeppelin thing on TV the other night [actually the 1990s collaboration between Jimmy Page, Robert Plant, and other musicians with Middle Eastern and North African sensibilities]. The similarity in the way Jimmy Page moved around and does stuff to the oud was so reminiscent of the way David did it that I said, 'Oh, man, it looked like he did rip him off.'" It should be noted that a guitarist in England—Eddie Phillips, of the cult mod band the Creation—was using the violin bow on electric guitar at least as far back as 1966, when he used it on the Creation single "Making Time," and that it's sometimes been claimed that Page ripped *him* off. There's also the theory that Page didn't learn the technique from a rock musician at all, but from a session violinist (film star David McCallum's father, as a matter of fact) in the mid-1960s, when Page was still making his living as a session guitarist. Darrow allows, "It could be two separate guys on two separate sides of the continent just working something out."

It is indisputable, however, that Page was a fervent fan of Kaleidoscope, as he proclaimed at length in an interview with *ZigZag*, in which he called the group "my favorite band of all time—my ideal band—absolutely brilliant. I saw them one time and they played all the numbers off *Beacon From Mars*, all that Moroccan stuff, changing instruments and having a whale of a time they were. They had such good roots and such a grip on their music—and that bloke Sol [Solomon Feldthouse] was a real traveler…the sort of bloke you'd meet on the road out in the East somewhere, and you knew there was no phoniness in him, because it showed in his music. One night I saw them playing the Avalon Ballroom, and he was doing a flamenco thing, which was so authentic—easily as good as you'd expect from a top concert guitarist …and then this line of flamenco dancers suddenly emerged from the wings and danced across the stage…just too much! It sounds a bit corny, just explaining it to you like this, but it certainly wasn't because the spirit and enthusiasm was so great."

Beacon from Mars, like *Side Trips*, was not a big seller, although it received the unusual critical accolade of a three-and-a-half-star review in *Down Beat*, the major jazz magazine of the time (as it remains today), which seldom reviewed rock albums. "I don't think Columbia, on a big picture level, had any kind of fucking idea of what they were doing, really," says Darrow, with less exasperation than detached analysis. "I think it was just [Columbia thinking], 'This is what's going on right now with the kids today.' And they did the best they could to try to figure out who they could get. Stu Phillips, the A&R director at Epic, didn't know heads from tails. He was like a movie soundtrack guy, and came from a whole other era; he didn't get us at all. The guys over at [Columbia's R&B subsidiary] OKeh, Johnny 'Guitar' Watson and Larry Williams—probably of all the guys in the company—got us the best. They thought we were really cool." He laughs with pleasure. "That's why they used us on that record. They were the ones that were really the most understanding of it."

"That record" was the late 1967 single "Nobody," one of the most unusual and satisfying collisions of superficially disparate styles coughed up by 1960s rock or soul. Larry Williams, the Little Richardesque '50s rocker with the hits "Bony Moronie" and "Short Fat Fanny," was a staff producer at OKeh a decade later, frequently recording with his buddy, the esteemed blues/R&B guitarist Johnny "Guitar" Watson. Their "Nobody" was a compellingly funky number with joyous harmonies, given lilting Eastern psychedelic accents by Lindley's harp guitar and Feldthouse's saz; top L.A. session man Earl Palmer played drums, and John Vidican played congas. Especially ear-catching was the freaky instrumental tag, created, to the best of Darrow's knowledge, with drums recorded in reverse, and "one of Lindley's overtones on his harp guitar, played backwards." Not only was it the rare instance of R&B-cum-psychedelia that worked, it was catchy enough to be a hit single. It wasn't, for reasons not entirely connected with the music in the grooves.

Williams and Watson, remembers Darrow, "were like best friends, and showed up at the session with matching Coupe de Villes, matching suits, and matching hats, with chicks on their arm. One of the cars was chocolate brown, and the other was deep burgundy. And the suits were deep burgundy and chocolate brown. They really liked us an awful lot. We were treated with respect. They wanted to be psychedelic R&B; they said, 'This is natural, man, this fits great.' I thought it did too, and I was very pleased to be able to be the bass player on it. Chester didn't get to play on that one, which was really too bad. They just didn't feel that violin and/or his keyboard thing was what they needed.

"I think both those guys [both of whom are now dead] were involved with dealing coke and all kinds of undercover stuff, drug use, and they were maybe even pimps too. There was some kind of thing that happened between Larry Williams and the stations on some payola level. It didn't get paid off, and that record just bombed. The radio stations refused to play it. Some kind of nefarious goings-on that had to do with those guys just sank that record. That was another one I thought, 'Man, this is a hit, what a great, beautiful record this is.' And it just never saw the light of day. I don't know if I've ever seen a copy that wasn't promotional." As a final strange twist, "Nobody" was later covered by a decidedly less adventurous California rock band, Three Dog Night.

Although *Beacon From Mars* endures as their strongest album, Darrow opines, "We didn't feel that record was even close to how good we were [as] a live performing band." By the time it was recorded, the members of Kaleidoscope were hitting the peak of their improvisational abilities, at a length which wasn't even reflected on the record's twelve minute cuts. Feels Darrow, "We weren't just playing the notes. We could play extended solos. All of us were soloists, so if something needed to go another five minutes, it could. It didn't sound like we were falling apart; it usually got better."

Concurs Crill, "We could do that for almost forty minutes and just change up how we did it. If we had to work three nights in a row, we'd never play the same set. We just changed it all the time, because it was boring. We disparaged people who would go out and play the same thing night after night; we'd see how listless and unexciting it'd get to be for them. I can't help but sometimes think there was a small influence on bands like the Dead, who at the time were playing songs four or five minutes [long]. The only band I saw do extended stuff in that period of time was Quicksilver Messenger Service."

The band's visuals were becoming more flamboyant too, with belly and flamenco dancers. Darrow wasn't enthusiastic about the dancers, and Kaleidoscope's general drift toward a heavier Middle Eastern influence would instigate his departure from the group in early 1968. "We had a big talk, and it was like, 'I think we gotta go Middle Eastern,' and that was not my total focus. Chester and I both opposed it. Because I was probably the most emphatic about it, I just said 'I'm leaving,' basically before David said 'you're fired.'" Kaleidoscope, once envisioned as a leaderless democracy, was getting into a situation in which some members, particularly Lindley, were more equal than others. (Lindley did not respond to requests for interviews that might have allowed him to voice his side of the story.)

Crill takes a balanced view of Lindley's strengths and weaknesses. "Lindley and I never, ever got along. David really wanted to be a star. More than anything. That drove him to hire and fire people. But the guy does have an appreciation of talent. I would say that's his strongest suit. He was always involved in trying to get the best players he could around him, which was one of the things that made me be interested in being involved in rock 'n' roll. Because to me, rock 'n' roll was a howling mess." He also credits Lindley for helping to ensure that the band members, unlike some other groups on Columbia, actually got to play the music on their records, in large measure because there weren't a whole lot of session musicians up to coping with Kaleidoscope's large arsenal of instruments. "All of the other bands that we watched being recorded in the same space we were occupying, that they were giving major promotion to, [Columbia] had studio guys play all their albums. One of the things David particularly concocted was, we would get stuff that they couldn't do that [to]."

Before Darrow left for good, he agreed to do an East Coast tour with Kaleidoscope in early 1968, as his replacement would not be able to start until after that commitment was completed. This jaunt became a tour from hell after their gig at the Cafe Au Go Go fell through, leaving a less than enthused band that, says Darrow, "ended up playing at this place called Fun City, which was this, probably, front for a whorehouse on 42nd Street. It was lined with go-go dancers, [we were] playing in the middle of the day to nobody, and chicks [were] running around half-clothed." The only fond memory he has is of his last gig, which he places in Boston.

"Chester was playing this C-3 Hammond organ, which was one of our big prized possessions. Apparently, we were being chased by the finance company, [which was] saying there was all this money owed on it. It was like either give it back, or pay all this money. This stage was probably eight to ten feet off the floor, and there was a big long dance floor, and then this sort of bleacher seating around. At the end of the last song of the last set, all of a sudden Chester pushed the entire organ off the stage and just left it there. We ended up just walking out. That was a very infamous ending to the C-3. I don't think there was ever a Hammond organ used in the band after that."

Crill remembers the organ incident somewhat differently, and recalls the drama as having unfolded at the Crystal Dog in Portland, Oregon. "The place had been a roller-skating rink. It was on the second floor, and it had a couple-feet thick ball bearings in the floor. Don't ask me why. They were going to repossess [the organ]. David had a succession of managers that he picked, were just fabulously bad. This particular batch had really soaked us, so I decided I'd throw it off the stage and destroy it, 'cause it was like an eight-, nine-foot stage. I tossed it, it hit the floor, and it *bounced*, I don't know, eight feet in the air. It was a Hammond M-3. It went down, across the floor, and people scattered like this fucking train was coming through. It must have got about twenty, thirty feet out onto the floor, and it didn't destroy the fucking thing! So I did it again the next night, and when it hit the floor, it separated in two halves, and they flipped off in different directions. It was very spectacular."

Darrow left to join the Nitty Gritty Dirt Band after completing the East Coast tour. He was replaced by Stuart Brotman, a UCLA ethnomusicologist who had played bass in Canned Heat and, as it happened, been involved in the early lineup of another Columbia psychedelic band, the United States of America. The replacement of Darrow also sparked a change of drummers. "When Christopher left, it really made it necessary for Lindley to make Vidican leave," believes Crill. "Because Christopher was a strong enough bass player to keep a lot of rhythm happening in the areas that it did. Vidican could not play multirhythms, or Arabic, or any of the really far-out things we wanted to try [Crill also says that Billy Mundi, and not Vidican, played some of the drums on *Side Trips*]. As a live unit, we got a whole lot better, because we added [Paul] Lagos, the drummer.

"We had open auditions. The two finalists were Jim Keltner [soon to become one of the most highly regarded Los Angeles studio musicians] and Paul Lagos, and we took Lagos, because he had a much broader range of drum styles than Keltner did. Keltner was great; hell of a drummer. But he only had two or three things he could do. Lagos could have done without a bass player. Hell of a talent, and his ability to assimilate the stuff Solomon had to teach him was instantaneous. We couldn't have gotten that from anyone else. He was a great jazz drummer, he was a great rock 'n' roller, and he was a real good fusion drummer." According to Crill, Lagos was so valued by his former employer, Little Richard, that the great early rock 'n' roller ran down Sunset Boulevard in a pink jumpsuit, leaped onto the dashboard of Feldthouse's truck, stuck his head in the window, and implored Lagos to rejoin his band. "I have never had more respect than I had for Paul Lagos at that time. Because Little Richard always had *two* drummers. But when Lagos played there, he had *one*."

The first album recorded with the new rhythm section (although Darrow says much of the material had already been performed live before his exit), *Incredible!*, was a notch below its two predecessors in quality and ingenuity, though still a worthy effort in most respects. There was a heavier, occasionally slicker rock aura to some of the arrangements, such as the group original "Lie to Me." However, the diversity of material remained impressive, even daunting, taking in the traditional Cajun tune "Petite Fleur," Howlin' Wolf's "Killing Floor," a devious hard blues-rock arrangement of the folk standard "Cuckoo," and David Lindley's instrumental showcase "Banjo." Both Darrow and Crill, as an aside, express regret that Lindley, known as a guitarist above all else, is not better known for his championship-winning banjo playing. "He was using fingerpicks, and using so much torque that he built these ganglions up in his wrist," reports Darrow. "There would be these little lumps that would be about as big as a Hershey Kiss. I think that's why he gave up playing banjo, 'cause it was affecting his ability to play. It's really a shame that he doesn't play [it] very much."

The album's piece de resistance was another epic twelve-minute piece, the group original "Seven-Ate Sweet," a match for any track Kaleidoscope ever did, and the band's prime combination of Middle Eastern music with rock energy and improvisation. Opening with funky electric guitar chords playing off violin riffs, it suddenly takes off into a faster section in which violin and distorted guitar leads become equal solo partners. Feldthouse introduces some vocals that may or may not be in a nonexistent exotic-sounding language (Crill is uncertain to this day whether they were phony or not), and Lagos demonstrates the adaptability cited by Crill with ever-shifting rolls and rhythms that weave together rock, jazz, and R&B. Navigating several surprise key changes and introducing new instruments in subsequent passages (notably Feldthouse's oud), it mounted, as most long Kaleidoscope tracks did, in freneticism as it approached the finish line. Unlike most other rock songs of the late '60s that crashed the ten-minute barrier, there was little repetition of basic riffs or ideas over the course of the performance, with a seamless melding of numerous dissimilar sections, any one of which would have been impossible for most bands to master.

Kaleidoscope's unceasing pursuit of genres to blend and bend seemed to have exhausted itself by the time of the final album by the band's original incarnation, *Bernice*, recorded around the end of the 1960s. In addition, although they had weathered the change of rhythm section fairly well on *Incredible!*, further personnel rotations weakened the band's distinctive identity on *Bernice*, with Jeff Kaplan added as singer, and Stuart Brotman replaced for part of the recording by Ron Johnson. The record's fatal flaw, however, was a switch of focus from the all-idioms-to-all-people ethos of the first three albums. *Bernice* could have even been mistaken for the work of an entirely different band, which was now concentrating on routine R&B-rock numbers and fitfully funny comic/satirical pieces in a sub-Mothers of Invention vein. The members of Kaleidoscope were not brilliant humorists, however, nor were they nearly as good when they were sticking to a consistent sound as they were when they were dancing among several.

Crill blames part of the record's woes on the abortion of its original concept. "What we had written collectively was 'The White Man's Suite.' It was kind of Zappaesque, in ways. If you listen to the fourth album, there are a couple cuts which did survive, like 'Lie and Hide' and 'Sneaking Through the Ghetto,' but I think there were, like, five or six of these things." Darrow, long out of the band by this time, remembers them doing similar, unreleased satirical material while he was still in the lineup that poked fun at white hipsters trying on black personas for size, such as "I'm White and I'm Liberal": "It was based on James Brown and 'I'm Black and I'm Proud, but it was say it strong, I'm white and I'm liberal.' That last album, basically, was the death knell for the band, and everybody went off to do their various things."

Darrow and Crill have had thirty years to think about why Kaleidoscope did not become bigger than it did, and what if any influence they did manage to have despite their cult status. They both have a lot to say about the subjects. Darrow: "The fact that the band was able to stick together as long as it [did], judging from the commercial non-success, was pretty amazing. We all thought this was a great combination of factors, and were willing to tolerate a bunch of stuff that might not have

[been] tolerated otherwise, for the musicianship and ability to play with these people. I do think we created something very unique and satisfying.

"In terms of all that stuff coming out of one band, it was almost too hard for some people to take. We always expected everybody to get it, but it was hard to even find musicians that could get it. I'm starting to realize in retrospect that it was maybe silly for us to assume that we were going to be some kind of huge commercial success, because it was hard enough to find musicians that could play the stuff, let alone people that knew how to listen to it. We were a lot more effective on musicians than on the populace. It's been a long time coming in terms of our appreciation; now we've been termed, in too many articles, the first worldbeat band, which I think we probably were.

"We all had pretty good taste in where we were coming from, and knew the music that we were borrowing from well enough to know the difference between good, bad, indifferent. We were lucky to have been as good musicians at a young age as we were. There weren't many guys that were as good as us, as a band. The people who saw us live realized that we could really play; it wasn't just a gimmick. The music was really more important than the personalities. People can still listen to the music today, and it still has a sense of urgency. It's dated, in some respects, but it's not dated in other respects." Darrow also sees Kaleidoscope's influence on a few bands of the 1980s and 1990s that took a multi-instrumentalist, multiethnic, multigenre approach, especially Camper Van Beethoven. For what it's worth, he notes that Steve Turner of Mudhoney is a big fan, although one's ears curl in vain to detect traces of a tasteful roots music smorgasbord in Mudhoney's grunge rock.

Crill thinks "a lot of people assimilated the risk-taking" typical of Kaleidoscope's performances, particularly San Francisco psychedelic bands. "In the initial years that we came on, even what ended up to be the most radical rock groups were very, very polite in their live presentations. The English guys weren't, but the American guys were. The first time I saw the first wave of San Francisco bands, they were trying to make a stage presentation that would please a record exec; the only one I would say would be an exception would be Moby Grape. Big Brother did, like, four three-minute songs in a row, and they were terrible. I think we did have an influence in that area."

Crill and Darrow agree that inappropriate management and unsympathetic record company executives kept the band from living up to its full potential, to phrase it mildly. "David picked two managers who were celebrities' sons," says Crill by way of illustration. "One was [jazz drummer] Chico Hamilton's son. He managed the Watts Band [Charles Wright's Watts 103rd Street Rhythm Band, which had big funk hits with "Do Your Thing" and "Express Yourself"], so we did, like, black dance clubs for three months. Then he got Milton Berle's oldest son. He got us all the strip clubs for three months. We couldn't have come up with worse management. But it never mattered. All of them ended up with lots of bills we incurred for them, I'm sure."

As for Epic Records, "In four years, all of these guys left in three months. I'd never know who was in charge. They'd phone us up and say stuff like, 'we've got a new singer, and we think you should be their band' all the time. The first meeting I ever had with the guy who was the head of Epic, he was a shoe salesman. He said, 'You know, what you guys need to do is record Bobby Vinton tunes. Because you've got it all. You play all the instruments, so you should record Bobby Vinton tunes, because we've got a catalog of 'em here.'"

Darrow has more war stories: "One of the guys who was our manager used to swipe my cough medicine because he wanted to get high. Those guys didn't know how to manage money, and I think they were probably selling drugs out the back door too. Albert Grossman [manager for Bob Dylan, Janis Joplin, and other big '60s acts] would have been the perfect manager for the Kaleidoscope. Because ultimately, when we got into doing folk festivals, we could really work the room. We were good at festivals, because we could project that weird stuff across for 20,000 people outside on a Saturday afternoon drinking beer and doing acid. If we'd had a Bill Graham kind of guy on our side at that time, I think it would have been a whole different story. But we didn't have that. We had a guy that worked with Tommy James and the Shondells that didn't know fucking nothing."

David Lindley has been by far the most visible Kaleidoscope alumnus, as a top session player since the 1970s, particularly as guitarist and arranger for Jackson Browne, although he's also played on albums by stars like Linda Ronstadt. Like Ry Cooder, he's valued for his ability to play in just about every type of popular and ethnic music going—a skill surely honed in his Kaleidoscope days, although many of the people who hear his licks have never heard of the band. Darrow has been another Renaissance music man, playing with Ronstadt, John Stewart, and Hoyt Axton; producing punk and surf records; writing for surf and action film soundtracks; and making solo albums (his "Whipping Boy" was covered by Ben Harper). He's also done records with Crill (who's still working under the name "Max Buda"), including the forty-five-minute instrumental suite "Harem Girl."

And it wasn't the end of the line for Kaleidoscope after *Bernice*, as it turned out. In 1976, Darrow, Crill, Feldthouse, Lagos, and Brotman—essentially, a combination of the lineups on the first three albums, minus Lindley (although Lindley did contribute steel and acoustic guitar to some tracks under the pseudonym De Paris Letante) and Vidican—reunited Kaleidoscope to record *When Scopes Collide* for Mike Nesmith's Pacific Arts label. Less urgent and intense than the original Kaleidoscope albums, it did find their unsurpassed range intact, encompassing covers of "Ghost Riders in the Sky" and classics by the Coasters, Chuck Berry, and Duke Ellington, along with originals that again covered the gamut from folk to Middle Eastern. The same lineup reconvened for the 1990 CD *Greetings from Kartoonistan* …, a more satisfying effort consisting almost entirely of covers. Again it drew from a piñata of sources, including Ellington, progressive jazzman Abdullah Ibrahim, and the Music Machine's garage classic "Talk Talk," ending with a Brotman-penned "Klezmer Suite."

"Whenever we can engineer getting together to play together again," says Crill, "it's just a revelation as to how much farther our own paths we've come down, and also how incredibly smooth it is to put together without any kind of the old hammer-and-tongs shit." At least that quasi-democratic division of repertoire that both gave rise to Kaleidoscope's peak achievements and led to its dissolution isn't so much of a problem anymore. "Now, they let me and Chris pick 'em all," confides Crill. "I try to get more and more instrumentals so none of us sing. By now we just all fucking croak anyway."

Recommended Recordings:

Side Trips (1967, Edsel, U.K.). An erratic debut that nonetheless has several of their finest concise tracks, whether somewhat conventional folk-rock ("Please"), psychedelic-tinted folk-rock ("Keep Your Mind Open"), or "Egyptian Gardens," an early excursion into Middle Eastern modes.

A Beacon from Mars (1968, Edsel, U.K.). Unquestionably their finest noncompilation album, with the twelve-minute psychedelic journey of the title track, the equally long Middle Eastern instrumental "Taxim," the quality folk-rock of "I Found Out" and "Life Will Pass You By," and the traditional folk cover "Greenwood Sidee." The other covers are less impressive and do dissipate the momentum of the record to some extent.

Incredible! (1969, Edsel, U.K.). Although the group sometimes sounds less distinctive than it did on the first two albums as it breaks in an altered lineup, the latter half of the program really picks up the pace with Lindley's instrumental "Banjo," the bluesy rock version of "Cuckoo," and the whirlwind Middle Eastern rock of the twelve-minute "Seven-Ate Sweet," perhaps Kaleidoscope's crowning moment.

Bacon from Mars (1983, Edsel, U.K.). Not to be confused with the similarly titled *A Beacon from Mars*, this is a compilation of their best short LP and 45 tracks, including the delightful 1967 collaboration with Larry Williams and Johnny "Guitar" Watson, "Nobody." It is a shame that this and its companion volume, *Rampé Rampé*, are not available on CD, as taken together they include every first-rate 1960s Kaleidoscope recording, without any subpar filler.

Rampé Rampé (1984, Demon, U.K.). A perfect supplement to *Bacon from Mars*, emphasizing their longer cuts, including all three of their lengthy tours de force: "Beacon from Mars," "Taxim," and "Seven-Ate Sweet." It also has "Greenwood Sidee" and the title track, a worthy non-LP B-side.

Egyptian Candy (1991, Epic/Legacy). A patchy collection that does include most of their best short songs, but yields an incomplete picture of the band by including only one of its three twelve-minute masterworks ("Beacon from Mars"). Completists will find it interesting for the inclusion of three previously unreleased outtakes of mysterious origin, two of which ("Egyptian Candy" and "Sefan") emphasize the Middle Eastern aspect of the group.

Blues from Baghdad: The Very Best of Kaleidoscope (1995, Edsel, U.K.). A fine seventy eight minute compilation that combines the contents of the previous compilations *Bacon from Mars* and *Rampé Rampé* onto one disc, with the exception of "Taxim." As "Taxim" was one of the group's more vital performances, however, its absence prevents this from being a definitive overview.

Rock Satirists

The field of comedy rock was sparsely populated in the 1960s, as it has been during much of rock history. Most performers who are very, very funny concentrate on theater, acting, or stand-up routines rather than music. It is thus unsurprising that the few excellent comedy rock bands of the period used theatrical elements in their performances. With video a much less common tool in the 1960s than it is in the present, our full appreciation of such outfits is unfortunately diminished. It's a testament to the genius of the Fugs and the Bonzo Dog Band that their records are able to make you laugh more than thirty years later, minus the visuals and guaranteed familiarity with some of the topical issues they satirized.

Neither the Fugs nor the Bonzos are too well known to the mainstream, but in a sense got further than could have reasonably been expected given the limited market for rock satirists. The Fugs took an album of songs with profanity, open sexual references, and fervid left-wing politics into the Top 100 in 1966, and served, as one of their songwriters likes to say, as a "USO for the left-wing movement" in the 1960s. The Bonzo Dog Band, formed for laughs by college students, got a number five hit in England in 1968, produced by Paul McCartney, and appeared on television productions with the Beatles and future members of Monty Python. There were major differences between the two. The Fugs were far more committed to political activism and a delivery that some viewed as lewd and crude; the Bonzos were far more whimsical with their updated version of British vaudevillian and musical hall forms. Yet both were far more musically accomplished than most critics have acknowledged, and for both the Fugs and the Bonzo Dog Band, no cow was too sacred to roast over an open flame.

The Fugs

Sex, drugs, and rock 'n' roll.

As the twenty-first century begins, that phrase is more of a cliché than it is a threat. In the mid-1960s, however, that holy trinity of elements was not considered merely diverting, but downright subversive. And no group of the 1960s celebrated the most revolutionary implications of sex, drugs, and rock 'n' roll as much as the Fugs did. "Sex, drugs, and revolution" might have been a more appropriate credo for the band.

Few rock musicians have been as politically and stylistically radical as the Fugs were in their first incarnation, which ran from about late 1964 to mid-1969. They were the first group to shatter taboos against explicit lyrics about sex, so-called profane and obscene language, and illicit substances in rock music, predating even the Velvet Underground. They were the first underground rock band to make the Top 100 album charts, recording on an independent label that specialized in underground music of all kinds. They were among the forerunners of the hybrid known as folk-rock that rewrote the rules of popular music. They played, estimates cofounder Tuli Kupferberg, more benefits for left-wing political causes than any other band of the era did. They suffered draining battles against censorship and harassment from high-ranking politicians, law enforcement officials, and right-wing cranks. They drew upon the poetry of William Blake, Allen Ginsberg, and others for some of their more literary lyrics. They were among the first rock artists to smash the barrier against songs running more than five minutes, with suites that took up more than ten minutes and, eventually, an entire LP side. Kupferberg was the first reasonably widely known rock musician to rise to fame in his forties. Along with the Mothers of Invention and the Bonzo Dog Band, they were the *funniest* band of the time, couching their political and social satire in wit that could be both ferocious and gentle.

What *didn't* they do? They didn't have a hit single, of course. With a name like the Fugs, that was not so much bad luck as a deliberate exclusion of the very possibility.

The Fugs have often been pigeonholed as rock primitives or proto-punks for their straight-up radicalism and their maximization of relatively little in the way of conventional musical skills. This is accurate to a point, and particularly true of their earliest recordings, when they sounded more like a punky jug band than professional musicians. Yet within a couple of albums the Fugs had taken long strides from their motley roots, and over the course of four or so years would employ musicians who would become some of the most highly sought after session players of the 1970s, collaborating with the likes of Carole King and James Taylor. They did about half of their records for a major label founded by Frank Sinatra, and made their most ambitious album with the help of Harry Belafonte's backup singers. Their message remained pure and uncensored, but the Fugs themselves were never dogmatic musical purists, rising to an appreciably higher level of sophistication and tautness than they've usually been given credit for, onstage and in the studio.

The founders of the Fugs, however, were *not* slick musicians when they formed the band in late 1964. Ed Sanders and Tuli Kupferberg, the two mainstays of the Fugs through to its present lineup in 2000, were poets with roots in the beat era. Age-

The core trio of the Fugs, in the 1960s. Left to right: Tuli Kupferberg, Ed Sanders, Ken Weaver.
Credit: Michael Ochs Archives.com.

wise it was an unlikely combination. Kupferberg was a veteran beat poet already into his early forties. An anarchist who had joined a Communist Front student organization in high school, he was old enough to have seen a gig by jazz guitar great Charlie Christian (who died in 1942) as a teenager. Sanders was a linguistics student a generation younger, who ran the Peace Eye bookstore on East 10th Street in New York's East Village, and whose poetry journal, *Fuck You/A Magazine of the Arts*, had published Kupferberg's prose. Sanders had played in his high school band and taken piano lessons as a kid. Kupferberg, as he still likes to say today, could play the radio.

There was more heart than chops at work when Sanders and Kupferberg began to write, not so much devising rock songs as putting their poems to rudimentary music, quickly accumulating several dozen tunes. "We didn't see the formalities that other people might have seen as being necessary to do something in the arts that we wanted to do," explains Kupferberg, now in his seventies, still in the Fugs, and still living in Lower Manhattan. "We were young people—I wasn't that young, actually," he allows—"who would try anything to see if it worked, were *ready* to try anything and see if it worked."

The Fugs had roots in the folk movement of the early 1960s, as well as the beat poetry of the 1950s. Sanders had participated in civil rights demonstrations and interracial peace marches in the South, getting blown away by Pete Seeger singing "We Shall Overcome," listening to Joan Baez while committing civil disobedience. "'We Shall Overcome' and 'Down By the Riverside,' stuff like that, we viewed as religious rev-up texts," he says in early 2000 from his Woodstock, New York, home. When he and Kupferberg began to rehearse in the Peace Eye, soon augmented by the poets Al Fowler and Szabo, "I viewed it as an outgrowth of the civil rights singing, where we all sang together in times of stress. Singing together when you were tense, worried, and angst[-ridden]…but also singing for fun." One example of these informal, nearly a cappella get-togethers-cum-rehearsals, "Spontaneous Salute to Andy Warhol," was preserved from February 1965, and is now available as a bonus track on the CD reissue of *The Fugs First Album*.

It was soon evident that a somewhat more professional outlook—i.e., managing to show up at performances on time—was needed on the part of Sanders and Kupferberg's cohorts if the Fugs were to start to play in public. For that reason Fowler and Szabo soon faded from the scene. When the Fugs performed at the opening of the Peace Eye bookstore on February 24, 1965—a gig attended by Andy Warhol, and authors George Plimpton, William Burroughs, and James Michener—the Holy Modal Rounders, a folk duo who shared the Fugs' thirst for zaniness, also played. Peter Stampfel and Steve Weber of the Rounders were soon aboard as Fugs, instantly multiplying the group's instrumental skills many times over; Ken Weaver joined on conga and buffalo hide drums. A real, albeit ragged, band was beginning to take shape. "We were poets, so we did our best to adjust the poetry to a song format," says Sanders of his early efforts to team up with other musicians. "We tried, by adding musicians and subtracting musicians. It was very much in flux."

What was coming out of their mouths, however, was *not* too much like "We Shall Overcome," "Down By the Riverside," Pete Seeger, Joan Baez, or even more modern and idiosyncratic folk songwriters like Bob Dylan and Phil Ochs. If the prolific Kupferberg sounded like a rabbi chanting surrealistic texts on "Nothing," "The Ten Commandments" would no doubt have gotten him thrown out of the synagogue, with its exhortation not to covet thy neighbor's ass. Ed Sanders adapted William Blake poems to music. Weaver—"the funniest guy you can imagine," according to Sanders—was proving a skilled comic songwriter with his hymn to a "Slum Goddess" of the Lower East Side, and frustrated howls for mind-altering substances in "I Couldn't Get High." Weber got in the taboo-smashing spirit with his lusty "Boobs a Lot," as did Sanders on "Coca Cola Douche." This was the sound of East Village bohemia, unadulterated. The sex could be raw, the language could offend, the sarcastic humor could be sharp, and even the protest songwriting could not just be earnest, but also confrontational (as on Kupferberg's roast of a "CIA Man").

"They totally preceded the punk movement by about ten years," says Peter Stampfel. "Sitting and writing sixty songs and knowing nothing about music whatsoever, just having an attitude and a concept and doing it, despite the fact that they didn't know shit about what they were doing. That's one of the things that attracted me to them: the idea that they had no ability whatsoever, and it didn't matter. That attitude was so totally wonderful. Frank Zappa was extremely resentful about the fact that [noted '60s music critic] Ralph Gleason compared the Fugs to the Mothers of Invention. Zappa was completely enraged by it: 'How can you compare super technical Mr. Chops to these cretins, these musical idiots?' And of course [Gleason] was talking about a similar irreverence, a similar spirit. But Zappa could only see himself as being identified with these people that were [the] antithesis to what he thought was a proper approach.

"The Fugs, I thought of what they were doing as smut rock. It was basically sex and drugs and counterculture. Setting classical nineteenth century poems to music, which is I think a very nice foil to things like 'Coca Cola Douche.' The Fugs were covering all sorts of ground that was, music-wise, virgin territory."

Even with their improved musical proficiency, however, it was not the kind of material that record labels, even independent folk ones, were eager to record and promote in 1965. There was, however, an established folk music label known in part for its willingness to record controversial artists. Folkways, run by Moe Asch, had released discs by political progressives since the 1940s. He had put out Pete Seeger product even at the height of that legend's struggle to find work in the aftermath of the McCarthy-era blacklisting of performers with left-wing sympathies. Asch had started a subsidiary, Broadside, in the early 1960s, as an outlet for topical songwriters such as Seeger, Phil Ochs, and Bob Dylan (who recorded a few tracks for Broadside under the pseudonym Blind Boy Grunt). Asch had also put out a series of albums in the 1950s of vintage country blues and folk music, assembled by ethnomusicologist Harry Smith and titled *Anthology of American Folk Music*. Smith, a friend of the Fugs, was the catalyst for getting the Fugs a recording deal with Broadside.

Even with such an apparent harmonic convergence of interests, Asch might not have known quite what he had on his hands. "Harry and I figured out the best way to float this past Mr. Asch was to call it a jug band," admits Sanders today. "The first session, we didn't even know that you were supposed to face the microphones. Moe did let us do what we want, and let Harry and I put whatever we wanted on the record."

The Fugs look more like an urban slum band than a jug band on the stark black and white photo that graces *The Fugs First Album*, recorded at two sessions, each lasting a single afternoon, in the spring and summer of 1965. This is the Fugs' most ramshackle LP (aside from the even looser *Virgin Fugs*, comprised of mid-1960s outtakes), but also one of their funniest albums, containing highlights of their early repertoire like the aforementioned "Slum Goddess," "Nothing," "Boobs a Lot," and "I Couldn't Get High." Sanders subverted the bathetic country-and-western tear-in-my-beer ballad with his "My Baby Done Left Me," with its key line, "I feel like homemade shit," not something apt to be sung in the average barroom. Kupferberg also came up with a winner in "Supergirl," his acerbic anthem to the impossible girl of the collective American male consciousness.

"Supergirl" and other tunes like "Slum Goddess" had been recorded at the second session for the LP. While the Fugs might have been a jug band of sorts, just barely, when they first entered the studio, the primitive electric guitar and rhythm section on the second session found them gingerly entering the world of rock 'n' roll. Multi-instrumentalist Stampfel was gone, which he eventually regretted, as "by '66, they were really a good band. Weber was getting too crazy and fucked-up, basically. In retrospect, I wish I wouldn't have quit playing with the Fugs at the same time, but I just was totally fed up with Weber." Weber was on his way out ("he had real instability problems," says Sanders diplomatically), and Vinny Leary and John Anderson came in on electric guitar and electric bass respectively. Ken Weaver had junked the buffalo hide drums and congas for a full drum kit. They might have still sounded like the Shaggs with much better songwriters, but they were becoming a folk-rock band.

Sanders and Kupferberg, like many folk musicians in 1965, were feeling the electric music bug at the height of the British Invasion. It wasn't solely a love for the Beatles, Rolling Stones, and a newly electrified Bob Dylan that made them plug in.

There were also the bottom-line considerations that have sparked many innovations in popular music. It had happened before when purist British blues and jazz musicians turned to rhythm and blues and rock 'n' roll in the early 1960s, or country-and-western singers adopted rockabilly in the mid-1950s, or Marvin Gaye ditched his ambitions to be a jazz crooner for soul music with Motown. "I needed a way of earning a living," confesses Sanders.

"I had just graduated from college. We had just had a baby. My bookstore made some profit, but not a lot at the time. It was more of a postmodern hangout center than an actual bookstore. I realized that to earn a living from one's art, one needed some sort of gloss of professionalism. We jumped on the electromagnetic steamboat to play clubs.

"When we formed, folk-rock had not become a hyphenated word. Nor had beat turned to hippies; we were in the pre-folk-rock, pre-hippie beat era. We evolved in a gallery performance space milieu as much as the folk club milieu. I had originally thought we could just get by with buffalo hide drums, maracas, and a couple Weberesque, weirdly tuned, space-tuned guitars. But it didn't happen." To share the bill with other artists playing the Cafe Au Go Go in New York, such as Richie Havens, the Blues Project, and Howlin' Wolf, more amplification would be obligatory.

Had Stampfel at least stayed on, Sanders reflects, "I think we might have evolved into more of what our original intention was: more of a string- and fiddle-based, Incredible String Band-type [group]. We could have done some of these longer suites we did acoustically. We could have gone proto-klezmer. We could have added Cajun, we could have had an accordion player. Probably should have. Didn't, though. And there ain't no time machine."

The Fugs, like the times, were changing fast in late 1965. A cross-country tour brought them into contact with emerging West Coast psychedelic bands like the Jefferson Airplane, and into the middle of anti-Vietnam War protests. At a club in San Francisco, their driver, Lee Crabtree, began playing a piano; the band hadn't even known he was a musician, and got him into the Fugs straightaway to further rock up their arrangements (some of which, like "Doin' All Right," he introduced with quotes from Bach). Sanders was arrested on New Year's Eve for possession of obscene materials at the Peace Eye bookstore (a case that Sanders eventually won). In early 1966, the Fugs signed to ESP, arguably the first truly "underground" label in the United States to enjoy wide distribution, with a catalog heavy on cutting-edge free jazz by the likes of Albert Ayler and Sun Ra.

The Fugs (titled The Fugs Second Album in its current CD reissue), recorded in early 1966, was a quantum leap from their debut, particularly in the power and relative tightness of the rock arrangements. Now a seven piece with the addition of another guitarist (Pete Kearney), the group had become a bona fide rock—and not even particularly folk-rock—combo, retaining enough of a garage rawness to refute any accusations of having sold out. Without diminishing the go-for-broke topical literacy and lunacy of their lyrics whatsoever, Sanders and Kupferberg (Weaver, oddly, wrote none of the material) had also developed into better and more tuneful singer-songwriters. The Fugs was indisputably the band at the peak of its powers, and at the optimum balance between its raucous, almost anarchic roots and the slicker studio rock sound toward which the band eventually gravitated.

The Fugs' second album also boasted the best balance of the group's sexual, political, and poetic facets, without dulling their humorous satirical edge. The urge for sexual expression and free love was at the forefront right from the opening bars of the first cut, "Frenzy," an all-out rocker that kicked off with pseudo-orgasmic wordless chants, like a cockeyed Lower East Side takeoff on the ascending harmonies that bring the Beatles' "Twist and Shout" to its climax. The same Ed Sanders that wrote "Frenzy" could also set Charles Olson's poem "I Want to Know" to gorgeous music that resulted in the Fugs' most affecting, melodic folk-rocker, complete with celeste by Crabtree. Kupferberg offered one of the most trenchant comments on the absurd madness of Vietnam in "Kill For Peace," and matched Sanders for folk-rock tenderness in "Morning Morning," adapted from the folk song "Morgen Morgen" with harmonies by non-Fug Betsy Klein (Ken Weaver's girlfriend). ("Morning Morning" would soon be covered by Richie Havens, on his 1967 album *Mixed Bag*.) The group wasn't averse to tapping outside songwriters for material, but again looked to the literary community rather than the Brill Building. Poet Ted Berrigan supplied the lyrics for "Doin' All Right," an uncommonly serious-minded statement of purpose that flew the flag for the counterculture lifestyle in general. In a lighter mood was another of the LP's cuts, "Dirty Old Man," donated by Lower East Side composer-poet Lionel Goldbart, which fought sociopolitical hysteria over left-wing subversives with jokes, not bombs.

Every song save one on *The Fugs* stuck to the two-to-four-minute length that was common currency in rock of the period, but those borders were shattered by the album closer, the eleven-minute "Virgin Forest." This was a suite-like concoction of poetic recitation, an orgiastic "Tarzan-Jane" satire (again with the participation of Betsy Klein), a fragment of material by the band's friend Allen Ginsberg (who also wrote the liner notes), and sound effects (Sanders is particularly proud of the frogs). Like many such tracks from the psychedelic era, it was a mixed bag, and not totally successful. However, the Fugs were the first to try such a long multipart song on a rock album. The only other cuts recorded around the same time of similar length by notable groups were the blues jam "Going Home" by the Rolling Stones, the avant-garde "The Return of the Son of Monster Magnet" by the Mothers of Invention, and the psychedelic instrumental "East-West" by the Paul Butterfield Blues Band.

The Fugs is also the album on which Sanders and Kupferberg's songs best complement each other. Special bands, whether the Beatles with Lennon and McCartney and the Buffalo Springfield with Neil Young and Stephen Stills, or more cultish ones such as the Bonzo Dog Band with Neil Innes and Viv Stanshall and the Move with Roy Wood and Jeff Lynne, are often made into something greater than their talents by the presence of two excellent songwriters who give the group diversity and feed off each other for inspiration. Both of the Fugs' chief composers have much to say when asked to compare and contrast styles.

"Tuli's more of a rhymer than I am," says Sanders. "He has an exquisite sense of line and rhyme. Tuli's more out of the English street ballads, a wonderful and noble tradition. He was more of a Guthrieite, in that he took existing melody lines right out of the Wobbly songbook. [Woody] Guthrie had taken that church hymn for 'This Land Is Your Land'; Tuli did the same thing, bringing new words, and then slightly mutating where it made sense. He also brings the shtetels, the keening sensitivities of

Hasidic music. Also, from his youth, his anarchism. In many ways [he's] much more radical than I am, politically. I'm more of a social democrat, I guess.

"I'm more quatrain-based as a poet, more in the school of Black Mountain Poets [like] Charles Olson, an open field where you try to create. You use the image of a high-energy grid, and try to make your lines fit into this grid. I like to take more chances with different song structures than [Tuli] does. My original intention with the Fugs was never to repeat. To deny the song form. I wanted to break free of the re-peated refrain A-B-A-B hook, bridge, A-B-A-B hook, bridge format. But it's very diffi-cult, working with musicians raised in the ballad and the folk-rock tradition, to break away from that. We did now and then."

"I was shocked at first by Ed's language," reveals Kupferberg. "But I swiftly caught up to the freshness of his so-called vulgarity and the honesty of his attitude to-wards sex. I had also passed through Reichian therapy. That was kind of liberating too. Just living in the bohemian atmosphere of Greenwich Village and the Lower East Side pushed you in a lot of free directions. Since you believed that the revolu-tion was about to happen, or could happen at any time soon, there was really no point in opting for a standard professional track.

"We brought a lot of things that were different, but [also things] that we all had in common. That was actually more important, I think, than our differences. Ed, I've always thought of him as a Mark Twain of rock 'n' roll. He came from Missouri, originally, or his folks did, and he grew up in Kansas, I think. There's an old tradition of Southwest humor, and sort of sagacious craziness.

"One thing about Ed's songs: The reason they're not well known is because they're sort of long. Most pop songs, that isn't really true of. That's the secret of the fact that Ed's songs aren't covered that often. But no one else can perform them the way Ed can."

Kupferberg is in general the gentler and less agitated songwriting voice of the band than Sanders is, but could still get worked up about major political issues, as in "Kill For Peace," the anti-Vietnam War tract done to a tune resembling "Twist and Shout." "It was during the Vietnam War. The postal service, I don't know if they do it any more, but they had a little slogan they would put on with their cancellation. One of them was 'pray for peace.' This was at the time when they were killing people by the thousands, or tens of thousands, or a million, or maybe more. So I thought 'kill for peace' could be applied to their slogan. I thought that would have been more ap-propriate then."

As for Ken Weaver, who despite his absence from compositional duties on *The Fugs* would be the member who did more songwriting than anyone besides the two cofounders, Sanders notes, "He was a brilliant comedian. He had studied very care-fully Lenny Bruce; we sang at Lenny Bruce's memorial. Weaver brought a kind of devastating wit to his routines, some of which were quite good, and some less than good. He was good at hook lines; 'I feel like homemade shit' was something he said in my bookstore, and we worked it out from that. 'Crystal Liaison,' he thought of that one day, and right then on the spot, we wrote this tune satirizing psychedelic lyrics. He was good at instant distillations."

All of the Fugs wrote graphically and enthusiastically about sex. In some respects these are the lyrics that have dated the most poorly, as the humor can seem juvenile several decades down the road, when such language in popular culture isn't as shocking as it once was. Kupferberg sees the Fugs more as a part of a continuum reaching back centuries, however, than as unique or deviant exponents of the form. "There's a long tradition of radical poetry and music, and there are also hidden traditions of free sexual expression in English literature. I have a collection of eighteenth century bawdy songs. Some of them are British, and some are by well-known songwriters of the period, or people who wrote classical songs. There was even a tradition of bars or taverns that men would go to, and sing bawdy songs to each other and get drunk. That was eighteenth century in London. I'm sure those songs existed in America too."

The Fugs crept inside the *Billboard* Top 100 albums in July 1966. It was a remarkable feat for an album whose airplay was severely curtailed by its controversial language and topics, and which didn't stand much chance of airplay anyway since album-oriented FM rock radio was still a year or two away from taking off. "I don't think there was any airplay," speculates ESP founder Bernard Stollman. "I think it was all word of mouth. With respect to the chart activity, it was interesting, because our sales did not reflect that. So it must have had admirers or supporters."

With increased notoriety came increased heat from the authorities. The FBI, the New York City District Attorney's Office, and the Postal Service conducted an investigation of the band, which Sanders learned more than a decade later after getting access to some files under the Freedom of Information Act. "We were very controversial," Sanders recalls. "People forget *how* controversial. People would call in bomb threats, they would raid my bookstores. Somebody sent me a fake bomb. Right-wing nurses picketing us. We would get thrown out of theaters. Carnegie Hall wouldn't rent to us. We played Santa Monica Civic, and they wouldn't rent to us again. We were always in trouble. My phone sounded like Miriam Makeba sometimes. So we ran a close ship. I learned that James Brown wouldn't let his band carry drugs, and I did the same thing, because I knew how close we were to being arrested at any point. So we never—on planes, for instance, or in our luggage—carried dope."

In spite of the heat, the Fugs did not retreat from the public eye or dilute their content, onstage or in the studio. In 1966 and 1967 they rented the Players Theater in Greenwich Village and gave, in Sanders' estimation, more than 700 performances during a year and a half. "We were really theater, you see," explains Kupferberg. "Ed had the idea that I shouldn't sing too much in the theater, so I started to do pantomimes. I only sang one or two songs a set, [but] I developed a routine for every song. I would wear six different shirts, one on top of the other, so I had to peel them off for the next number."

The routines were not always family entertainment, and Kupferberg runs down one that illustrates exactly why the Fugs made both government authorities and lowly venue managers nervous. "My most highly developed one was in 'Kill For Peace.' I came out dressed as a Vietnam soldier lost somewhere in the jungle, and I had a very torn khaki uniform. I had a machine gun, and a huge navy gunner's helmet. As the song would develop, I found this Vietnamese baby doll with no clothing on, and it didn't have a leg. I picked it up, cradled it. I had chocolate-covered jelly candies, and I would offer this candy to the kid, who was dead. Since the kid wouldn't react to the candy, I would take the jelly and smash it into the kid's mouth, and then the audience would go, 'Uggggh!' Then I would run around sort of out of my mind, and my U.S. Navy [helmet] would fall off. Underneath I had an authentic World War II German helmet that was easily recognizable. I would realize that, suddenly be discovered, and run off the stage."

The routines didn't have to be so blatantly antiestablishment to make an audience nervous. One of their more imaginative ones placed Weaver in a coffin, to be interviewed by Sanders while "Crabtree would play appropriate funereal music," says Ed. "He would pretend like he was on his deathbed, and he would be disinheriting all his ingrate relatives. Or we would talk to Otis. It was the end of 1967 at the Players Theater, right when Otis Redding died. So we were channeling Otis."

Rock as theater, or even performance art, was another area in which the Fugs were pioneers. It certainly seems like they influenced Frank Zappa and the Mothers of Invention, who would do their own wild, if less avowedly political, routines when they took up a long-running residency at the Garrick Theater in the Village in 1967. In strictly musical terms, the Fugs were influencing important artists too, although sometimes in subtle ways that they were unaware of at the time. Sanders, for instance, remembers seeing and liking the Velvet Underground, a band that broke lyrical taboos against sex and drugs in a darker fashion, when the Velvets were first making the rounds. Yet he wasn't certain if the Velvets were influenced by the Fugs, although Velvet Underground guitarist Sterling Morrison once said (in *Up-Tight: The Velvet Underground Story*), "We often played together at shows and benefits, and liked and were liked by the same people. The Fugs, the Holy Modal Rounders and the Velvet Underground were the only authentic Lower East Side bands. We were real bands playing for real people in a real scene…I have a complete collection of Fugs albums and they bring me great joy." More surprisingly, perhaps, a then-unknown David Bowie got hold of *The Fugs* through his manager and put "Dirty Old Man" into his act in 1967, praising the band in one of his first press interviews that same year.

In some ways, the Fugs and the ESP label were good fits. ESP, despite a low budget that usually limited its covers to newspaper-quality black-and-white graphics, had managed to get them onto the charts. More important, it was the kind of label that put out music so daring, or just plain weird, that few other companies would touch it. Tuli Kupferberg, for instance, did a rare solo album for ESP (since reissued on CD), *No Deposit, No Return*, in which he read ads, word-for-word, for products such as "The Hyperemiator" and "The Sap Glove" from newspapers, magazines, and direct mail, backed by nothing but sound effects to emphasize the ridiculous nature of the source material.

Sanders, however, wrote in the liner notes to the CD reissue of *The Fugs* that "the Fugs' relationship with ESP Records was, mildly to state it, turbulent. We were told, for instance, that the Mafia was illegally manufacturing Fugs records and selling them. We can be forgiven for not really believing the Genovese crime family would bother with the Fugs, when there were the Beatles, the Stones, Mantovani, and Petula Clark to rip off." Bernard Stollman declines to cite Mafia involvement, but says the Fugs' second album "should have been very profitable for us. It wasn't, because the [pressing] plants were doing business through the back door with distributors."

"I didn't allow record executives, or people associated with the label, around," says Sanders. "I must say I had great quarrels with the people that owned ESP over the years, but they did stay out of the recording studio, except when I had the gigantic fight with them over the mixing. They tried to remix 'Doin' All Right.' Ted Berrigan's line, 'I'm not ever gonna go to Vietnam, I'd prefer to stay right here and screw your mom' — 'screw your mom' was a big problem with the owner of ESP. Because I think the woman bankrolling this whole shot *was* his mom. She was always around. I know that when we signed with ESP, I think Mom was right there in the room.

"He wanted to dip 'screw your mom' [Sanders' voice lowers an octave or two] *waaay down there*, sort of underneath the bass. That was the only censorship the Fugs ever suffered." Even with the offending line mixed down, ESP couldn't get off scot-free from the guardians of morality. "At one point, our distributor in Indiana called me, or I called him," says Stollman. "He was a very genteel, very nice man. But he said, 'Bernard, I got a problem. I was playing golf the other day with the governor. And he turned to me as we were on the links and said, "I don't want those dirty Fugs in my state."' There were no sales." And according to Kupferberg, no cash for the band either: "They let us do everything we wanted. What was bad was that we never got any money out of them. They were notorious for that."

Tension between the Fugs and ESP was exacerbated by an album of outtakes, *Virgin Fugs*, "which considerably incensed Ed Sanders and was part of the reason for the breakup," Stollman continues. "They separated from us and went their own way. I guess they wanted the kind of exposure they could get through a major label. It was the one instance in which I broke with the credo that I had established for the label, which was the artists alone decide what you will hear on their ESP disc. In that instance, I violated that, I must say. And it was very stupid on my part. It was highly improper. I think Ed had every reason to be enraged that we had put out material that he had not previously determined that he wanted to have out. Subsequently, he did take the material and in fact licensed it. So perhaps on mature reflection, he decided [it] wasn't a bad idea. But at that time, I guess they were a little bit nervous about songs like 'CIA Man' being issued." *Virgin Fugs* was comprised of outtakes from the sessions for *The Fugs First Album* that were even rawer and more cacophonous than those selected for the debut LP. It did, however, have some material of historic interest, such as the first version of "Coca Cola Douche," the Peter Stampfel-penned "New Amphetamine Shriek," and Sanders' adaptation of Allen Ginsberg prose into "I Saw the Best Minds of My Generation Rot."

The upshot was that in 1967 the Fugs signed with Atlantic. An entire album was recorded. Right after it was finished, the group was dropped from the label. "They were happy to get us off the label, because they thought we would retard their sales price from Warner," believes Sanders. Ironically, "It turns out that that's the label we signed with," as the Fugs were taken by Warner Brothers subsidiary Reprise, the label founded by Frank Sinatra. The Warner transaction might not have been the only reason behind the album getting axed. Atlantic, according to Sanders, "didn't like the title *The Fugs Eat It*. See, I shouldn't have leaked the album cover to the *Village Voice*. I let Howard Smith run with the proposed album cover, which was my wife and...." Sanders leaves the no doubt colorful details up to the imagination. "Anyway, I guess the Erteguns [Atlantic executives Ahmet and Nesuhi Ertegun] couldn't go with it."

Three of the songs from the rejected Atlantic album do appear as bonus tracks on the Fantasy CD reissue of *The Fugs*, and show them moving to a more standard, cleanly executed folk-rock style. Some of the songs intended for the Atlantic album show up on the Fugs' Reprise debut, *Tenderness Junction*, although Sanders is not entirely sure whether the tracks on the album are the original Atlantic tapes, remixes of the Atlantic tapes, different rerecordings, or some combination of the above. *Tenderness Junction*, like the unreleased Atlantic tracks, was also notably muted in comparison to the ESP recordings, with more psychedelic influences at play in cuts like the highlight, "Turn On/Tune in Drop Out." Although the familiar Fugs trademarks were there—a five-part suite mixing sex and poetry ("Aphrodite Mass"), antiwar protests on "War Song" and a live recording of "Exorcising the Evil Spirits From the Pentagon October 21, 1967," and even a vocal by Allen Ginsberg on "Hare Krishna"—the level of manic inspiration had definitely cooled down since *The Fugs*. The arrangements were, unexpectedly, about as professional as most in 1967 rock, in part because the band now had entirely different personnel, aside from the frontline trio of Sanders, Kupferberg, and Weaver.

Indeed, the Fugs' personnel was quite instable over a five-year run, with more than a dozen members playing with the band in all. Their proto-punk image to the contrary, quite a few virtuosos passed through the lineup, foremost among them Peter Stampfel, one of the most eclectic multi-instrumentalists in folk music; bassist Charles Larkey, who would marry Carole King and play on her early solo albums; guitarist Danny Kortchmar (aka Danny Kootch), who became one of the top L.A. rock session guitarists of the 1970s, frequently recording with Carole King, James Taylor, Linda Ronstadt, and Jackson Browne; Stefan Grossman, who subsequently established himself as a top acoustic folk and blues guitarist; and guitarist Allan "Jake" Jacobs, later to play in Jake & the Family Jewels. "We were looking for bright, very creative people who had a kind of integrity," says Sanders of the qualifications to be a Fug. "I was trying to get the best minds of my generation together in a way where we could produce art that combined poetry and some decent, more or less in-tune renditions of songs. I wish I knew then what I know now about recording, harmony singing, and undoing a few mistakes. 'Virgin Forest' was an example of what I really wanted to have happen, which was group creativity. It was truly an example of each band member rising to the occasion."

"Ed became a very good arranger," elaborates Kupferberg. "He really arranged the music, and picked the instrumentation. I think he hears every note. So he knew what he wanted. There were a lot of excellent musicians who played with us. If they could establish the mood of the song and go with it, it satisfied me, or if they didn't interfere with the lyrics, that's all I asked for. Ed asked for more.

"Ed was sort of running the band. It could be upsetting when someone left or Ed fired [them]. It was more of a personal thing. I didn't like getting rid of people. I thought maybe things could be worked out. [But] I don't think we were ever held back, [or] our performances were ever injured, when we changed personnel." It must be noted that not all of the personnel changes were due to Sanders' vision; bassist John Anderson was drafted to serve in Vietnam, and guitarist Jon Kalb (brother of the Blues Project's Danny Kalb) left to go to college.

"I was trying to get quality songs by quality players who had a lot of pizzazz, but were reliable," resumes Sanders. "What I wanted was a group that could sing great, interesting harmony live as well as in the studio. I was slowly permutating the band to get it. I finally succeeded in '68, I had felt." That was the year that the Fugs issued their finest Reprise album. *It Crawled into My Hand, Honest* was the best realization of their yen to experiment with more sophisticated arrangements and maximize the possibilities of the studio, while retaining the characteristic intensity and humor of their compositions.

The mere presence of half a dozen arrangers and conductors on the LP guaranteed a diverse and expansive sound unlike any other Fugs record. There were maudlin country tunes with surrealistic or viciously satirical lyrics, none more so than "Wide Wide River," better remembered by most for its chorus "river of shit." "Burial Waltz" had a classical choral arrangement; "Crystal Liaison" was druggy psychedelic folk-rock that worked either as a send-up of psychedelia, or pretty groovy sounds on their own terms; and Kupferberg's "Life Is Strange" was an almost anachronistic throwback to the tuneful folk-rock ballads that appeared on *The Fugs*, such as "Morning Morning." The group pulled out all the stops for the suite of tracks, varying in length from three seconds to four minutes, that comprise the whole of side two, veering from more country cock-ups ("Johnny Pissoff Meets the Red Angel") and a Gregorian chant about "Marijuana" to more abstract, poetic ruminations such as "When the Mode of the Music Changes" and the memorably titled "Claude Pelieu and J. J. Lebel Discuss the Early Verlaine Bread Crust Fragments." Although not as cohesive and brilliant as the flawlessly segued strings of song fragments employed by the Mothers of Invention on *We're Only in It for the Money*, this LP side does rate not far below that Mothers album as one of the most successful radically structured extended pieces of the psychedelic era.

Sanders is eager to credit the group's recording engineer and (with Sanders) co-producer, Richard Alderson, as "the unsung hero of the Fugs," who was crucial to the construction of such ambitious pieces (as he had been previously with "Virgin Forest"). "He was our George Martin. We could just suggest something to him, and he would be able to realize it." Other unsung heroes of *It Crawled into My Hand, Honest's* suite were, believe it or not, Harry Belafonte's backup singers, who were responsible for many of the grand choral vocals that dot the album.

And what did Reprise and its Chairman of the Board think of a record with stately choruses crooning "river of shit"? "When we went to Reprise, I mean, that was the deal," emphasizes Sanders. "[Warner's president] Mo Ostin, to his great credit and our great gratitude, just said, 'Go record.' Never censored us. I guess he played our tape for Frank Sinatra, I remember that. He told me that Frank said, 'I guess you know what you're doing,' and allowed him to."

Sanders was happier with the band, musically speaking, in the late 1960s than he had ever been, and continued to permutate the format, for a time featuring two drummers. The stress of leading a group on the front lines of both musical and social change, however, was wearing him down. Threats from right-wingers and difficulty in renting venues continued to be hassles, and the band members were no less visible targets in 1968, as they were among the few musicians (the MC5 and Sanders' friend Phil Ochs were others) to make their presence felt at the violence-ridden 1968 Democratic convention in Chicago. Also, Sanders declares without self-pity, it's "a lot of work to be famous. I would get up in the morning and have to do press releases. We had sort of lost steam by '69. We lost our vision. It was a kind of ghastly year in American history."

The inspiration was somewhat parched on *The Belle of Avenue A*, the final studio album the Fugs did for Reprise. A retreat from the psychedelic experimentation of *It Crawled Into My Hand, Honest*, it was in some ways a throwback to the rawer sounds of the pre-Reprise era, but the political punch and humor weren't on the same level. Sanders also feels the absence of Alderson particularly hurt. Even when the songs were moving or witty (as on Kupferberg's ballad "Flower Children," and the title song about a "horny truck driver who falls in love with a bra-less hippie," as the liner notes state), the production was thin and the energy was on the flat side. The album was concluded shortly after the Fugs shared a bill with the Grateful Dead in Pennsylvania in early 1969—the last show the Fugs would play for 15 years.

Kupferberg for one was disappointed that the Fugs didn't stay together longer. "I thought we were really needed most at that period, when everything was going down. We were sort of the USO for the left-wing movement. We probably played more benefits than any band I can remember."

Sanders, however, "wanted to be a poet and go back to my beat roots, and have my little bookstore." Before stepping down from the music business entirely, though, he recorded a couple of rare solo LPs for Reprise, *Sanders' Truckstop* (1969) and *Beer Cans From The Moon* (1973). The first of these in particular highlighted his oft-overlooked debt to country music, rooted in his childhood exposure to Roy Acuff and Hank Williams, which had started to bloom on several *Belle of Avenue A* cuts. His solo LPs served to emphasize, however, just how much better and funnier Sanders was in the context of the Fugs, and how whiny his pseudo-country voice could be as a soloist. At any rate, by the 1970s Sanders was becoming better known as a writer than he had been as a musician, authoring a popular biography of the Charles Manson family, *The Family*. (He also did a 900-page biography of the Eagles, strangely enough, titled *This American Band*, that has never been issued, as the Eagles own the rights: "They hired me to follow them around, and I did" is Sanders' comment.) Then he decided "I hated my voice, so I was going to escape into the world of poetry and short stories, which is more or less what I did for around eight, ten years."

Sanders and Kupferberg couldn't let the Fugs go entirely, however, reforming the band for periodic reunion performances and recordings beginning in 1984. "A career is a fifty- or sixty-year thing, and I didn't want the Fugs to be totally known by those tapes we did in the '60s," remarks Sanders. The Fugs' 1980s and 1990s albums, which have a focus on social change and sex that is similar to, but more easygoing than, their 1960s work, reflect a "broader worldview." And Sanders is happy that the Fugs have a more constant personnel of supporting musicians and vocal harmonizers than they used to, including Steve Taylor, Coby Batty, and Scott Petito. These musicians were all on hand when the Fugs recently played three days running at Real Woodstock II—an alternative, more grassroots-conscious alternative to Woodstock '99, the highly commercialized extravaganza celebrating the thirtieth anniversary of the 1969 Woodstock festival. A notable absentee from any Fugs reunions was Ken Weaver, who, unbelievably from a musician in a group that once lampooned the "CIA Man" in song, eventually *became* a translator for the CIA. Weaver's worldview is "a little to the right of Tuli and me," understates Sanders.

Sanders is also pleased with the opportunity to integrate some of his musical inventions, such as a combination necktie-synthesizer, into the reunited Fugs performances. He's thinking of others, such as a "brainlyre," a device that could "demultiplex compound brainwaves to get a sequence of brainwaves with enough on an oscilloscope or some monitoring device that can be translated into musical notes or drumbeats. 'Cause it's very technically possible to have a synthesizer or another instrument that can be played by the brain. There's a woman in L.A. that can turn on and off a light bulb with her brainwaves, so it's just a matter of time before some handsome young woman or young man will be standing in front of a crowd and thinking their music through devices that pick up and demultiplex brainwaves."

"There was more excitement, energy, and potentiality at the beginning," acknowledges Kupferberg. "We were also more simple. Our songs became more complicated, intricate, subtle, and general, and in many ways more interesting and universal, maybe. I think our later work is just as good, but maybe it doesn't have the effect the earlier work had. Which was more valuable, I'm not going to say. We had a greater effect in those days than we have now."

Sanders, a well-known author whose *Thirsting for Peace in a Raging Century: Selected Poems 1961-1985* won the 1988 American Book Award, is certainly as active in the arts and community as he's ever been. He and his wife own and publish the *Woodstock Journal* in Woodstock, New York. In early 2000, he's about to have published an installment of his in-progress seven-volume history of the United States in verse, as well as a book on Allen Ginsberg. He's completed volume three of *Tales of Beatnik Glory*; the first two volumes, comprised of short stories based on the literary and political community of Greenwich Village in the late 1950s and early 1960s, were published together in a single book by Citadel Underground in 1990. And now he's a quarter through volume four, although volume three hasn't been published in English yet. "In the nineteenth century, Dickens, other people liked to print multivolume works of fiction," he observes. "Now they would rather go to the dentist for the rest of their lives."

As for the legacy of the Fugs to twentieth century culture, "There was a strong emphasis on [the] satirical, but also very strong on social change, sharing the wealth. I actually believed there would be a revolution, that poverty and racism would be gone by now. But hey man, fucking and revolution? Still valid."

Kupferberg, still a cartoonist, poet, and public access TV host in Manhattan, offers that "until the '60s, except for country and western, American pop music, in the mainstream, was 99 percent courtship music. We threw politics into the arena of popular song. Some other people did it too; a lot of folk singers did, and still do it. The Beatles did it, the Stones did it, and Billy Bragg does it. But we did it too, and we also were part of making pop music able to sing about *anything*, every aspect of human life. People in the community, work, life, family or lack of family, and sex—we were part of opening up pop music to anything people wanted to write about. I think that was very important for human culture.

"We haven't retreated from 1968. Almost everything we believed in is correct. We're biding our time, and still keeping in shape. The world is going to hell in a computer; we need radical changes. The problem is no one knows quite what to do, since the old theories of Marxism and anarchism are rather inadequate. So we need a lot of new ideas and ways of putting them into reality.

"And everybody who is reading this better get to work. That's my message."

Recommended Recordings:

The Fugs First Album (1965, Fantasy). The group's unschooled and sometimes hilarious beginnings, performed with the élan of musicians just learning to sing, play, and plug in electric instruments. "Slum Goddess" and "Supergirl" are the best rockers on an album more notorious for songs that ventured into language and content rarely heard in pop prior to its issue, such as "I Couldn't Get High," "Boobs a Lot," and "Nothing." Get the CD reissue on Fantasy, as it doubles the length of the album with a smattering of erratic but interesting outtakes and live recordings, highlighted by "The Ten Commandments," "CIA Man," and "I Saw the Best Minds of My Generation Rot." For even more rickety rock, find *Virgin Fugs*, comprised of outtakes from the debut LP sessions.

The Fugs Second Album (1966, Fantasy). The group's finest hour, for both hormone- and politically charged-rockers ("Frenzy," "Kill For Peace") and melodic, poetic folk-rock ("I Want to Know," "Morning Morning"), topped off with the innovative eleven-minute musical collage "Virgin Forest." Originally called *The Fugs*, it was retitled *The Fugs Second Album* for its CD reissue on Fantasy, which again is the configuration to get as it has five bonus tracks. These include a couple of live 1967 performances and three previously unreleased songs (among them an early version of "Wide Wide River") from their rejected 1967 Atlantic album.

It Crawled Into My Hand, Honest (1968, Reprise). Their best album for Reprise has a potpourri of sounds that fit well into the psychedelic vibe, including the mock cosmic rocker "Crystal Liaison," the notorious "Wide Wide River," the operatic "Burial Waltz," and the sweet overlooked Kupferberg folk-rocker "Life Is Strange." That's just side one; the whole of side two is occupied by a suite of sixteen songs and song fragments, a jarring and freaky assemblage in the mold of the early Mothers of Invention. Like all of their Reprise output, this is unfortunately not available in the U.S. on CD as of this writing, though there are hopes to put the Reprise Fugs catalog on CD in the near future; you might have better luck finding a British LP reissue on Edsel than the Reprise original.

Golden Filth (1969, Reprise). Recorded live at the Fillmore East on June 1, 1968, this is valuable not just as a document of the Fugs onstage (with much explicit between-song patter), but also for its updated arrangements of compositions from 1965. All but one of the songs, in fact, were originally recorded at the Folkways sessions for the first album; the full rock versions of "Slum Goddess," "Saran Wrap," "Coca Cola Douche," and others are much tighter and fuller than the studio ones, and for that reason perhaps superior.

Part of the Bonzo Dog Band, during rehearsals on the *Do Not Adjust Your Set* set at the Rediffusion studio, Wembley, London. Left to right: Viv Stanshall, the top of Rodney Slater's head, Roger Spear, one of the floor crew (not a band member) on piano, and Terry Jones (later of Monty Python's Flying Circus) watching the monitor. Credit: Courtesy Dave Clague.

The Bonzo Dog Band

It is very difficult to be funny. It is also very difficult to create good rock music. It is exponentially more difficult to create rock music that is both very funny and musically good. Add intelligent satire, a mesmerizing stage show, and an ability to translate the humor and theater into recordings that stand the test of time, and you've got a pretty rare bird indeed.

In the 1960s, many rock bands were funny some of the time. Only a few, however, made humor about as much of the act as music was. In the United States, only two such bands did so with consistent brilliance: the Mothers of Invention from Los Angeles, and the Fugs from New York City. The international, and kinder and gentler, branch of the triangle of major rock comics was represented by England's Bonzo Dog Band.

The Bonzo Dog Band had one major hit in the U.K. with "I'm the Urban Spaceman," and some Beatle-glamour-by-association due to a cameo appearance in the *Magical Mystery Tour* film. In the United States in particular, however, they remain a cult band, even in comparison to bigger cult band the Fugs. Sometimes compared to the Mothers of Invention, particularly in their zany onstage behavior and facility for parodying multiple pop genres, the Bonzos lacked the savage cynicism that powered Frank Zappa's brand of wit. As compensation, they offered a more whimsical, surreal take on the absurd that was in some ways more sonically versatile, encompassing not just rock but also prewar music hall, jazz, and spoken word.

The benign lunacy of the Bonzos' live performances, with their outrageous costumes, exploding robots, outsize props, and anything-goes unpredictability, may have been impossible to fully capture in the studio. Throughout the erratic course of their five albums, however, they lampooned vaudeville, trad jazz, French romantic crooners, psychedelia, and even the British blues scene with both affection and irreverence. As they got more experience as recording artists, they also developed a certain pop-rock sensibility that both colored some of their most inspired work, and led to some of their most leaden tracks when the heavy rock elements began to outweigh the comic ones. Their droll wit was also a substantial—and, certainly in America, largely overlooked—influence upon British humor as a whole, particularly Monty Python.

The Bonzos' eventual emergence as a beloved presence on the late '60s British rock scene was highly unlikely. They didn't play rock for the first four years or so of their existence, during which they didn't even have much serious ambition to become professional musicians. The nucleus of the Bonzos took shape in the Bonzo Dog Dada Band in the early 1960s, formed in art schools, and dedicated to reviving and deconstructing vaudeville and novelty tunes from the 1920s and 1930s.

Should a family tree of the Bonzos ever be attempted, a forest will be needed. In their early years especially, they were more a floating ensemble numbering about nine or ten, joined from time to time by friends and hangers-on sitting in, than they were a project with a set lineup. Saxophonist Rodney Slater and singer Vivian Stanshall were aboard from about the very beginning. With three recruits along the way—Neil Innes (guitar and piano), "Legs" Larry Smith (drums), and Roger Spear (saxophone)—they would form the core quintet of the Bonzos throughout the band's career, during which many more musicians would pass in and out. Stanshall once told *Rolling Stone*, in fact, that "thirty or so people" were involved in the outfit when they began fooling around.

"We used to look for funny songs, learn them, and play them in pubs," remembers Neil Innes in the summer of 1999 at a London cafe not far from BBC headquarters, where he's just done a radio show. "We used to go to flea markets and things, and look for old 78 records that had silly song titles, 'cause you couldn't play them until you got them home. On the plus side, they didn't cost more than a penny, or sixpence at the most in old money. If you saw a record that said, for example, 'I'm Going to Bring a Watermelon to My Girl Tonight,' then you'd buy it on the off chance that it would be fairly humorous." "I'm Going to Bring a Watermelon to My Girl Tonight," in fact, would become their debut single in 1966.

The Bonzos finally evolved from a student band to a professional one that year, taking an edited version of their pub act on the road to cabaret clubs in Northern England. By this time they had become the Bonzo Dog Doo Dah Band, dressed in gangster suits and two-toned shoes to affect a 1920s look. Yet there were some Dada, or at least surreal, parts to their presentation, as when they held up cutout boards of the sort of speech balloons that appear in comics, emblazoned with logos like "Wow, I'm really expressing myself." There were some precedents for this blend of music hall and oddball humor in Britain, the Temperance Seven (produced by George Martin) and the Alberts, that are far less known than even the Bonzos are in the United States.

Explains Innes, "The Alberts used to do the most insane things. Someone would climb into a fake cannon, and they'd be shot from the cannon. They'd just push a dummy out and there would be this huge painted canvas drum about sixteen feet across with a painting of the Highlands of Scotland, and Dougie Gray would play the bagpipes, marching on the spot. The scenery behind him would be revolved, so it looked as though he was walking along through the Scottish Highlands. The Temperance Seven were much more musical than either the Alberts or the Bonzos; they played really well. I suppose we were a kind of mixture of the two in the early days."

In 1966 the Bonzos began recording for Parlophone, famous as the Beatles' label, but also a company with a history of producing comedy discs, including hits by the Temperance Seven and Peter Sellers. Their first two singles were entirely comprised of covers, three of the four tunes ("I'm Going to Bring a Watermelon to My Girl Tonight," "My Brother Makes the Noises for the Talkies," and "Button Up Your Overcoat") being slightly goofy covers of pre-World War II numbers, the other being a none-too-riotous version of the early 1960s rock novelty "Alley Oop." In a way the Bonzos were like the white blues revivalists of the era, digging up obscure and forgotten items from decades past, sometimes discovered on flea market 78s, and giving them a somewhat more modern interpretation. Indications were that their label thought of the group as a novelty act at a time when rock, and Parlophone's own Beatles, had clinched a stranglehold on the collective pop consciousness. Parlophone dropped the band after these releases, and had the Bonzos never recorded again, they would probably only be remembered as an aberrant footnote.

However, the transatlantic success of a corny vaudeville update in late 1966 by the New Vaudeville Band, "Winchester Cathedral," set off a chain of events that would propel the Bonzo Dog Doo Dah Band from the 1920s into the 1960s. The New Vaudeville Band was just an ad hoc studio ensemble, not a real group, which prompted an offer to Bob Kerr, who briefly played trumpet in the Bonzos. According to Innes, "This chap rang Bob up and said, 'You're working with a daft band. Ask them if they want to become the New Vaudeville Band!' Bob sort of rushed in and said, 'Hey, we could have a number one! It's already in the Top Ten, this record.' And of course, we all said, 'No!' Bob said, 'Well, I'm going.' We said, 'Go! Never darken our towels again!'

"When the New Vaudeville Band appeared on television, they got a bunch of people together, and they took the whole look. So you saw these people with these suits, the two-tone shoes, the comic balloon things, and a singer in an army suit. We'd hardly finished our six weeks of cabaret when people would come up, having seen the New Vaudeville Band on television, saying 'Hey! You're like that New Vaudeville Band!'

"This caused quite a rage within Viv and Legs that this had happened. I think it was Legs Larry Smith who said, 'Why don't we play anything?' 'Cause he'd been batting on about that. And we said, 'Yeah, why not?' So we just turned our sights on the whole musical scene, and that's how it evolved.

"We'd been quite happy playing all this old nonsense stuff. So it was quite a good thing, in a way. 'Cause we then developed songwriting, got electric guitars. The lineup actually eventually changed because of that, because [bass, banjo, and sax player] Vernon [Dudley Bohay-Nowell] and [percussionist/spoons player] Sam [Spoons] were sort of squeezed out. They couldn't really adapt."

In the transition from trad to rock, the Bonzos' lineup contracted from the unwieldy nine-piece seen in the first widely circulated photo of the group from 1966—including members that soon drifted out of the picture, like Big Sid Nicholls and Lenny Williams—to a six-man setup more characteristic of rock bands. The bass position remained problematic for a while, Dave Clague and American Joel Druckman serving short stints before Dennis Cowan finally settled in around 1968. Most important, the band's repertoire shifted toward original material, written almost exclusively, either separately or together, by Stanshall and Innes (although Spear chucked in a tune now and then).

Nonetheless, the Bonzos' first album, *Gorilla* (in late 1967), found them still negotiating the passage between eras. There were still a few covers of moldy standards like "Cool Britannia," "I Left My Heart in San Francisco," and "The Sound of Music." These were considerably more absurdist in conception than those on their 1966 singles, done not so much in tribute as in aborted versions that seemed determined to cause as much embarrassment to the composers as possible. In fact, on "The Sound of Music," the interpretation was downright anarchic, with an insufferably stuffy spoken narration preceding a racket far more reminiscent of the sound of broken crockery than of the Rodgers-Hammerstein song.

Some of the original material retained echoes of their trad jazz and vaudeville roots, especially on the instrumental "Jazz, Delicious Hot, Disgusting Cold." The humor was more on the subdued side than the uproarious. Yet the band members were also learning how to use the studio to their advantage. Well-timed unpredictable sound effects—laughter, roaring crowds, cocktail-party applause—were dropped in to set the juxtaposition of the good-time and the bizarre in bolder relief, as top musical comedians such as Spike Jones had. Viv Stanshall's deadpan spoken delivery on the spy satire "Big Shot," as well as his atonal quasi-upper-middle-class sing-speak on "I'm Bored," unveiled a knack for loquacious yet ridiculous voiceovers that would serve him well in various media in the next twenty-five years. Nowhere was it more effective than on the album's highlight, "The Intro and the Outro," in which he introduced the Bonzos, augmented by an all-star celebrity band on all manner of inappropriate instruments—Eric Clapton on ukulele, Adolf Hitler on vibes, Brainiac on banjo. "It's a classic, isn't it?" says Innes. "Someday they ought to do a video of it. Pull back to reveal all of these people on a wonderful bandstand, look-alikes and whatnot."

Neil Innes, by contrast, offered a more (relatively speaking) normal songwriting voice. "Piggy Bank Love" and "The Equestrian Statue," the latter of which somewhat resembles the Kinks in its Edwardian tunefulness, were getting in sync with the British pop-rock melodicism of the period. Not that this ruled out intelligent silliness on his part. "One of the first songs I wrote was 'Equestrian Statue,'" Neil remembers. "Being an art student, I'd been reading Jean-Paul Sartre's *Nausea*, which was existentialist rubbish, really. I just thought, who is this guy worried about whether a lamppost exists more than he does? Why not choose something a little more interesting, like an equestrian statue?

"I see my role in the Bonzos as being the straight man, in many ways," he continues. "Because it got so crazy, somebody had to say, 'Well, no, we have to play this sequence for this long. It would be nice to sort of be able to stop together and change together sometimes, you know. We can't all be free-form.' We weren't by any means like the Grateful Dead or something, who could just roll on and on and on."

Around the time of *Gorilla*, the Bonzos got what seemed to be their first huge break by appearing in the Beatles' *Magical Mystery Tour* film. They had first met the superstars at Abbey Road back in 1966, and friendship between the Bonzos and Paul McCartney in particular led to the Bonzos' cameo as the band in the movie's cabaret sequence, providing the musical accompaniment for stripper Jan Carson. Brief as it was, it could be argued that Viv Stanshall in particular stole the show from those funding the project, singing his sub-Elvis impersonation "Death Cab for Cutie" with supreme unctuousness. The scene didn't do the Bonzos loads of favors, however, as the BBC showing of the film was critically panned in Britain, leading to cancellation of its planned television broadcast in the U.S. The Beatles connection, however, would work to their benefit nearly a year later.

Before then, the Bonzo Dog Band (the "Doo Dah" getting dropped sometime after the release of *Gorilla*) made its primary impact live, rather than on record. They shared bills—usually at the second tier or lower, it must be said—with many hot and hard-rocking late '60s bands, some known for an overt sense of humor (the Who, the Kinks), some not (Spirit, the Byrds, Joe Cocker, Cream). The Bonzos went over well, not just because of their music, but also because of their presentation, which was much more visual and off-the-wall than that of their colleagues.

Roger Spear's wacky robots, animated bubble-blowing dummies, and exploding heads and trouser presses are probably the most fondly recalled props; eventually these became so complex that they were physically difficult to cart around on tour. Legs Larry Smith tap-danced and, as reported in Lillian Roxon's *Rock Encyclopedia*, "wore Shirley Temple outfits and large wobbly plastic breasts and blew little kisses (*before* Tiny Tim)." Viv Stanshall wiggled in lamé suits and was well on his way to becoming one of British rock's frontline "loons" with his increasingly erratic behavior. In her *I'm With the Band: Confessions of a Groupie*, Pamela Des Barres breathlessly describes a show where Stanshall "came out in a massive muumuu with a gigantic lion's head on, beating a hand painted drum, and when he whipped off the lion's head, he was wearing a sheep's head, and he kept taking masks off until the finale when he had bloodshot ping-pong balls stuck into his eye sockets." Even in his short time with the band, bassist Dave Clague pitched into the oddness by wearing a newspaper jacket.

"Dave was a very competent bass player, but sort of kind of stood there," recalls Innes. "We needed everybody to be daft, you know. Dennis [Cowan] was a really solid musician, and we really needed somebody who could play bass like him. Because Larry, by then, was a drummer who would sort of get bored and tired, and rather stand up and blow kisses to people. So we needed the bass to sort of drive along.

"In fact, once when we were playing the Isle of Wight [festival], Larry was late, 'cause he'd been mucking around with Keith Moon, and we had no drummer. Jim Capaldi [of Traffic] said, 'I'll come up and do it.' And it was great, the first four or five numbers. Jim's sort of whacking into it, and Dennis and I are looking at each other, saying, 'We can play off the beat, around the beat, do whatever we want.' And Larry turns up, and sort of waggles a tambourine for a bit. Then we get to 'Canyons of Your Mind,' and Larry goes over to Jim Capaldi and says, 'I think I'd better do this one,

Jim. It's a bit complicated.'" Innes laughs at the mise-en-scene. "Dennis and I went, 'Oohhh, stay there, Jim!'"

At the Fillmore East, the group warmed up the crowd by doing gymnastics as a recording (not of the Bonzos) played on the sound system, going offstage after finishing their exercises, and returning to play a set as the Bonzo Dog Band without explanation. That earned them an invitation to the Fillmore West, where they cut off their version of "Blue Suede Shoes" and began miming sans music; Stanshall kicked the stage, and the music started up again, as if the Bonzos were a dying phonograph. Playing a stadium in New Jersey with Sly and the Family Stone, and lacking sufficient sound equipment, Stanshall sang through a megaphone (a burst of ingenuity that did not go down well with the fans). At the Albert Hall, they fed yards of plastic balloons out to the audience; at one venue, Stanshall staged a fight in the gallery that ended with a dummy being thrown over the edge. It is unsurprising that Keith Moon of the Who sat in with the band on drums on a few occasions.

A less obvious fan was Jimi Hendrix, who checked out the Bonzos in a Los Angeles club and met Innes in the bathroom. "It was just the two of us, sort of taking a leak. And he said, 'You know, we're doing the same thing.' I said, 'What, you mean, taking a leak?' He said, 'No—I mean, onstage.' 'Cause he felt part of his act getting almost as daft as the Bonzos, with having to light things.

"It was definitely a show to watch, and it's really difficult to describe. It really, really is a shame that it's not on film anywhere." The brief bits that circulate of the band miming on television do not, according to Innes, do them justice. "On TV we were like caged animals, really. But onstage, we *were* the animals. We were free to do what we needed to do. We didn't have to worry about cameras, or staying in one space. The whole show just seemed to dovetail from one thing to another, and you were always kept guessing.

"It became like a well-written sitcom. There were regular characters. Larry was a flamboyant, show business character—'look at me, I'm wonderful,' tap-dance with false breasts on and things like that. Viv had this kind of stage presence you couldn't ignore. He walked onstage, he looked dangerous; you just didn't know what he was going to do, and for the most part we didn't either. Roger was crazy with his robots. Rodney used to hurl himself into blowing every kind of thing that had a hole in one end, and a noise that came out the other. You had bass saxophones, bass clarinets, tenor saxophones." Not all of the mayhem made it to record. In the Bonzo Dog Fan Club magazine *Doo Dah*, Legs remembered the unrecorded "It Was a Great Party 'Til Someone Brought a Hammer" as an instrumental where "we used to sing the one line (the title) and then we would just scream for a bit."

In 1968, the challenge was getting some of their mushrooming rock-friendly experimentalism onto record. "The main problems with recording *Gorilla* was not a shortage of ideas, because we had plenty of ideas for sound jokes," observes Innes. "In fact, we were probably a little bit ahead of the engineers in what we could do. The problem was, in fact, Gerry Bron [their manager at the time], who was our producer. After three hours, he said, 'That's it. We've got to move on to the next track.'

"It was because Gerry was like this…in fact, that's how Paul McCartney ended up producing 'Urban Spaceman.' Because the record company was saying, 'Well, what about a single? What about a single?' And we couldn't care less. We were just still being silly art students. We didn't feel that we were in the same business as everybody else. We didn't have teenage fans or anything like that, we were just out for a good time.

"Viv was down [at] the Speakeasy Club, I think, with Paul, talking generally; he used to hang out quite a bit. Viv was complaining about the fact that Gerry was sort of, 'Right, three hours of that, move on.' And [Viv] said, 'Now we gotta go in and record this bloody single.' So Paul said, 'I'll come and produce it if you like.' And that was perfect, because that was the only way we were going to get [Bron] off the control desk, to have somebody like Paul, who wasn't known as a record producer. But he was *known*. So he came and produced that, and took eight hours." Innes' "I'm the Urban Spaceman," by far their most commercial outing to date with its sing-along melodies and coy lyrics that could be interpreted as lightly psychedelic, was their only big hit single, reaching number five in Britain.

Innes picks up the story: "It took eight hours because Paul's used to spending hours in the studio and hanging out. He sat down on the piano and played 'Hey Jude' all the way through. No one had heard it then. He'd only just written it. And of course, the people watching the clock are going absolutely ape shit. We did things like double-track the drums, and Viv wanted to blow his trumpet mouthpiece into a garden hose, with a plastic funnel on the end, whirling around his head. The engineer said, 'I can't record that.' Paul said, 'Yeah you can. Just put a microphone in each corner.' So that took twenty minutes.

"Anyway, it was a really good time. He played Viv's ukulele, and Gerry's wife Lillian came up to him at one point and said, 'What's that you've got there? A poor man's violin?' And he said, 'No, it's a rich man's ukulele.'" McCartney's admiration for the band was unquestionably serious, however, as expressed in *MOJO* in 1995: "They were on the cusp between humor and music. In a way I don't think they ever got it sorted out. They didn't ever fall fully into music or into comedy, but that was their charm really."

Were there any thoughts of having McCartney produce an entire Bonzo Dog Band album? "He probably would have loved to. But it didn't cross our minds. All that crossed our minds was so we could annoy Gerry even more by sort of refusing to allow Paul's name to go on the record. So we came up with the name Apollo C. Vermouth, and we kept it like that for a good four or five weeks. In fact, the single actually got up to about number seventeen without anybody knowing he'd had anything to do with it. But by then, the management snapped and leaked the story. Then it shot up to number five. But by then, it had sold over a quarter of a million records in the U.K. alone."

On the heels of "Urban Spaceman" came the album *The Doughnut in Granny's Greenhouse*, whose opening track, the most definitely self contradictory "We Are Normal," brought the Bonzos into the psychedelic age. Murmured non sequiturs and creepy witches' brew sounds suddenly exploded into a heavy rock track. Organ, thrashing drums, glissando electronic blips, and the group's chants of "We are normal and we want our freedom!" carried the cut to its conclusion, nodding to the band's roots with the dissonant horns near the fade. "That's the first time we kind of workshopped something," says Innes. "Viv drew a kind of graph and we'd start off with sort of like a primordial soup noise. Things come out of it, and it just turned into a kind of terrible row. We actually did it live with Roger wearing his black-and-white-striped T-shirt like a four-foot-long chimney over his face. He had an extra long arm, and an extra long guitar. In the middle of this Zappaesque thrashing and jamming, his head would explode; the top of the chimney would explode. That would be a signal for Viv to come in, and we'd all go into 'Blue Suede Shoes.'"

The Doughnut in Granny's Greenhouse was inarguably the Bonzos' most daring, eclectic, and successful work. There was silly sci-fi satire in Innes' "Beautiful Zelda," a campy 1950s rock tribute to an extraterrestrial lover; brutal deflation of the British blues boom with "Can Blue Men Sing the Whites"; more ludicrous marriages of '50s dance craze rock to daffy words on "Kama Sutra" and Roger Spear's "Trouser Press" (whose title would be taken by *Trouser Press*, the premier American alternative rock magazine of the 1970s); and "My Pink Half of the Drainpipe," with its boatful of seasick French crooners bewailing British suburban neighborly complaints. Stanshall's peerless mastery of straight-faced narration of events that mixed the mundane and the mad peaked on "Rhinocratic Oaths." His "11 Mustachioed Daughters" closed the record on an ominous note, with its jungle beats and disturbed, distraught recounting of what sounds like a pagan-satanic ritual.

Innes offers a few thoughts on a couple of the album's more popular cuts, starting with "Can Blue Men Sing the Whites?" (in which Stanshall cuts off the soon-to-depart Druckman's harmonica solo with a "not yet, man"): "There were *so* many British blues bands. It was just us lampooning our own peer group, saying, 'Well, hey, where did this stuff come from? And where do British guys get to be so good at it suddenly?'" As for the Stanshall-Innes collaboration "My Pink Half of the Drain-pipe," "I've always adored French music. I was just trying to do some sort of French melodies, and that suited Viv's flow. 'You who speak to me across the fence' [he mimics Viv's opening vocal] it's sort of Edith Piaf, isn't it, really. Those little snippets [of dialogue that punctuate the tune], again, were things we liked to do—suddenly bring a bucket of cold water on the general flow, put something else in, and then come back to it."

With its jump cuts through a kaleidoscope of styles, rib-tickling wordplay and overall purposeful mayhem, *The Doughnut in Granny's Greenhouse* is the Bonzos record most apt to provoke comparisons with the late '60s albums by the Mothers of Invention. "I certainly was aware of the Mothers of Invention," Innes owns up. "Maybe *we* were the Mothers of Convention. One of my favorite albums is *We're Only In It For the Money*. But Zappa's far more musical than the Bonzos ever were. Some of the Mothers, who we met in L.A. and got to know quite well, were quite close to the sort of wackiness we used to do onstage. But we were nowhere near them musically. We had our own quirky thing, where we didn't really care. If somebody played a bum note, it didn't matter. Whereas I think Zappa would have gone through the roof."

The album further distinguished the styles of the two principal composers from each other. Generally speaking, Innes was the more tuneful and poppier of the pair; Stanshall was the odder and more verbal of the two. "Viv was never much of a musician," Innes confirms. "He could think of a tune, but he always needed help to put the chords together and whatnot. His strength was words. My strength was the musical side." Innes and Stanshall did collaborate on some of the Bonzos' best songs, like

"We Are Normal" and "My Pink Half of the Drainpipe," in which case Neil "used to help Viv with the chords and melodies sometimes. If I helped him a lot, we'd share the song. Viv used to suggest lyrics on my songs. And if he only changed a couple of words, *he'd* take half the song."

Was it hard for the notoriously mercurial Stanshall to put his ideas into a finished composition? "No, he was disciplined. If he had a fault—it's like a chimpanzee painting. He'd get it really good and you'd say, 'That's really good, Viv.' No one had the power to take it away from him. He had to keep fiddling and changing words, and in fact, he'd often smudge up it again."

While *Greenhouse* was only a mildly successful seller in the U.K. (reaching number forty), the group's profile was much higher in Britain than its chart success would lead you to guess. This was due in large part to a long-running gig as the house band of sorts on the British television series *Do Not Adjust Your Set*. Although supposedly a children's show, its comic sketches were often sophisticated and daring, the writing and acting dominated by cast members Eric Idle, Michael Palin, and Terry Jones. This trio would go on to Monty Python's Flying Circus almost immediately after *Do Not Adjust Your Set* finished its run, and many of the ideas that surfaced in Monty Python were floated in this earlier series. The Bonzos provided musical interludes by miming to many of their early songs, usually with the expected strange oversize and mobile props. They also had minor roles in some of the sketches; Roger Spear, for instance, did a cameo as a human plant watered by Eric Idle. Twenty-six episodes, plus a Christmas special, of *Do Not Adjust Your Set* were broadcast between late 1967 and early 1969. Unfortunately, few have been seen since, particularly in America, where only a handful of dedicated collectors have had access to poor-fidelity copies.

Similarities between the humor of the Bonzos and the silly-but-surreal future Monty Python sketches could already be heard on early Bonzo Dog Band albums, especially when Viv Stanshall took center stage to deliver spoken word curios on "Big Shot" and "Rhinocratic Oaths." "There is a link," believes Innes. "When the band first met Eric and Mike and Terry, there was a certain mutual suspicion, 'cause we were crazy guys just coming off the road. They'd come from Oxford and Cambridge, and were young, up-and-coming writers; they'd written stuff for David Frost. It was a kind of cross-fertilization that took place over a couple of years. We all became very good friends.

"I think Eric's acknowledged that there was an influence from the Bonzos in terms of the anarchy. Python wouldn't have been Python, I think, if a lot of them hadn't worked with the Bonzos. I'm not saying that the Bonzos taught them everything they know. But we certainly had the anarchy ingredient, which I think they found attractive, or useful to them. But they were more disciplined than the Bonzos. They knew how to get cameras to point at things."

The Bonzos' third LP, *Tadpoles*, was less a proper album than a collection of songs that had been performed on *Do Not Adjust Your Set*. The less serious regard with which the record was held was perhaps reflected by the inclusion of only three songs by Innes and Stanshall, all of which had already appeared on singles. As a whole it was a retreat, though a well-done one, into the prewar jazz and pop of their early repertoire, with off-kilter covers of odd ditties like "Laughing Blues," "Ali Baba's

Camel," "By a Waterfall," and "Hunting Tigers Out in 'Indiah.'" In a more contemporary style, there was the "Urban Spaceman" hit and its Elvis-from-hell B-side "Canyons of Your Mind" (with one of the world's most deliberately awful electric guitar solos). There was also the flop follow-up to "Urban Spaceman," "Mr. Apollo"; the band might have been better advised to try "Beautiful Zelda" for the singles market. Roger Spear's "Shirt" was the clearest antecedent in the Bonzos catalog to Monty Python, largely consisting of a befuddled interviewer asking passersby in the street about "Shirts" ("Are they still necessary? Do you think they should stop making shirts?") before the gang broke out into a jolly sing-along about…shirts.

Tadpoles was another modest charter in the U.K. (reaching number thirty-six), but none of the Bonzos' 1960s albums so much as made the Top 200 in the U.S. Although they were very well received by live audiences on American tours, they were (and remain) very much a cult act in the States. Innes blames this partially on bad timing and business pressures. "I think because we went in 1968, it was overkill. Agents and managers were killing each other for places to play. It was a bad year to go to America. If we'd gone in '67, it would have been better. But the manager at the time, he thought it was impossible. It was like he hadn't heard of airplanes.

"We were always really a Dada band. We only ever had the one hit, and we didn't really want that; we were more of a live act. We weren't going to play the showbiz game, and be obsequious. So when we found out [during an American tour] that Roger's wife had had a miscarriage and they hadn't told him, Roger said, 'Well, I feel like going home.' And I said, 'We're all with you.' We needed just one little thing to sort of make it, 'That's it. Had enough of this scrambling, scuffling.' We turned our back on a coast-to-coast TV show when we left. They said, 'This is national TV!' 'So?'" Innes does *not* think that the Bonzos' humor was too British for American tastes. "Monty Python's British humor certainly didn't affect [the troupe's success in the States]," he notes (although Monty Python would not take off in the U.S. until five years after its British debut, as the TV series was not broadcast Stateside until the mid-1970s). "They were worried about it too, you know. 'Cricket jokes? Who's gonna get cricket jokes?'"

For the Bonzos' fourth LP, *Keynsham* (1969), the group concentrated more on the music, and less on the comedy. Although it's sometimes been described as a concept album, the concept was so vague as to be indeterminate, unless all the songs were meant to take place in a town of Keynsham. In *Comstock Lode*, Stanshall described Keynsham as "the only never-never land, the only tangible Shangri-La." Regardless of its intent, *Keynsham* was a letdown. While they were becoming better rock musicians, the serious compositions were not on the level of the comic ones that were their stock-in-trade, and even some of the comic numbers on the album were pedestrian. Some Innes penned cuts, like "Keynsham" and "You Done My Brain In," found him gravitating to a pensive, melodic direction akin to the Kinks and Beatles, and Stanshall's "Look at Me I'm Wonderful" was something of a signature tune for Legs Larry Smith's showbiz parodies. Stanshall's contributions were more frivolous than Innes', and the divide between their writing seemed to be widening.

Keynsham was not the only 1969 endeavor in which the Bonzos grappled with a muddled concept. Stanshall and the god of hellfire, Arthur Brown, were at work on a

"Brain Opera," reportedly about German scientists who get offered large cash prizes to work in the United States. Thirty years on, Brown confirms that the Brain Opera was not completed. "It was shortly after Viv came out of a mental home. He came down to visit me, and we had some good fun in the pub, slinging words backwards and forwards. We'd done a lot of concerts together before that.

"We came up with all these strange ideas. There was going to be a silver slug that came across the stage. It was going to be a very surreal and adventurous piece. We discussed, about, the first act. I said to Vivian, 'Look, most of my stuff at this time has a sort of mystical content. So it's going to have a mystical content, which would be carried by the surreal element of it.' And then of course, with it being Vivian, it was also going to be quite funny. But that was about as far as it got, really. He was at the time drifting in and out, and I was doing one of my bands, and we got temporally pulled apart."

Was this a Stanshall project, a Stanshall/Brown one, or a Bonzo Dog Band one? And was it intended for the stage, an album, or both? It's still uncertain. The Bonzos would have been involved, thinks Brown, "and we would have had other people as well. Some female parts. Really, we didn't get around to discussing the sort of technicalities or too many of the actual personnel. It was a very interesting prospect. And then, you know, some of those things just disappear. Not because you decide they're not good or you're not going to do them, it's just things carry you other ways."

That sentiment would soon apply to the Bonzo Dog Band itself, which broke up in early 1970, not so much out of rancor as fatigue. "We were worked so hard," says Innes. "We didn't really have a holiday in five years. Three managers, no holidays—that kills off any group. Viv certainly burnt out." It couldn't have helped that Stanshall's mental problems, which as Brown mentioned had already led to some hospitalization, were getting worse.

"We'd felt we'd gone as far as we could. Viv and I talked about it and said, 'We're pretty high now. If we go on without any real ideas and things like that...let's leave it while we're at a high point.' We weren't destined to go on for year after year like the Stones, no way. One of the problems is, I think, we stopped arguing with each other. We became better friends. We were more sympathetic to each other. But before, we used to fight tooth and nail for ideas. The only way to get an idea in was just to do it and not tell anybody. If it got a laugh with the audience, it stayed in."

Although the Bonzos were immediately at work on solo endeavors, they weren't quite finished with each other. As they owed a few more tracks to their record label before they could be totally free to do as they willed, they reformed for a contractual obligation album, *Let's Make Up and Be Friendly*, released in early 1972. In actual fact this was primarily the work of Innes and Stanshall, with contributions from the rest of the band that ranged from extensive to ephemeral. They were aided by several outside musicians, including drummer Hughie Flint (ex-John Mayall), Stevie Winwood, saxophonist Dick Parry (who would play on Pink Floyd's *Dark Side of the Moon*), and Yes keyboardist Tony Kaye. Unsurprisingly it boasted their heaviest rock sound to date, and wasn't bad, but was only fitfully inspired.

Most would agree that the high-water mark was Stanshall's nine-minute "Rawlinson End," one of his characteristic music-with-monologue pieces. Built around eccentric protagonist Sir Henry Rawlinson, it would eventually be expanded into a radio series, a solo album, a stage presentation, and finally a full-length feature film. Neil Innes' faux-Beatles "Fresh Wound" was an early forerunner of his Fab Four satire in the Rutles in the late 1970s, while "Slush," with no vocals but repeated snippets of manic laughter, concluded the Bonzos' career on a suitable note (though there would be a "reunion" single, "No Matter Who You Vote For the Government Always Gets In," recorded in the late 1980s but not issued until 1992).

To cover the various post-Bonzos careers of their core membership would take at least another chapter. Neil Innes was the most visible, certainly in the United States, as an auxiliary member of sorts for Monty Python. Solo warm-up gigs for their TV audiences led to work with the troupe in their stage shows, writing some musical and comic material for their series and movies, and supporting acting roles in *Monty Python and the Holy Grail* and *Life of Brian*. He also collaborated with Python's Eric Idle for a television series and, most memorably, the Beatles spoof *All You Need Is Cash*, in which Innes played the "Ron Nasty" (i.e. John Lennon) role in the Rutles and wrote the pseudo-Beatles songs for the soundtrack. For the last few decades he's racked up numerous comic/musical acting and writing credits for television, radio, records, and live one-man-show performances.

Roger Spear toured with his Giant Kinetic Wardrobe of robots and such in the 1970s, even opening for the Who in 1971; he also did some solo records, and taught interior spatial design at Chelsea College of Art. Legs Larry Smith, like Stanshall, became one of Keith Moon's (and George Harrison's) running buddies, and toured as a gowned tap-dancer with Elton John and Eric Clapton in the 1970s. Rodney Slater became a psychiatric social worker, of all things; Dennis Cowan died of peritonitis in the '70s. Viv Stanshall was a well-known personality in Britain, and not just for dressing up as a Nazi with Keith Moon. He made records as a soloist and with short-lived bands (Eric Clapton was on the Vivian Stanshall Sean Head Showband's 1970 single "Labio-Dental Fricative"). He did lots of comic and voiceover radio, worked on the various Sir Henry Rawlinson projects, painted, and sculpted. Yet in the States, his only well-known work was a cameo: as the silver-tongued narrator of the march of instruments that concluded side one of Mike Oldfield's huge progressive rock opus *Tubular Bells*. After struggling with mental illness for many years, he died in a fire in his flat in 1995.

Innes acknowledges that Stanshall's decline began back in the Bonzos days. "Before we went on the second tour to the States, something must have happened. Because we went to pick him up, he came out of the door, and his head was completely shaved. That sent a shiver through me. I thought, this is 1968, and you've shaved your head bald: that's a statement. I don't know whether he was starting to have a kind of crackup then or not. But he certainly got the wrong prescription from the doctor. The doctor prescribed him Valium, 'cause he was having anxiety attacks I think he became addicted to Valium. And he liked to drink, and drink and Valium just don't go together. He began to have more and more periods where he was completely inaccessible. And then he'd pull himself out of it. He had this constitution like an ox; he'd go from being overweight to really skinny.

"Gradually what happened was the periods of inaccessibility got longer, and the periods of lucidity got shorter. He was terrible to everybody who tried to help him. He was beyond help in the end. It's one of those tragedies of life. Somebody who has so much talent, who couldn't actually handle it himself. How he died was a shock, but it wasn't a surprise."

Does Innes have any regrets about the Bonzo Dog Band, together for about a decade but only committed recording artists for four years or so? "I wish we could have spent more time getting a little bit better. We could have had a more disciplined approach to the business. But that wouldn't have been us. I mean, the whole thing was a laugh. Until we got tired. And when we decided to end it all, it was a laugh again.

"It wasn't designed to be a career band. It was anti-art. It was letting off steam from art school. It would have been wrong to suddenly say, 'Oh no. Really, we're serious.'"

Recommended Recordings:

Gorilla (1967, One Way). The group's most traditional (as in jazz and vaudeville) and in some ways quaintest outing. Restrained only in comparison to their later work, it's jolly good fun, including the disorganized interpretations of "Cool Britannia," "The Sound of Music," and "I Left My Heart in San Francisco"; the more surreal "I'm Bored" and "The Intro and the Outro"; and the first airings of Innes' pop bent ("The Equestrian Statue") and Stanshall's narrations ("Big Shot").

The Doughnut in Granny's Greenhouse (1968, One Way). Their best and most musically satisfying album, with a hefty chunk of their finest and funniest songs: "We Are Normal," "Beautiful Zelda," "My Pink Half of the Drainpipe," "Rhinocratic Oaths," and "11 Mustachioed Daughters." Like those early Mothers of Invention records, it's also thoughtfully constructed and sequenced for maximum comic flow and diversity, so that the sum is greater than the parts.

Tadpoles (1969, One Way). An uneven mixture of the rock and trad sides of the band, though still of a pretty high standard. The British hit "I'm the Urban Spaceman" is here, as well as the hilarious "Shirt," which would fit in well on a Monty Python record.

The History of the Bonzos (1974, BGO, U.K.). There have been several best-of Bonzos compilations. With thirty-five songs (including a few items from solo projects) this is the most comprehensive, although it's marred by the inexplicable omission of quality cuts like "Beautiful Zelda." That's on Rhino's twenty-four-song *The Best of the Bonzo Dog Band*, which has its own flaws, like the absence of "My Pink Half of the Drainpipe."

Cornology (1992, EMI, U.K.). Three-CD box set contains all five of the Bonzo Dog Band's albums, as well as both sides of their two 1966 Parlophone singles, the B-side "Ready Mades," a German version of "Mr. Apollo," and a solo cut each by Stanshall, Innes, and Spear. It's not quite the last word on their catalog. Diehards can seek their compilation of radio performances, *Unpeeled*, and the erratic collection of late '60s demos and rehearsals, *Anthropology*. The various-artists anthology *By Jingo It's British Rubbish*, in addition to a few Bonzos cuts (including the previously unreleased 1966 outtake "On Her Doorstep Tonight"), effectively illustrates their roots by surrounding them with material by trad jazz funnymen the Alberts and the Temperance Seven.

Unheralded Heroes

The performer/recording artist is the public face of popular music, receiving virtually all of the adulation and praise, if definitely *not* all of the money. Those who get deeply enough into the music to scan the fine print on albums, and certainly those who even dip their toes into the music industry from the business or media ends, know that behind each great record and show lies an incredible machine of supporting players. The "backroom boys," they're sometimes called (although it should be "backroom boys and girls"): the producers, publicists, managers, engineers, label owners, and others who are vital cogs of the wheel of music production and distribution. Sometimes they're essential to the success of the artists with whom they work; sometimes they, with the best or worst intentions, obstruct that success; sometimes they do both. Often bad-mouthed by the artists themselves, most would nonetheless agree that they do not receive due credit for their work.

There were enough such characters in the 1960s (and in any era of pop music you care to examine) to fill several entertaining books. Only two are spotlighted here, linked by their massive contributions to the 1960s British rock scene. Producer Shel Talmy and producer/manager/promoter-and-more Giorgio Gomelsky make for an interesting pair, for their similarities and their differences. Entering the music business more than 5,000 miles apart from each other, they were each fortunate enough to converge with British rock at the precise time at which it began to unexpectedly explode. Neither, oddly, were British themselves; perhaps it took figures with a different cultural perspective to appreciate exactly how special U.K. rock of the time was. Both were essential to shaping the sound of superstar and cult bands that, taken together, represented much of the best music of the 1960s: the Rolling Stones, the Yardbirds, the Kinks, the Who, and more. Both gained more leeway within the industry by establishing themselves as independent producers who worked on their own terms, not those of a studio or record label; both formed record labels themselves. While Talmy was content to make most of his contributions in the studio, there was little that Gomelsky *didn't* try to boost the bands he believed in: management, production, running clubs, festival promotion, filmmaking, reading dirty limericks to placate restless crowds waiting for the Rolling Stones, you name it. Both are also raconteurs, pulling few punches in their enthusiasms for and criticisms of the huge talents, and equally huge egos, with whom they collaborated.

The Rolling Stones, as they appeared in early 1963, when they were the resident band at Giorgio Gomelsky's Crawdaddy Club. Left to right:Charlie Watts, Bill Wyman, Brian Jones, Keith Richards, Mick Jagger. Credit: Wayne Knight Collection/Chansley Entertainment Archives.

Giorgio Gomelsky

"I'm a creative person!" exclaims Giorgio Gomelsky with pride. "I'm not a businessman. Never was a businessman. Never wanted to *be* a businessman."

As he later takes pains to clarify, Gomelsky is not necessarily annoyed by business as a fair exchange of goods and services. He finds it more objectionable when it's used as a means to accumulate capital, exercise power, and exploit. Nonetheless, you will have a hard time finding other rock 'n' roll managers and promoters who dealt with money for creativity's sake, rather than the other way around. Let alone someone who managed one of the bigger, and certainly one of the most influential, British groups of the 1960s. Or, yet more improbably, was as close as anyone to being a manager of sorts for the Rolling Stones before they were whisked away by Andrew Loog Oldham in April 1963. A man who worked in some capacity—manager, promoter, producer, general cheerleader—with, seemingly, almost every important British rock star or cult artist of the 1960s, from the Beatles on down. And a figure who, unlike many of the movers and shakers of that decade, continued to work with artists on the cutting edge in the 1970s, in France and New York City, if anything becoming more avant-garde in his vision than he had been as a champion of British and European jazz and blues in his youth.

Giorgio Gomelsky, few would argue, is a colorful, controversial, and above all gregarious figure, even by the exaggerated standards of music industry management. Above all, he is known for managing and producing the Yardbirds from late 1963 to early 1966, a span which saw the band drag purist blues into psychedelia at a frightening speed. There were also associations with the Animals, Soft Machine, Rod Stewart (as a member of the Steampacket), John McLaughlin, the Rolling Stones of course, Jimi Hendrix, British stars that were barely known in the U.S. like Julie Driscoll, great cult groups like the Blossom Toes, budding talents like future members of Traffic and 10cc, way-out-there experimentalists like the Spontaneous Music Ensemble, trad jazz stars such as Chris Barber...the list goes on and on.

In the 1970s, he handled leading French progressives Magma, and after emigrating to New York was among the first to recognize the potential of names like Bill Laswell and Fred Frith, now venerated icons of the NYC "new music" scene. His artists have sometimes griped about his eccentric promotional stunts, his erratic business acumen, and a restlessness that left some projects unfinished. Yet, as one independent label owner explained to me back in the early 1980s, in many cases—particularly in that crucial stage between formation and wide recognition— "Giorgio's enthusiasm is the only thing that keeps those bands going."

Gomelsky was one of the very few important nonmusicians of the 1960s rock industry who, to most appearances, was motivated more by creative vision, love of music, and a hunger for innovating artistic and social change than he was by financial considerations. He is very much an ideas man, less so a conventional entrepreneur. That's immediately evident upon entering his loft office in Manhattan, north of the Village and south of midtown. Seated in front of a curving array of computer, video, and audio equipment as several screens flash television footage, animated images, and computer graphics simultaneously, he would seem far more comfortable on the deck of the *Starship Enterprise* than behind an office desk. Conversations about his illustrious past flit from name to name, anecdote to anecdote, with unnerving eclecticism, moving from Herman's Hermits to recordings of pygmies by Belgian musicologists in a heartbeat. Hanging out with the Beatles or commandeering French youth halls for Magma concerts, traditional jazz concerts by Chris Barber and memories of Jeff Buckley, whose band rehearsed in Gomelsky's building and who sat in the same chair I occupy just a few days before his death...all are discussed with a turbocharged enthusiasm, all considered part of the same global mosaic of significant twentieth-century music.

Now sixty-five and a repository of more than four decades' worth of musical memories, Gomelsky has changed little in some respects from the man who did more than any other nonmusician to get the British blues movement off the ground in the early 1960s. He is still a fountain of ideas and schemes, some up and running and some at the notion stage. Projects that, one would think, would require the time and energy of several men to execute. Organizing users of the Amiga computer to create their own platform. Starting a netcasting station. Filming material for his public access TV show. Creating a floating ensemble of New York jazz and experimental musicians for live netcasts. Having a lottery for artists that would enable them to afford to live in New York City. Trying to decide whether to write his autobiography. But he's glad to set aside an afternoon—it winds up being two afternoons, actually, after he gets going—to talk about his career. Throughout those years—even as far back as the early 1960s—he attempted, with varying degrees of success, to innovate business, promotional, and creative strategies that would still be considered futuristic in the fall of 1999, the time of our interview.

Gomelsky was, to say the least, an unlikely agent for revolutionizing the British pop scene. Raised on the European Continent, he developed a love of American jazz and indeed all music and art that was rejected by the mainstream. His sympathies lay with the subversive, fueling a desire to champion the underdog that persists to this day. It was his love of jazz that brought him to England in January of 1955, fluent in French, German, and Italian, but not in English. He "had convinced someone to give me money to make a jazz documentary. It was a lot of money at the time—four hundred pounds. I had to go somewhere where jazz was being played."

The question is, how did this aspiring documentary filmmaker with a thick foreign accent, arriving in Britain with a bagful of leftist and Marxist books, become one of the U.K.'s leading rock impresarios within eight years? It must be borne in mind that the British trad jazz of Chris Barber, Kenny Ball, and Acker Bilk—which sounds staid and corny to so many listeners born after 1950—was, in its day, something of a subversive movement. British pop was innocuous and tame in the extreme, and trad jazz did represent an attempt to capture, at a continent and several decades' remove, a sense of authenticity in its replication of New Orleans jazz and Dixieland from the early 1900s. It was also the trad jazz players—Barber foremost among them—who introduced skiffle music to a mass audience, and then blues music, both by bringing over American blues singers to tour the U.K., and by devoting part of their sets to blues music, as played by emerging British bluesmen like Alexis Korner and Cyril Davies. Barber, Korner, Davies, and others were beginning to foster a British blues movement that, once younger players and more electric instruments got involved, would spearhead a full-on explosion of British blues, R&B, and finally rock music.

Gomelsky was heavily involved in the British jazz scene as a fan and filmmaker, and especially interested in making movies featuring live jazz. This had rarely been done prior to 1960, particularly in Europe. At the same time, by the early 1960s, he could sense change in the air. "The traditional jazz thing was kind of dying. It was overexposed, overcommercialized, milked to death. And I saw this as a big opportunity to start a new scene. As far as I was concerned, it was definitely going to be blues.

"Also, the audience for traditional jazz was older. After that, skiffle was for a while young people's music. But, like trad, it was limited thematically and milked to death, and then they got fed up with it too. So we needed a new audience. Alexis [Korner] and Cyril [Davies] had a very dedicated blues connoisseur-type following. That was fine. But I felt that we needed young people to play this music, in order for it to get to young people and *their* need to identify with a musical style. The Stones became the breakthrough."

Blues was starting to take away some of the action from jazz in London's still-sleepy live scene, at central London venues such as the Marquee and the 100 Club, in the face of much resistance from both jazz musicians and club owners. Gomelsky was convinced of the potential of blues, and "to prove my point, I would find me a place as far away from the Marquee as possible, so I would not be accused of taking advantage of their audience. I found a pub, the Station Hotel, which, like most London pubs, had a room for dancing in the back. Some young jazz guys, the Rustics, were running a venue there on Friday nights. They introduced me to the publican and I asked, 'Any time available?' He said, 'Oh yeah, Sunday nights aren't doing too well, so I'm prepared to take a chance on you if you can fork out a pound rent.' Of course I had to print some 200 flyers and put an ad in the *Melody Maker*, a total of about five pounds (or some $25) which I didn't have. So I had to borrow the money from a friend, Ronan O'Rahilly, later founder of Radio Caroline, the famed U.K. pirate radio station. So, on what is perhaps the worst evening of the week, we started this rhythm and blues club."

Originally called BRRB (British R&B), this was soon named the Crawdaddy Club, in the Station Hotel, in the western part of town known as Richmond, well away from the center of nightlife in London's West End. At first the gig belonged to Dave Hunt, a traditional jazz player trying to make the leap to R&B (Ray Davies was his lead guitar player at one point, before joining the Kinks). When they didn't show up one day, Gomelsky remembered a young musician he'd recently met. "A guy came up to me and said, [here he adopts a lisp] 'I've got the betht blueth band in the land, you must come and listen.' 'What's your name?' It was Brian Jones, bending my ear about giving this band a gig. Which I did." Jones' band, the Rolling Stones, would take over as the Crawdaddy's resident act, probably playing their first show there in February 1963. They earned a grand total of four shillings (about a buck) each for their debut performance.

"The first time the Stones played, only three people showed. They didn't have a following. Brian Jones was saying, 'There's six of us on stage. There's only three of them. Do you think this is worth playing?' I said to him, 'Brian, how many people do you think we can fit in this place? A hundred? Just play as if there were a hundred people here.' And it was one of the best shows the Stones did, very genuine. That's why I rarely go to see them in the stadiums, because I saw them sweating it out face-to-face.

"The three guys that came that night, I said, 'Did you like the music?' 'Oh yes, the blues, that's our music all right.' So I told them that if they knew two people each they could bring next time, they would get in free. So the week after, nine showed up, six paid. We did the same thing with them. And twenty-seven people, and the same thing again. So in six weeks to eight weeks, we had 300 people in the joint. Word of mouth."

The timing was right for one of those rare explosions—also happening several hours' drive to the north in Liverpool, where the Beatles had built a rabid following at the Cavern Club—that irreversibly changes the pop and rock world within months. The Crawdaddy was not just where the Rolling Stones built their following; it was also one of the key venues igniting the British Invasion, and the rock counter-culture in general. "After quite a few weeks, we had all this crowd in there…it even got to the point where girls were only allowed to come in if their boyfriends carried them on their shoulders." There was little reference point in Britain for the Stones' raw R&B, still exclusively devoted to covers of songs by greats like Chuck Berry, Bo Diddley, Muddy Waters, and Jimmy Reed. And there was no room for conventional partner dancing in the Crawdaddy's cramped confines.

"Nobody knew how to react. At the end of the evening, there'd be some very ferocious Bo Diddley covers going on, and people were standing there like dummies, not knowing how to express themselves. My good friend Hamish Grimes, a photographer, had an adventurous sense of fun. So I said to him, 'Hamish, get up on a table and start waving your arms around, we've got to do something.' He got up on a table, started waving. So all the guys and the girls [here Gomelsky pauses to mimic their waving arms] started swaying back and forth because that was the only thing they could do, wave their arms!" he laughs. "Little by little, they'd add all kinds of stuff, holding on to these [overhanging] steel bars and shaking their bodies. If you dropped, somebody'd pick you up before you hit the floor. It became totally ritualistic, particularly in the second half of the show."

As the spring of 1963 approached, the Rolling Stones were still without a record deal, and Gomelsky took advantage of his multimedia background to devise a vehicle for press attention. "I couldn't get any of the journalists to come and see the Stones. I had to finally convince them that I was doing something important by making this film of this unknown band. So finally, Peter Jones [of the *Record Mirror*] came down. That was the whole beginning." The film, intended as a short subject, was unfortunately never finished, although shots of dancing at the Crawdaddy were done, including glimpses of early girlfriends of Brian Jones (Linda Lawrence) and Mick Jagger (Chrissie Shrimpton). The Stones recorded a couple of songs for the soundtrack, Bo Diddley's "Pretty Thing" and Jimmy Reed's "Baby What's Wrong" [not "It's Alright Babe," as has been previously reported, says Gomelsky]. The thought of live footage of the Stones in early 1963 is enticing, but mythical; Gomelsky admits that "we didn't have the equipment to record live. We knew how to do it, but we didn't have the money to install [live recording equipment]. So I went to the studio and recorded two songs with the Stones, to shoot to playback." And Gomelsky does not know where those songs and footage are today, if they still exist. "Be worth something now!"

As an ironic consequence of Gomelsky's film project, however, his influence over the career of the Rolling Stones would diminish. Peter Jones, according to Roy Carr's *The Rolling Stones: An Illustrated Record*, told aspiring young pop manager Andrew Oldham that Norman Jopling was going to give the Stones an enthusiastic notice in *Record Mirror*. Oldham, at the end of April 1963, saw the Stones at the Crawdaddy. Almost immediately, while Gomelsky was in Switzerland burying his father, Oldham signed them to a management contract (along with partner Eric Easton). Some members of the Stones, and Giorgio himself, have made it clear that Gomelsky was never considered the official or unofficial manager of the Rolling Stones. However, their decision to sign with Oldham spelled the end of some ambitious endeavors that Gomelsky had in mind for the band.

"I had no presumption, assumption, or desire to have a career in the music business," proclaims Gomelsky now. "I had no idea about that side. I had no intention to become a magnate. I was a filmmaker. I had my vocation, my calling. I just wanted to prove a point. I was passionately interested in change, and change was needed.

"There was a commercial jazz scene. I didn't want the blues people to fall into that. My idea, at the time, was to form a sort of collective; to have the bands, the artists, get together and run their own agency, promotion, and publishing company. 'Rhythm & Blues Associates' was to be the umbrella organization. Independent recording studios started at about that time, and independent production became possible. Before that, unless you were signed to a label, you couldn't get into a professional studio, because all of them were actually owned by the labels. I knew that art and money were very uneasy bedfellows, so my big dream was that"—Gomelsky pauses and dives into the heart of the matter—"it's easier for an artist to become his own businessman than for a businessman to become an artist. A very simple axiom. Guess it's close to the idea of the cooperative or guild. It goes back quite a few years and makes a lot of sense. It would certainly offer more equality and equity. Out-and-out capitalism does not lead to equality.

"I said, 'Let's form our own entity.' With the Yardbirds, for instance, I formed Yardbirds Ltd., which was a fully fledged limited company. Since some of them were underage I asked some of their parents to be on the board of directors and oversee the transactions. I had wanted to do this for the Stones, but Brian Jones did not understand the concept at all and was too keen to be taken care of. My idea was for the artists to build their work into a patrimony, so that when the big time came, it would be protected and no one could take it from them.

"But it was too early. Brian Jones—he wanted to have this made-to-measure suit, which was fashionable at the time. Did not want to wait for the rewards; he wanted it all there and then. Fundamentally, Brian sold me down the drain, for a made-to-measure suit," he opines, referring to the Stones' decision to sign with Oldham (at this point Jones was pretty much the leader of the group, wielding considerably more power than he would in later years) and pursue a much more conventional course to widespread popularity. For the most part, it was a very successful one; within two weeks, the Rolling Stones were recording their debut single for Decca Records, and within a couple of years or so, they were the biggest band in the world except for the Beatles.

Still, believes Gomelsky, "If an *artist* owns his own corporation even in strict business terms, he's a lot more powerful and can negotiate from strength. David Bowie has even gone 'public' now! In later years, the Stones got into all kinds of money trouble. I remember one time in a nightclub, Andrew Oldham saying to me, 'Giorgio, we really hit the jackpot now. We've just done this great deal with an American business manager.' I had no faith whatsoever in American business managers and said, 'Andy, I wish you all the best, but it's not going to go like that. Ten years from now, you'll see what a mess you've signed yourself into.'" Gomelsky was correct; that American businessman was Allen Klein, whose handling of various affairs on behalf of the group eventually led to considerable strife between him and the Stones. (Still later, Klein's involvement in the management of the Beatles would play a strong role in that group's breakup.)

Although he remains diffident about his role in the early Stones' career, Gomelsky is careful to claim his due credit. "Some people say it would have happened anyway, but other people say, 'Perhaps, but where, how, and when, and who made it happen?' Keith Richards, every time he sees me, introduces me to people: 'This is our first manager, couldn't have made it without him.' You ask Mick Jagger, and that's probably not his view. But the fact is that I was there, and nobody else was there. As regards to Oldham's contribution, the Stones' image was all set up before he came on the scene. It was pretty obvious they couldn't compete with the Beatles' charm, wit, and experience with audiences; they had to become the antithesis to the 'cuddly' Liverpudlians. He just took it to the mass media. If I'd been there, it would have unfurled in much the same way, except they wouldn't have needed to piss on a gas station to attract publicity." (Three of the Stones did use gas station grounds for this purpose in 1965, and much publicity did result, whether that was the goal of the action or not.)

As the Stones began to tour and drift out of the Crawdaddy orbit, Gomelsky did not withdraw from the pop fray, but actually intensified his promotion of the blues movement. The Crawdaddy Club "ended up with like 15,000 members. It ran for like five, six years. We had Crawdaddys all over London and were able to give serious work to bands. In a way, it was self-run. Members also worked the door, did the sound and the lights, posted the flyers. Many of them got careers as roadies, sound engineers, tour managers. It was kind of like a community-run sort of situation." Gomelsky expanded his activities beyond Richmond and the Crawdaddy, helping the Animals get a foothold in London by doing a sort of trade whereby the Animals would play in London on the Crawdaddy circuit and his new protégés, the Yardbirds, would play the clubs frequented by the Animals in Newcastle, the Animals' hometown, during that same time. He organized the first blues festival in the U.K. in Birmingham in February 1964, featuring both British newcomers (like the Yardbirds, Long John Baldry's Hoochie Coochie Men featuring Rod Stewart, and the Spencer Davis Group) and veteran American original blues great Sonny Boy Williamson.

As a promoter, Gomelsky was instrumental in shoehorning local blues bands into the National Jazz Festival at Richmond, again in the face of resistance by jazz hounds who felt threatened by the new, loud guitar music. In 1963, he convinced Harold Pendleton (owner of the Marquee and founder of the festival) to get some R&B acts into the program. "Kenny Ball and his trad band [who had a big hit in the early '60s with "Midnight in Moscow"] were playing on the main stage, top of the bill. At ten o'clock at night, in the tent set up at the other end of the field to feature 'young bands,' the Stones started playing a Chuck Berry number *loud*." Gomelsky emits a mirthful chuckle. "Now you're live at prime time on a Saturday night on BBC TV, for the first time ever covering the festival, a big feather in the cap for the organizers. And you see people gently nodding their heads looking at the main stage. Then suddenly, from the other side of the field, this loud guitar chord reaches the main stage and gets into the PA and recording mikes. [People were looking around]—'what IS going on?' During a long shot you saw quite a lot of people, probably energized by the Stones, leaving their seats to go and find out. Very embarrassing!"

By 1964, the National Jazz Festival, originally modeled on the famous American jazz festivals in Newport, had become the National Jazz & Blues Festival, and was well on its way to becoming a largely rock festival. Gomelsky's duties sometimes extended into doing whatever was necessary, even at the risk of looking absurd. "We had added a Friday night show dedicated to the 'new' scene, and the Rolling Stones were top of the bill. That day they were also appearing on some BBC radio show uptown and now it was 9:30 and they were late. I feared the audience might start throwing things at the stage, so I jumped up there and I started telling stories. Somebody had thrown a booklet at me, and I picked it up. It was full of dirty limericks. I started reading it, and before long people were [in] convulsions, it was really funny. I was in fact *very* surprised how the audience sort of took to me, despite my thick and even unintelligible accent. I guess most of the audience that night were from the Crawdaddy and knew me. Twenty minutes into the thing, I feel somebody patting my back, and I turn around. It's Mick Jagger. They had set up, all ready to go. But nobody had noticed them coming in. I must have really gripped them with these dirty limericks."

In a more serious vein, Gomelsky stresses how vital it was to promote groups like the Stones, and venues like the Crawdaddy and the Jazz & Blues Festival at Richmond, in view of the stale and silly British pop scene it was counteracting. Popular music in England, he notes, prior to the emergence of the Beatles, "was a total disaster. It was an imitation of an imitation of Elvis Presley and Brenda Lee. Pop music was in fact in the hands of the wrestling people."

"The wrestling people?" I ask incredulously.

"Yeah, the people that organized wrestling matches. They were promoting the pop thing. What did they have to do with music? Nothing, but they had a hold over the venues, the halls." Gomelsky's efforts in directing the National Jazz Festival to a more contemporary sensibility, incidentally, had repercussions far beyond the 1960s; the Richmond festival, forced out of Richmond after 1965 by community complaints, continued to thrive at other locations and is still thriving as the Reading Festival, one of the most popular rock and pop festivals in the world.

"My mission," Gomelsky elaborates about those days when jazz was making way for blues and rock, "was to innovate, to push envelopes, to get a new thing established, to allow the underdog, the underground, to come forward and up. To have the kind of influence that would leave those seeds. Put it this way: I was determined to make that scene work. And I was the one pushing it more than anybody. Nobody else was pushing it as hard as I was, '61, '62, '63."

Gomelsky was also among the very few people in England with any sense that history was being made by the emerging rock and R&B bands, and should be preserved. His appetite fired by an on-the-spot decision to tape the Animals and Sonny Boy Williamson at the Club-A-Go-Go in Newcastle at the end of 1963, he recorded numerous live shows and demos throughout the 1960s. Several of these were released in the 1970s, and were the source of some of the earliest recordings, live or studio, by the Animals, the Spencer Davis Group, and the Yardbirds. These also included some of the earliest available performances of then-obscure musicians that went on to fame in other contexts, including Jack Bruce and Ginger Baker of Cream (as members of the Graham Bond Organisation) and Rod Stewart, Brian Auger, Long John Baldry, and Julie Driscoll (as the Steampacket). There were also valuable studio tapes of important cult musicians such the Soft Machine and folk-blues-raga guitarist Davy Graham. Albums from the Gomelsky tape archive, issued and reissued (by pirate or unauthorized labels, he says) too many times to count, are erratic in both fidelity and performance, though occasionally brilliant. Yet they are of undeniable historical importance, especially considering that some of these acts (the original Soft Machine with Daevid Allen on guitar, the Steampacket) barely or never recorded otherwise.

"My motivation was sheer enthusiasm about catching this sort of moment," says Gomelsky. "I've been accused a lot of having recorded people in a sneaky sort of way, and then released this stuff. I swear to god, I've never done it. I mean, I never recorded anybody without their consent. Most of these recordings happened on the spur of the moment, and the bands were glad to participate and hear themselves. It was sheer enthusiasm. Like Graham Bond at Klook's Kleek [club], which was next door to the Decca studio. I knew an engineer there, and I said, 'Listen, why don't we run a cable into Klook's Kleek?' Which we did, without permission from Decca of course! It was a cable that ran from the window of Decca's control room into Klook's Kleek."

And Gomelsky, despite the somewhat sour aftermath of his association with the Rolling Stones, was still nurturing bands in a hands-on manner. "Once the bands that were playing in the Crawdaddy on a residential basis were safe in their audience, I'd introduce the next band as a supporting act. Once I had the Muleskinners [whose keyboardist, Ian McLagan, went on to the Small Faces]. We had a whole bunch of them. It was like, grow bigger and stronger." The most famous of those resident Crawdaddy bands was the Yardbirds, who began playing the venue in 1963, the same year Gomelsky began managing them. They would do a great deal to pull Gomelsky—and to some degree, British music as a whole—away from blues, and into eclectic pop, rock, and psychedelia.

Although the Yardbirds began as an R&B band that covered songs by many of the same icons—Bo Diddley, Chuck Berry, etc.—as the Rolling Stones did, there was a crucial difference. "The Yardbirds were chosen because they had one thing that the Stones didn't have," explains Gomelsky. "They had the concept of altering the material. I went up the stairs where they were rehearsing, and I said, 'That's the band.' They were doing the rave-ups, speeding up. [Gomelsky mimics their trademark accelerating and decelerating rhythms.] I said, this is good for me, because I like the idea of pushing the envelope further. And I saw how rhythm and blues could then be connected with jazz, which connected with ethnic music. Little by little, I wanted to get to the point we are at now, planetary popular music"—as an aside, he adds, "we're not really at now yet—where you had a sort of living and ongoing synthesis of world music, that would reflect all the cultural riches of this planet.

"With the Yardbirds, I felt, this could be possible to go that way. The Stones couldn't; they were very set in their own format. The area of solos, improvisation—nobody in the Stones would have tried. Brian [Jones] had a great gift for instruments; he would pick up an instrument and two hours later, he would sort of make it work. But he was lazy, he did not practice, he was not a virtuoso in any way. So with the Yardbirds, there was a possibility of expanding form. You had to start somewhere, and blues was just a good place to start. It's a great form of music that allows you, with little technical knowledge, a little effort, to actually compose. Everything else had started there. Jazz, for instance."

The Yardbirds, as mentioned previously, entered into an agreement with Gomelsky as a limited company; Giorgio, mindful of the way things had turned out with the Stones, had contracts this time, and a share. When it came time to record, he and the Yardbirds opted to do so in a way that was uncommon in Britain at the time. Rather than recording under the supervision of a staff of a big label such as Decca or EMI, their tracks would be cut as independent productions, and then leased to a large label (the U.K. Columbia branch of EMI, as it turned out), with ownership of the tapes reverting back to the band after a few years. This gave the group—or producers, such as two U.K.-based ones of the time, Joe Meek and Shel Talmy, that frequently operated in this fashion—more creative freedom than they probably would have had otherwise. It also enabled Gomelsky himself to become a record producer, fulfilling that duty on all of the Yardbirds' releases through early 1966. "I became a record producer for lack of record producers!" he declares, not unhappily.

One of Gomelsky's first inspired brainwaves in this capacity was to make the Yardbirds' first album live—an uncommon practice for a group's debut release, both in the mid-1960s and now. Gomelsky always had a passion for recording musicians live, dating from his quest to capture jazz musicians in concert for his film documentary. Having already recorded the Animals live in Newcastle with engineer Philip Wood, "I convinced him to install himself in the back room of the Marquee, so he could do live recordings. The Yardbirds was like a demonstration of the possibility of doing this. Because I heard so much good music that was gone, evanescent. So I said, why not record it?" *Five Live Yardbirds*, recorded in March 1964 with Eric Clapton as lead guitarist, is the only quality document of a major British Invasion band playing in a club in front of its fans. It also allows us to hear them developing their trademark "rave-up" improvisations, particularly on Howlin' Wolf's "Smokestack Lightning" and Bo Diddley's "Here 'Tis."

Yet Gomelsky also realized that "playing live on stage is one thing, and being in the studio is another. You have to translate to a space-time-reality measure, or it's just not the same. We had to work at this." Gomelsky is credited as producer on all records done by the Yardbirds through their early 1966 "Shapes of Things" single, and Yardbirds bassist Paul Samwell-Smith is often credited as musical director. Some critics have theorized that Samwell-Smith, as an accomplished musician and later a successful producer of acts such as Cat Stevens and Carly Simon, took a greater role in the proceedings than Gomelsky did. Without denying Samwell-Smith's contribution, Gomelsky is quick to claim some innovations as his own, as the Yardbirds went from R&B to experimental pop and psychedelia that incorporated harpsichords (on "For Your Love"), sitar-like fuzz guitar ("Heart Full of Soul"), Gregorian chants ("Still I'm Sad," one of whose chanting voices belongs to Gomelsky himself), feedback (stumbled upon, according to Giorgio, by accident in the studio), social commentary ("Shapes of Things"), and manic tempo changes and hypnotic, haunting melodies throughout. "Direction is important, somehow or other. Oftentimes, musicians are so involved in their own thing, they can't see in front of their noses.

"I had ideas," continues Gomelsky. "The harpsichord [on "For Your Love"], for instance. The sitar [on "Heart Full of Soul," discarded in favor of Jeff Beck's sitar-like fuzz lines] was my idea." (Speaking to Harold Bronson in 1982 for the Rhino interview LP *Afternoon Tea*, Yardbirds drummer Jim McCarty remembered the harpsichord as being Samwell-Smith's idea, but Gomelsky offers that Samwell-Smith "is unlikely to have ever heard or seen such an instrument. I was a Wanda Landowska fan [Landowska was possibly the most renowned harpsichordist of the twentieth century], a friend of mine was a harpsichord restorer in Paris.") Gomelsky was conscious of the needs to both have hit singles *and* be creative—a difficult tightrope walk from the time musicians began making records. "We had to have singles, because singles was the way to carry the band forward onto the next step. The dilemma was how to take advantage of the situation that would allow us to get to a bigger audience. We had to do something that's going to be played by the radio." When Gomelsky heard a demo by a young Manchester songwriter, Graham Gouldman, "I resisted it. [I thought], 'We could use a harpsichord, it would be a commercial record, but it would have some innovation.' Which was in fact the approach that we used in the Yardbirds. So it's cross-pollination, cross-fertilization."

The record was "For Your Love," a big hit on both sides of the Atlantic. Gouldman would write two more smashes for the Yardbirds, "Heart Full of Soul" and "Evil Hearted You," which exhibited a similar mastery of unpredictable minor melodies and tempo variations, particularly in the context of 1965 commercial rock. Gomelsky and Samwell-Smith would also be involved in the production of a little-known single by one of Gouldman's early bands, the Mockingbirds, "You Stole My Love," which had a moody-yet-melodic feel, and abrupt tempo and chord changes as the verse yielded to the bridge, similar to those heard on Gouldman's Yardbirds-penned hits. "He had this Middle Eastern-Manchester, kind of a weird, very interesting synthesis. His father was a cantor. He spent a lot of time in synagogues. That's where he had this kind of Eastern [influence]. I always encouraged Graham to have a band."

It's often been reported that Eric Clapton found "For Your Love" too commercial for his blues sensibilities and left the Yardbirds in protest, but in Gomelsky's view, "Eric wanted out before that. Eric was bored by the whole thing. But the fact there was no part for him [on the single] to play..." In any case, his replacement, Jeff Beck, was more than up for the Yardbirds' adventurous approach. "Jeff was much more of a daredevil, much more of a wild man. If Eric had stayed on, he would have worked in that kind of stuff. But he never did, really. Perhaps that was not really his sensibility. When Jeff came, we pushed him—*I* pushed him—like *hell*, to the limits. He was very willing to experiment. He was quite brilliant."

As an example, Gomelsky remembers how the guitar intro on "Heart Full of Soul" was originally played on sitar by Indian session musicians. "When we were using the sitars, the problem we had was the Indian musicians could not count bars like we do. And you're doing this semi-live on a four-track machine. I was trying to tell them when to stop, and they couldn't stop. Jeff was there listening to all these things. He went to the bathroom and started working. An hour later he came back and says, 'Giorgio, come listen.' I went to the bathroom, and he played me this sitar sound, through a fuzzbox. So I said, 'OK, you do it.' It was Jeff doing the sitar [effect]. In just an hour, he got it. Brilliant!

"Using sitars—nobody knew what a sitar was. In fact, Jimmy Page came to the recording session and saw this sitar. He was still a session man, and his mouth was like…he actually went up, bought the sitar we were using on 'Heart Full of Soul' for fifty pounds off the Indian guy. He walked home with a little piece of carpet around this thing. The next day he had it at a session with [fellow British session guitarist] Big Jim Sullivan, and shortly after, somehow, the news got to George Harrison."

Some of Gomelsky's promotional brainstorms struck members of the Yardbirds as gimmicky. In 1977, drummer Jim McCarty told Chris Welch (for the liner notes of Charly's *Shapes of Things* compilation), "The psychedelic things we did were Giorgio's ideas. He even had ideas for light shows, but he couldn't always put his ideas into practice. We used to think a lot of his ideas were quite funny. I think he wanted us to be like the Monkees!"

"That is totally absurd," Gomelsky comments. "I had no respect for stuff like that." However, he did have a memorable idea for stirring up publicity that the Monkees probably wouldn't have dared to execute, unless it was on one of their TV shows. "In the mid-'60s the entire question of youth having its own culture exploded. Ted Willis, a Socialist then Home Secretary, had given interviews where he strongly excoriated the new generation. I thought that his views were lopsided and needed confronting. So we thought up a surefire plan to express our side of the question. One calm, news-dead Sunday afternoon, the Yardbirds took their gear and thirty followers to more-or-less the U.K. equivalent of suburbia, where Ted Willis lived in pastoral surrounds. On the strike of four, traditional tea time, they set up their gear opposite Willis' house and started playing the loudest stuff they knew! Of course, Willis had to come out, open his gate, and talk to us. Matter of fact, we had a good conversation and came to reconcile our views. We had alerted the sympathetic faction of the press, so the next day this incident was all over the front pages, including big pictures. The Yardbirds and the 'scene' got a good dose of confidence. They had to let us pursue our interests, at least for a while, until the drug busts started."

On the sleeve notes of the bootleg *More Golden Eggs*, Yardbirds singer Keith Relf remembered, "We had this mad manager, you know, who was very European in his attitude to music. He thought he'd get the group to be the first R&B group to ever play at the San Remo Song Festival, which is a very straight thing, like tiaras and a sort of black tie thing. So he…oh, fuck it all…got me to sing this song…. This is why we got rid of that manager. It's because he pushed us into playing such…." Not only did Gomelsky send them to Italy's San Remo Song Festival, he also had them sing "Paff … Bum" and "Questa Volta" at the event (also recorded on a single for the Italian market)—bouncy and sentimental pop tunes (the latter actually sung in Italian) far from the styles the Yardbirds favored.

Counters Gomelsky, "I spoke Italian, I spoke French. I was trying to get my revenge on the English xenophobia. So with the Yardbirds, I had the idea of having them go to different countries, and whenever the occasion arose, to do something to show the country that they can come to them cap in hand, so to speak. Humble." He had done this in the United States by cajoling Sam Phillips, founder of Sun Records, into recording the Yardbirds at Sun in Memphis, resulting in one of their greatest tracks, the proto-psychedelic "Mr. You're a Better Man Than I." As for the tunes performed by the band in Italy, "There was as yet no 'rock' in Italy, so that was a way of sparking it off. The songs were written by two guys who later became the most influential new artists in Italy, Lucio Battisti and Lucio Dalla, who totally transformed

Italian pop. They remember the Yardbirds at San Remo as a big breakthrough for themselves and rock in Italy.

"The Yardbirds," Gomelsky points out, "sold more records in Italy than any English group, including the Beatles, for a number of years. They were the first English band that went toward *them*. People remembered that we had done this for them." He emphasizes that the Italian adventure "is not the reason we parted company. Actually, before he died I had met Keith in London, who in retrospect practically apologized for not having understood what was in fact going on at that time, and put it down to being a very snotty and green twenty-two-year-old."

The Yardbirds fired Gomelsky in early 1966, a move instigated, Giorgio believes, by Samwell-Smith, under pressure from his wife-to-be, who wanted Samwell-Smith to be home more often; Gomelsky also thinks she thought the band would do better with a friend of hers, Simon Napier-Bell. (Ironically, Samwell-Smith quit the Yardbirds altogether just a few months later.) The Yardbirds continued for a couple more years, under different managers, before disbanding in 1968 (Beck having left in late 1966, his spot taken by Jimmy Page, who originally came on as bassist and moved into a dual lead guitar role with Beck before taking over as sole lead guitarist). Had Gomelsky's association with the band not been terminated, he believes, "They would still be going now. They certainly would have done things with…not symphony orchestras, necessarily, but other ensembles. They would probably be doing techno stuff now, of some kind."

"The Yardbirds?" I ask, surprised.

"Oh yeah! With chants and stuff, and a Bulgarian women choir…I mean, there was like, every possibility, to go anywhere at all. 'Still I'm Sad' was modeled on a Gregorian chant; remember, recently some Spanish monks had a hit record doing Gregorian chants?" Indeed you can hear some strange chants and Middle Eastern influences on the album the Yardbirds recorded, *The Yardbirds* (also called *Roger the Engineer*), shortly after Gomelsky's exit. According to Giorgio, "I had started that album. I was keen to experiment with modal stuff—John Coltrane had initiated that—so I started playing the Yardbirds Middle Eastern, polyrhythmic shit. The conception and organization of the material on the album, I did with them. We did the rhythm tracks, the backing tracks, and then we stopped. When we split, those tapes came to me. So they had to rerecord them, which is what they did. It was the same studio, the same engineer, so they didn't have much of a problem doing it. They had quick, provisional mixes tapes, so it wasn't a big deal for them to pick up without me being there." The existence of alternate versions of several songs from the album on Gomelsky-produced tracks that surfaced on compilations after the Yardbirds disbanded bears out this contention.

"There had always been a connection to the blues, obviously," summarizes Gomelsky as to voyages upon which he and the group might have embarked. "But they would have been, perhaps, extending into other areas. The fact that the Yardbirds were a band capable of improvising, and capable of arranging different structures for their songs, indicated quite clearly that you could go toward more compositional zones, more compositional fields. In which case, it could bring in all kinds of stuff. I was into musique concrete, I was into Stockhausen, I was into all this Stravinsky of course, and all of that dissonant stuff. And I thought that we would have, sooner or later, gotten to that. And bands did. Look at Sonic Youth. Sonic Youth is a band that came not far from…they were a sort of New York blues band to begin with."

While the Yardbirds took up much of Gomelsky's time and creative focus in the mid-1960s, he did manage and produce other bands, such as Gary Farr & the T-Bones, a far more journeyman British R&B act. Another of his protégés, the Steampacket, was a supergroup before its time, including singers Rod Stewart, Long John Baldry, and Julie Driscoll, as well as keyboard whiz Brian Auger (who had played the harpsichord on the Yardbirds' "For Your Love"). All four of these musicians would have big British hits within two or three years, but were fairly unknown when they came together as the short-lived Steampacket. "The Steampacket was my idea of trying to get unemployed people to work together. Long John Baldry had no job left; he went through a bad personal spell and got kicked out of every band. Rod Stewart [was] hanging in by the skin of his teeth. And there was Brian and Julie, doing their thing. I said, 'Why don't we [put] all of you together and do a show. Like a soul revue. I mean, none of you are cutting records. None of you are ready for the prime time. In the meantime, we can have a lot of fun.' I rehearsed them, I had them do gestures, walk on. Brian's major skill defined it—he was a steamy improviser, he steamed when he played. So I called it the Steampacket, without knowing that was a word describing a Mississippi steamer."

Gomelsky "sent them off to St. Tropez for a couple of months in the summer, when I considered that a band in order to really improve needed to play a lot and give me a break [from] their problems. I would send them [to] a friend of mine [who] had the number one nightclub in St. Tropez. During their stay there, they would play every night and rehearse most afternoons, and go to the beach and eat great food. They would come back two months later, man, they would be a real band and look like a million bucks. If a band plays every night, you get *good* after a couple of months. You get tight as a mosquito's ass, as Sonny Boy [Williamson] used to call [it]. That's what happened with the Steampacket. When they came back, they were an amazing live band. They stole the show everywhere. You can imagine. Three great singers, great rhythm section." The Steampacket chugged to a halt shortly after its birth, its progress impeded by business complications (although Gomelsky managed Driscoll and Auger, Stewart and Baldry were under different managment). Nor did the band make any proper studio recordings, although some Gomelsky-produced demo tracks were eventually issued, done live with few overdubs, that do not capture the group at its best.

Gomelsky may have gotten his footing as an R&B champion, but he was not a purist, and his general yen for mixing media and mixing with the cream of British musical talent led him into some high-rolling company. You couldn't get any higher than the Beatles in the 1960s, and Gomelsky got into their circle early on, showing them around the town during their first London visits in early 1963, and arranging for them to see and meet the Rolling Stones at a Crawdaddy show that April. According to Gomelsky, after getting to know the Beatles, "I had the idea of doing this kind of strange documentary, sort of a 'how did you meet,' and a shot of each one of them coming down one road and banging into each other at the intersection. I was working with a writer called Peter Clayton, who ended up being a columnist for the *Sunday Telegraph*. He was this very funny man. So he and me started writing the script, and I remember the Beatles coming to my house on a number of occasions.

"Rohan O'Rahilly [manager of Graham Bond, who also helped the Animals get a foothold in London and founded the pirate station Radio Caroline] was going to produce it. I was going to direct it. Peter and me were going to write it. We had, like, a budget of £10,000, which was about $30,000 or something. It was going to be a B-feature, but, be a really funny, totally different type of thing, much based on the *Goon Show* sort of humor of the absurd: later, Monty Python. Well, in the end, they got too big too fast, and [Beatles manager Brian] Epstein decided that he had offers for four films, for this, that, the other. So they took a writer from Liverpool [Alun Owen], who had a successful play running at the time." The Beatles' first film would be *A Hard Day's Night*, directed by Richard Lester.

"A lot of the ideas were ours," claims Gomelsky. "Brian Epstein, a couple of years later, realized that he done a little bit of something strange. He wrote me a letter—I wish I had that letter—where he apologized for having done this, for having shown them our treatment. Because that obviously gave them the angle. The kind of musical [film] things that were made before then were a joke! You know, the school wanting to put on a dance, that kind of stuff. If that treatment hadn't been there, I think it would have ended up like that, because nobody had thought of connecting that kind of abstract, absurd humor with the music."

Gomelsky surmises that as compensation, the Yardbirds got to play on the same bill as the Beatles for several weeks running at their 1964 Christmas show in London, as well as open for them in Paris in June 1965. "For music lovers there, we kind of stole the show, because the Yardbirds played, like, amazing. We were totally unknown in France. Normally, these shows, the people would not even listen to an opening act; they'd go, 'BEA-TLES, BEA-TLES!' They did that, but after five minutes, they shut up. [The Yardbirds] did a pretty good version of 'Smokestack Lightning,' explosions going on—not physical explosions, musical explosions. And we won the audience over."

Not that Gomelsky bore serious grudges against the Beatles; he fondly recalls how during the Christmas shows, Paul McCartney tested a new composition called "Scrambled Eggs," which would evolve into "Yesterday." "Scrambled eggs...I don't want no more scrambled eggs," Gomelsky sings. "He was living with Jane Asher at the time, and she couldn't cook. All she could cook was scrambled eggs. And he had enough scrambled eggs!"

All this schmoozing with the rock elite stood Gomelsky in good stead when he began working for the public relations company Paragon, which did publicity on behalf of Polydor, Track, and Atlantic Records, among others. During the several years Gomelsky worked there in the late '60s, he says, Polydor's share of the U.K. record-buying market rose from about 1 percent to 15 percent. "We nicked the Who from Decca, we set up [hugely successful manager and record executive] Robert Stigwood. Unfortunately he had no taste, and no idea as to what was going on in music. We'd given him the Cream on a platter practically and Polydor gave him the Bee Gees." Gomelsky also remembers helping set up the Jimi Hendrix Experience's first European tour by helping him get a slot in France as support to French pop star Johnny Hallyday.

However, his most creative outlet was his label, Marmalade, distributed by Polydor. From about 1967 to 1969 it boasted a remarkably eclectic roster, including Julie

Driscoll, Brian Auger & the Trinity, who had a big British hit with their cover of Bob Dylan's "This Wheel's on Fire"; the Blossom Toes (whom Gomelsky managed and produced), one of the very best obscure British 1960s bands, capable of both charmingly whimsical orchestrated psych-pop and heavy, moody guitar rock; the first solo album by giant fusion guitarist John McLaughlin, *Extrapolation* (produced by Gomelsky); the avant-garde Spontaneous Music Ensemble; modern jazz pianist Keith Tippetts; and, as a nod to his roots, Chris Barber and his wife, singer Ottillie Patterson.

The catholic wingspan of Marmalade's talent was a reflection of Gomelsky's desire for an "ecumenical" label that embraced all forms of quality musical expression. He agrees that Julie Driscoll, Brian Auger & the Trinity's Marmalade albums were the closest embodiment, on recordings, of this outlook. This is particularly true of their second Marmalade album, *Streetnoise*, a mixture of jazz, soul, rock, and some folk, gospel, and improvisation. It was also something of an ensemble effort, as opposed to featuring a relatively set lineup, in which the focus could be either upon Driscoll, Auger, or band instrumentation.

"I wanted to find that which was authentic in each form of music, sort of throw it together somehow, and see what would emerge. Pay tribute to the old guys, and then help the new people. I wanted to have genuine talent, and give them the space to develop. So I would not say to people, first you have to do a single, then another single, and an album. You work on trying to capture your essence into a hooky type of single, and/or you can extend to a wider spectrum. The idea was to do a farming system. I knew that talent had to be developed. You don't, overnight, become an expert at recording, or organizing your material, or doing stage performance. You had to grow into this, you had to sort of acquire the knowledge."

Warming to the topic, he continues, "it was the idea of having a bit of a family," likening the atmosphere he was striving for to that of the famous Stax/Volt label. Using singer-songwriter Graham Gouldman (whose future 10cc band mates, Kevin Godley and Lol Creme, recorded for Marmalade as the oddly named duo Frabjoy & Runcible Spoon) as an example, "the idea of Marmalade was for Graham to produce his friends from Manchester. Up there in Manchester, it would be to start their own studios, to create kind of a network." And, by extension, Gomelsky had visions to make Marmalade "to effect, a *worldwide* network. I had a project going on with Belgian musicologists who had played me tapes once of pygmies in the Belgian Congo. It sounded like John Coltrane. It was unbelievable! So with an engineer, my friend Eddie Offord who worked with me on most of my projects and later became producer of Yes, we were working on a twenty-four-track portable thing that we could take on location. Like the Belgian Congo, Brazil, Siberia. Wherever there was music to be discovered."

Brian Godding of the Blossom Toes remembers how Gomelsky's remarkably wide interests and enthusiasms could work both for and against his clients. Their Gomelsky-produced debut album, *We Are Ever So Clean*, was distinguished by its deft orchestration, perhaps the best expression of Gomelsky's love of composers such as Stravinsky. Yet the band members, not wholly pleased by having many of the parts arranged and played by other musicians, insisted on performing everything on their second album themselves. "He's actually a creative person, which is his strength," Godding told me in 1996. "His weakness was that he didn't know how to handle people, which is common. He had lots of great ideas, lots of enthusiasm, and he could in fact get things together. He had influence, and he was able to communicate with people. But I think he always found it very hard to communicate on a long-term basis with musicians.

"Technically speaking, he probably wasn't a very good manager, but he was an entrepreneur, and he could be very inspirational; a team coach, really. If he was in the mood, he could really inspire you to get on with something, and not just sit around drinking your beer and having a good time. He could actually make you think, go out and do some work, get some stuff together. But other times, he could be very negative, where he could make you feel like you were just wasting your life. I think he found it very, very hard to cope with the business side of things. He had to, but I don't think he enjoyed that side. In my opinion, he probably would have been better off in a band himself, rather than trying to produce them. Except nobody could have taken him for much more than half an hour. Because he wanted to tell everybody what to do," Brian laughs.

Although Arthur Brown was managed by Gomelsky for only a brief time, shortly after the Crazy World of Arthur Brown had split, he hails Gomelsky as "every bit as much a figure as any of the stars. He also is a very cultured person. He put things onto a different level. On our French tour, we had meetings with the heads of the Communist Party. He knew all these great artists; that was his milieu. So his thinking about things was not terribly closeted. It was much more available to true musicianship. *Strangelands*, the first [album] after the Crazy World, where I auditioned people and we just improvised—he wanted to put that out on Marmalade. It would have been nice for him if there were big hits. But as long as he could get the money to get the artists he wanted to have adventurous music, that was satisfying. It wasn't necessary to have hundreds of hits."

Guitarist Daevid Allen worked with Gomelsky on several occasions, first as part of the original Soft Machine in 1967, and then with progressive rockers Gong in the 1970s. "He was an incredible oiler of wheels, Giorgio. Extraordinary social genius, one of the great connectors. He got me involved with doing some kind of loop project with Paul McCartney that never really finished up getting anywhere, but still it was interesting to talk to him about it. He also has ability with money, but he doesn't waste too much time with money. He mostly uses it in a good sense, in the sense of creativity, ideas, inspirations. He always seems to be able to add some kind of extra energy to any idea you've got. But if his vision doesn't come through, he gets impatient with people, because he wants to see that vision, just like I do, like anyone else does who's driven by an idea and determined to see it through.

"He got involved with almost everybody that was going to shake the system. He had a real natural attraction to anyone who was fundamentally revolutionary. What fascinates him is not mainstream stuff. What fascinates him is new ideas." Allen, in fact, credits a Gomelsky production, the Yardbirds' "Still I'm Sad," as the single that made him feel like he could be in a band like the Soft Machine that would play rock music, but not be averse to avant-garde explorations.

"He can see the grand picture, and where the grand picture can go. He's very valuable to everybody in that sense, like some kind of adviser. He's not all that good at getting his hands down and doing it. He needs to find people to do that for him."

Allen laughs heartily. "Giorgio's one of these managers that needs a manager! [To] take care of details."

In addition to commissioning Allen to write a poem called "The Death of Rock," performed in London with keyboardists Zoot Money (in a coffin) and Brian Auger (actually on keyboards) during the Summer of Love, Gomelsky recorded him as part of the Soft Machine in April 1967. The Soft Machine, along with Pink Floyd and Tomorrow, was among the first major underground British psychedelic bands; unlike Pink Floyd and even Tomorrow, the Soft Machine did not get to record much in 1967, its output limited to a solitary single. Had not Gomelsky recorded nine demos with them (issued and reissued under numerous titles since the 1970s, usually as *Jet-Propelled Photograph*), there would be just three tracks available by the band's first incarnation, during which it was at its most melodic and whimsical. These demos—nine of the twelve extant Soft Machine tracks with Allen on guitar (as the Australian left the band later in 1967 after being refused reentry to the U.K.)—are the most important of Gomelsky's live/unreleased 1960s archive recordings, none of which would see the light of day during that decade.

The Soft Machine tapes are a bit rough sound- and performance-wise, but fascinating for their blend of rock, jazz, psychedelia, and absurdist wordplay. They came about, according to Gomelsky, when Henry Henroid, assistant to Animals/Jimi Hendrix manager Mike Jeffery, "came to see me. He says, 'Mike Jeffery is thinking of signing this band. You should hear them, because they're *so* weird. And I know you like weird stuff. They're there for you to do something with if you want to.' So I went to hear them. I loved Robert Wyatt's singing, and I liked them. I was saying to Henry Henroid, 'The best way to do this is to do a demo record of some kind. This is not a band that's a singles, a commercial band. This is the wrong way to go for them.'

"Now I knew that America had FM radio stations. I'd been there a couple of times and knew they played entire sides of albums. I felt this was a great breakthrough—the fact that you could get played without a single on the radio, in America. And hence, everywhere else, because unfortunately, everyone had always copied the Americans. The purpose was to convince whoever held the purse that this is an LP type of band, and they should be encouraged to do this that way. I produced some kind of a single, as well. 'Fred the Fish' [a song that later appeared on a Daevid Allen solo album], or something." In the event, however, the Soft Machine with Daevid Allen never recorded a proper album, with Gomelsky or anyone else; when their first LP came out in 1968, they were a trio, playing more atonal and jazz-influenced music.

Regrets Allen, "The decisions [for the Soft Machine] were usually made by [managers] Mike Jeffery or Chas Chandler, neither of whom really had anything like the same vision or ability to understand what Soft Machine was, that Giorgio had. But at that point, I don't know whether Giorgio really had the right relationship with the other members of the band or not. We were four heavyweight egos, all battling for supremacy. It wasn't an easy band to deal with. That's why it blew up and became four different bands.

"I'm not 100 percent sure that I totally liked what he did in terms of the production of the Soft Machine, because I was dissatisfied with my guitar playing, and I thought a good producer might have wheedled some better guitar playing out of me. Maybe it's just that lack of attention to details. I felt sort of as if I'd been closed down when I was very dissatisfied with what I'd done. The reason I got shut down when I did, they were demos. I think he was real limited by time. Nobody really realized at that time how valuable all this stuff would be in the future."

Would Gomelsky have liked to have done an official LP with the Soft Machine? "If Polydor would have gone for the album, yeah, I would have worked with them." How might that have come out? "I don't know, I lost track. I had so many…I was so busy. At the time, for instance, the MC5 came to London and asked me to help them. I really wanted to work with them, and never got the time." As to why a number of promising Gomelsky-associated artists never yielded many recordings—the Steampacket, the early Soft Machine, Frabjoy & Runcible Spoon—he responds, "You had to go to where things concatenated. One thing followed another. If there was any stoppage on the way, you had to abandon the project. There was ten other things that were going on. I was just one person."

Gomelsky has a story to illustrate his point at every turn, and this one concerns yet another talented group that didn't get to the finish line, Deep Feeling, with singer Gordon Jackson, Jim Capaldi (later of Traffic), Poli Palmer (later of the Blossom Toes and Family), and Luther Grosvenor (later of Spooky Tooth). "This is the band I spent eight months doing a major production bit on. We recorded like ten, twelve tunes. We never finished, because Dave Mason kidnapped Capaldi for Traffic. They took all the ideas from the Deep Feeling demos, because that's where we had African percussion, vibraphone, a sort of flowing, waving rhythm. For instance, we put a vibraphone in the stairwell and miked it on the last floor; it gave it a very languid, atmospheric sound."

Gomelsky does not recall every obscure, unjustly overlooked group he produced with delight. In the late 1960s the intriguing Danish psychedelic-progressive rock band Savage Rose was brought to London for sessions with Gomelsky by Polydor. Only one little-known single resulted from the collaboration. "In the studio, we just didn't get to the place where our kind of creativity started," recalls Savage Rose keyboardist Thomas Koppel. "We felt like the road was blocked somehow. It didn't work out. In situations like that, we became anarchists. We were never really the typical kind of artists that wanted a producer at all."

"That's BS," retorts Gomelsky. "The drummer [Alex Riel] was a professional musician, he knew a lot about music. You could talk to him. He saw very clearly what the ideas were. Annisette—great singer. We had no problems. With one of the brothers [Thomas and Anders Koppel, founders of the band], I had terrible problems. One of them thought of himself as some kind of Viking god. Big-headed, big chip on his shoulder and knew zilch. It was very difficult to get anything out of them and by consequence out of the session. He opposed everything, he stopped everything, he stopped work from flowing. We were getting nowhere.

"In London at the time, remember, we were flowing. We were in a groove. The engineers were hot, everybody was hot, we worked and went out and we celebrated. It was such an 'up' kind of situation. And there came this guy with this sort of negative kind of resistance. It just didn't make for any agreeable environment. So I said, 'I can't do anything.' But on the way there, we had some really good ideas, because

Alex Riel—a pleasure to work with—was open to anything that made sense to him. Annisette, she was waiting, ready to wail away at the least opportunity. One of the brothers was cool. But then there was the other one. So it was not a happy experience. Truth to be known, you can pinpoint why."

By the end of the '60s, Gomelsky had left Paragon, tired of London, and was ready for a change of scene, leaving England on December 31, 1969. Moving to France in the early '70s, "I wanted to just relax. I wanted to get back to my film career, really. I thought I'd done enough managing artists and helping people out." However, while doing an interview with a French music magazine, he heard a tape of a new French progressive rock band, Magma. After reading Gomelsky's favorable comments about them in the subsequent article, a Magma member contacted him and convinced him to check them out. "I'm a real sucker for talent. When I saw them, I was totally won over. I said, I got to do something. That was '71."

As a manager and producer for Magma, and a producer for Gong—the latter actually comprised in large part of musicians from the British progressive scene (including Daevid Allen), but often based in France—Gomelsky was instrumental in getting the experimental French rock movement off the ground. This is a genre that is still relatively unknown to the English-speaking world. Given the challenging nature of bands such as Magma—who fused jazz, avant-garde, classical, and rock, and invented their own language in which to sing—it is likely to remain so. In order to create an audience in France itself—which had an undernourished rock and pop circuit, particularly for the underground—Gomelsky made typically imaginative use of the available alternatives.

"One day I'm going to pick up the singer of Magma, Klaus. He's teaching cartoon design in a youth center. They had a gig every four months. So I'm walking around, and I find, in the back of this youth center is a little hall. 'Ah—this would be a good place to do a Magma concert.' I found out that there were like 600 youth centers in France, about twenty-five in [the] Paris region. I went to talk to all of them and said, 'Why don't we do it like this? We come in, we organize the concert, 20 percent is for your expenses, the rest is for us. You don't have to do anything. Just lend us your printing Xerox machines.' Within three months, I'd organized twenty-five shows all around Paris. There were about a hundred or so venues, in all of France, for this music to exist and grow. But I soon found out we were being watched by the National Security Police.

"We had a lot of resistance. Whenever we went to a gig, we always got there two hours late, because we were stopped and searched for drugs at the entrance of the throughways. Then we were stopped at the exit and searched again. Getting this music out was not something that was easy to do. It was a political, almost, kind of struggle to have freedom to play this music. Because it was very subversive music, very aggressive.

"After we did this show, I created this circuit. This allowed Gong to follow them [Daevid Allen credits Gong manager Bob Benamou for helping to trailblaze this circuit as well]. I then all of the bands that were doing alternative stuff at the time, like the Art Bears, Henry Cow, we got them gigs—Faust came to our gigs—Can, Univers Zero. Every European band that was into original music was able to [take advantage of it]. We changed the whole face of music in France. France used to be much maligned by the British and Americans as being a bunch of people who can't play any music. I was from the Continent, and proud of it. After fifteen years in London, I thought, this is the occasion for me to now go back to my roots, and to help original stuff from here." Gomelsky formed an agency, Rock Pas Degenere (or Rock Pas Gaga, "rock not soft-brained," as it became known), with a roster of about twenty alternative bands.

Gomelsky also found some time to do production, incorporating as usual some unconventional methodology. "In the Gong trilogy [a series of conceptually linked albums done by Gong in the early '70s]," remembers Allen, "he was sitting in the studio with the engineer saying, 'Look, look. It's the beginning of the record, right? It's dark. There's a desert. Look, over here, the sun's coming up. Here comes the sun. OK, in comes the synthesizer. The sun's coming up, first rays of light hit the mountain. OK, here comes the little bit of guitar there and the first cymbals.' This was his thing. He's a very visual, pictorial person."

Gomelsky moved from France to New York in the mid-1970s, after coming to the city to collect money owed by CBS for the Yardbirds. RCA executive Ken Glancy offered Gomelsky a label, Utopia, which Giorgio envisioned as he had Marmalade. "My idea was to become a sort of alternative label. Even in baseball, you've got farming systems. In the theater, there is off-Broadway. It doesn't exist in the record world." However, he fell out with his partner, Kevin Eggers, and Utopia's deal with RCA—which offered millions of dollars of advances, subject to periodic renewal—was terminated. Glancy offered him a high-paid research position at RCA, which included finding New York talent, such as bassist and future producer Bill Laswell, whom Gomelsky came across playing in a band at CBGB's. He also presented a report to RCA, as Glancy had requested, about what the label was doing wrong, "and the picture came out of a very old, slow, pterodactyl, dinosaur-type record company. Ken Glancy resigned," he laughs sympathetically. "Now I'm stuck here, involved with the New York scene."

Gomelsky got involved with the forerunners of what has come to be known as New York "downtown music"—that confluence of rock, avant-garde, contemporary composition, and jazz that has come to characterize the New York experimental scene. "My idea," says Gomelsky, "was to connect the alternative music in Europe with the alternative music here." John Zorn and Fred Frith played early improv gigs in his building; Bill Laswell lived in the building for more than a year. Gomelsky brought Frith, Chris Cutler, Daevid Allen, and members of Magma to play in New York, Laswell ending up in Allen's band for a time. He mounted the Zu Manifestival in New York in 1978, which showcased emerging progressive talent. He produced the first record by Material, the funk-prog rock band in which Laswell played bass. "The idea of Temporary Music [a phrase used in the title of several Material recordings] and Material was that you didn't bind yourself, tie yourself, into a format or formula. So that it could be people coming and going; it would be ensembles. It would all be one-off-type projects. My old dream, of pulling together this kind of collective-type situation.

"After the Zu Manifestival I thought, OK, let's do the same thing we did in France. Let's get a[n] alternative music circuit in America. The year after, I bought a school bus, I put twenty-four musicians in there, and off we went to California. It took us three months to go there and back. And found out that it was a very different alternative circuit here and all remained to be done. But, apart from some college radio stations, we got no support and I ended up doing everything myself, a lot of work. Nevertheless, in three months, we did thirty-five concerts across the country. Sometimes we played in front of a thousand, two thousand people; other places we played in front of one hundred people. So it was very, very difficult. I found out that people who were into progressive music fifty miles from each other didn't know about each other. People that were running college radio stations didn't know about each other. I was trying to make this huge effort to put everybody together and establish an alternative circuit everyone would have benefited from. That's where Bill Laswell and company started sort of sabotaging the whole thing."

After the passage of about twenty years, this seems to be among the experiences that has caused Gomelsky the greatest sadness. "I understood one thing: that the college radio stations played this European music a few years back highly intensely, and there was an audience there. We used to get mail from America in France about, 'oh, when are you coming to'.... So I said, 'These guys got radio stations, they got university halls, they know the local scene—lean on them to organize our circuit.' Everybody was very enthusiastic about this, and then it kind of fell apart. People were very suspicious. Even Fred Frith, whom I wanted to be one of the leaders of the movement, and whom I knew from way back, started accusing me of being a manipulator. What?"

Gomelsky turns unusually critical at this point. "These people that are now so respected, like Laswell and Fred Frith, acted like traitors to the cause. They looked for what advantaged them. They never thought of giving back. Fred Frith was a complete self-serving guy. Bill Laswell, to this day, has never had an original idea. All of the kind of synthesizing ideas about music...for instance, he didn't know who [jazz guitarist] Sonny Sharrock was until I told him. But when we split, he went to Rochester and found Sonny Sharrock. Laswell and the others in Material had nothing, knew nothing. Laswell was a bass player from Detroit, playing at CBGB's, in a Led Zeppelin imitation band. I turned him on to all the music, all the records, but instead of contributing to the common good, he appropriated it all for himself. To this day he hasn't paid back anything to the scene."

Gomelsky "feels the U.S. is so caught in the competitive mode it has lost all sense of cooperating for the common good. People have no hesitation nicking ideas and fucking them up. The Zu Manifestival was the first event of its kind and meant to independently support a wide array of alternative music. Instead it turned into the foundation/art authorities/cliques-sponsored New Music USA, obviously favoring only a small section of artists. That's where I gave up on music activism and started looking elsewhere for inspiration. One day, I woke up and a thought appeared on the horizon: 'Get a computer'"

In the 1990s, much of Gomelsky's efforts have been directed toward computer technology. In addition to trying to organize users of the Amiga computer into building their own platform, he is an accomplished computer animator and is working on "a web site which would allow, through a device that might be an interactive game, to get to the path of finding the information that really services your pursuit, your research. First of all, defining the problem as it really is, and secondly, finding the solution."

Gomelsky has not entirely curtailed his support of cutting-edge music. He lets out the ground floor of his building as inexpensive rehearsal space for musicians (a scarce commodity in Manhattan) who are felt to have creative potential, and not just the financial means to pay for it; the most noted of these has been Jeff Buckley. And "it would be really great to put sort of [a New York] ensemble together that would be a temporary ensemble. It would go from one-off to one-off to one-off, where you have people to write for this kind of ensemble, and someone else to write for another setup and so on, and put it all on the Net. I know enough musicians who 'owe me' to perhaps be able to do something all together once more. That would be a dream of mine," he reiterates.

As to why more of his dreams haven't been realized over the last forty years, he laughs, "if I'd found an honest business partner and an honest lawyer…I wouldn't have gone through all this heart-wrenching disappointments and setbacks. They *were* setbacks. Not that I'm playing my own trumpet. But I think having started that stuff off, I somehow wasn't allowed—or otherwise disabled myself—to finish it as it was perceived in the first place. With the exception of France, perhaps. There it really worked and changed things."

At the core of Gomelsky's checkered career has been a tension between art and commerce, and the struggle that ensues when the former is weighted more than the latter. In England in the 1960s, he observes, there were only two other nonmusicians (now dead) in the entire industry who were in it more for the music than the money or the ego. These were Guy Stevens (one of London's first rock and soul club DJs, and later producer of Mott the Hoople, the Clash, and several others) and, surprisingly, Peter Meaden, the early Who manager who "really drove them on to be in the music business," only to have his position usurped by Kit Lambert and Chris Stamp.

Musicians have also gladly abandoned idealistic principles for money and fame as well, Gomelsky is careful to observe. "I did believe that success could afford one more independence and choice. Unfortunately, artists were somewhat short-sighted, and rather than practicing more long-term strategies, preferred to see their need for approval gratified instantly. Just as a comparison, they say that Peter Grant [who managed the Yardbirds just before they broke up, and then Led Zeppelin] was a good manager because he knew how to collect monies on his artists' behalf and was able to see through promoters' schemes and other scams. At my time, these hadn't been invented yet, and my major concern was accessing sufficient resources to consolidate our independence and allow the band to give up their day jobs and make a living playing music."

There is also the enormous difficulty in implementing collective, aesthetically radical, even anarchist strategies—ones which Gomelsky repeatedly voices support for in our conversation—within an entertainment industry, and society, which is unabashedly capitalist and profit-minded. What, ultimately, were the most important *artistic* qualities—rather than the financial benefits—he impressed upon the remarkable roll call of artists he produced, managed, promoted, and otherwise encouraged?

"Daring," he answers. "To explore, to dare, to search. Not to accept anything that had been fixed. There are rules, but once you got no rules, try and break them. Or find new rules."

Recommended Recordings:

By the Yardbirds:

Greatest Hits Vol. 1: 1964-1966 (1986, Rhino). The best of the material Gomelsky produced for the band, with Jeff Beck or Eric Clapton on lead guitar, through the debut R&B singles to the futuristic, feedback-laden "Shapes of Things" and "Mr. You're a Better Man Than I." This represents his peak as producer, with the introduction of Middle Eastern melodies and sounds into rock 'n' roll with "Heart Full of Soul" and "Still I'm Sad"; the transcendental rave-ups of "I'm a Man," "Smokestack Lightning," and "The Train Kept A-Rollin'"; and great Graham Gouldman songs like "For Your Love." If you want a more complete set of the Gomelsky sessions, there are the two double-CD compilations on Sony (*Smokestack Lightning* and *Blues, Backtracks and Shapes of Things*), or the Charly box set *Train Kept A-Rollin': The Complete Giorgio Gomelsky Productions.*

Five Live Yardbirds (1964, Columbia, U.K.). Reissued since the mid-1960s on innumerable labels, whole and piecemeal (the Rhino edition will be among the easiest to find for U.S. residents). Although the fidelity is only average, this is the prime live document of the mid-1960s British R&B scene. With Clapton on guitar, the Yardbirds charge through covers of classics by Bo Diddley, Chuck Berry, Howlin' Wolf, and others, demonstrating their penchant for, as Gomelsky has said, altering material. That's especially exhilarating on their lengthy rave-ups of "Smokestack Lightning" (with brilliant exchanges of harmonica and guitar riffs), Bo Diddley's "Here 'Tis" (whose rippling, percussive guitar solo verges on musique concrete), and the Isley Brothers' "Respectable" (whose ska-like nursery rhyme break typifies the Yardbirds' unpredictable eclecticism).

By the Rolling Stones:

Bright Lights, Big City (1973, Trademark of Quality, bootleg). First issued as a bootleg in the 1970s, this unreleased material, largely dating from 1963-64, has since shown up under a variety of titles and labels. Among the tracks are five unissued songs from early 1963 that show what the Rolling Stones sounded like just as they found their footing, and just before they rose to fame. There are raw and ready covers of great Bo Diddley ("Roadrunner," "Diddley Daddy") and Jimmy Reed ("Bright Lights, Big City," "Baby What's Wrong") tunes that the Stones would never release officially, as well as an earlier version of Muddy Waters' "I Want to Be Loved," which they would rerecord for the B-side of their first single. Gomelsky did not produce these, but they best capture, more than anything else the Stones would record, how the group might have sounded at Gomelsky's Crawdaddy Club in early 1963.

By the Blossom Toes:

Collection (1988, Decal, U.K.). The Blossom Toes' records were the best, and most accessible, records to appear on Gomelsky's Marmalade label in the late 1960s (though some might argue for the ones by Julie Driscoll, Brian Auger & the Trinity). This double-LP has almost everything from their brilliant 1967 debut album, *We Are Ever So Clean*, with its Kinks-meet-the-village-brass-band sound; their second and final album, 1969's *If Only For a Moment*, with its contrasting ominous, serious words and multi-guitar-line hard rock arrangements; and two non-LP songs from singles. Gomelsky produced all of these.

By the Soft Machine:

Jet-Propelled Photograph (Charly, U.K.). Also issued as *At the Beginning,* or under other titles, these are the nine demos Gomelsky produced with the band in April 1967. In addition to being historically important (comprising most of the available material by the early version of the band with Daevid Allen on guitar), it's also enjoyable and innovative early British psychedelia, with incessantly inventive tempo and melodic shifts, alternately goofy and affecting lyrics, and Robert Wyatt's soulful singing. There are strong hints of jazz and the avant-garde, though these are still subservient to a hummable pop sensibility. That invigorating collision of elements is best heard on "Jet-Propelled Photograph" and the emotional ballad "Memories."

By Julie Driscoll, Brian Auger, & the Trinity:

Streetnoise (1969, Disconforme, Andorra). One of the most eclectic productions by a producer committed to eclecticism as part of his overall modus operandi. Brian Auger's smoldering jazz-rock organ, and Julie Driscoll's emotive vocals (sounding like a more soul-oriented Grace Slick), share the spotlight on this seventy-four-minute disc, originally a double LP and now a single CD. With its panoramic blends of progressive rock, jazz, soul, and some folk and gospel, it is the best reflection of Marmalade's aesthetic: to bring all types of musical expression under one umbrella. It also expresses Gomelsky's conception of a band as an ensemble with a rotating focus, some cuts featuring Auger's instrumental talents, some containing only Driscoll's voice and acoustic guitar, and some capturing Driscoll and Auger interacting in a group context.

Shel Talmy

If the British Invasion was a hurricane that wiped out everything in its path, the flashiest leaders of this sonic blast were the English guitar heroes of the mid-1960s. Jeff Beck, Pete Townshend, Dave Davies, and less heralded figures like Eddie Phillips of the Creation—all were playing power chords and fierce solos that were louder and more frenzied than anything before heard in rock music. Their riffs leaped off the records with such a grab-you-by-the-throat immediacy that you feared that the needle would shudder and jump off the turntable (back in the days when there *were* turntables, of course).

No producer was more responsible for capturing the guitar revolution on disc than Shel Talmy was. No, he didn't play the guitars or write the songs; he couldn't have done it without the immensely skilled, if somewhat raw, young talent in his charge. What he had was the vision and courage to allow rock music, and guitars in particular, to be played and recorded with more force and power than was thought decent. If he had done nothing else than produce the early hits by the Kinks and the Who, Talmy's place in history would be secure in this regard. "You Really Got Me," "All Day and All of the Night," "My Generation," "I Can't Explain"—all were Talmy productions. The irony was that Talmy, one of the principal architects of some of the British Invasion's greatest moments, was not British, but an American expatriate who might have never gotten a job across the Atlantic in the first place if someone had bothered to check his resume. Perhaps it took an American—someone raised on the raucous rock 'n' roll of the 1950s, and brash enough to surmount staid British music business conventions—to fully exploit the most uninhibited qualities of the first generation of British rockers.

The power chords that open "You Really Got Me" and "I Can't Explain," the almost-careening-out-of-control guitar solo on "All Day and All of the Night," and the feedback on "My Generation" and "Anyway, Anyhow, Anywhere" may be the most distinctive aural imprints on Talmy-produced recordings. Yet Talmy's skills were hardly limited to guitar madness. Although his association with the Who did not last past the band's first album and first hit singles, he worked with the Kinks as they changed from raw ravers to gentler pop satirists and ironists. He also produced the Easybeats' power pop classic "Friday on My Mind," some of David Bowie's earliest sides, and Whoesque cult rockers the Creation. There were intermittent associations with British Invasion hit-makers Manfred Mann, Chad & Jeremy, the Fortunes, and the Nashville Teens. And although Talmy oversaw his share of guitar mayhem, he also produced the earliest and best albums by one of Britain's premier folk-rock groups, the Pentangle, proving as adept at recording acoustic guitar duels as he was at working with distorted and heavily amplified electric axes.

In spite of his impressive track record, Talmy was not universally admired within the industry. He fell out with the Who and its management in a conflict that ended up dragging everyone involved through the courts; Ray Davies and the Kinks have claimed that he could be callous in the studio, and retroactively questioned his judgment on classic singles; and Talmy himself cheerfully admits to clashes with managers who tried to interfere with the recording process. When members of the obscure American psychedelic band Mandrake Memorial were being difficult in the

Shel Talmy behind the boards.
Credit: Courtesy Shel Talmy.

studio, Talmy simply walked out on the second day. No one, however, builds such an impressive catalog by accident, and there can be no doubt that Talmy played a significant role in some of the best and most enduring British rock records of the 1960s.

There was no hard evidence that Talmy would have a lot of rough diamonds to polish when he moved to Britain in 1962, before the Beatles had launched the British Invasion. Frankly, Talmy had no business even crashing the upper echelons of U.K. record production in the first place. Born in Chicago and raised in Los Angeles, he had trained as a recording engineer in L.A. in the early 1960s before bluffing his way into the producer's chair in England. A vacation turned into a job, in a way that would be all but impossible to imagine anyone getting away with these days, when accountants and bureaucrats have lots of paperwork to process before anything gets done, and telecommunications have made contact between the continents instantaneous.

"I thought it would be nice to go to Europe, work if I could," remembers Talmy. "I expected to be over there about a month or so and figured I could go and see a couple of people and get a job to pay for my trip. So I prepared myself. My friend Nik Venet was at Capitol producing [stars like the Beach Boys]. He said, 'Take what you like.' I took a bunch of lacquers that he had just finished, and went to see Decca when I went to London. I thought, what the hell, I'm not going to be here long, I might as well be brash as possible. I said, 'I am arguably the greatest thing since sliced bread was invented,' and reeled off a whole string of hits I hadn't done. The two things I selected to play for [Decca's] Dick Rowe were the Beach Boys' 'Surfin' Safari' and Lou Rawls' 'Music in the Air.' Rowe said, 'Thank God you arrived, you start next week!' So I did."

So Decca didn't even bother to check out Talmy's bogus claims? "Nobody picked up the phones those days to find out if you were bullshitting or not," he points out. "They wrote letters, a couple of which went to people [in the U.S.] that knew me. And so they wrote back, saying, yes, of course he had done all these things. By the time they found out it was all bullshit, I'd already had my first hit, and they were very gentlemanly. Never mentioned that they knew that I knew that they knew."

Talmy had some success right off the bat with pop singer Doug Sheldon and Irish trio the Bachelors, whose hit "Charmaine" Talmy admits to disliking, despite having produced it. However, the future of British pop would not lie with faux folk-country groups like the Bachelors. It would lie with the tide of guitar rock groups — first from Liverpool, then from all over the U.K. — that would refashion the British music industry in a matter of months in 1963. Talmy was lucky enough to be in on the ground floor, although when he first arrived, he had no inkling of the incoming beat boom: "Hadn't a clue. There was no indication whatsoever. However, by the time I was there six months I *certainly* knew.

"In fact," he claims, "I came back here [to Los Angeles] in September '63 and I still didn't know a lot of people, nor did I have a lot of money. I went to see everybody that I could see in town and said, 'There's going to be a big explosion of British bands. All I need is $5,000, and I can tie up every British band there is.' I could have gotten the Stones for about $500, the Beatles for maybe $1,000, and everybody else for about $100 each. They said, 'sure kid,' patted me on the head, and that was the end of that. I knew, but nobody believed me. I, of course, subsequently got loads of apologies."

Talmy had arrived, somewhat by accident, at a changing of the guard of British music. When he first started working in the U.K., he explains, "The main problem at that time was really the musicians. There was one set of session guys who could play sort of like American musicians, and if you didn't get them you might as well forget it. If you wanted anything in sort of a soul feel, there was just no way. Unless you got this one set of guys, and it was more rote than instinctive. There were several of those around, really good guitarists, but they came out of either swing or jazz or something and were not rockers. They played great, immaculate notes with no soul whatsoever.

"As an engineer, I had been used to using people like Steve Douglas [who played on numerous Duane Eddy and Phil Spector sessions, among many others] as a great sax player. There was nobody there who could play funky sax. To some degree there still isn't. They've never seemed to completely master it over there, for whatever reason. The guitar is a different story. Big Jim Sullivan was the guitarist I was using. He was really the only one at the time who was *worth* using.

"Of course, not that much later, a whole bunch of kids that had grown up with American rock 'n' roll really started playing well. From going to nobody who could really play music from feel, they went to hordes of 'em who could, in a very short period of time — two or three years. I can only assume that this age group of kids, who when I first got there were probably sixteen or so, had been growing up for the last several years with American rock 'n' roll, and all came of age at the same time."

Talmy, familiar with the concept of the independent producer from his experience in America, also worked as an indie producer in Britain, where such positions were far rarer. As such he arranged to get royalties from the records made from his sessions, and was on the lookout for promising bands to bring into the studio. He says he brought both Manfred Mann and Georgie Fame into Decca to cut a few sides, only to have Decca turn them down; both artists would shortly go on to become consistent hit-makers. "What I felt I could do over there was give an American sound to a really good rock 'n' roll band, and I was on a constant lookout for rock 'n' roll bands. Originally I couldn't get those kind of bands—they didn't exist. I guess the Kinks were the first one I found that I thought were really sensational. They were not nearly as good then as they eventually wound up being."

The Kinks were still called the Ravens when Talmy liked what he heard on a demo and started recording them for Pye. After a name change and a couple of Merseybeatish flops, they got a huge international hit with "You Really Got Me." Just as importantly, the record—with its incessant fuzzy chord riffs, full and raunchy backup, and soar-into-orbit guitar solo—gave the Kinks an identity, and Talmy his first important triumph. Many of Talmy's subsequent productions in the 1960s would emphasize a crunchy, raucous guitar-driven sound that was also wed to hook-laden riffs and harmony vocals. These differed, however, from the American garage rock of the mid-1960s in the far greater sonic clarity of the production, as well as, particularly in the case of the Who and the Kinks, the superior songwriting and instrumental skills of the bands.

So accomplished and frenetic was the guitar solo on "You Really Got Me," as well as its similar but equally great follow-up "All Day and All of the Night," that many have speculated that Jimmy Page, then a star session musician, was responsible for the fretwork. Was it Page or Kinks lead guitarist Dave Davies playing on those early Kinks records? "You know how many times I've answered that question?" sighs Talmy. "I wish I had a buck for each one. Jimmy Page did *not* play the solo on 'You Really Got Me,' he played rhythm guitar. He never played anything *but* rhythm guitar on that plus [the Kinks'] first album session. On 'You Really Got Me,' the Kinks had just added Mick [Avory, drummer], and I used Bobby Graham on drums. [Page] played rhythm guitar because at the time Ray [Davies] would not play rhythm guitar, he didn't think he was good enough. So I said, fine, let me get a rhythm guitarist, 'cause Dave was playing the leads. We had Jon Lord [later of Deep Purple] on organ."

While the Kinks' early records helped establish new levels for high-energy rock 'n' roll, Talmy made an even greater find with the Who, a group that took the high-octane guitar-and-pounding-rhythm-section ethos to dizzier heights. It is probably no coincidence that the Who's first hit single, "I Can't Explain," is quite reminiscent of the early Kinks sound, especially in its declamatory opening guitar riffs. And, as on the Kinks' early recordings, Talmy used some session musicians on piano, guitar, and backup vocals, a decision which would spark some controversy when Who histories began to be written, many years later. Talmy takes great pains to justify his use of outside musicians, not just on "I Can't Explain" but in general.

"As far as the Who were concerned—again, I talked to them about it beforehand, and memory's terribly selective when you want to do these kind of things—their backing vocals sucked. That's why I got the Ivy League doing them. Perry Ford was the pianist, who was in the Ivy League, on that session [for "I Can't Explain"]. So I didn't arbitrarily bring guys in without telling anybody what was happening. I've never done that, 'cause I don't think that's right. I've always gotten along with musicians real well. Of course bands and musicians aren't necessarily mutually inclusive. A band has their own individual-plus-group ego. Nobody will do more for you than a band before their hit, and less afterwards. I'm not bitter, just realistic."

It's sometimes been written that Jimmy Page played rhythm guitar on "I Can't Explain," essentially doubling Pete Townshend's chords to fatten the sound. It's also been reported that he played the fuzztone guitar riffs on that single's B-side, "Bald Headed Woman," a blues tune whose composition was credited to Talmy himself (and which had been previously recorded by the Kinks as well). Page was already one of the premier rock guitarists in England, yet waited until 1966 to join a top rock group (the Yardbirds), Talmy recalls, "because he was making a lot of money as a session guitarist. You've got to remember, he was in a working-class family. He was seventeen or eighteen when he started, and all of a sudden he was doing three sessions a day, earning during one of them what he would have earned during the course of a week if he had a regular job as a working-class individual. He was very much in demand."

In fact, Talmy used Page often, not only for the Kinks and the Who, but for obscure British R&B-rock acts that only cut a few flop singles, many of which are now coveted by collectors. At times, indeed, Page's solo is the one thing about those records that lifts them out of the ordinary. The First Gear's "Leave My Kitten Alone," for instance, is a fairly routine R&B cover until it explodes with a sizzling solo by Page in the instrumental break, which segues from early wah-wah effects to fingers-on-fire leads.

"Jimmy initially didn't want to go out on the road. He still was living with his mother," chuckles Talmy, "and I don't think he really liked to travel at that time. So he played sessions. He was very reliable. And I think he liked playing sessions. It's not an onerous job. You walk in, you see all your pals there, because there was by that time a fair-sized group of session guys who could do this; there was probably fifteen to twenty guys that all worked the same sessions. They were all very good friends. One of my very best friends was Clem Cattini, the drummer, who was one of the great senses of humor of our time. Not only is he a great drummer, but he lifted a session because he was so funny. John Paul Jones was [also] playing a lot of sessions." And while Page would not play with the Who again as far as anyone knows, another ace British session cat, Nicky Hopkins, played such invaluable piano on the Who's *The Who Sing My Generation* album that he could have been considered a fifth member of sorts on that LP. (Hopkins also played on 1960s sessions by the Kinks.)

While the Who's "I Can't Explain" was very much a proto-power pop classic built around chunky chords, the group's second single, "Anyway, Anyhow, Anywhere," employed guitar feedback (by Pete Townshend) that was different from anything else that had ever been recorded. This was particularly true of the solo, a white noise explosion of Morse code beeps, airplane swoops, shock waves, and shrieks, all simulated with a guitar. "I got a cable from [the American branch of Decca Records] after we sent it in, saying, 'We think we got a bad tape, it seems to have feedback all over it,'" laughs Talmy. "I assured them that was the way it was. Of course 'My Generation' followed that, which had as much or more feedback on it."

These singles were not hits in the U.S., though they (especially "My Generation") were big sellers in Britain, and it would take much longer for the members of the Who to become stars Stateside than it did in the U.K. "The Who was funny, because I brought them to Decca America, who were a very nice bunch of guys, older men who had no idea what rock 'n' roll was. They didn't understand what the hell I was doing, but they said, 'If that's what's supposedly selling, then we'll go out and try to sell it.' They didn't really understand, but they stuck to what they knew best, which was selling a record.

"This still holds true today," adds Talmy. "If you speak to any number of producers, they'll probably tell you the same thing—it's really great to get tied up with a record company who lets you do your thing while they do theirs. It is almost nonexistent. With a couple of exceptions, I don't think I've ever run into sales and promotion in a record company who didn't think they were A&R people. If they know how to do it better—and I have said it on more than one occasion—'Why don't you go out and do your own records? Why tell me how to do mine?'

"I certainly am open to criticism. If somebody has some valid suggestion, I'll be very happy to take it. In fact, always in the studio, when I walked in I had about a 90 percent idea in my head of how that finished record should sound, before we got one note down. I always left 10 percent for flexibility if suggestions came up, and often they did—from a musician, or somebody who did something by accident. I kind of resented promotion people—when the record was finished, after it had already started selling—telling me how the record should have been."

Talmy was at the helm for all of the Who's 1965 recordings, comprising the three British hit singles "I Can't Explain," "Anyway, Anyhow, Anywhere," and "My Generation," as well as the excellent *The Who Sing My Generation* album. Dissatisfied with the terms of Talmy's production deal, however, the Who and its managers broke away from Shel in early 1966 to record on their own. Talmy sued for breach of contract, having signed the band to his own company and spent his own money on making the Who's records, leasing the results (which appeared on Decca in the U.S. and Brunswick in the U.K.). Disputes over the Who's contracts soon brought everyone involved into court, and for a few months in 1966 the Who was even prohibited from recording. This led to a ludicrous situation in which the instrumental "Waltz for a Pig," the B-side of the band's first 1966 single ("Substitute"), had to be cut by the Graham Bond Organisation (with the pre-Cream Jack Bruce and Ginger Baker) under the pseudonym of "the Who Orchestra."

In the subsequent settlement between the group and the producer, Talmy was awarded a 5 percent royalty on the money generated by the Who's recordings for the next five years, although his production deal with the band ended and he would never produce the Who again. Five percent might sound like a small amount, but as it encompassed the huge-selling 1969-71 Who albums *Tommy, Live at Leeds*, and *Who's Next*, it was enough to make Talmy a multimillionaire, according to Tony Fletcher's biography of Who drummer Keith Moon. Shel retains ownership of the multitrack tapes of the Who's first album and first three singles, which have yet to appear on a CD mastered from the best existing tapes (Talmy's). In mid-2000, with no sale having been arranged to the current administrators of the bulk of the Who catalog, he took the unusual step of putting twenty-four of his three-track Who tapes up for auction on the Internet site e-bay, at a minimum price of half a million dollars.

"The Who et al., including underaged band members who needed parent permission, thought this was a wonderful idea as I was putting my money where my mouth was," says Talmy now of his arrangement with the group. "[Who comanager Kit] Lambert, who was a lot older than all of us, became jealous of my alleged influence with 'his boys,' and along with Polydor abetting him, breached my contract. Note that Polydor came on the scene to foment discontent only after the Who were already a huge band. So where were they when I was looking for a deal!

"I had always felt that the so-called Who sound, on record at any event, was a good deal my creation," Shel declares. "And I *don't* think that's an ego trip. All you have to do is listen to the record they did before I was with them, the High Numbers record ["I'm the Face"/"Zoot Suit," released in 1964 when the band was briefly called the High Numbers], and compare the difference. And I certainly felt that after I stopped recording them, they weren't being recorded nearly as well. But I'm probably prejudiced," he admits.

"My problems with the Who were with Kit Lambert, who was out of his fucking mind. I think he was certifiably insane; if he hadn't been in the music business, he would have been locked up. The problem with him was his giant-sized ego-plus-paranoia. He felt I was usurping his authority because I was producing these recordings."

Talmy was able to continue working with the Kinks for a couple of years after his split with the Who, however. In his semiautobiography *X-Ray*, Ray Davies, dissatisfied with the first session for "You Really Got Me," claims that he had to lobby for a rerecording of the song over the objections of Talmy and others. Writes Davies of the second go-round, "I asked Shel if we could do another take. Shel, slumped in his chair, looked down at me from the glass booth, gave a giant sigh down the intercom and reluctantly agreed… If I had asked for another take, I'm convinced that Shel and the engineer would have left the building." Davies also remembers Shel refusing to rerecord a flawed bass part on "Sunny Afternoon" with the remark, "Nobody will notice, it's just a fluff on the bass." In his Kinks biography, Johnny Rogan writes of the classic single "Waterloo Sunset," "Ray secretly entered the studio with the Kinks and laid down a third version which was reputedly used on the record, though Talmy denies this."

Talmy, again, has a different take on things. "The Kinks' sound, and the concept of what they were known for on record, certainly had a lot to do with me. I was with them from inception, and after we stopped working together, I think it's certainly fair to say that they went through a period where they did not have a lot of hit records. It wasn't until [Ray] finally returned to the old formula, which was basically 'Lola,' that he got another smash.

"I suppose I was sort of spoiled because the Who, musically, were as good as you were going to get. The Kinks, although not quite as good, were still good, and had, in my opinion, the best songwriter in England. Ray, who certainly was one of the most prolific writers I've ever known, would go away and come back the next day with about forty songs he'd written in the last hour. We'd sit down at the piano and he'd start going through the songs and I'd say, 'that one still needs some work,' or 'that's great, that's a number one,' which is what happened with 'Sunny Afternoon.' I heard about four bars of that. I said, 'That is definitely a number one record.'"

The Who and the Kinks, not to mention their volatile band members and management, should have been enough on their own to keep Talmy's hands full in the mid-1960s. He produced several other groups, however, with a similarly raucous feel. Even though these bands lacked songwriters on the order of Townshend and Davies, outfits like the aforementioned the First Gear, the Untamed, Mickey Finn, the Talismen, and the Zephyrs made some outstanding singles stamped by Talmy's touch, which crafted tight tracks that did not compromise the raw energy of the musicians. Of all the groups Talmy worked with that didn't make it, he is fondest by far of the Creation. Featuring guitarist Eddie Phillips, who was almost the equal of Pete Townshend in combining thrashing power chords with innovative sound effects and distortion, the Creation got only a couple of modest hit singles in England. Though they had more success on the Continent, they are still almost unknown in the United States. Phillips is particularly known for pioneering the technique of playing an electric guitar with a violin bow, as heard on their most famous song, their debut single "Making Time" (which finally reached the masses in the late 1990s via its use in the film comedy *Rushmore*).

"I wished they had gotten bigger," says Talmy. "Eddie Phillips deserves to be up there as one of the great rock 'n' roll guitarists of our time, and he's hardly ever mentioned. Jimmy Page stole the bowing bit of the guitar from Eddie. As I recall, [Eddie] was practicing guitar at somebody's house and there happened to be a violin bow around, and he picked it up and started messing with it. I heard it, and I said, 'Christ, let's use that. I've never heard that sound before.'" Talmy even briefly had his own label, Planet, of which the Creation was the mainstay. Planet folded soon after the Creation's first releases, and although the group kept recording, they too threw in the towel after a couple of years.

One star who crossed Talmy's path five years too early was David Bowie, known as David Jones when the singer made his second and third singles with Talmy in 1965. Jones/Bowie was still an average R&B-rock singer at this stage, and apt to be riding other trends rather than developing his own style. Indeed the second Talmy-overseen single, "You've Got a Habit of Leaving," begins like a Kinks outtake and tears distorted guitar riffs almost wholesale off the Who's "Anyway, Anyhow, Anywhere" for the instrumental break and ending; the similarity is not surprising given that Talmy produced all three artists. Bowie also did some demos with Talmy that hinted at a more personal vision; these surfaced on the *Early On: 1964-1966* CD compilation in the early 1990s.

"I always liked him," maintains Talmy, decades after the singles flopped. "I always thought he was incredibly talented. He was extremely bright; he impressed me as knowing exactly where he was going. He was seventeen when I first recorded him, with the Manish Boys. I honestly didn't think that what he was writing at the time had a snowball's chance in hell of making it, but I thought, he's so original and brash, let's take a flier. So we did a bunch of them, and of course they didn't make it, and it wasn't until seven or eight years later that a window of opportunity opened for his style of music. And he made the most of it, of course. There wasn't a whole lot of difference between what I did with them and what he did seven or eight years later, just that at the time we put it out nobody wanted to know. It was weird music."

Traces of the Who and the Kinks can also be heard in the Easybeats' "Friday on My Mind," an international hit that blended classic staccato guitar riffs with the more familiar Talmy trademark of thick, emphatic power pop chords. The Easy-beats, already superstars in Australia, had just come to England in an effort to break into the worldwide market. Talmy helped them do so with their first attempt on this 1966 single. It was his suggestion to put in the brief dramatic bit near the end of the song where all of the instruments and vocals drop off save for a few bass drum taps, which kick the song back into full gear again. Talmy's association with the band was brief, though, as he soon found himself at odds, he says, with someone in the group's management.

Around this time, Talmy helped revive the career of a group he had tried to push back in 1963, Manfred Mann. "They approached me after Paul Jones left and Mike d'Abo became the lead singer. Of course, the whole music press had written them off as dead because Paul Jones was the band, etc., etc., and so I was given this thankless job of doing a record with Manfred Mann sans Paul Jones. I've always liked challenges, what the hell. So it worked out fine. We continued to make hits.

"I think it's fair to say that I contributed, but really Manfred Mann's the guy who led that band, not Paul Jones or Mike d'Abo. He kept making hits, after I was gone, after everybody else was gone. They've had several versions of good bands, and Man-fred is certainly a talent. He is a very good chooser of material, that's really where his strength is. He's not a wonderful writer, but he sure can pick material. He loved Dylan material, and quite frankly, I think we did it a lot better than Dylan did." In-deed, the first single Talmy did with the band was a cover of Dylan's "Just Like a Woman," which became a hit in Britain but not in the U.S. "And he's very good at putting bands together. He's got a concept of where a band should go, and he cer-tainly *is* the band. It was never Paul Jones."

Talmy is, deservedly, known for records with hard guitar textures. It's not as well known that he has an equal passion and skill for recording acoustic guitars, best heard on the early albums by the Pentangle, whose lineup included perhaps the two finest British folk guitarists of the 1960s, Bert Jansch and John Renbourn. Talmy also did Jansch's fine late '60s solo album *Birthday Blues*, a couple of late '60s albums by cult British folk-rocker Roy Harper, and a precious folk LP by the brother-sister duo the Sallyangie; the brother, teenaged Mike Oldfield, reemerged five years later as a prog-rock superstar with his *Tubular Bells* opus. "I love recording acoustics," en-thuses Talmy. "One of my first loves was folk music. I grew up in that kind of music, when I was going to high school. The [famous L.A. folk club] Ash Grove—I used to practically live there.

"I have evolved a way of recording acoustics that I know nobody else quite does. The concept I was striving for, and on which I did a lot of experimentation, was to record an acoustic sound that had both space and clarity. Today that sounds like a no-brainer, but in the '60s it was another Everest to climb, given the level and limitations of the gear available. What evolved was a combination of mike place-ment, the type of mike used, and enhancements I added from the board, fairly primitive at that time, but it worked. Also as far as the Pentangle in particular were concerned, I was recording two of the best acoustic players in the country, making everything a lot easier.

"In fact I did try early on [to record an acoustic] duo called Jon and Allen, and Jon became Jon Mark of the Mark-Almond Band. [Jon] was a great innovator. He's the first person, come to think of it, who ever told me about Bob Dylan. He said, 'Watch—this guy's going to be sensational.' Jon was the first guy that ever brought Indian music to my attention, and in fact wrote a song that was sort of based on a drone, a folkish type song, that I recorded with him. I played that to Ray Davies, who was so enamored with it that he went out and wrote 'See My Friends' [one of the first Indian-influenced rock songs].

"It was very interesting recording [the Pentangle] because their various musical tastes were so diverse that we did a little bit of everything. [Drummer Terry Cox] in particular and [guitarist John Renbourn] were very into medieval music, and consequently we did a fair amount of medieval music. [Guitarist Bert Jansch] was particularly interested in eighteenth and nineteenth century English ballads, which were fun to do. I knew all that stuff from my folk days. So it was great; I really enjoyed them."

Get Talmy going on the subject of managers, and you can let the tape roll for quite a while. "My problems I don't think were ever with the bands, or if they were, they were never voiced there in the studio. My problems have been with the managements. For the most part, producers never or very seldom have problems with the bands, but usually with the support troops. If you have to nail a reason down, if you think about it, what is a manager? It's some untalented asshole who has got a piece of talented property to do things that he—normally it's he—has no ability to do himself. Basically, managers are warts on the backside of society. They really don't do a lot. Of course there are some very good managers. I have been unfortunate to run into the ones that weren't.

"Bands—especially back then, when that whole rock revolution started—were really young and extremely impressionable. All the managers that I knew were guys at least in their thirties, and they were sort of father figures in many ways. They had access to the band on a full-time basis. You got these young kids who were thrust into the limelight, most of them from working-class backgrounds, most of them with very little money, and they were incredibly impressionable. These guys were making five quid a week or something, and all of a sudden they're getting a thousand pounds a night for playing an instrument that they really liked to play in the first place. Of course they went crazy. It's understandable from a sociological point of view. It doesn't mean I loved it."

On several of Talmy's famous records, his engineer was Glyn Johns, who went on to become a hugely successful producer in his own right, working with Talmy's former clients the Who in the early 1970s, as well as with the Beatles (on *Let It Be*), Eric Clapton, and the Eagles. However, in Talmy's view, "We had a lot of mutual respect for each other, but I don't think I can fairly say that I worked on a record *with* him. I was producing the record, and he was the engineer. And maybe that's my personality fault. I could not produce a record, I think, *with* someone. It would be very difficult to do. Somebody's got to steer the damn ship, and I don't think you can have two captains trying to steer in two different directions. That's certainly the way I always worked."

That's a launching point for some observations about the role of a producer in general. For Mickey Most (who produced the Animals, Herman's Hermits, Donovan, Lulu, and other big British stars in the '60s), Talmy observes, "His major strength was picking material. The absolute reverse of Glyn Johns, who perhaps produced the best *sound* records there ever were, but could not pick a hit record if it came and bit him. On balance, I'd rather have a Mickey Most, because records are really 75 percent the song, I think. Maybe more. It is certainly a fact that you can have a great song with a lousy band that's a hit, but never the reverse.

"If I can't have any fun doing it, it's really not worth doing. I would rather not do a session with somebody that is going to be strictly a grind who I didn't like, and we weren't going to have any laughs during the session, because I think that gets on the tape. Part of what I'm supposed to do in the studio is provide for, or at least enhance, an environment where everybody can work, accomplish things, and have some fun while we're doing it. In my experience, the longer you go on, the worse it sounds. There've been very few records who've managed to sound better after eight months than eight weeks. And even eight weeks would be too damn long."

As a producer, Talmy will always be linked with the British rock of the 1960s, although he moved back to the U.S. at the end of the 1970s. He continues to do some projects here and there, and in fact in 1999 was working with "a seventeen-year-old Australian girl named Brooke Anderson, who I'm as sure about making it as I was with the Who or the Kinks. I've cut several tracks with her and will be doing some more before we get into serious shopping, but the buzz about her has started, so who knows." But he has only sporadically been involved in recording since the early 1970s. Not that he seems to have many regrets about it. "I probably should have come back [to the U.S.] at the end of 1970-71. I knew it was all over, and I didn't."

"What do you mean, 'it was all over'?" I ask.

"The music scene was pretty much all over as we knew it. The '60s were gone, and the early '70s went through a very fallow period. Everything started getting corporate and all that kind of stuff."

So what, then, made the 1960s different? "It's one of those rare things that happen from time to time," he responds. "Apparently, the same thing happened, I'm told, in Paris in the '40s after the war, and in Greenwich Village in the '50s. I consider myself extremely fortunate to have been in the right place at the right time. When I got there, I moved to Kings Road in Chelsea. At that point in time, Chelsea consisted of probably, seriously speaking, 400 people who knew each other who more or less traveled around in one huge rat pack. If there was a party, all of us would turn up. And it consisted of every type of creative endeavor that there was—photographers, models, actresses, actors, writers, all that kind of thing.

"What it eventually turned out to be was what I had been told college was going to be like, where you were going to sit late into the night and discuss the meaning of life and all that kind of shit, which didn't really happen to me in college. But it happened to me in Kings Road. We sat late into the night and discussed how we were going to make it and what we were going to do, and all of a sudden everybody bloody did!" Talmy—the self-described "slave driver" in the studio, the man Ray Davies variously recalled as an uninterested clock-watcher and "smart producer" in *X-Ray*—laughs with pleasure. "It just kind of exploded. It was a real fascinating experience."

Recommended Recordings:

By the Kinks:

Greatest Hits (1989, Rhino). There is a lot of great Kinks material from the Shel Talmy (1964-67) era. This means that any single-disc compilation of early Kinks cuts will omit a lot of good stuff. This eighteen-track overview of their 1964-66 output inevitably leaves off quality performances. Yet it does have the major monsters—"You Really Got Me," "All Day and All of the Night," "Tired of Waiting for You," "Well Respected Man," "Dedicated Follower of Fashion," and "Sunny Afternoon" are the most famous—with which both the Kinks and Talmy established their reputations. The absence of the innovative 1965 raga-rock British hit single "See My Friends" is the only unforgivable omission. The final three albums the Kinks and Talmy made together—*Kinks Kontroversy* (1966), *Face to Face* (1966), and *Something Else* (1967)—are all excellent, and now available on CD with bonus tracks.

By the Who:

The Who Sing My Generation (1965, MCA). The best British mod-rock album has lots of fine songs besides the classic title hit, like "The Kids Are Alright," "The Good's Gone," "Much Too Much," and "Out in the Street." Critical reviews have usually focused on the incredible aggression and energy of the record, best projected in Keith Moon's nonstop drumming and Pete Townshend's powerhouse guitar chords and flights of feedback. These are also fine *songs*, however, with a keen sense of pop hooks and harmonies. Should the rest of the sides the group recorded with Talmy in 1965—particularly the earlier 1965 British hits "I Can't Explain" and "Anyway, Anyhow, Anywhere"—be added as bonus tracks to create an expanded CD version, it would stand as a definitive document of the Who-Talmy era.

By the Creation:

How Does It Feel to Feel (1982, Edsel, U.K.). The best of several Creation compilations has twenty tracks from 1966-68, including the group's modest British hits "Making Time" and "Painter Man." They recall the Who in their mix of harmony vocals and textured guitar distortion, which is at its most inventive when Eddie Phillips plays his instrument with a violin bow, as on the aforementioned cuts and the droning, psychedelic "How Does It Feel to Feel."

By the Pentangle:

Basket of Light (1969, Reprise). The best record by this innovative folk-jazz-rock group is a reflection of the band's astonishing eclecticism, including the small hit "Light Flight," the excellent rendition of the traditional folk song "Once I Had a Sweetheart," the rehaul of the girl-group classic "Sally Go Round the Roses," and the superb original "Springtime Promises." Excellent interplay between acoustic guitars, a light jazz rhythm section, and sincere folk vocals (particularly by Jacqui McShee and Bert Jansch) throughout. Their first two Talmy-produced albums, *The Pentangle* (1968) and the half-live double album *Sweet Child* (1968), are also fine and well worth acquiring.

Two-Shot Wonders

One of the reasons this book is not called *Unknown Legends of Rock 'n' Roll Part 2* or some such thing is that not all of the artists could be fairly described as unknown, even to the general pop and rock listener. Bobby Fuller, the Beau Brummels, and Mike Brown of the Left Banke all had big hit singles; one of them is undoubtedly playing on an oldies radio station near you at this very moment. Indeed, all of them had more than one hit single, although each one tends to be remembered for one song: Bobby Fuller for "I Fought the Law," the Beau Brummels for "Laugh, Laugh," and the Left Banke for "Walk Away Renee." Throw in Bobby Fuller's "Love's Made a Fool of You," the Beau Brummels' "Just a Little," and the Left Banke's "Pretty Ballerina," and you have not one-hit wonders, but two-hit wonders. Right?

Nope. One of the aims of scholarly dissection of rock history is to disprove lazy assumptions among some rock writers and listeners. One of the most common of those is that rock groups known mostly for one hit single, or two if you push it, concentrated all of their art into that two- or three-minute piece of plastic, and have nothing else worthy of your time and money. That is in fact true of many such artists, but it's sometimes the case that those singles are merely the fountainhead of a substantial body of quality work, including flop singles, albums, and side projects that have never received the exposure they merit. Dig beneath those radio oldies, and you also discover other facets to these artists—sometimes merely other good songs in the same vein, sometimes detours that prove they were quite capable in other styles, and sometimes downright experimental ventures.

That's certainly true of Bobby Fuller, the Beau Brummels, and the Left Banke. Each was helmed by a superb songwriter and instrumentalist. Together they comprise the most pop-friendly trio of acts in this book, no surprise as each for a time blanketed the AM radio with a song or two. Beneath that facade, however, beat the heart of an artist, even an auteur, with a dedication to artistic expression equal to that of any of the more avant-garde musicians in this volume.

Bobby Fuller

When Bobby Fuller was found dead in his car on July 18, 1966, the twenty-three-year-old had just one big hit single—and that single was a cover version. If there was ever a 1960s singer with one big hit whose story was worthy of a movie, however, Bobby Fuller was the man.

Dig deeper into the Bobby Fuller story than that big hit, and the vigor of his art and intrigue of his career path become progressively absorbing. Here was a triple threat: a dynamic singer, songwriter, and guitarist who was also a skilled engineer and producer. An artist who hit the big time with a cover of "I Fought the Law," but whose catalog contained dozens of largely overlooked self-penned gems. A musician who was at once behind his times and ahead of his times, building his own studio and releasing his own records at a time when the DIY ethic was unlabeled, yet favoring 1950s and early 1960s rockabilly-influenced styles that had long passed out of fashion by the time "I Fought the Law" charted in 1966. Someone

Bobby Fuller in his too-brief prime.
Credit: Courtesy Bryan Thomas, Del-Fi Records.

who was a studio perfectionist when it came to production and mixing, yet who insisted that his records were simple enough to be closely replicated live. A Buddy Holly acolyte who recreated the sound and style of the oft-imitated rock pioneer with more accuracy than any other rock 'n' roller did, but had to compete with the British Invasion, Motown, and psychedelic trends that were totally revamping the rock field by 1966. And most sadly, a guy who, like his idol Holly, died tragically just at the point at which his career and music were becoming established, leading to an endless query of "what-if" questions in the following decades.

In the 1980s and 1990s, Bobby Fuller's unsolved death got some retroactive media attention that, while making many aware of his music for the first time, also overshadowed the surprisingly extensive catalog of good-to-great records he did complete in his brief lifetime. Fuller has sometimes been classified as a Buddy Holly imitator, and there is some truth in that assertion, particularly in his earlier recordings. Unlike almost all rockers whose source of inspiration is worn on the sleeve, however, Fuller sounded almost as good as the prototype. At his best he sounded like Holly himself might have had Buddy survived into the 1960s. At his very best—on "I Fought the Law" and much more obscure nuggets like "My True Love," "Fool of Love," "Never to Be Forgotten," and "Only When I Dream"—Fuller was starting to sound like himself. Which is the one trait, above all, that a musician must acquire to become a major artist.

At the time of his death, it was little known (and has remained so since then, actually) that Fuller had been recording and releasing quality discs for about five years. From his preteens he had exhibited a wealth of musical talent, becoming proficient on several instruments, starting to write songs, and recording material on his parents' reel-to-reel. By the early 1960s, still in his teens, Fuller was recording himself, as a solo artist and as a member of the Embers, in the El Paso, Texas, family home. The reverb-drenched, rockabilly-pop cuts "You're in Love"/"Guess We'll Fall in Love" were soaked in the Buddy Holly ethos, and released as a single on the local Yucca label. It was a chart-topping hit in El Paso, which nonetheless meant sales of only 3,000 to 5,000 or so.

Perhaps Fuller knew that bigger connections would be necessary to break him out of West Texas. Or perhaps it was his worship of Buddy Holly that led him to record his next single at the Clovis, New Mexico, studio of Norman Petty, who had produced Buddy Holly & the Crickets' greatest tracks. "Gently My Love"/"My Heart Jumped" was also released on Yucca, and did even better, approaching the 10,000 sales mark. He and Petty did not, evidently, get on like a house on fire. Although they might have seemed a natural combination given Fuller's sonic resemblance to Holly, it was to mark the only occasion the pair worked together.

By this time Fuller's younger brother Randy had joined his sibling's band on bass. "Norman Petty was trying to promote Jimmy Gilmer [who had a number one hit in 1963 with "Sugar Shack"]," remembers Randy. "He still probably had all the rights to Buddy Holly's stuff, and he was making money on it. So he didn't really need another Buddy Holly artist. Petty left a bad taste in our mouth when we left there, as far as him wanting to do anything with us. But as time went on, Bobby became as good an engineer as Norman Petty ever thought of being, and had more creativity about it. That's where he was headed, so he didn't really have any reason to go back with Petty."

So Bobby, with the help of Randy and others, went to the unusual—for 1962—step of building a fairly elaborate studio in his parents' home, complete with Ampex tape recorders and a mixing board. There was even a primitive echo chamber, formed by leaning a four-by-eighty-foot block of concrete against a wall outside the house. Over the next couple of years he would record and release singles on his own Eastwood and Exeter labels, for whom he would also produce singles for other regional artists. He also opened his own club, the Rendezvous. He was the entrepreneur of El Paso rock 'n' roll, a promoter, producer, and performer wrapped into one.

The full trajectory of Fuller's musical development during the years 1962-64 would not become evident until about twenty years later, when several dozen selections from the mounds of unreleased tapes he cut started to become available. Fuller was pretty selective in what he chose for official release, with only five singles coming out between his first Eastwood single and his late 1964 move to Los Angeles. Even some of these 45s were not among his most distinguished efforts of the period, and an equal number of Eastwood and Exeter singles were devoted to his productions of virtually unknown groups like the Sherwoods, Pawns, and Bill Taylor & the Sherwoods.

In a way, Fuller could be described as the very first rock 'n' roll revivalist, or roots-rocker, as such performers are now called. The same age as the Beatles and most of the British bands about to invade the American charts, he was just too late to ride the wave of the rockabilly and early rock 'n' roll that was his obvious true love. Pop and rock were changing enormously even in the years just before the Beatles' first hit, and Fuller was among the few young musicians devoted to preserving and emulating the styles of the 1950s giants (although the British bands were also doing so, to a less devout degree). The five years between Buddy Holly's death in a February 1959 plane crash (which also claimed Ritchie Valens' life) and the Beatles' first American smash have often, and unfairly, been tabbed as a time when rock 'n' roll was tamed, or even died. Bobby Fuller's music proves the fallacy of this assertion. No one could have known this at the time, but in looking back to more vital sources and writing and performing his own material with a guitar band, he was also following the model that the British Invasion greats were employing to breathe more life back into rock as they readied themselves for their assault on the charts.

Buddy Holly was boss in the Fuller pantheon, of course. Listening to the early singles and numerous unreleased studio and live tapes that surfaced in the 1980s and 1990s, however, one can also detect his love for Eddie Cochran and Ritchie Valens, and to somewhat lesser extents Chuck Berry, Little Richard, Roy Orbison, the Everly Brothers, and Jerry Lee Lewis. Randy Fuller even cites Valens' "La Bamba," and particularly its electrifying Danelectro bass intro, as "the main reason I started playing bass." The big question, especially for those new to the Fuller discography, is why exactly a listener should care about him if his style was so close to that of Buddy Holly in particular.

The answer is not easy to pin down in words, but evident to most upon hearing the songs (and much more so on the original compositions than on the numerous covers he recorded during the era). Fuller had both brash vocal confidence—a quality that brother Randy repeatedly refers to as unstoppable "drive"—and, at the same time, immensely likable sincerity, not afraid to admit to vulnerability or even romantic rejection. While he was obviously aping Holly's vocal style in some early tracks, his voice was clearer and he was less apt to build hooks around catches, stutters, and hiccups. He could celebrate partying with wild abandon on "Keep on Dancing," "Shakedown," "Bodine," and the close Eddie Cochran knockoff "Saturday Night." He could also sing about tenderness and pain with heartrending passion, as on "A New Shade of Blue," "Fool of Love," "You're in Love," and "Unreliable Irresistible Girl." On paper the words, like so many rock 'n' roll lyrics, could seem banal; it is the emotion in the delivery, rather than the literal meaning, that so powerfully impresses.

There was also an intangible Tex-Mex border sound to many of Fuller's melodies and arrangements, attributable almost certainly to El Paso's position just across the Rio Grande from Mexico. Fuller and his band mates were exposed to both the searing electric blues of Long John Hunter, who played in the Lobby Bar in Juarez across the water, and the Mexican-American music of Hispanics on both sides of the border. The galloping rhythms and sad, dramatic chord progressions of "Nancy Jean," a personal favorite of Randy Fuller for its "desert" feel, make it the best early example of Bobby's penchant for rockaballads that could have fit snugly onto Western movie soundtracks. It was a talent he would tap until his death.

"We were like the Beatles in El Paso, before they knew who the Beatles were," claims Randy Fuller. "But it was hard, without distribution and a large label, [to] have the power to distribute records, get 'em played. That's one reason we came to California, was to get with a big label." For all his love of retro rock, and his determination to write and record his way, Bobby Fuller knew this. He was also not immune to pop and rock trends outside of Texas. Had he somehow faded away after 1964, he would be a very interesting, yet mightily obscure, cult figure, esteemed for a handful of neat singles and somewhat anachronistic approach. However, he had, as Randy Fuller says, the drive that wouldn't settle for that. So it was that in the summer of 1963, he got a month of shows booked at a hotel in Hermosa Beach, a Los Angeles suburb, and also hawked his tapes to several L.A. labels. One of them was Del-Fi, home of one of Bobby and Randy's heroes, Ritchie Valens. Del-Fi chief Bob Keane told Bobby to come back when he had something better.

"We went to Del-Fi and places and let 'em listen to our stuff, and Bob Keane said that we weren't quite ready to do anything, to go home and practice," laughs Randy Fuller. "So we did. We *were* ready. *He* just wasn't ready, I don't think. 'Cause we were playing as good as the Beach Boys were. We drew a bigger crowd than [original surf instrumental guitar great] Dick Dale, partly because of our versatility and knowledge of music, and not just [being] stuck in one bag. We liked it all. And it wasn't just Buddy Holly. It was Elvis, Chuck Berry, and Ritchie Valens."

The year 1964 was a time of considerable artistic and commercial headway for Fuller. His singles "King of the Beach," "Fool of Love," and above all his first version of "I Fought the Law" were, to make an awful pun, fuller sounding and melodically stronger than his previous releases. With "Saturday Night," he got a one-off deal with a label he didn't run, Todd, although the disc stiffed. Deeply impressed, even enamored, with Californian surf music, he started incorporating original and outside surf tunes into his repertoire, enriching the twin-guitar attack he developed with Jim Reese.

The British Invasion made things tougher on homegrown acts of all sorts, but Fuller couldn't have been too down on the Beatles, as he covered several of their early songs on live tapes that survive from the mid-1960s. And after running through numerous lineups in the early 1960s, he had assembled a tight, killer band, with Jim Reese on guitar, Randy on bass, and Dalton Powell on drums. In late 1964, they returned to L.A. to make another assault upon the music business capital of the West Coast, Dalton Powell deciding to stay in Texas and getting replaced by DeWayne Quirico. "We had a lot more material at that time, a lot more stuff, and saw Bob Keane again," says Randy Fuller. "He signed us up."

Bobby Fuller's brief and, in hindsight, controversial stay at Del-Fi got off to a slow start with three singles in late 1964 and early 1965, variously credited to Bobby Fuller & the Fanatics, the Shindigs, and finally the Bobby Fuller Four (the first on Del-Fi subsidiary Donna, the second on another subsidiary label, Mustang, which would issue almost all subsequent Fuller product). Some of the tunes were surf instrumentals; some were pleasant but slight pop-rock songs that uneasily bridged early '60s American pop with British Invasion-meets-Four Seasons harmonies. The Bobs Fuller and Keane (the latter of whom produced Bobby at Del-Fi) seemed to be groping for a style more current than Fuller's Buddy Holly soundalike ditties, without establishing a comfortable new identity.

In the meantime, however, the Bobby Fuller Four were becoming a hot attraction on the L.A. club scene via long residencies at the Ambassador Hotel and PJ's (where they recorded a live album, not issued until after Fuller's death). Phil Spector sat in with the band on piano once, and it's been theorized that he was interested in signing them to, and producing them for, his Philles label. Although the matchup sounds intriguing, it would probably in fact have been a mismatchup. Spector was known for grandiose productions that bore far heavier stamps of his artistic vision than those of his actual artists; Bobby Fuller favored straight-ahead, if immaculately produced, guitar rock that could be reproduced to near-perfection onstage.

In any case, the Bobby Fuller Four's breakthrough on record arrived in mid-1965 with the single "Let Her Dance." This was actually a rearrangement and rewrite of the single Fuller had done in 1964 in El Paso, "Keep on Dancing" (indeed several of the strongest tracks Bobby did for Del-Fi were remakes of songs originally cut in Texas). It could be said that Fuller was at once returning to his roots of powerful, Hollyesque rock 'n' roll, yet marrying them to a fatter, more textured, and above all more modern, radio-ready production sound with Bob Keane.

Fueled by Randy's thick, propulsive opening bass line, reverbed vocal harmonies, and even a beer bottle tapped by Randy for extra percussion, it actually ended up a bit Spectoresque. ("We had a little Wall of Sound going with Bobby as it was," responds Keane when asked about Spector's interest in the singer.) Keane used an echo chamber to fill out the sonic canvas without drowning the band's personality in masses of orchestration and echo, as Spector might have done. "Let Her Dance" was a big hit in Los Angeles, and almost got to the national Top Forty. Its B-side, "Another Sad and Lonely Night," was an excellent song in its own right, again showing Fuller's ability to adapt to more modern textures on a song that showed the more introspective, forlorn sides of his moods.

Keane singles out "Let Her Dance" as the tune that had whatever it was he found lacking in the first batch of material Fuller had played to Del-Fi: "In those days we were mainly interested in singles. We weren't really thinking albums so much." As for most of the original songs Fuller had cooked up in El Paso, "I thought it was kind of corny, personally. I was trying to get away from the Buddy Holly sound that he had. That was my main objective with Bobby. He had a lot of talent, and his songs were, I thought…they weren't Buddy Holly songs, exactly. He could have recorded them like that, I suppose. But I said to him, 'Well, even if you copy Buddy Holly, who's to say you're better? Buddy Holly is an institution, and you're just starting out. Get your own stuff out there.'"

Randy Fuller goes as far as to surmise that "Let Her Dance" and its follow-up, "Never to Be Forgotten," boast "almost like a classical song type of sound." That was more evident in "Never to Be Forgotten," which cranked up the reverb and massed background vocals used for "Let Her Dance" another notch, and added some wicked fuzz bass, its anthemic melody driven by a series of unexpected key changes. The guitar lick opening the track was another riff that would have been suitable for kicking off epic Westerns; particularly at the end of the verses, Bobby's vocals sometimes threatened to drift off like the passing fog. A fine and adventurous release, but perhaps not too ready to wear as an AM radio hit—which, as Keane stated, was his primary goal at the time. It would take a simpler, more direct song to get them into the Top Ten.

"I Fought the Law" was first done by the Buddy Holly-less Crickets, buried as an album track in 1960, and written by Cricket Sonny Curtis (a rock and country songwriter whose varied career encompasses both the Everly Brothers hit "Walk Right Back" and the theme song of the *Mary Tyler Moore* TV show). "I'm the one that wanted to do 'I Fought the Law' from the very beginning," notes Randy Fuller. "I was the one that picked it off an album, and actually the one that kind of turned it into the kind of Motown groove on it."

Bobby Fuller had already recorded and released a fine version of "I Fought the Law" back in 1964 that was only heard regionally. As with "Let Her Dance," it was decided to refine a previously recorded song with more sophisticated production, beginning with the long descending drumroll that kicks off the tune. "I Fought the Law" has been recorded dozens of times, if not more, since 1966, most famously by the Clash. The Bobby Fuller Four's 1966 rendition remains the definitive interpretation, though, with its authoritative Tex-Mex power strums, handclaps, that bit right before the line "six-gun" where all the instruments drop out except the drums, and Bobby's own defiantly proud vocal. Although similar in arrangement to the thinner-sounding Crickets original, it added a lot of punch, particularly in the percussive boom and rich backup vocal harmonies. It became a number nine national hit, and is still a much-played standard on oldies radio. As with "Let Her Dance," believes Keane, he and Fuller had taken the music Bobby had developed in Texas, "refined it a little bit, and got it out of the Buddy Holly sound into the Bobby Fuller sound."

It also marked Fuller's group as an American band that could be successful without attempting to draw heavily from the Beatles and the British Invaders. "We did a few Beatles songs," concedes Randy Fuller. "We could copy them down to a T if we wanted to. I don't think that they could copy *us* down to a T; I really don't. I can't really say that the Beatles influenced us, except maybe on a couple of records [where we said], 'Well, the Beatles got that sound, let's get that sound.' But no, I think we were trying to really stay in the rockabilly thing, like 'I Fought the Law' and stuff like that." They certainly stayed the rockabilly course with their follow-up, a straightforward cover of Buddy Holly's "Love's Made a Fool of You." Perhaps not as imaginative a choice as it could have been given Keane's desire to wean Fuller away from Holly's influence, it did become the group's second-biggest hit, making number twenty-six.

Some of Fuller's best tracks, and particularly his best original material, were actually appearing on B-sides and LPs. These tended to be his most sensitive and melodic songs, and not coincidentally, ones that he cowrote with Mary Stone, mother of his Texas high school classmate (and eventual road manager) Rick Stone. Highlights of the Fuller-Stone alliance included "Only When I Dream" (which would have done the Everly Brothers proud), "Don't Ever Let Me Know," and the great "My True Love," a haunting piece that is something of a rock "Greensleeves" (which Fuller, believe it or not, did a juiced-up version of live, as a posthumously released recording reveals). There were also remakes of songs from his 1964 Texas singles, "Saturday Night" and "Fool of Love" (both on his second Mustang LP, *I Fought the Law*), that (as with "I Fought the Law") muscled them up without tampering with their strengths. "Fool of Love," which Randy Fuller mentions as one of his faves, was a relatively ignored classic, Hollyesque but up to the standards of Buddy Holly's greatest songs.

It might seem odd that some of Fuller's finest songs were composed with Mary Stone, someone an entire generation older than he was. "She wrote a lot of love type of songs," explains Randy Fuller, "and Bobby was really into pleasing the young girls with his music. Bobby had the charisma to the young girls. They *loved* him. And he didn't mind playing the corny music, which I call it. I wanted to play harder music, more blues, more like 'I Fought the Law.' But he liked the things that made hit records. The girls' stuff. Mary wrote that kind of way, and she just kind of fit into his way of thinking and writing. [She was] kind of young at heart. I don't think he could write with just any old person, but he had a way with dealing with women, you know. He didn't have any problems or hang-ups."

Fuller had just six months to live after "I Fought the Law" began to hit—months that were packed with touring, recording, and tension. In weighing the differing retrospective viewpoints that have been put forth about Fuller's final days, it is important to bear in mind that the rush of events was such that it will be difficult, and probably impossible, to ascertain with certainty the precise details of his activities in 1966, let alone what he might have had in mind for his music and career. No one was anticipating Fuller's death, or keeping a running record of grievances and disputes that have built up over the years. It seems fairly certain, though, that he was frustrated to some extent in deciding what sounds he should explore, and how he might have the best opportunity to get what he heard in his head onto vinyl.

"We tried to play with four pieces and all our harmonies, live, all the time, just like what was on the record," says Randy Fuller. "What you hear on the record, a lot of times, is what we sounded like live. We tried to duplicate that sound as close as we could live. My brother believed if you couldn't play it live like the record, pretty much, then people weren't gonna like it as much." On the Bobby Fuller Four's records, "It seemed like I wanted more bass, and that Bobby wanted the bass to be up louder. We wanted our bottom to be up.

"It seemed like every time Bob [Keane] would mix something, you could hear the kick drum and the bass kind of down. That was bugging [us] a lot. Plus, you got two engineers in a booth, you're gonna have that. But Bob Keane, he's pretty much into his own world. What Bob wants is what Bob does, and you don't have much say in it. That was kind of driving Bobby crazy. It was always a thing of having to do it, but yet it always went Bob Keane's way. That's one reason he wanted out of the Del-Fi situation. Ahmet Ertegun [of Atlantic Records], I think, was very interested. He would have signed us in a minute at that point. We could have gotten on any label we wanted to get on. They [Del-Fi] knew that, and they didn't want to let go, I imagine."

Keane sees things differently. "He [Bobby] had knowledge of how to make a band and get the right guys playing the right parts, and he was really good in the studio. He kind of objected to [some mixing and production decisions], but didn't object too strenuously. In fact, he never really said much to me about the sound. There's a lot of stories around about Bobby this, Bobby that in the studio, and Keane this and Keane that, and it's all bullshit. We got along fine in the studio. I never had any problems with the guy." As for the Fullers' wishes to boost the bass and kick drums, "I thought that was also *my* idea. That's the way I feel, too; I think the bass and the kick are the things that make it happen. Although Randy played a very busy bass, and you had to be careful with that. But that was cool, because that's one thing that made 'Let Her Dance' go, that bass line. That was a killer.

"The one problem was that other guitar player [Jim Reese]. He was a real asshole. He caused a lot of problems. He was always bitching and bellyaching about this and that." Reese was an underrated component of the Bobby Fuller Four, a colead guitarist to Bobby rather than a second or rhythm guitarist, and as Randy acknowledges, Jim "contributed a lot with his knowledge of music and guitar. But he was kind of a stubborn guy."

Rifts widened in the Bobby Fuller Four as their success grew—not a good portent, for even as Bobby was the unquestioned star, his sound was very much a group product. "We all had our jealousies of Bobby, because he was getting most of the recognition. My brother could get onstage and had the charisma, [could] project himself as the man. They really pursued to make him a star, which was kind of understandable, the way I thought. I'd always get upset when we never got mentioned or anything, and my brother would tell me, 'You gotta show them something [if] you want to be mentioned.' And I look back now, he's absolutely right. You can't be self-conscious and then don't project yourself." Just after "I Fought the Law," the first member of the winning team departed, as DeWayne Quirico got fired for missing or coming late to rehearsals and engagements. Johnny Barbata of the Turtles filled in briefly until Dalton Powell came out from Texas to rejoin, although Randy admits Quirico "was probably the better drummer for us at the time."

There had been petty disappointments over the past year or so that frustrated the group members, such as their sole film appearance, in the low-grade American International Pictures flick *The Ghost in the Invisible Bikini*, in which they had to mime to songs they hadn't even written or recorded. There was a mishap that saw "Let Her Dance" released twice on Mustang, and once on Liberty, deflating its momentum. Their two Mustang LPs did not do the band full justice. *KRLA King of the Wheels* had some filler hot-rod tunes and a title track calculated to get them the airplay and support of one of Los Angeles' top radio stations; *I Fought the Law*, while better, duplicated no less than seven cuts from the previous album. It was a progressively hectic touring schedule, however, that aggravated the quartet the most, cutting into time they, and especially Bobby, would have rather spent writing and recording new material.

"We didn't really want to do anything but record and play concerts, spend all our time doing that," reasons Randy. "And here we had to go on the road to New York and play every joint in town. There was a few really good gigs that we did, but some of it was really just Mickey Mouse. Booking us at gigs that didn't really matter, just to get their percentage of the booking." Del-Fi was involved in setting up bookings for the band, "so a lot of things were down to get us, Bobby, wanting out of that label."

It should be borne in mind that while Fuller's wish to concentrate on recording rather than touring was not unreasonable, it *was* unusual by the standards of 1966. Even the Beatles were still making lengthy, tiring tours through the end of that summer; it took a nervous breakdown to get Brian Wilson of the Beach Boys off the road and into the studio most of the time. Zigzagging six-week national tours such as the one Fuller undertook that year, though hardly conducive to artistic growth, were pretty standard fare for acts with hit records, from Motown and the Beatles downwards.

Keane, again, has a different perspective. "These guys were all from a whole different bag. They probably weren't into the regular rock 'n' roll image that was out there with the big bands, the touring bands. They had a different idea about their music, about what they wanted to do. Of course, touring is the only way you're really going to make any money. You gotta tour a band in order to make 'em happen. Somebody has to get the band promoted, and that was my job. I had to do it with all our acts. None of them had managers. I was just trying to get exposure for Bobby the best way I could.

"So I don't know what they were thinking about, that they didn't want to tour. I never heard that from any of those guys. But he was successful wherever he played, except New York. When he was in [the New York club] Ondine's, they weren't ready for him. New York, as against Southern California in those days…it was very difficult to get a California record played east of the Rockies. They didn't dig California music.

"Bobby was wonderful in personal appearances and talking with fans. He was very gracious. The chicks loved him, because he didn't hit on 'em; he respected them. That was terrific. But *working* with him was a different story. A lot of times, he wasn't a very warm guy. He wasn't communicative. So there was a lot of things I didn't know about Bobby. He was kind of introverted in that respect. So a lot of things you're asking me that people said, I don't know about 'em. Because maybe he said it to somebody else. But he didn't say it to me. We really didn't hang out together too much.

"The thing about Bobby Fuller was that he wanted to have his own music. That's what really got him upset, that we didn't record but one of his songs, or a couple maybe [as singles]. But there was only one [of his compositions] that happened, 'Let Her Dance.' The rest were all other people's songs. And he wanted to be known for his songwriting. So he was unhappy about that, as far as I know. The stuff that he wrote was all kind of pretty, pretty stuff. He had some rockers, too. Good songs, and great for albums. I don't know what it was, but I just didn't feel that any of those he had, like 'Saturday Night,' that stuff that kicks out, was really big hits.

"But when you come time for another release, and you don't have anything, you don't think, strong enough to follow up, then you gotta get it from somebody else. And that's what we did."

In New York, Fuller and Keane had gone to the Brill Building for suitable material, choosing the songs "The Magic Touch" and "I'm a Lucky Guy." It has sometimes been written that Fuller disliked "The Magic Touch," actually a pretty decent song with a heavier contemporary soul vibe than anything he had previously done. The young Barry White, then learning the ropes of record production at Del-Fi, helped out at the session, although his role, says Randy Fuller, wasn't too big (White would also play drums on Fuller's final B-side, "It's Love, Come What May"). "Bobby wanted to do the song," clarifies Randy. "There was no problem with that. He was frustrated with how it was mixed. It didn't sound right. It didn't have enough oomph. Too thin-sounding. That's what he was upset about. That was the one he wanted to really try to develop and mix. I think Bob Keane was leaning more toward getting into a Motown thing."

Keane again counters: "I wouldn't *want* to copy Motown. It would be the most stupid thing in the world to do. Bobby had his own thing going by that time. By the time we did 'Magic Touch,' it was all Bobby's stuff. He really put it together in the studio with the band; Barry didn't."

By July 1966, problems between Fuller, the rest of the band, and Del-Fi were rising to the point that changes were probably inevitable. A booking at a San Francisco club was so disastrous that Fuller canceled the gigs to return to L.A. Jim Reese got his draft notice. The band members were disappointed that a possible European tour had not come through ("I Fought the Law" had made a little noise on English radio and charts). It's been speculated that the Bobby Fuller Four were on the verge of breaking up, with Bobby reorganizing the band, or going solo. "I look back on that now, and it was the stupidest thing for them not to put money into sending us overseas," asserts Randy Fuller. "We were aware that if we went to England, we would be over there what the Beatles are over here. That's what was happening, P. J. Proby and [American] guys like that were doing great over in England." For what it's worth, according to a *Kicks* magazine article on Fuller, "George Harrison did cite the Bobby Fuller Four as his most listened-to group in an early 1966 interview"—a more important British fan the band could hardly hope to have.

Keane says he does not remember plans for the band to tour in Europe, "but if it was canceled, it was because the deal didn't go through. Maybe we were trying to get 'em a European deal. But that would have been too soon, I would think, because they wouldn't do well over there, 'cause nobody would know who the hell they were. At that point, their record was not overseas at all, as far as I know."

A band meeting was scheduled for the morning of July 18, in which some of the issues troubling the group members and their relationship with Del-Fi would most likely have been discussed. Bobby Fuller never showed up. That afternoon, his mother, who had moved to L.A. to be close to her sons, found his body—bloody and beaten, covered in gasoline—in the front seat of his car.

The unsolved mystery of Bobby Fuller's death may be the closest equivalent to the JFK assassination in the history of rock 'n' roll. It was ruled as either an accident or a suicide by the Los Angeles police; the autopsy report determined the cause to be "asphyxia due to inhalation of gasoline." As with the single-gunman theory that the American government settled upon after President Kennedy's death, many familiar with the case doubt the LAPD's conclusion. In fact, no one who knew Fuller seems to have thought it a suicide, or even that Fuller was close to a suicidal state of mind. Many also can't see how he could have met his fate accidentally, given the mutilated condition of his body when it was found.

There have been dozens of theories propagated, some plausible, some bizarre, concerning Fuller's death, the puzzle enduring despite the LAPD's lack of interest in reopening the case (and when Del-Fi and Randy Fuller asked the department to locate Bobby's file in the 1990s, it was reported as having gone missing). There were even segments devoted to the incident on *Entertainment Tonight* in the 1980s, and the *Unsolved Mysteries* series in the 1990s. There has been periodic interest from Hollywood in making a movie based on Fuller's life, and if one is ever made, for better or for worse, it will probably center around his premature demise.

Some thought that Fuller was the victim of a jealous boyfriend of a girl with whom he might have been involved; some thought he could have been done in by the mob. There was even speculation that Jim Reese (who died in 1991) could have had something to do with it; or that someone wanted to cash in on Fuller's life insurance policy. An entire book could probably be devoted to the tragedy; Dan Epstein's lengthy essay on Fuller's death in the liner notes to the Bobby Fuller Four box set *Never to Be Forgotten* is the best place to familiarize oneself with the details.

Within days, Reese and Powell were on their way back to El Paso with a loaded pistol in the seat of their car, frightened by three armed men who had shown up looking for Jim at Reese's apartment. A final Bobby Fuller Four track, "It's Love, Come What May," came out under Randy Fuller's name (with Randy doubletracking his voice with Bobby's). Randy did a few recordings with a Randy Fuller Four and joined Blue Mountain Eagle, which had an album for Atlantic. Del-Fi wound down its operations by the end of the 1960s.

What has only become clear with time is the magnitude of the loss for rock music as a whole with Fuller's passing. Bobby Fuller's cult following continued to expand, particularly over the last twenty years, when reissues made virtually all of his recordings (and many previously unreleased ones) available. Which leaves that galling question: what if?

Fuller, despite having recorded prolifically for five years, was only just maturing as a musician. At the same time, he was a throwback in many ways, not in sync with current British Invasion and Motown trends, let alone the psychedelic and hard rock music that was just emerging. There were mild touches of sonic experimentation on the reverb and layered composition of tracks like "Never to Be Forgotten," and the fuzz guitar on his group's cover of Sonny Curtis' "Baby My Heart" (not released until long after Fuller's death), but little that was in keeping with 1966 folk-rock or early psychedelia. Could he have adapted? Would he have wanted to? Would he have even had to?

"The way I figure it, we were in a bad place right after the rockabilly era ended," says Randy Fuller. "We weren't Motown, and we weren't English. My brother always said we were ahead of our time. I really kind of believe that now. I think if we were together now, him and me especially, I think we'd be right on top of it."

Would Bobby have continued with the Bobby Fuller Four, or tried his luck as a solo artist, as has sometimes been mooted? "I don't think we'd have had the Bobby Fuller Four as it was. I would have still been there, but I don't think the other two guys [would have]. I think he'd have finally had to do that, just for his own health. I think it would have driven anybody about half batty to have to deal with two other musicians that really didn't give a hill of beans about nothing but themselves.

"He'd probably [have] built a studio, either in El Paso or in California, and started producing his own stuff—our own stuff. It probably would have broke the band up, though." Randy had written a few Bobby Fuller Four songs with Bobby, and couldn't envision that he and Bobby would not continue to work together as musical partners. "We might have gone our ways for a while. We might have taken some time off, got into a different label, somebody that really wanted to produce and promote us right, like Ahmet Ertegun at Atlantic. Del-Fi didn't really have the power to do that much, even though [Del-Fi partner Larry Nunes] had a lot of money; he did a lot to get us recognized. But he didn't book us in the right things, with the right shows.

"Once you had blood harmonies and rhythms, it's hard to replace that. You can never replace blood harmony. We couldn't replace each other's harmony, 'cause we lost our sound. A lot of times, Bobby would put his voice on the top of the harmonies, or do two-part harmonies, just to keep that sound. Just like the Beatles. You hear their harmonies, you don't really want to hear anything but *their* harmonies. If you put some black girls in there singing the harmonies, it wouldn't be the Beatles, would it? It sounds kind of silly or something.

"I think he would have ended up as a real good and fair businessman, because of knowing how people get screwed. I think we would have excelled musically. One-hit wonders have one song and can't find another one. We could have found another song. We could have written a *thousand* songs.

"I always thought we would have been something like Creedence Clearwater after that. We were headed that direction. We could do any music we wanted to do as far as play it. But we were trying to get more stuff like 'I Fought the Law.'" The Creedence Clearwater Revival comparison is not too far-fetched. In 1966, Creedence, then a struggling outfit known as the Golliwogs (whom Bobby had suggested Keane sign after hearing them at a TV show), were far behind Fuller in evolution, yet steeped in much of the same roots rock ethos. No one would have guessed that they, and John Fogerty in particular, would have become *the* major American earthy rock 'n' roll artists. Another musician whom Fuller admired, fellow Texan Doug Sahm (then of the Sir Douglas Quintet), also proved able to expand into progressive directions after the mid-1960s while maintaining a roots music base.

"I don't think Bobby would have ever been happy with where he was at. Where he was headed—I don't know. I just cannot say, because it could have been that we'd have given it all up, and he'd have gone just into producing. He could have ended up being a great singer. His voice was developing better and better and better. He had a hell of a lot of drive, and when a person's got that, man, there's just no limitations to what they can do. He had the faith that everything he did was good." Adds Barry Tashian of the Remains, who met Fuller in 1966 when Bobby was in New York, "In my opinion he would have remained a roots artist because he had a genuine connection to these roots. He was too authentic to ever change his style and go with some new music craze."

"Bobby would have gone on, I'm sure, to be one of the top groups," chips in Keane, still involved today with a revived Del-Fi label, which has put out comprehensive reissues of released and unreleased Fuller material. "I think he'd have a band that would be in the neighborhood of the popularity and image of maybe the Stones, or some of those kind of groups. He was creative. He would have probably developed himself a lot, in his writing. He would have just gone on and on and on."

Randy Fuller has started making music again recently, working in his home studio with guitarist Billy Webb and drummer Larry Thompson, both of whom passed through the band in the early 1960s. Along with the pleasant surprise of a steady stream of fan mail from around the world extolling the Bobby Fuller Four, there are the less pleasant trips down memory lane, particularly when it comes to recounting Bobby's death for the media. "As far as what happened to Bobby, I don't like to go there too much anymore, unless I have to. I get calls like this all the time I have to go through. I agreed to do this for the sake of all of us, 'cause I feel like he would want me to. He's still my brother, and I'd give my right arm if he'd come back now. It's like part of you's gone. Part of your talent is gone."

Recommended Recordings:

The Best of the Bobby Fuller Four (1990, Del-Fi/Rhino). The best of the Bobby Fuller best-ofs. Eighteen songs from his mid-1960s stay at Del-Fi, almost every one a gem, including "I Fought the Law," "Love's Made a Fool of You," "My True Love," "Fool of Love," "Never to Be Forgotten," "Let Her Dance," "Saturday Night," "Only When I Dream," and other goodies.

Shakedown! The Texas Tapes Revisited (1996, Del-Fi). First-class double-CD set of more than fifty songs from Fuller's "Texas" era, recorded in 1961-64 prior to his signing to Del-Fi. Generally overlooked and underrated, it's stellar rockabilly, Hollyesque pop-rock, and straight-ahead rock 'n' roll. Original versions of songs he rerecorded in the mid-1960s like "Fool of Love," "I Fought the Law," and "Saturday Night" are here. Equally rewarding, though, are gentle, tuneful, and haunting originals like "Guess We'll Fall in Love," "Unreliable Irresistible Girl," "A New Shade of Blue," and "Nancy Jean," along with his storming hard rocker "Shakedown."

Never to Be Forgotten (1997, Del-Fi). This three-CD box set has everything he did for Del-Fi, as well as unreleased tunes, alternate takes, Randy Fuller solo tracks, and an entire bonus disc of the live material they recorded at PJ's in the mid-1960s. Not everything is great, and many may find the 1990 best-of CD enough. It's cool to have the mid-1960s Del-Fi legacy in one place, though, enhanced by a sixty-four-page booklet of liner notes.

The Beau Brummels

Compared to most of the artists written about in this book, you could say the Beau Brummels got a pretty good deal. They had not just one but two big hits that people still remember thirty-five years later, especially the first of these, "Laugh, Laugh." And they're still remembered as one of the first—perhaps the *very* first—American band to successfully emulate the sound of the British Invasion. Indeed, when "Laugh, Laugh" first hit the airwaves, many listeners simply assumed the musicians were British, what with their foppish name, and melodic harmonies that strongly recalled the Beatles, Zombies, and other U.K. hit-makers of the mid-1960s.

You could say, however, that few bands were dealt a rawer deal by conventional rock history than the Beau Brummels were. They were the first significant San Francisco rock band, their sweet-sour tunes setting the table for the Bay Area folk-rock and psychedelic scenes that exploded into national prominence. They were one of the first groups from anywhere to play in the style that would be identified as folk-

The Beau Brummels, the thinking man's pop group. Top left, John Petersen; top right, Sal Valentino; bottom left, Ron Elliott; bottom right, Ron Meagher. Credit: Courtesy Sundazed Music.

rock, predating even the Byrds. A few years after their commercial prime, they helped pioneer country-rock. They had one of the greatest lead singers in rock, and one of its most underrated songwriters. They didn't just have those two classic hit singles; they had albums of quality, often superb, material, some of which never even got released until the 1990s.

History tends to forget most of this, reducing them to a footnote, or almost a novelty act of sorts that fooled listeners into thinking they were a British band, before better and hipper acts from San Francisco and elsewhere took their place. Those who have bothered to wade through their extensive catalog know better. The campaign to rehabilitate their reputation won't be spearheaded, though, by either of the two Beau Brummels mainstays—singer Sal Valentino and guitarist-songwriter Ron Elliott—both of whom are modest to a fault, almost self-deprecating, about the music they made together in the 1960s.

When the Beau Brummels began recording in 1964, there were few guitar rock bands in San Francisco who wrote and sang their own material. What little muscle the local music scene had was due largely to the entrepreneurial efforts of Tom Donahue, DJ on pop station KYA. With his partner Bob Mitchell, he formed Autumn Records to record regional acts. With the advent of the Beatles in the United States, they, and most other labels in the United States, were looking for an American answer to the British Invasion. They were lucky enough to stumble upon the first good one, the Beau Brummels, when a hooker known to Donahue recommended that he check the band out at the Morocco Room in San Mateo, a short drive south of the big city.

As the earliest photos of the group testify, none of them (save bassist Ron Meagher) even had the Beatle hairstyle down at the outset. They did have one asset few other U.S. bands of the time had—a genuine British accent, or nearly one, courtesy of guitarist Declan Mulligan, who had moved to the States from Ireland in the early 1960s. A more durable weapon, however, was their chief songwriter, Ron Elliott, who had a knack for penning songs that sounded somewhat like the Beatles' folkiest early efforts—'64 Beatle tunes like "I'll Be Back," "Things We Said Today," and "I'll Follow the Sun"—without sounding like rewrites.

Elliott, oddly, had little interest in rock until the Beau Brummels formed, although he'd been writing music since his preteens. His influences were theatrical composers—George Gershwin, Jerome Kern, Rodgers and Hammerstein—and the country music of Lefty Frizzell. "I'd never really listened to popular music until we started to put a band together," he reminisces as he finishes breakfast at a cafe a few blocks from Golden Gate Park. "The first thing I heard when I turned on the radio listening for that format was the Four Seasons. And I turned off the radio and wrote Laugh, Laugh." Elliott does not remember the exact Four Seasons song, and it's difficult to imagine what tune of theirs may have inspired "Laugh, Laugh," in spite of the minor chords in some 1964 Seasons hits like "Rag Doll." "Laugh, Laugh" did not sound like the Four Seasons, George Gershwin, or country music. It sounded like the Beatles, with its adroit shifts from major to minor chords, eerie harmonica, and rich vocal harmonies.

Yet "Laugh, Laugh," and most of what the Brummels would record for Autumn over the next couple of years, was not merely a Fab Four photocopy. There was a surfeit of yearning melancholy, emphasized by the sad melodies and straining harmonies, that both made the band instantly identifiable and distanced it from the armies of Beatles copycats springing up on both sides of the Atlantic. There were also the trembling, but full-throated, lead vocals of Sal Valentino, one of the few rock singers able to sing with as much resonance in the lower register as he had on the high notes. Helped, most likely, by an understandable perception on the part of many that they were a British band, "Laugh, Laugh" rose to number fifteen in the national charts in early 1965.

Introducing the Beau Brummels, produced by a young Sly Stone, was comprised mostly of Elliott originals, and hinted at the depth of a group just beginning to find its feet. While some of the tunes were transparent if enjoyable Beatlesque ditties, others reflected a more serious state of mind. The brooding "They'll Make You Cry" was embryonic folk-rock, with its descending acoustic guitar strums and lonesome harmonica, while "Not Too Long Ago" betrayed Elliott's debt to country music in its narrative tone and close harmonies. "I probably used too many minor keys," says Elliott now of his early work. "But I always enjoyed them. It adds a touch of mystery to the music. Like all the James Bond things; there was a lot of minor in those, which I always liked."

The album also had their second and biggest hit, "Just a Little," which brought the incipient folk-rock of the band to maturation. Introduced by haunting acoustic guitar strums and ascending minor-key harmonies, then exploding into an uplifting chorus with shimmering electric guitar chords, it took the best from both folk and rock music. With its vocal blends and mix of electric and acoustic guitars, it anticipated—barely—the official birth of folk-rock, usually ascribed to the Byrds' "Mr. Tambourine Man," which entered the charts a month after "Just a Little." Not that the Byrds were too appreciative of the Brummels' advance guard: in a *Rolling Stone* interview, Byrds leader Roger McGuinn claimed that the San Francisco group "had a little trouble singing in tune."

Elliott sees the folk-rock label attached to some of the Brummels' recordings as more a product of accident or coincidence than deliberation. "We only had acoustic and electric guitars, so every chance we got, we'd try to add some variety. We couldn't do it much with playing or style differences, because everybody had limited chops, including myself. We weren't professionals in that sense, where people could jump from style to style or do a flashy thing. The only way you could get variety was to go [to] a harmonica during this song, or get an acoustic in this space, get different moods that way.

"I had to de-complicate my music and get it simpler and simpler, so that we could play it and make it sound popular. [The Beau Brummels] weren't top-of-the-line musicians, they were good musicians, just solid and simple. Whenever you have a format like that, it sounds folky, because it's not glitzed over with anything. If it had been a group of different players, it would have had a totally different thing." Sal Valentino, for his part, feels the Byrds "knew the folk thing much more than we did. I don't know that Elliott knew it that well."

A big boost to the group's early sessions was producer Sly Stone, then in his early twenties and something of the Autumn house producer. In view of what he did with the Family Stone, it may be hard to imagine the flamboyant psychedelic soulster cutting catchy British Invasion mimics and early folk-rock. Elliott, though, thinks "he pulled a lot of loose ends of the band together. He was the most talented musician in the room. He was just a joy, it was really fun. He would be dancing in the studio as we were playing tracks. He could play a lot of things, knew a lot of stuff. Tom Donahue gave Sly free access to studio time, so he had experience, when we had none. His influence was very positive. And at the time, he was clear-headed."

In retrospect, the group might have been well advised to put out a superb new Elliott song, "Sad Little Girl," as its third single. With its reverbed guitar lines, it fit well into the jangly sound that became a craze as the Byrds and others brought folk-rock to AM radio in mid-1965; its story of its sad-hearted protagonist built to an intense climax with a steadily more ominous march of tambourines and drums. Elliott believes "it should have been done more like a bolero than what it was done as; it could have been very powerful." Valentino is still not sure of the reason, but it was passed over in favor of the lower-key "You Tell Me Why," a song "I thought was going to be great too." It just made the Top Forty, and started a downward sales trend that would not be arrested for the rest of the band's stay on Autumn.

Musically, the Beau Brummels continued to grow throughout 1965, as evidenced by their second album, the none-too-imaginatively-titled *Volume 2*. In addition to "Sad Little Girl" and "You Tell Me Why," it had "Don't Talk to Strangers," which perhaps was a little too close to the Byrds for comfort with its ringing circular guitar lick and harmonies that were nearly identical to those heard on the Byrds' "The Bells of Rhymney." "I Want You," also closer to the jangly sound of folk-rock than their earliest recordings had been, was as good as any song the Beau Brummels ever did, with its dense humming harmonies and spellbinding melody. While not as good as the albums being made by the Byrds in 1965 and 1966, *Volume 2* wasn't much worse either, although Sly Stone's involvement had decreased to the point that Elliott and Valentino don't really remember any producer being in charge.

The lack of a firm production hand on *Volume 2* was symptomatic of a general unraveling of the band throughout 1965, businesswise if not musicwise. Around the middle of the year, Dec Mulligan was fired or quit, reducing the band from a quintet to a quartet. More seriously, Ron Elliott's diabetes made touring difficult, especially with the punishing schedules one- or two-hit bands were expected to keep in the mid-1960s, when there was often little concern for career longevity from managers or record companies. At times the Brummels had to hire replacements for live shows, although Elliott continued to play on all the recording sessions. In addition, Autumn Records—a small independent that was fighting an uphill battle to get national hits in the first place—was becoming increasingly uninterested in promoting the Brummels, or indeed anyone. Rumor had it that by this point, Tom Donahue and Bob Mitchell were spending most of their time and money at the Bay Meadows racetrack.

"The record company was coming apart," says Valentino. "Nobody was working our stuff like they were before. Maybe Tom and Bob were out of favors. They did have a lot to do with the first two [singles], but I don't think they had much to do with the third and fourth and fifth and sixth. They may have been losing interest because Ron and his father were after them for more, or wondering why this, why that. They were a force that way that the rest of us didn't know about."

In spite of the tumult, Elliott continued to write at a blazing speed. The Beau Brummels were only on Autumn Records for about a year and a half, yet the band cut more than forty Elliott compositions (some written with high school friend Bob Durand) during that period, only about half of which made it onto their first two LPs. Songs such as "I Grow Old" and "Gentle Wandering Ways" went into a darker, more complex and philosophical frame of mind than Elliott's early Beau Brummels tunes had. The much brighter "Dream On" had wonderful harmonies that hinted strongly at country-rock, a fusion that was two or three years down the line from getting labeled by the media. All of these songs would have most likely ended up on a third Beau Brummels album for Autumn that Valentino feels "would have had a mixture of the darkness and some of the lighter stuff; it might have gotten a little more country, too." In addition, Valentino himself was starting to write quality songs like "Love Is Just a Game," "This Is Love," and "Hey Love" that were strongly reminiscent of Elliott's work in melody and tone, though more romantically-minded. (All of the aforementioned material can be heard on the three-CD box set San Fran Sessions, a compilation of the group's Autumn demos and outtakes.)

The third album didn't happen. Shortly after the Brummels' final Autumn recording session in early 1966, the rug was pulled out from under them. The entire Autumn Records roster was transferred to Warner Brothers, and its back catalog auctioned off. The Beau Brummels were suddenly on Warner Brothers and recording, through no plan of their own, an album consisting entirely of covers of mid-1960s Top Forty hits.

"Tom Donahue lost interest in everything he started," speculates Elliott. "A brilliant guy. Not focused. [Autumn] was more like a toy, something he could run and meet chicks; that was my impression. He'd start something, then something else would interest him, and that would be the end of it. There was no continuity.

"Donahue was a big reason why we didn't make it. Because when we got through with Autumn, we could have gotten a good deal somewhere, like on Warner Brothers. But he sold the band to Warner Brothers, he sold our tapes to somebody else, and they sold the publishing to somebody else. By the time Warners figured out what they didn't have, we were a tax write-off more than an act."

As a bitter consequence of this division, Warners did not want the band to record its own songs—songs, in other words, for which Warners did not control the publishing. Instead, for Beau Brummels '66, the label had them do hits of the day such as "Mr. Tambourine Man," "Louie, Louie," "Hang on Sloopy," "Mrs. Brown You've Got a Lovely Daughter," and "These Boots Are Made for Walking." Given that the best thing the band had going for it was its strong original material, this counterproductive cutting off the nose to spite the face was nothing short of idiocy.

Valentino takes pains to put the best possible face on this disaster. "When we went to Warner Brothers, they were just anxious to get a record out, to capitalize on the success we had. That record was the wrong one to do at the time. We had a third album, and they just weren't of a mind to do it. Warner Brothers wasn't the record company that they were fifteen years later. In a lot of ways, they were laughable as a record company.

"Everything considered, I was happy to go to Warner Brothers. I was relieved that we were going to be somewhere and able to make records. That record was their idea, and I thought they knew what they were doing. I'm sure Ron objected to it."

The Beau Brummels lost an enormous amount of ground in 1966, and not just because of the Warner Brothers album. San Francisco rock was rising from a rumble to an earthquake, as the Jefferson Airplane started to record and groups such as the Grateful Dead, Big Brother & the Holding Company, and Quicksilver Messenger Service cultivated local followings that would soon lead to national exposure and major label recording contracts. Some of these musicians—like the Grateful Dead, Grace Slick (as part of the Great Society), and Sly Stone—had made pre-fame recordings and demos for Autumn.

The Beau Brummels should have been there to share the wealth as the Bay Area scene, centered around the Fillmore and Avalon ballrooms, started to explode. Although on the surface their music may have seemed dissimilar to that of the San Francisco psychedelic bands, it is not unreasonable to postulate that the Beau Brummels—rather than the Airplane or, on a more underground level, the Charlatans (commonly cited as the first true San Francisco hippie group)—were the true forefathers of the San Francisco sound. If most of the diverse San Francisco rock acts of the era shared anything—at least in the mid-1960s, as folk-rock moved toward psychedelia—they had in common bittersweet melodies, chord structures and harmonies that often derived from folk music, and a shift from standard love songs to more reflective and serious lyrics. All of these traits were bountiful on the Beau Brummels' mid-1960s recordings, and it is not so far a leap from these to the folk-rock songs that dominated the early repertoire of the Jefferson Airplane.

The Beau Brummels, however, were considered comparative lightweights in the counterculture, partly because they had already had big hits, and also because they weren't able to play much in the city anyway, owing to their frenzied touring schedule. As to their failure to get in on the burgeoning psychedelic underground circuit, Elliott offers, "The best explanation I've ever heard was that Tom Donahue and [leading San Francisco promoter] Bill Graham didn't like each other. As soon as Graham got popular, we were not on his list.

"We happened before the drug scene happened. We were on the periphery of it, not in the center of it. We were too early, I guess. But the caliber of players we had, I don't think would have been good for the Fillmore anyway. We were playing a much simpler kind of music—actually, a very complicated music in a very simple expression. There was no flash, no psychedelic riffs or anything like that to excite the crowds. Possibly Graham just didn't think we would fit into his format."

"When I saw the Great Society I thought they were a bunch of artful kind of people who wanted to be a band," comments Valentino. "I didn't get the feeling they were musicians that were on their way to being entertainers. Neither were we, as a matter of fact, but we were looking that way. I don't think the rest of these bands were. We were into selling records, selling a lot of them.

"The San Francisco scene, I have to say I was a little envious of it," he confesses. "When I'd come back here, I'd go to the Fillmore or the Avalon and see this society growing up with this music, or this music growing up with this society. It looked like it was great fun, but the Brummels weren't part of it." In fact, they weren't even strictly a San Francisco band anymore, as Elliott and Valentino moved to Los Angeles in 1966, although the rest of the group remained up north.

Fortunately, after the *Beau Brummels '66* debacle, the group found a sympathetic ear at Warner Brothers in producer Lenny Waronker, who produced their next two albums and allowed the band to resume recording original material. By the time of 1967's *Triangle*, the departure of Brian Jones look-alike drummer John Petersen reduced them to the trio of Valentino, Elliott, and Ron Meagher, fleshed out by session musicians such as Van Dyke Parks (who played harpsichord on "Magic Hollow"). The beat group arrangements of the Autumn years were gone, replaced by more arty orchestrations and subtle songs with a gauzily introspective aura. The exponentially high "haunt count" of the early Beau Brummels records was replaced by a growing interest in country and western music, especially audible in Ron Elliott's masterful acoustic guitar work. For the first time, Elliott and Valentino collaborated on much of the songwriting, though Ron wrote some of the tunes with his occasional cocomposer Bob Durand. Elliott calls the album "sort of a mood swing into the world that was around us at the time. It was sort of dissolving into this drug culture. So the music became very ethereal, mystic, and mysterious."

The album also allowed Valentino's always exceptional voice to reach new levels of expression, especially when he worked the lower notes and delivered hazy yet evocative lyrics, as on "The Wolf of Velvet Fortune," "Only Dreaming Now," and "Magic Hollow." "That came with Ron's writing," asserts Valentino. "Ron had a great low register. He knew how to write in the best keys for me. If you listen to Stoneground's [Valentino's subsequent band] stuff, it's a different guy, different songs, different styles. Some people don't think much of it at all, especially people that like my singing at the beginning. From the time I started singing in bands, I didn't really sing too many other people's songs other than Ron's. Being able to sing just one person's writing, who was a pretty able writer with ability to adjust to what he's working with, had a lot do with the way I sang."

Elliott on Valentino's singing: "I think I helped Sal a lot because, [with] my theater background, I'd tell him not to be so free with phrasing or something, or stick to a melody. We were very compatible during those days; we were working together and he wanted to sing. And he would sing and sing and sing and sing and sing and sing," he laughs. "I remember one time he came over to my house, and he went, 'Summertime'—it took him about half a minute to get up to the note. I made him realize how to focus. I didn't teach him how to sing at all. He taught himself. But I taught him how to maybe project the music I was writing, how to get it across better."

Triangle won the Beau Brummels some credibility with the underground, although it only made the very bottom of the Top 200 (peaking at number 197). For the follow-up, as Elliott recalls, "Waronker wanted to go to Nashville to record an album He thought country was a good place to go for us, to try out. So we went and recorded at Bradley's Barn"—one of Nashville's top studios, named for producer Owen Bradley—"and boy, those players were unbelievable. It was so much fun to do that.

"But it wasn't so far from the *Triangle* approach. We weren't trying to do country. We were trying to do *Beau Brummels* country, which was a totally different thing. But it didn't catch on."

Valentino agrees: "We pretty much did a Beau Brummels album, Ron doing the writing and playing, and my doing the singing. It wasn't, 'Let's go in and do a country-rock album.' The idea was basically to do a record there with some of the best players available. It worked. Once again, through all of this time, we're still trying to come up with a single. With that album and *Triangle*, kept thinking that we had one. But we never got one, for some reason."

By the time of *Bradley's Barn* (1968), Ron Meagher had left and there were only two Beau Brummels remaining, accompanied for the recording by grade-A Nashville musicians like drummer Kenneth Buttrey (famous for playing on Bob Dylan's 1966-69 records) and guitarist Jerry Reed. The album was one of the better early country-rock efforts, though as Elliott says, it wasn't too different from *Triangle*, just a little more country-accented. On "Bless You California," you can hear Elliott's long-suppressed love of American theater coming to the fore.

One happy consequence of the Nashville experience for Elliott was getting introduced to the Everly Brothers by Waronker. He ended up writing, playing guitar on, and arranging their 1968 single "Empty Boxes," and also wrote two of the songs on the Everly Brothers' own 1968 country-rock album, *Roots*. Indeed *Roots* and *Bradley's Barn* sounded rather similar to each other, which was unsurprising as both had been produced by Waronker. And neither sold too well, despite getting belated acclaim by rock scholars as quality country-rock pieces.

The Beau Brummels—which had been more a recording project than a working group since the end of 1966, anyway—finally drifted apart at the end of the 1960s, never having managed to get another hit record after 1965 despite continuing to musically progress. For Elliott, working solo on the laid-back, country-rock *Candlestick Maker* (1970) brought a special satisfaction, although it was heard by few. "One side of the album is a suite. Years later, I had some guy walk up to me after a gig. He said he was in Vietnam, he played that album every day, and it saved his life. I always thought it should have been in a documentary of Vietnam or something, for vets, because that's what it is. It's a story about the butcher, the baker, the candlestick maker and I; all of these forces around this guy going through this madness. And it has a healing quality to it. But hardly popular, again."

Elliott and Valentino had a low profile throughout the 1970s. Valentino sang in the group Stoneground for a while, and Elliott did session work (including tracks with Randy Newman, Van Dyke Parks, Van Morrison, and Little Feat), as well as producing and writing all the songs for the album by Pan. Elliott: "Clive Davis signs Pan, they fired him, and our album was down the tubes within three days of release. That was the best album I've ever written, period. That, to me, was what the Beau Brummels [should have sounded like], but never did." There was a Beau Brummels reunion album in 1975, but in Valentino's view, "We hadn't performed at all, it showed that we hadn't, and we were out of place."

Elliott did do an album as part of Giants in 1976, but has stopped playing music in the latter part of his life, partly as a result of his diabetic condition. "As the decades progressed, when you take insulin it attacks your nervous system. Gradually the music that was in me began fading, and now it's gone altogether. But in place of the songs, I'm doing paintings, computer graphics, and art. I walk by my guitar twenty times a day, and I never even think about picking it up."

Although he is still proud, to a modest extent, of what he did with the Beau Brummels and other musicians, he realizes he was never a good fit for the rock 'n' roll business, partially because of his health, and partially because of his attitude. "The music business is run by tone-deaf shoe salesmen," he states matter-of-factly. "They're great business people. But most of them have no knowledge of actual music. Lyrics to them is 80 percent of the song, so the music is always handicapped. I never really got into understanding that [rock] mode of popular song as much, because I was coming from a totally artistic point of view. I probably would have been better served to go to New York and write scores.

"I think I could have had more success staying in the background, and not trying to be a player. I kept telling the record executives, 'I'm a songwriter.' And they kept telling me, 'You're a guitar player.' They *needed* a guitar player, so that's what they wanted me to be. I was pretty adequate on guitar; I wasn't great. But I was a *songwriter*. Since they listen to lyrics and not music, they had no way of knowing that, or even caring about it."

Elliott also lacked the gregarious nature necessary to make the business and music connections that might have enabled him to subsist principally as a writer and studio recording artist without playing live, a la Nilsson. "People would have to put me together with other people. Unless I was physically introduced to someone and had my guitar and could play 'em something, I was never hanging out with the crowd. Otherwise I would have never talked to them or known them. Because I was either writing, or adjusting my blood sugar, one of the two. When the gig ended, my day was over. I'd go back to my room, no parties, no socializing. If I was still conscious, I would be writing. That was my life on the road; anything outside of that, I was not in contact with.

"I always tried to write good lyrics, but I wasn't a great lyricist. Should have keyed up with a real quality lyricist, a real master of words, which I never had access to. When I tried to get that, it never really worked." He pauses, then illustrates his analogy about tone-deaf shoe salesmen with vigor. "It worked one time. I met this guy from Oregon, we wrote a song, and submitted it to [Richard] Perry when he was producing Barbra Streisand. He heard the song and told me, 'Barbra would love this song. She would do it in an instant. That's why I'm not showing it to her. 'Cause I don't want her to do this kind of material.'" He laughs. "That was the story of my life."

Sal Valentino takes a more cheerful, though equally realistic, view of the hand the band was dealt. "We were at Warner Brothers ten years too early, or seven years too early. Because sometime after we left, it became the best record company." He returns to his comment about how the San Francisco rock explosion saw society and music growing up together, though "the Brummels weren't part of it." He clarifies: "We did that at Warner Brothers, but I think it was the wrong place to do it at." The group had managed the difficult trick of being old-fashioned and ahead of its time simultaneously.

"We were obviously a little ahead, or a little behind. No matter how you look at it."

Recommended Recordings:

The Best of the Beau Brummels (1987, Rhino). A decent eighteen-song overview of their 1960s recordings, though one could dispute the song selection, particularly the absence of "I Want You." Contains a few Warners-era tracks that do not appear elsewhere.

Introducing the Beau Brummels (1965, Sundazed). A somewhat callow but oft-charming debut with the big hits "Laugh, Laugh" and "Just a Little." Other songs like "Still in Love with You Baby" find the group at its most Merseybeat-soaked, but "They'll Make You Cry" and "Not Too Long Ago" herald a more sophisticated brand of folk-rock.

Volume 2 (1965, Sundazed). This overlooked quality folk-rock album has a few songs that could have been hits given a fairer world: "You Tell Me Why" (which *was* a small hit), "I Want You," and "Sad Little Girl." "Don't Talk to Strangers" is an enjoyable Byrds clone, and even the filler is of a pretty high standard.

San Fran Sessions (1996, Sundazed). A three-CD set of "rarities, demos, alternate takes, and unissued performances" from 1964-66 that includes almost everything they did for Autumn that did not appear on their first two albums. Certainly the size of this package will dissuade the casual fan, but for those in love with the Brummels, it's not just a collector's item. It has plenty of excellent tunes on par with their better Autumn cuts—such as "Love Is Just a Game," "This Is Love," "Dream On," "Hey Love," "No Lonelier Man," and "She Sends Me"—and even the more marginal alternate takes and leftovers are usually fun listening. Lots of Elliott (and, to a lesser extent, Valentino) compositions here that never found a home elsewhere.

Triangle (1967, Warner Brothers). A substantial departure from their earlier work, trading the instantaneous hooks and spooky vocal harmonies for greater lyrical sophistication and more expansive arrangements, with some strings, harpsichord, and accordion. Some of this is early country-rock, including a superb cover of Merle Travis' "Nine Pound Hammer." It's more memorable, however, for the wispy and wistful tunes, like "Magic Hollow" and "The Wolf of Velvet Fortune," which are like mood music for deep forest walks.

Bradley's Barn (1968, Edsel, U.K.). More muted than, but similar to, *Triangle* in its countrified rock. "Loneliest Man in Town" is as barroom Nashville as the group got, though by contrast the mystical and moody folk-rock of "Love Can Fall a Long Way Down" would have fit in well on *Triangle*. The suite-like "Bless You California," on the other hand, looks forward to the more ambitious and theatrical pieces Elliott would devise on his solo album *Candlestick Maker*.

Mike Brown

"Music's meant to be felt, not analyzed."

That could be a credo of sorts for keyboardist and composer Mike Brown. He's just broken off his explanation of the fusion of rock and classical music that has characterized his work since the Left Banke's "Walk Away Renee" became a hit in the fall of 1966. Rarely interviewed, rarely heard from on disc since the mid-1970s, he's much more comfortable *making* music than he is *talking* about it. And if he's going to talk about music, he's far more interested in talking about the present than about an illustrious past, in which he wrote and played on both hit singles and lesser-known projects by the Left Banke, Montage, and the Stories that have accumulated a devout international cult following.

Brown's sensitivity to media attention is understandable in light of his occasional portrayal in the rock press as a one-hit teen prodigy. Although he was indeed just seventeen when "Walk Away Renee" became a smash, this ignores the scope of his discography, slim in size but long on artistic depth. The Left Banke, in any case, was not a one-hit wonder; the group had a second big hit ("Pretty Ballerina") of equal quality to its predecessor, and an outstanding, overlooked debut album on which Brown was the principal writer and creative force. After leaving the Left Banke, Brown was the producer and chief composer of a mini-gem of an album by Montage, continuing in the same gorgeously melodic, deftly arranged vein as his earlier work. In the early 1970s he proved adept at incorporating heavier rock and power pop elements into his recordings as a member of the Stories. Since the sole album by his subsequent band, the Beckies, however, the public has heard little Brown music, although much, he says, has been written.

The marriage of classical and rock music has been attempted by many, but rarely with as much success as Brown has had. When the Left Banke emerged in 1966 and 1967, its style was dubbed by publicists and press as the hybrid baroque rock. The sobriquet may have been ham-fisted, but certainly there were many baroque elements in the Left Banke's pop—the stately arrangements, the brilliant use of keyboards and harpsichords, the soaring violins, and the beautiful group harmonies. The melodic genius of the band's best work was largely down to Brown, and that knack for classical-pop composition has been a constant of his work, to varying degrees, throughout his career. He has rarely sung on record, however, and to fully translate his compositions to disc, has needed to team with other vocalists, particularly the Left Banke's Steve Martin and the Stories' Ian Lloyd. His perfectionism, and his unwillingness to abide by some of the compromises usually demanded by the record business, contributed to a near-total absence of releases over the last quarter-century or so. The contrast between the magnitude of his talent and his microscopic public profile was in a sense reminiscent of that enjoyed, or suffered, for many years by one of his closer artistic counterparts in the rock world, Brian Wilson.

When I speak with him by telephone in the fall of 1999, Brown is friendly but wary. He is proud of his work from the 1960s and 1970s, including that of the Left Banke, but not too interested in discussing the specific details—songs, sessions, and stories—so dear to those that collect his records. "The time is now," he emphasizes more than once. His tone rises from matter-of-fact to passionate when he talks about

Mike Brown, keyboardist and composer.
Credit: Courtesy Ken Schaffer.

his new music, or, conversely, when he berates the impersonal and aesthetically sterile machinations of today's music industry. Clues are slipped as to how some of his classics were conceived and recorded back in the day, and what he's been up to during the 1980s and 1990s, but the precise details remain for the most part unexplained. Some of those will need to get filled in by the scraps of information that have appeared in those scant other interviews, and, thankfully, by the records themselves, which articulate his vision as no words can.

Brown got an early start as a musician, not only via studying classical music as a youngster, but also via the good fortune of having a father, Harry Lookofsky, who ran the production company World United in New York. In his mid-teens, Brown was already helping out at World United as an engineer's assistant. He was also starting to compose, cowriting a song ("Do You Remember When") that appeared on an album by one of his dad's clients, the girl group Reparata and the Delrons. It was at World United studios that the nucleus of the Left Banke formed, with Brown, bassist Tom Finn (who had been in a band, the Magic Plant, that Lookofsky produced a single for on Verve), guitarist George Cameron, and singer Steve Martin.

Influenced by the most harmonically sophisticated British Invasion bands of the time—the Beatles, the Zombies, and the Kinks—as well as the Beach Boys, the group began to work up material emphasizing the three-part harmonies of Martin, Finn, and Cameron, Martin getting singled out as the primary lead vocalist. Talking to Jon Tiven for the liner notes of Rhino's *The History of the Left Banke*, Finn confirmed that Brown was the main musical brain behind the ensemble at this point. "We couldn't play instruments; except Michael, who played a classical piano," he recalled. "We would stand around Michael at the piano and filter our ideas through him; he would use all our ideas, it was a collaboration. Michael had the musical background to interpret what we were doing, and that was the creative essence of the Left Banke."

The group (with Warren David on drums at this point) was recording well in advance of the mid-1966 release of its first single, laying down the first tracks around late 1965/early 1966. After this initial batch, there was some question as to whether the group even existed any longer, as these first efforts did not attract any record company deals. Brown and David left for California, although Lookofsky, Finn has recalled on more than one occasion, had them stopped when they got off the plane. The backing track for "Walk Away Renee" had been completed, however. Martin, Finn, and Cameron overdubbed vocals, and Lookofsky (who produced or coproduced all of the Left Banke's recordings through early 1967) placed it with Mercury's Smash subsidiary, after quite a few other labels had passed. The record entered the Top Forty in September of 1966, peaking at number five. Brown, who cowrote the song, was only seventeen.

It was in some ways the typical story of sudden success, common in the days before rock got so corporate that it would be almost impossible for an independently recorded single by an unknown band to make it big within months. "Walk Away Renee," however, was not your typical single, by an unknown group or anyone. With its beautiful descending melody lines, violins, harpsichord, and flute solo, it was pop-rock as played by a chamber music ensemble, an ambitious combination that nonetheless felt organic, not forced. Steve Martin was unveiled as one of the best upper-register male rock singers of the 1960s, sympathetically supported by bursts of harmonies and drums on the chorus. It is not well known that Lookofsky was a noted and prolific session violinist for several decades, contributing to recordings by jazz greats Wes Montgomery, Gil Evans, and Sarah Vaughan, and bossa nova great Antonio Carlos Jobim, among many others. While ambiguity surrounds the extent of his contributions to the Left Banke's recordings and arrangements, certainly his experience at adding strings in various nonclassical contexts couldn't have hurt.

"When you study classical music, it allows you a bigger dimension," says Brown now. "If you just listen to rock and roll music, you're not gonna get a very big dimension of possibilities; you're not gonna do as much as you can with classical. So it leaves more room for creativity." Yet, he is careful to note, it was not a deliberate strategy on his part to combine classical and rock. "I wasn't really conscious of it then. Now I am, but at the time, I just had those two things bleeding together." He also points out that this notion was not unique in rock of the era, citing the Beatles' "Eleanor Rigby" and, more unexpectedly, the Stone Poneys' (Linda Ronstadt's first group's) use of cellos. He makes no great claims for "Walk Away Renee"'s intricacy: "'Walk Away Renee,' interestingly was very simple in its accompaniment of voice in the track. The strings were very, very simple. And the flute line was very, very simple."

Perhaps unsurprisingly, adds Brown, "one of my favorite records is 'Macarthur Park'"—another song from the era (actually from almost a couple of years later) with a quasi-classical air. "It takes you places. All these good songs, they take you somewhere. If it takes you to the subway station, it's not the greatest thing. But if it takes you somewhere higher, it's a good thing."

A great arrangement and performance do not necessarily a standard make. One of the reasons "Walk Away Renee" was frequently covered (notably by the Four Tops, who took it to number fourteen in early 1968) and remains in the collective pop consciousness is the emotional tug of the lyrics, an eloquent ode to heartbreak and unfulfilled desire. It is by now well known that the song was inspired by a girlfriend of Finn's, Renee Fladen. In *Rolling Stone*, Brown once elaborated, "It's the ultimate love song. It's not a love song about possession. It's about loving someone enough to set them free. There's a certain purity to 'Walk Away Renee,' and its purity comes from the idea that a dream lives, even if it's just as a fantasy…My hands were shaking when I tried to play, because she was right there in the control room. There was no way I could do it with her around, so I came back and did it later.

"The truth of the matter," he continued, "is that I cheered 'Walk Away Renee' up the charts so that 'Pretty Ballerina' would have a better chance." "Pretty Ballerina," like "Walk Away Renee" (and a third tune that appeared on the first Left Banke album, "She May Call You Up Tonight") has also been reported to have been inspired by Fladen, all the songs pouring forth in a matter of weeks. Although "Pretty Ballerina" was nearly as big a hit as its predecessor, reaching number fifteen, it is for some reason not nearly as well-remembered, perhaps because it (unlike "Renee") did not manage to become a staple of oldies radio.

That is unfortunate, as if anything it was even better, with its hypnotic melody, Steve Martin's masterfully sensitive and soaring vocals, the adroit interplay between Brown's piano and a buzzing organ tone, graceful violins, and its mysterious lyric of a ballerina as beautiful and ethereal as a vanishing dream. Brown's skill with descending melodic lines comes to the fore in the unexpected instrumental break, whose tune is completely different from that heard on the sung verses. An orchestral crescendo dissolves, leaving only unaccompanied plucked low tones, the notes bouncing off each other as if they're settling in the bottom of a cavernous drum; the break is brought to a finish by Martin's yearning scat vocals. All in all, quite a lot of ideas to pack into, and pull off within, a two-and-a-half-minute single.

On the heels of "Pretty Ballerina" came the Left Banke's first album, unimaginatively titled *Walk Away Renee/Pretty Ballerina*. The packaging did the band no favors either, with large-type liners hyping the baroque-pop label ("in their effort to go for Baroque, they've succeeded in making many trips to the bank(e)"). The music it contained, however, was of a much classier standard. In an era when many debut albums by young groups were rush jobs stuffed with covers and derivative originals, the LP—including both sides of the first two singles, and seven additional tracks—was almost uniformly stunning, with several treasures that remain undiscovered by those who think of the Left Banke as a one- or two-song act.

It is fair to claim that no pop-rock album of the 1960s combined rock and classical elements as well as *Walk Away Renee/Pretty Ballerina* did. The Zombies had used some classical-friendly flourishes and vocal harmonies in their own magnificent body of work. The Beach Boys had also done this on occasion, and devised complementary arrangements of orchestral sweep for leader Brian Wilson's music, particularly on their classic 1966 album *Pet Sounds*. In these groups, however, the classical part of the equation was far more subordinate to the pop-rock part than it was in the Left Banke. Mike Brown, in addition, is an underacknowledged pioneer in using the harpsichord (as well as piano and other keyboards) in rock music, as he did throughout his stint with the Left Banke. Again, this was not totally virgin territory—the Yardbirds had used a harpsichord (played by Brian Auger) on their hit "For Your Love," and the Beatles had achieved a harpsichord-like effect on "In My Life" by using a double-speed George Martin piano solo on the instrumental break. With the Left Banke, though, the harpsichord was not an occasional novel touch, but an integral ingredient of the mix.

Among the delights on *Walk Away Renee/Pretty Ballerina* were "Shadows Breaking Over My Head," with its astral harmonies and lovely orchestration; the aforementioned "She May Call You Up Tonight," the most upbeat and up-tempo of the trio of songs allegedly inspired by Renee Fladen; and "Barterers and Their Wives," quasi-medieval in both lyrics and vocal/instrumental arrangement. The Left Banke is sometimes thought of, not without reason, as a genteel group owing to its gift for lovely ballads and mid-tempo tunes. Yet they could rock out on occasion without losing their baroque flavor, as demonstrated by the almost raunchy "Evening Gown," with its almost manically rapid harpsichord, and the moody "Lazy Day," anchored by thrilling exchanges of doomy piano runs, fuzz guitar, and explosive harmonies on the chorus. Although the lyrics, as usual for the time, were largely love songs, there was a pensive, uncertain tone which gave them emotional resonance. The album only fell flat on the atypical country-rocker "What Do You Know," with a rare Mike Brown lead vocal that illustrates exactly why he needed to collaborate with other singers.

It is important to note that although Brown was the visionary behind the band, in much the same way as Brian Wilson was behind the Beach Boys, the Left Banke was a real group whose other members also made important contributions. Martin, Finn, and Cameron were responsible for vocal harmonies, and Martin and Cameron helped write some of the tunes (indeed one, the quite respectable "I Haven't Got the Nerve," was a Cameron/Martin collaboration on which Brown did not get a composer credit). Certainly Martin, a singer of mysterious background (it has been reported that he came to New York from either Spain or Puerto Rico), was the most vital component of the Left Banke's magic other than Brown, particularly in his skill at handling high vocal lines without breaking into falsetto. Martin also cowrote some of the band's better tunes with Brown ("Lazy Day," "Shadows Breaking Over My Head," and "She May Call You Up Tonight").

Mike Brown reserves more praise for Martin than for any other musician with whom he has worked. "He was a catalyst. He blew it wide open. He had a very, very good voice. And it was a lot of fun to write for, because he was such a great singer. He would sing Little Richard better than Little Richard. That's hard to do. I still have cassettes here of him imitating 'some fun tonight' [from Little Richard's "Long Tall Sally"]…I'll tell you, there's nothing more exciting than hearing a lot of songs that he sang.

"See, he was able to sing what you *wrote*, and he did it in the key that you wrote it in. You'd [be] like, 'little lower.' 'No no no…let me try it in *that* key.' He was like a wild stallion, and he really got into music; that was really the *most* important thing to him. And if you have that kind of enthusiasm, it's very exciting. With Steve, it was an exponential growth of the song, the music, and he was able to do it. Some people *think* about doing it, and they have the right ideas. He was able to *execute* it. And when you've got a situation like that, it's unbelievable."

With one of the best young composer/instrumentalists *and* one of the best young singers in rock, one would think that the Left Banke had unlimited potential. However, the band had an unusually fractious history considering the brevity of its existence. Even before the *Walk Away Renee/Pretty Ballerina* album, the group's personnel had shifted several times. Original drummer Warren David (who became "Lisa" after a sex-change operation, Tom Finn told *The Bob* in 1986) was fired by Brown after the first recording sessions, although David had devised the drumbeat used on "Walk Away Renee." Cameron switched from guitar to drums, and Jeff Winfield came in on guitar for a while, only to be replaced by Rick Brand by the beginning of 1967; session man Hugh McCracken plays guitar on much of the Left Banke's first album, with Brand contributing to just one cut (although he is billed as a full member on the sleeve).

No matter what the musical lineup, the inexperienced musicians had a hard time matching the quality of the Left Banke records onstage, particularly as those discs relied so heavily on precise orchestration. Brown stopped touring with the group, and according to other members, envisioned a Brian Wilson-like role whereby he would stay with the group and concentrate on recording, writing, and production. Others in the Left Banke felt their songwriting ambitions curtailed by Brown's relative dominance in this area.

There were also problems between the band and its management, particularly as the group's affairs were handled by Harry Lookofsky, Brown's father. In the 1986 Left Banke article in *The Bob* magazine, Rick Brand told Dawn Eden, "He paid the group a very, very tiny percentage of recording royalties—something like one-and-a-quarter percent, to be split among the entire group. The problem was that he was our manager and our producer and our publisher. There's a tremendous conflict of interest, because your manager should be the one who is trying to get you the best deal from your publisher and producer, and since he has all three functions, he was managing all of those functions to his benefit."

Things came to a head in early 1967 when Brown—with vocalist Bert Sommer, a few other musicians, and Harry Lookofsky as producer—recorded a single, "And Suddenly"/"Ivy Ivy." Although Brown was the only musician who had played on prior Left Banke material to appear on the 45, it was issued as a Left Banke single. This drew the wrath of the other guys in the band, who used the group's own fan club newsletter to point out that some of the musicians on the recording were "strangers none of us have ever heard of." In the wake of the controversy, Smash Records withdrew support of the single, which only made it to number 119.

In any case, the songs did not represent Brown at his best, although Mike remembers the composer of "A Taste of Honey" exclaiming "that's a hit!" when he heard Brown playing "And Suddenly" on piano. The happy-go-lucky "And Suddenly" was more frivolous and disposable than the best of the Banke's previous releases (although a cover version by the Cherry People made the middle of the Top 100). As for "Ivy Ivy," even Brown admitted (in the liner notes to *The History of the Left Banke*) that "I didn't like the way it was arranged, and that was very unfortunate for [cocomposer] Tom [Feher] and Bert [Sommer]—his voice wasn't entirely suited for it, he was a little bit feminine sounding on the thing."

It would be six months before the Left Banke got back in the studio, a lot of the band's momentum deflated by the personnel and business conflicts. Mike Brown did come back into the fold for one last single, "Desiree," recorded in September 1967. This was a return to the quality of the *Walk Away Renee/Pretty Ballerina* era, with one of Brown's most haunting melodies and more prominent use of brass than the group had previously employed. When I ask Brown which of his songs he wishes had become more widely recognized, he instantly replies, "'Desiree.' It's a really nice musical piece. I produced the song. That song never reached what it should have been, and I blame myself." Although major flaws are not evident on hearing the track, it did underachieve commercially, topping out at number ninety-eight.

Given the acrimonious circumstances in which the group became embroiled, and Brown's reluctance to speak at length about the Left Banke in interviews, you might assume he holds little affection for the band. This is not exactly the case. "We were so tight, the Left Banke. We were the very best of friends. We knew each other. We were like brothers. It was incredible. It was accidental, lucky, that we all came together at the same time."

Still, Brown is modest, even a bit dismissive, of all those fine songs he did with the Left Banke that remain known only by fanatics. "All these other songs in albums and everything else, I feel, didn't make it for a reason. If they *were* good enough to make it, somebody would have found it and done it."

Several of the songs from the first album other than "Walk Away Renee" and "Pretty Ballerina," I offer, seem like eminently good candidates for cover treatment. "Shadows Breaking Over My Head," for instance. "Yeah, that could be done over," he concedes. "There are a lot of them that could be.

"There were people following me, I guess, for a few years at least anyway. Every time something came out, they scoured through it." Even many Left Banke fanatics, for instance, don't know that "Anne Murray did a song of mine, 'She May Call You Up Tonight,' in Canada; it was a big hit. 1970, Capitol of Canada. It sold a lot, and I got a nice royalty check. That was very nice. I had heard it, it was exciting, you know? It was good." (For Brown/Left Banke obsessives, the track, retitled "He May Call," is on Murray's 1969 album *This Way Is My Way*.)

The Left Banke was not entirely finished after Brown left, and Brown was not entirely finished with his band mates (more of which later), but in the meantime he linked up with other musicians for his next undertaking. The self-titled album by Montage, issued by Laurie in early 1969 (and preceded by a couple of singles during 1968), is an oddity in that Brown—who produced, played keyboards, and cowrote all but one of the LP's songs—was not actually a member of the group. In other words, he dominated the band's music about as much anyone not actually *in* a band could. He is pictured, alone at the keyboards, in the actual montage of photos (some of the group, some not) on the inner gatefold sleeve. None of the quartet of musicians that actually comprised Montage did any notable projects after the album's release.

For all its obscurity—both in terms of whether it was meant to be a bona fide band or a front for Brown's music, and its low commercial profile (it passed almost unnoticed at the time, and has still not been reissued on CD)—the record is a must for Brown/Left Banke fans. More subdued than *Walk Away Renee/Pretty Ballerina*, it's nonetheless quite similar in its enchanting baroque melodies and small-scale orchestral arrangements. With one exception, Brown cowrote the tracks with either Bert Sommer or Tom Feher, both of whom he had already worked with on the "And Suddenly"/"Ivy Ivy" single (Feher, in fact, joined the post-Brown Left Banke for a while in the late '60s). Brown also took the opportunity to try "Desiree" again, as well as a song he had recorded, but not released, with Bert Sommer in 1967, "Men Are Building Sand" (the original 1967 Brown-Banke version was finally issued in 1992 on the Left Banke compilation *There's Gonna Be a Storm*).

A record of considerable fragile beauty, *Montage* was also, however, not as grand in production scope as the Left Banke was. Montage's singers were not up to the Left Banke's stellar vocal standards, either as lead singers or harmonizers, as is particularly evident on some off-key notes in "Men Are Building Sand." Brown himself does not hold the album in high regard, and, as with the Left Banke's "Desiree" single, was dissatisfied with his performance as producer. "I had three groups that I was working with," he recalls. "I was about nineteen years old. I was really pounding away and I wasn't sleeping right, and I did too much at once. Without having excuses, though, I am not a producer. And that album, wholly, was produced by me. Mixed by me, which is even worse. I can't tell you how sorry I am, but let's leave it alone. It wasn't my best effort." In *The Bob*, he was only slightly more charitable in his view of Montage: "They were my friends more than they were people who could really do an album. Some people like the Montage album, and I love a couple of cuts on it, but one swallow does not a summer make, right?"

As Montage faded away, so did the Left Banke, which had continued without Brown to make a second album, *The Left Banke Too* (1969). With the aid of some session musicians in the studio and additional personnel on the road (Emmett Lake played keyboards with them live, and as mentioned above Tom Feher was part of the group for a while), the band straggled on until it finally split sometime in 1969. *Left Banke Too* had some fair moments, as well as a couple of tracks from the can with Brown ("Desiree" and "In the Morning Light"), but was generally a pale continuation of its debut, the band seemingly at sea without its original keyboardist. Future Aerosmith star Steven Tyler sang some backup vocals, and told *Musician* in 1990, "I'll never forget being in their apartment one day and one of them saying, 'What's the date today? Are we recording tonight? What are we going to record?' It turned out that they were: 'Don't worry, we'll come up with something.' I couldn't believe they were taking it so lightly. I remember thinking, 'There's got to be a better way of doing this.' But I was just so into those guys, Steve [Martin] and his voice."

The group may have already broken up by the time Martin and Brown reunited to record the Left Banke's "Myrah"/"Pedestal" single in late 1969, which featured none of the other musicians that had been part of the Left Banke in the past. "Myrah" was a fair Brown-Martin composition; neither were involved in writing the less impressive, harder-rocking flip side (which doesn't even have Brown on keyboards). Whether Brown and Martin intended to relaunch the Left Banke is unclear; a miffed Tom Finn said of the cuts in *The Bob*, "All that stuff was Steve Martin on acid at Elephant Five Mafia studios, being fed cocaine and (they) said, 'Sing, kid, sing!'"

The notion of reforming the Left Banke, however, seems to have persisted until the early 1970s, when the four most important members—Brown, Martin, Finn, and Cameron—reconvened for a 1971 Steve Martin solo single, "Love Songs in the Night"/"Two By Two." This was the original Left Banke reunited in all but name, and the songs were nice, low-key efforts that retained much of the majesty of the group at its best, even if they may have seemed anachronistic in 1971's rock market. The baton was not picked up, however, as Brown never did release anything else with the musicians, moving on to his next important band, the Stories.

In the Stories, Brown had his most productive collaborator save Martin, Ian Lloyd. Lloyd, like Martin, had a wide upper range that suited Brown's compositions, and sang lead and cowrote (with Brown) most of the material on both Stories albums in which Mike participated. The self-titled debut (from 1972) was not devoid of Brown's trademark classical-influenced melodies and keyboards. However, it was in a harder-rocking mode than his 1960s groups, although not exactly hard rock; indeed, it was far lighter and poppier than most American bands of the early '70s were. Echoes of British bands such as the Kinks, Beatles, and Badfinger could be heard, and Brown's predilection for harpsichords and such was largely eschewed in favor of standard piano.

Yet much of the music could not have come from anyone but Brown. The instrumental break on "You Told Me" approached chamber music territory, and songs like "Winter Scenes," "Nice to Have You Here," "High and Low," and the ballad "Kathleen" boasted passages of intricate and unpredictable, yet accessible, progressions and harmonies. In a link to the Left Banke days, Harry Lookofsky contributed some violin. But 1972 was not a prime time for pop-oriented bands that had more to say than could be contained on a single or two a year, and *The Stories* was not a smash. It demands reinvestigation, however, by power pop (or, perhaps more accurately, mid-power pop) fans who may well have missed it the first time around.

"I *hated* the '70s," confesses Brown. "I had to withdraw from all the music around me and try to write things, and try to hold my ears, hold my nose, and jump in the pool. I had to do something that wasn't what was happening. I had to do something different. With Ian Lloyd, I liked his lyrics. His voice per se, I don't know...but [it] matched the lyrics, and that's very important. It sounded like you wanted to listen to what he had to say. In that sense, he was very good."

Brown's memories of the Stories, however, are mixed, due in part to bumpy experiences in the studio. The Stories, he stresses by slowly enunciating every word, were a band that "never, was, in, the, studio, before. I'd *been* in the studio before, and I had been on the road. If you've never been in a studio before, it's very, very difficult. It's really tough, getting involved in the production in the studio, and then to have everybody resent...everything you do is just thrown back, 'you didn't do it good enough.' Meanwhile, nothing was done at all before you started it."

His voice rises into frustration, not so much at the Stories as with the least palatable aspects of commercial music making, when he remembers one incident in particular with a producer during this time. "He wanted to put a pick on the bass and electrify it. Ian plays bass, Ian is a team player; it's not negative or positive connotation to that phrase, but he was a team player. So he changed what he was playing to accommodate the engineer, to accommodate the producer, and then I heard these weird notes coming out, whereas before it sounded great. I said, 'It was better before.' And [the producer] goes, 'What do you want, good music or classical music?' Think about that one for a while. He meant it."

Brown resumes, "There was a lot of politics around us at the time, and there was a lot of pressure. We went to England to record that second album, and it was the best of times and the worst of times." Largely written and recorded in England, *About Us* took on more hard rock trappings than *The Stories*, with Brown making more use of synthesizer and mellotron than he had on the first album. *About Us* was not as affecting, or emotionally tender, as the band's debut, though it did have some decent pop tunes, verging on the McCartneyesque when Lloyd sang his highest notes. The Stories, oddly, were about to get their big break by covering a song by the British soul group Hot Chocolate, "Brother Louie." Not at all similar to anything else they had done, it was cut just after Brown left the group, and went to number one in the summer of 1973. When casual rock fans think of the Stories, they only think of "Brother Louie"; the quality pop they did with Brown remains largely unknown.

Still, his stint with the Stories was as high as he would register on the visibility meter in the 1970s. His last full-fledged album to date was the self-titled 1976 album by the Beckies on Sire, on which he played keyboards and coproduced. More pop-oriented than any of his other discs, it was also less distinguished, sounding similar to the Stories albums, but with weaker material and singers. The scepter of the Left Banke continued to hover in the guise of guest vocals by Tom Finn on one track.

According to a contribution by engineer and producer Les Fradkin to a Left Banke fan page on the Internet, he was approached by Brown, Steve Martin, and George Cameron in 1978 for help on a possible Left Banke reunion. Brown left that endeavor early on, however, to be replaced by Tom Finn. The album resulting from the ensuing sessions was finally released in the mid-1980s, doomed to failure not just by the absence of the Left Banke's best musician, but also by a music business that had long since moved on from the epoch in which the group made its impact.

Brown's writing is not easily imitated, and he hasn't seen his influence on many other artists, other than perhaps "a lot of chromatically descending bass lines in songs," such as B. J. Thomas' "Hooked on a Feeling." He muses that the Boxtops seemed to have some traces of the Left Banke, but if such groups were influenced by Brown, "I don't think they got the inspiration from the inner beanpole. The inner beanpole is a very sacred, special place. And nobody understands what it is, when it clicks with millions of people. Millions of people want to identify with you, and it's something—you don't even know what it is. It's different for everybody, in a way. It's magical, it's very, very special."

Other than contributing keyboards and songwriting to a release by his wife, Yvonne Vitale, in the 1990s, Brown has barely been heard from since the 1970s. He hasn't died or vanished into a black hole. He lives not far from New York, and recently became the father of twins. The music hasn't stopped; he calls himself "a truly prolific writer," and acknowledges the existence of "two suitcases full of cassette tapes of songs that came from the '80s and '90s. Two *large* suitcases. Which, through a bit of struggle, I've been able to push in the back of the closet, barricaded, and cover 'em all up." He is not resentful of the admiration for his recordings from decades ago: "I'm just tickled pink that people, even a few people, could be that wonderful to keep these things somewhere on our conscious level." He does not go into specifics as to *what* exactly he wrote in the last twenty years, and *why* he did not release any of it. What he does talk about is *why* he feels incompatible with the current music industry, and *what* he is working on now.

"I was very young when this all started," he reflects. "A lot of people were managing me, getting me apartments and telephones and setting up Command Central, and I really didn't understand what was happening. I was seventeen. I was more interested in girls than I was in anything." He chuckles before his tone becomes more vituperative. "Basically, I just was being put in a machine, washed, and tumbled. I'm rolling around, and everybody's pushing the buttons. Finally, when they're through with you, they spit you out. Then you have to tumble out of the machine for a while, until you get your clothes, stand up, brush yourself off, and keep going.

"The times change and we change with them. Yet I didn't change, really, with the times. And I still haven't. My trouble has *never* been writing. It's always been conflicts with the ideology of my music." Recently, he says by way of illustration, "I had somebody here who said, 'Well, you can add this to make it more commercial.' 'What, are you kidding me? At this point, you're really crazy to tell me to start changing it now. Leave that to the inevitable changes that people make later on.' How can I change my writing now? Am I going to aspire to be commercial? I'll go crazy doing that. In any shape or form, any way, that somebody is trying to change my music, almost before the sound hits their ears from the piano—that is *really* sick.

"I'll be frank with you. I've cut off just about everybody I know. I feel a lot better, having said the truth and telling these people to leave me alone. I need people—but these people I don't need. In music, all I need is myself."

Toward that end, what really puts him in a more positive mood these days is the solo instrumental music he's writing and playing now, and his plans to get "a really beat-up Steinway" piano. "I think I can make a CD with just piano and absolutely nothing else, and it would ring, it would work. The more instruments you add to it, the worse it gets. I may modify my position. But I don't think I need another musician to play along with. If I wanted bass, I'll play a synthesizer or something. I don't want to produce. I want to find somebody who wants to work with me, and is excited about it." He's considering working on the record in England, where he enjoys the appreciation of some especially supportive fans in the record collecting community who have become personal friends.

"I don't expect it to be a major, major success, but I think I can get a cult following. I want to intermingle with myself in a simpler, musical journey. And it's very special, if you can do that instrumentally, without lyrics. It's a very difficult thing to do, because it's a very gutsy thing to do. And I'm not going to *do* it like a cult record. I'm going to do it to come out as five-star number-one album, if I can.

"I'm not easy to get along with at all times," he allows. "But usually I'm saying something a little vociferously because I'm defending the music. I'm not out to attack people. Leave the music alone. Pick on me, but don't try to change this music."

To close that circle, he draws a similarity between his present situation and the key axis of the Left Banke. "I have something to say, the way Steve Martin had something. He had a voice; I've got the writing ability. We tolerated his eccentricities to the point where we really were ready to hang him. Whatever's wrong with him, he did it, and everybody was glad in the end that he did it, whatever they had to go through. I hope that what's wrong with me *can* be endured, and I hope that what shines in me can be celebrated after we all do it."

Recommended Recordings:

By the Left Banke:

There's Gonna Be a Storm (1992, Mercury). This invaluable twenty-six-song disc has everything recorded by the Left Banke in the 1960s, including the entirety of *Walk Away Renee/Pretty Ballerina* and *The Left Banke Too*; the non-LP singles "And Suddenly"/"Ivy Ivy" and "Myrah"/"Pedestal"; and the previously unreleased "Men Are Building Sand," which would be rerecorded by Montage.

The History of the Left Banke (1986, Rhino). An odd compilation mixing together Left Banke, Steve Martin, and Stories cuts. It draws only sparingly from the Left Banke's best work (although it includes the band's chart singles) and concentrates on ephemera: the non-LP singles, two Stories tracks (one of which, the hit "Brother Louie," has no Brown/Left Banke connection at all), and the unreleased 1969 cut "Foggy Waterfall" (which does not appear on *There's Gonna Be a Storm* for a reason, as aside from Martin's lead vocals, there is no evidence of participation on the part of Brown or other Left Bankers). It's worth finding, however, for the inclusion of the rare Steve Martin "Love Songs in the Night"/"Two By Two" single, which is a worthy postscript to the Left Banke's 1960s discography.

By Montage:

Montage (1969, Laurie). Not that much less essential than the Left Banke's *Walk Away Renee/Pretty Ballerina*, this is one of the best obscure pop albums of the late 1960s. So similar in mood to the Left Banke that it might be considered the band's missing second album, it is perhaps daintier and less forceful than Brown's work with his first band, but still jammed with grand and unusual melodies. "I Shall Call Her Mary" and "Tinsel and Ivy," for instance, are as achingly tuneful as anything he's played on, and the remake of "Desiree" is in about the same league as the Left Banke original. Unfortunately this has not made it onto CD, although Bam Caruso did reissue it on vinyl in the U.K. in the 1980s.

By the Stories:

Stories (1972, Kama Sutra). A pretty successful effort, with much help from singer and cowriter Ian Lloyd, to put Brown's frail sensibilities into the heavier (though not much heavier) rock of the early 1970s. As is the case with most of Brown's work, it's most pungent when it's at its lightest, airiest, and most melancholy, as on "Winter Scenes" and "Kathleen."

About Us (1973, Kama Sutra). Harder rocking and less pleasing than *Stories*, this still has a number of shining melodies in "Words," "Love Is in Motion, and "What Comes After." "Please Please" is one of the most musically complex of Brown's co-compositions, with its ever-shifting keys.

Blue- and Brown-Eyed Soulsters

6

Blues, R&B, and soul music influenced virtually every rock band of the 1960s, regardless of their color. Some non-African-American groups, however, took the soul music gospel more seriously than others did. The term blue-eyed soul, according to *The Blackwell Guide to Soul Recordings*, was coined by black DJs to describe white acts soulful enough to get on their playlists, such as the Righteous Brothers and the Rascals. The term was not quite as appropriate for Latino soul-rock groups who certainly weren't black, but weren't Anglo, and the much lesser-used label brown-eyed soul has been devised in their honor.

One could argue whether soul and rock should be separated at all, in favor of treating soul as one important subgenre of what we call rock 'n' roll. If "rock" is defined as more group- and guitar-based than "soul," though, there were a number of fine bands — we could call them "soul-rock" acts, creating more fodder for debate — doing their best to bridge the forms in the 1960s. Everyone knows the Rascals and Boxtops, as they should. The Rationals and Thee Midniters were also stars and are also remembered well today. The problem for them is that the Rationals are remembered well only in their native Ann Arbor-Detroit region in Michigan, and Thee Midniters only in Los Angeles (and primarily East Los Angeles at that). They had the talent to make a bigger splash. They didn't have the distribution, timing, or luck.

The Rationals and Thee Midniters were almost unequaled in their facility for mixing American soul with British Invasion-inspired guitar rock. Yet to pigeonhole the Rationals strictly as blue-eyed soul, and the Mexican-American Thee Midniters as brown-eyed soul, would turn a blind eye to the larger scope of their musical vision. Each band failed to reach a bigger market, in part, because their progressively widening range in the late 1960s — including garage rock, psychedelia, and in the case of Thee Midniters, some pop ballads, Latin jazz, and Mexican bolero as well — made them difficult to sell. In an age in which fragmented diversity is prized rather than scorned, the time for each of those bands to reach an international audience may have finally arrived.

Thee Midniters, a seven-man band with a correspondingly wide musical vision. Left to right: Ronnie Figueroa, Willie Garcia, Larry Rendon, George Dominguez, Danny LaMont, Roy Marquez, Jimmy Espinoza.
Credit: Courtesy Jimmy Espinoza, Blue Nova Entertainment.

Thee Midniters

No, that's not a typo. That's Thee Midniters, with two e's in the Thee. A vexing problem for those retailers who agonize whether to file Captain Beefheart under C or B, or put the Marshall Tucker Band under M or T. The same goes for Thee Midniters: do you put them in the T section or the M section? Where are the customers going to look, and will they give up if they go to the wrong letter first?

For Thee Midniters, the best Latino rock band of the 1960s, the struggle has not been so much to figure out where to alphabetize themselves as to make sure they're in the primary pop-rock section in the first place. Despite huge local popularity in their native East Los Angeles, and a couple of big regional hits (which became small national ones) in the mid-1960s, they could not make that step into national and international viability. When they are referred to at all, they're usually hailed as the pioneers of Los Angeles' Mexican-American rock heritage, or as a brown-eyed soul act.

For Thee Midniters bassist Jimmy Espinoza, the ghettoization into the East L.A. Chicano rock world can generate both pride in his roots, and consternation at the limits imposed. "The '60s wasn't segregated," he stresses. "The '60s were *integrated*. The whole peace, love, black, white, brown, we're all the same: that's who *we* were. We were a crossover group, and we really loved it. It's extremely frustrating for me to get put into the Latin bag, because Thee Midniters aren't."

Thee Midniters were not so much fighting to break down barriers of racial segregation as to bust the barricades of segregation between *musical* styles. Few rock
groups at that time or since were as versatile. The band combined blue-eyed soul (or,
as it's sometimes dubbed in their case, brown-eyed soul) with Rolling Stones-styled
rock on both raw bluesy stompers and teary ballads. They mixed in psychedelic
music, Mexican-style boleros, Latin-jazz instrumentals, quasi-political statements,
and even goofy comedy. Utilizing a horn section in their permanent lineup, they
predated the more famous and, dare it be said, much inferior horn-rock bands
Chicago and Blood, Sweat & Tears by four years or so.

Listening to a Thee Midniters compilation tape is an almost unnerving experience, as the band hip-hops from the soul cover of "Land of a Thousand Dances" to
the Rolling Stones-with-horns of "Whittier Boulevard," the mariachi satire "The Big
Ranch," instrumentals fusing garage blues-rock guitar with big band brass, slow-
grind make-out soul ballads like "That's All," breezy pop-psychedelia on "Breakfast
on the Grass," a version of jazz singer Oscar Brown Jr.'s "Brother, Where Are You,"
nasty garage punk in "Jump, Jive and Harmonize," and Chicano power chants on the
obviously titled "Chicano Power." By the time more than a dozen songs have passed,
you half-expect the lads to launch into an Irish jig next. They don't, but they do pull
out the stops for the Spanish-sung corrido "Tu Despedida," with heartrending operatic vocals and maudlin violins ensuring that there's not a dry eye in the house by the
time the last note is plucked. The temptation is to draw out the old cliché and say it's
like hearing a tape of several bands, not one. Unlike most such genre-blenders, however, Thee Midniters had a consistency of taste, musical excellence, and a certain
soulfulness—derived in part from, but not exactly like, soul music—that ensures that
they can't be mistaken for anyone but themselves.

More than anything else, the key to making Thee Midniters sound like no other
group, from East Los Angeles or elsewhere, was lead singer Willie Garcia, aka Willie
G. One of the best non-African-American soul vocalists of the 1960s, Garcia had ex-
ceptionally rich and supple pipes that were best heard emoting the lower and bluesier end of the register on slow ballads. Yet he could also pick up the pace for
full-throated shouters and up-tempo rockers. The versatility was a partial result, perhaps, of working gigs from the time he entered his teens in the late 1950s, playing
"R&B, a lot of boleros, and corrido [Mexican ballad]-type music" for Latin audiences at weddings and parties.

When Garcia was first performing and future Midniter Jimmy Espinoza was
playing in other bands, Espinoza remembers, Willie "was like a pledge rushee, because there was a point where he couldn't even sing. We used to say, 'Oh, here
comes Willie, god.' We used to play these dances, and Willie would always be popping in. Boy, he was the most persistent guy. Always wanting to sing the blues. But he
was always flat. Thirty years later I asked him, 'What did you do to get good?' He
went and locked himself in his room, listened to records, and practiced all day, just
sang to the records. He's virtually self taught."

In the early 1960s Garcia was working in the Gentiles, whose name, almost as
surely as a moniker like the Fugs, would have probably ruled out much radio airplay.
They wisely decided to opt for Thee Midniters, in honor of one of their favorite
bands, Hank Ballard and the Midnighters, who had done much to midwife the tran-

sition among black vocal groups from R&B to rock 'n' roll with hits like "Work with Me Annie," and recorded the original version of "The Twist." The odd "Thee" spelling originated to avoid conflict with the other Midnighters, as did the mutation from "Midnighters" to "Midniters." At the first show they played under the Midniters name, the band came out in Lone Ranger-style paper masks, ripping off each in turn as they were introduced by Garcia during their opening number, "Green Onions."

As that incident shows, in the early 1960s Thee Midniters were still a fun high school band rather than a serious career endeavor. That began to change as some of the top young musicians in East Los Angeles began to enter the lineup, including bassist Benny Lopez, saxophonist Larry Rendon, trombonist Romeo Prado, lead guitarist George Dominguez, and rhythm guitarist Roy Marquez. Although Lopez would leave Thee Midniters in 1965, he and others feel he had an underappreciated role in helping shape their music and image, taking the lead in redoing their hair and wardrobe in the British Invasion style. "I feel I formed the group," says Lopez today. "[In] '63, we were just a weekend band. In '64, I decided to change the band, and replaced members with friends of mine. If I would have kept that original group, I don't know what destiny would have brought forth. I don't think it would have done anything, really. It didn't have a personality."

Both Rendon and Prado had studied under Salesian High School music teacher Bill Taggart, who was known for directing one of the best high school bands in Los Angeles. Taggart also put on rock 'n' roll shows at the school, and it was at one of these in 1964 that the band got its big, and rather accidental, break by making a live recording of "Land of a Thousand Dances." The song, an infectious lyrical catalog of dance crazes, was first recorded by New Orleans singer Chris Kenner, best known for the early 1960s hit "I Like It Like That." Kenner couldn't make "Land of a Thousand Dances," which he wrote with Fats Domino, a hit. Somehow, though, it caught on with the legions of Mexican-American rock bands springing up in East Los Angeles in the mid-1960s, including Cannibal & the Headhunters.

"The only reason we recorded 'Land of a Thousand Dances' that night in October of 1964 is because the second half of our set was to back up Cannibal & the Headhunters," explains Garcia. "'Sad Girl,' 'Land of a Thousand Dances,' and a few other songs that we did that night were actually to be sung by Cannibal & the Headhunters. They had gotten stuck in the fog coming from Fresno, and didn't show. So the stage director, Taggart, peeks out the curtains, because there was a lull. We kept looking in the wings to see if Cannibal & the Headhunters were set to come out. He said, 'Keep going, they're not here.' The only songs that we really had rehearsed tight enough were those, so we went into 'em. The rest, as they say, it's kind of like history."

Well, not exactly. Thee Midniters' live version of "Land of a Thousand Dances," turning Kenner's New Orleans R&B song into a raw rocker with powerhouse drumming, chanting, and blasting horns, did well locally and made number sixty-seven on the national charts—as high as Thee Midniters would ever get. However, they were outdone, certainly on a national level, by a competing version from none other than Cannibal & the Headhunters, who took it to number thirty and rode its success to national tours, including some 1965 dates supporting the Beatles. Both East L.A. groups were then commercially blown out of the water by Wilson Pickett, whose own superb cover made number six in 1966, and is the one remembered by most lis-

teners today. Still, the song had given Thee Midniters a foothold in the music industry, inaugurating a fairly lengthy and at times inscrutably diverse recording career.

By 1965, East Los Angeles housed a thriving Mexican-American rock scene that
remains woefully neglected by rock historians, and indeed largely unknown to those
not living in Southern California at the time. Two Chicano rockers from the Los Angeles area, Ritchie Valens and Chris Montez, had made some national hits in the
late 1950s and early 1960s, but for the most part Mexican-American musicians from
the region were unable to cross over into the national rock mainstream. This is unfortunate, as the East L.A. bands had cultivated an exciting hybrid of rhythm and
blues, Latin music, jazz, and newly felt influences from British Invasion bands into a
distinctive sound. R&B from the 1950s, particularly as sung by black vocal groups,
has always been hugely popular in L.A.'s Latino community; it remained a component of the area's rock bands in the 1960s, but the success of the Beatles and the
Rolling Stones was inspiring more musicians to grow their hair long and write their
own material. The best of their records, usually issued by small indie labels without
powerful national distribution, can be heard on Varese Sarabande's four-volume *The
West Coast East Side Sound* series, and to a lesser degree on Rhino's three *Brown
Eyed Soul* volumes. Were Thee Midniters only able to do covers such as "Land of a
Thousand Dances," they would be a footnote on the order of most of the bands that
fill up those compilations, such as the Blendells, who had a small national hit by
covering Little Stevie Wonder's "La La La La La," or to a lesser degree Cannibal &
the Headhunters, who never matched the success of "Land of a Thousand Dances"
again.

Thee Midniters were different, certainly from the other East L.A. bands, and
eventually from most other rock bands from anywhere. To begin with, there was the
horn section, which gave them the depth of a jazz big band without diminishing
their rock energy. Rather than employ only saxophone (by far the most common
horn instrument in rock ensembles before the mid-1960s), the group widened the
breadth and range of their brass by matching Larry Rendon's sax to Romeo Prado's
valve trombone. Prado's choice of the valve trombone was specifically inspired by the
music of the Jazz Crusaders, and by Benny Lopez, who asked Prado to switch from
trumpet. "I didn't want to do that, but he convinced me," admits Prado. "That's
when Larry and I developed a sound of our own. I brought the Latin jazz aspect into
the band, [and] I tried to bring [the] big band sound." Garcia claims much more for
his band mate: "He has got one of the most fertile imaginations, musically, that I've
ever heard. I'd put him right in there with Marty Paich [who did arrangements for
Chet Baker, Stan Kenton, Frank Sinatra, Ray Charles, and many others] and Quincy
Jones."

Until such time as Thee Midniters could write their own material, they were re-
liant upon cover tunes. Again they distinguished themselves from the pack by astute
judgment, the risky eclecticism of their repertoire, and the discovery of nuggets so
obscure that it's rather impressive they were able to find all of the songs in the first
place. There was "The Town I Live In," by Chicago-based cult "deep soul" singer
McKinley Mitchell; "That's All," by Nat King Cole; "It'll Never Be Over for Me," by
New York soul diva Baby Washington; "Brother, Where Are You," by socially conscious jazz singer Oscar Brown Jr.; "I Need Someone," by pop crooner Lenny

Welch; Jerry Butler's "Giving Up on Love"; and Jay Wiggins' "Sad Girl," a whopping number 116 hit in 1963 that nonetheless got adopted as a radio oldie in Philadelphia and some other cities. Garcia really came into his own as a heartbreaking vocalist on sad and sentimental ballads like "The Town I Live In," "Sad Girl," and "That's All," ideal for smoochy slow dances, on which the band could sound a bit like a lost Philly soul outfit. "The caliber of musicianship we had in the band made it interesting for us to select songs, and put horn arrangements to 'em," states Garcia. "We liked these songs so much that they actually became ours, if you understand my meaning. We *made* them ours. We bought into them; we personalized them."

It is one thing to simply assemble an obscure and wide-ranging set list; anyone with a big record collection can do that. It's another to put your own stamp on material as an interpreter, and Thee Midniters did so by sounding not so much like a soul group as a soul-rock one, not quite falling conveniently into either the soul or rock column. Often they could sound as if they were trying to cross the Righteous Brothers with the Rolling Stones, projecting the same sort of foggy blue-eyed soul textures as were heard on classic mid-1960s Righteous Brothers singles like "(You're My) Soul and Inspiration," but with more rock spontaneity, particularly in the bass lines and George Dominguez's slicing blues-rock guitar. You could hear this on their chugging 1965 cover of "Heat Wave," the studio version of "Land of a Thousand Dances" (rerecorded for their first LP), and their marching-tempo rendition of the obscure early Rolling Stones composition "Empty Heart," which as Garcia notes boasts a "killer horn line" in place of the expected guitars. Thee Midniters loved the Beatles and the Rolling Stones, but seemed to love the Rolling Stones more, at least insofar as what influences showed up on their recordings. And nowhere was the Rolling Stones influence more audible than on "Whittier Boulevard," their second monster local hit and, like "Land of a Thousand Dances," something of an accident.

Whittier Boulevard was the main drag in East L.A.: *the* place to go see music, shop, and, above all, cruise in cars. Now signed to the small L.A. indie Chattahoochee, whose big success was the Murmaids' 1963 one-shot girl-group smash "Popsicles and Icicles," Thee Midniters were placing their bets on a single called "Evil Love." The typically (for the group) soul-rock admixture, written by their friend Sammy Phillip (who as Hirth Martinez would record a Robbie Robertson-produced album for Warner Brothers in the mid-1970s), was recorded as an A-side and hoped-for-hit. Something was needed for the flip, and the group tossed off a jam based around the classic bass riff that piloted the Rolling Stones' great instrumental "2120 South Michigan Avenue."

"It's something we just used to do at rehearsal," says Garcia. "Benny Lopez would just start playing that line, and eventually, the song just started taking on a personality. We were in the studio, thinking, well, what are we gonna do as a B-side? I think it was pretty much unanimous. We said, 'Let's do that riff Benny's always playing.' And we just started exchanging ideas about the boulevard itself, trying to capture some of the excitement and things that were happening on the boulevard at the time. So the little screams in the background and what have you—that's how the song actually evolved. We were quite surprised when we heard it on the radio."

Confirms Lopez, "I kind of liked that one song by the Rolling Stones, I liked that bass part, on account of he was going into a second change without changing the whole structure of the chord. So I started playing that little bass part. Roy's the one that kind of started the rhythm with me. So I said, 'We're gonna play this.' Nobody [else in the band] liked it [initially], really. Mick Jagger, they interviewed him back then and he did mention about a group recording a [song] similar to '2120.' But he wasn't even concerned about…you know, he had so much money already, he didn't care."

"Whittier Boulevard" *was* very close to "2120 South Michigan Avenue," despite Prado's observation that "the bass line was similar to the Rolling Stones tune, but everything else was entirely different. The Rolling Stones changed a chord or two; we didn't. We stayed on one chord, and that was it. It was just a jam." Thee Midniters did add an exultant shout at the beginning, "Let's take a trip down Whittier Boulevard!," reminiscent of the shout "let's go trippin'!" that kicked off Dick Dale's classic surf instrumental "Let's Go Trippin'." Followed by yells of "Arriba! Arriba!," bleating car horns, and laughter that can only be described as manic, the mood was set for an instrumental that, unlike "2120 South Michigan Avenue," was made for anthemic status among East L.A. youth. Hyena cackles continued to punctuate a track brought further into the American garage band norm with skittering organ and raw blues-rock guitar, given that special Thee Midniters touch by periodic fanfares of brass. In mid-1965 the single got to the Top Ten on one of L.A.'s biggest radio stations, KRLA, although it could hardly be said to have had much national impact, reaching a mere number 127 on *Billboard*.

In retrospect it was fortuitous that DJs had flipped over the single to make "Whittier Boulevard" the plug side. The little-known "Evil Love," with its almost jazzy chord changes and an odd (for pop) structure without easily demarcated verses and bridges, was a rather cool song, but stood little chance of catching the immediate attention of listeners in the fashion "Whittier Boulevard" did. "Evil Love'"s hooks were subtle; "Whittier Boulevard" was *all* hook. "Whittier Boulevard'"s almost nonexistent national chart placement, and good but not great ranking on L.A. radio, did not reflect the enormity of its lasting impact in the Latino community of Los Angeles, where it (like many Thee Midniters tunes) remains a beloved oldie today. According to Lopez, that audience even made a dance out of it, copying the band's onstage choreography, in which the musicians would move their right feet forward and slide them across in time to the insistent trombone riffs that dot the track.

"Whittier Boulevard" is also a point of some dispute among the group. Lopez and Marquez feel that they were the key writers of the track, are not happy that the song is currently credited to Willie Garcia and Jimmy Espinoza, and want their names added to the composition credits. There are also different recollections of when exactly Lopez dropped out of the band to get married and pursue a different course. Asked if there were any Thee Midniters records on which he didn't play, Espinoza names only the early singles tracks "Ball of Twine," "Heat Wave," and the first version of "Land of a Thousand Dances"; Lopez and Marquez say that some of their first album, including the track "Whittier Boulevard," was recorded while Benny was still in the group. "I should get recognition for it," states Lopez regarding "Whittier Boulevard." "I don't feel that anybody who wasn't even in the studio, or wasn't even in the group, should get credit for it."

Again in retrospect, "Whittier Boulevard" was part of a pattern in which the songs Thee Midniters became most famous for were not necessarily the ones most representative of the band, or the ones for which they most wished the band to be known. "Some of the music that we recorded which became popular, I didn't care about," admits Prado. "'Whittier Boulevard,' for example. I hated that song. Speaking for myself, I wanted to do more Latin stuff." Prado wouldn't get as much opportunity to influence the repertoire as he would have liked, due to circumstances beyond his and the band's control. In August 1965, he was drafted, and spent the next two years in the service, only coming back for a few shows and recording sessions while on leave. (Garcia would take trombone parts, onstage and on record, during much of that time.)

The tug of different, and not necessarily competing, interests in Thee Midniters both fueled their innovations and made them a difficult group to market, perhaps, in their time, and a difficult one for history to easily grasp. There was no predicting what the next Thee Midniters single could be, and no predicting what moods and styles would be navigated over the course of one of their albums. Even within many of their individual songs, soul rubbed against jazz, blues, Latin music, and British Invasion music, alternately or all at once. Jimmy Espinoza, who replaced Benny Lopez on bass sometime in 1965 and still leads a version of Thee Midniters today, has given much thought to the congruence of elements that made the group unique.

"We opened the doors to each other's heads as much as we were able to without brushing each other's egos too much. We had these alliances. I had an alliance with Romeo for jazz; he had an alliance with me for jazz and Latin. But also, I had an alliance with him for Frank Sinatra and Johnny Mathis. That's how we started filtering down those ballads to Willie, who was the soul guy. He brought the soul and R&B really strong; he's the one who introduced 'Town I Live In,' 'Sad Girl' to the band. But we're the ones who introduced 'That's All,' 'Strangers in the Night.' We were exchanging musical baseball cards, if you will.

"George Dominguez was a hot blues guitar player, [and] had been playing weddings and parties with his father, so he had the Spanish influence also. He knew how to play mandolin. On 'It'll Never Be Over for Me'; that's making the pick [go] up and down in sixteenth-note fashion to get that mandolin effect on a lead guitar. Roy [Marquez] wasn't a good lead guitar player, but was fascinated with jazz chords, so he gave us that full guitar chordal effect. Danny [LaMont, who replaced George Salazar on drums after Thee Midniters' first LP] and I had been in a surf band, yet Danny was a great jazz drummer. He loved Louie Bellson and Buddy Rich, as well as Hal Blaine. Danny's influence definitely put us right into surf, white English pop studio sound.

"He would do incredible things with the drums. In fact, we used to do a routine, where he'd take a drum solo at the end of 'Whittier Boulevard' or whatever tune, and I would hit the bass. He would play his sticks on the bass, and I would move my finger up and down the string to get the different tones, and he would play the rhythm on it. I'd never seen anybody do that before. We just did it intuitively. He used to get up off his drums and walk around his kit and play every part of that set. I mean, he'd play things that you don't normally hit, like the stands, the chromium parts that hold the cymbals." If that wasn't enough to bring the house down, Larry Rendon could play the tenor and alto saxes simultaneously, like a rock counterpart to famed jazz musician Roland Kirk.

"We were all on a high. Everybody brought something brand new, and we just jumped on it, because it was pretty pure. If Roy brought a nice new chord, or George Dominguez brought a wonderful blues lick, or Willie came up with a new song or something, or Romeo and Larry brought their savvy from the horn section standpoint, or I came up with a bass line with Danny or whatever, we were all on the same page. But we all came from different parts of the computer, so to speak. I doubt, minus any of the elements, we would have had the same effect. It was just the rightness of the chemical equation."

Be that as it may, Thee Midniters' first two albums stuck mostly to rock, soul, or somewhere in between, with a few ballads like "Strangers in the Night" thrown in to vary the pace. The LPs did contain some high-class covers that are among their best tracks, such as the lounge-lizard reading of "That's All" and one of Garcia's great soul vocals on Jerry Butler's "Giving Up on Love." The studio remake of "Land of a Thousand Dances" (on the self-titled debut LP) totally outdistanced the original live 45 version with its urgent horns, too-short demonic guitar break near the end, and a truly lunatic peal of laughter from original Thee Midniters keyboardist Ronnie Figueroa (who left after the second album). There were also run-of-the-mill versions of well-known rock and soul hits—the Righteous Brothers' "Soul and Inspiration" was an obvious choice given the similarities between the groups on yearning ballads. By side two of the second LP, *Love Special Delivery*, the all-things-to-all-people credo seemed almost willfully perverse, as an overlong "Strangers in the Night" was immediately followed by an ear-piercing James Brown scream that led off a kick-ass cover of Them's "Gloria." Few tracks from 1966 are any stranger than "I Found a Peanut," with its dumber-than-doofus Garcia vocal, apparently mimicking some half-wit kid looking for…a peanut.

At least "I Found a Peanut" and three other tracks on *Love Special Delivery* had Thee Midniters picking up the gauntlet thrown to them by manager Eddie Torres and starting to write their own material. "We knew that we were going to have to start stepping up to the plate, and start to deliver in that area, if we were gonna get any longevity out of our career as a group," acknowledges Garcia. "Eddie Torres just challenged us. He goes, 'You know what? I'm going to go grab a burger, and if you guys can't write a song…if you guys can't come up with an original idea by the time I come back, I don't even think we should go in the studio and start another project.' And he just walked out. There was a deafening silence in the room as we looked at each other, and we sort of got this attitude, 'Well, we'll show him.' So we wrote [the single "Love Special Delivery"] like in about ten minutes."

"Love Special Delivery" was another mix of brass and blues that somehow worked instead of collapsing into schizophrenia. The LSD acronym of the title might lead some to see it as an allusion to the blossoming drug culture, but in truth it had a standard soul lyric, alternating a bursting horn hook with sizzling blues-rock guitar, and driven by a descending bass line not too dissimilar from the one in "Whittier Boulevard." "If you listen to 'Love Special Delivery,' you'll hear 'Whittier Boulevard' in there, all over the place," declares Marquez. "Not vocally; I'm telling the bass, 'Remember what Benny did. C'mon, try and give it that same feel.' Then," in the instrumental break where all instruments drop out except the bass and drums before reentering one by one, "we'll have this open thing. Just like in 'Whittier Boulevard,' that whole space of nothing."

"One of the good things about Eddie, he insisted we keep recording and putting material out," says Espinoza, who as we'll see has some pointed criticisms of Torres as well. "That's a real positive, because I don't know if we would have done that." Everyone in Thee Midniters seems to agree that their third album, *Unlimited*, represented their biggest stride from talented interpretive band to something truly original, especially as eight of its twelve songs were penned by the group. "That third album, that was the bomb," continues Espinoza. "That was the cookie. 'Cause we were really out on a limb with ourselves. We were really paddling out in our own creative waters, and we didn't know if we had something or if we didn't." Marquez feels likewise: "The first album was just a showboat. The second we were searching. The third started showing what Thee Midniters could have really went on to be."

On the best of *Unlimited*'s original compositions, the band started to come into its own with songs that integrated the musicians' soul, rock, jazz, and pop influences with more grace than they had ever managed on their previous recordings. "Cheatin' Woman," for instance, was just a nice R&B/pop tune until it suddenly segued into a nearly full-on jazz instrumental break with flute, the kind of transition that wouldn't be attempted with much regularity by rock bands for another two or three years. Romeo Prado (pictured on the back cover in military uniform as "Thee 7th Midniter in Service") got enough time off from the service to add a compelling Latin-soul-jazz instrumental, "Chile Con Soul," which stood up to the best of the similar "boogaloo" hybrids concocted by 1960s East Coast acts like Joe Cuba, Hector Rivera, Pucho & the Soul Brothers, and Willie Bobo. Most impressively, Willie Garcia was maturing into a first-class soul songwriter on "Dreaming Casually" and "Making Ends Meet," each of which had the tender, introspective aura of a sensitive voice crossing the threshold from adolescence to adulthood. Rendon, who helped Garcia polish both of those tunes, was compensating for Prado's absence with delicate flute passages on "Dreaming Casually" and elsewhere, adding yet further to the band's virtuosity.

Garcia's development into a quality songwriter for *Unlimited* came about partly due to the kind of unexpected accident that so often sparks an artist's evolution. "I had developed tonsillitis really bad, and that attributes for a lot of those rough-sounding vocals on *Unlimited*. Ultimately I had 'em removed, and was off for three months, two of those in complete silence. The doctor said, 'Don't speak, get a notepad for two months. Let it heal really, really well.' I was going nuts. So I rented a piano; my parents helped me get it into my bedroom. During that time, I was disobedient to the doctor, sat at the piano, and wrote 'Dreaming Casually' and 'Making Ends Meet,' both in the same day. You can probably notice the difference in my vocal texture. I was playing it intentionally in a real low key, and that's how both two songs came about."

"Making Ends Meet" had all the makings of a soul classic that never became the standard it deserved to be, with Garcia's admonition that you can't make ends meet by leaving love out of the middle. The key line came to Garcia in a nonhallucinatory vision that, perhaps, foreshadowed his current occupation as an evangelist.

"I was driving home one night, stopped at a red light, and looked over at the church marquee. It said, 'You can't make ends meet by leaving God out of the middle.' And the scripture verse came to me that God is love, and I said, 'God wouldn't mind if I used that.'"

Unlimited, for all its virtues, showed a band only partially down the road to fulfilling its potential. The covers included inessential remakes of "Yesterday" and "Devil with a Blue Dress"/"Good Golly Miss Molly." Even the good covers—the superb rendition of McKinley Mitchell's deep soul gem "The Town I Live In," and a raucous run-through of the Solomon Burke-by-way-of-Rolling Stones track "Everybody Needs Somebody"—were throwbacks to approaches the band had already explored on its first two albums. To develop further as artists and obtain the musical freedom to explore, create, and experiment, a national audience and heavy label and managerial support were not absolutely essential, but certainly advantageous. The national audience, and even the opportunity to record further albums, did not happen. The group members have a definite theory as to why these did not.

"I had RCA come down to see us at a concert, and Jose Feliciano was on the bill," says Espinoza. "He had been on RCA also. So they also scouted us, and liked the band. Neely Plumb, the A&R guy at that time for RCA, wanted us. Our manager rejected it, because he wanted to form Whittier Records." Eddie Torres, according to several members of the band, was trying to build a huge independent record company with Whittier Records, using Herb Alpert and A&M Records as his model, and Thee Midniters as the band upon which to build its success.

"I was so torn apart when Eddie didn't see the wisdom of going with RCA," Jimmy adds. "The concept was that Herb Alpert did it, so why couldn't we? Conceptually, I agreed with him that sure, if we can keep our own record company to do it, great. But I knew he didn't have the expertise to take it to that next level. You have to know your marketing, your promotion. I don't care if you have the greatest product in the world, if you don't know how to market it and make those connections on a higher level, you're not going to do it. I knew he didn't have that clout. Just because we established our own record company didn't translate itself into him being any more able than he was. He was a great beginning manager, a great personal manager. He knew how to talk, he had a lot of charisma. We all liked him. But then he became stubborn."

As to the RCA contract, Garcia chimes in, "I think it was just a matter of getting our signatures. I really believe the label was already grooming us for their audiences when that all fell through. As a group, we were in the dark about what was going on contractually. Our manager kept it from us." Prado believes "they offered [Torres] some serious money just to walk away, and they would take us. They wanted to make us an international group, from what I understand. When Jimmy told me about the RCA deal that went sour, I cried my damn self."

Had RCA gotten the band, Garcia thinks, "musically and careerwise, we probably would have been placed in a situation where the counsel and advice pertaining to direction and musicality would have enhanced what was already in our DNA. Probably would have brought out the best in us; the creative process probably would have had a real chance to manifest." Garcia also ascribes the failure of Thee Midniters to reach an international audience, with RCA or someone else as the vehicle, on "limited vision. I'm not blaming Eddie Torres for this. I really believe he did the best that he possibly could for us. But that probably was our biggest obstacle."

Torres did not respond to requests for an interview that might have allowed him to present his view of the situation. In *Land of a Thousand Dances: Chicano Rock 'n' Roll from Southern California*, however, David Reyes and Tom Waldman wrote that Torres "says that RCA wanted *Love Special Delivery* 'given' to it, without agreeing to pay Torres or the band either money up front or production costs. Torres says he could not possibly go along with these terms. Besides, he adds, Thee Midniters did not possess the writing skills necessary to become a top-of-the-line rock 'n' roll band. 'The one thing RCA wanted above all was for Thee Midniters to write their own material,' said Torres. 'I always had to fight to get the music out of them.'"

Had the band members signed with RCA, that would by no means have guaranteed getting them to the next level. RCA may have had the least impressive track record of any major American label in the late 1960s for developing creative rock artists, with notable exceptions like the Jefferson Airplane, the Youngbloods, and Nilsson. Some good bands that signed to RCA and made excellent music did not have it effectively promoted or distributed, such as the Kansas folk-rock act the Bluethings. It's also possible that with a major label, Thee Midniters would not have enjoyed the relative freedom they had in choosing and writing the material they issued on Whittier.

What *does* seem certain is that Thee Midniters were *not* going to rise to international fame on Whittier Records, which lacked the distribution necessary to even break them outside of California. Whittier also undersold the band by using dime-store graphics on their LPs that seemed more appropriate for 1956 than 1966. Additionally, although production on Thee Midniters recordings is generally decent, there were some curious decisions that indicated they could have done with more time and professionalism in the studio. The studio version of "Land of a Thousand Dances," for instance, cut off just as Dominguez ripped into a whiplash Keith Richards-type riff. The "Jump, Jive and Harmonize" single was recorded on a two-track at a theater where the band rehearsed, and faded abruptly just as the group reached the apex of a Yardbirds-styled rave-up. (Marquez does take care to praise Bruce Morgan, engineer on many of their early recordings: "He knew that we needed that echo, he knew how to not lose things, and he knew that we couldn't sing background real well. He made Willie sound very professional.") And there were no more Thee Midniters albums in the 1960s after *Unlimited* (other than *Giants*, which except for two songs was comprised of previously released material), which in itself seems like a sign that the band, the label, and the management were not maximizing their opportunities.

The band *was* extremely active on the live circuit, with a greater reputation and popularity among both Latino and non-Latino audiences than the obscurity of many of the group's recordings might indicate. Marquez says they played "every town from San Diego to San Francisco, Bakersfield, Sacramento," and although they didn't get out of California much, they did play as far west as El Paso, Texas, where "we became very big," and as far north as Washington. Often they did two or three shows a night, saving time by chartering private planes to get them between gigs and using the equipment that had already been set up by the previous band. They played for what Espinoza terms "three levels of audiences" in East L.A.—"the hard-core low-riders, middle-class Catholic school kids [called Jetters in the local lingo], and the young college crowd, people that are today politicians."

They also performed at a lot of concerts and dances promoted by DJ and future national radio personality Casey Kasem, then on KRLA in Los Angeles, who described them (in *Land of a Thousand Dances*) as "the best band I ever hired…The most consistent and the most visual." They played at the Rose Bowl with Herman's Hermits, the Lovin' Spoonful, and Bobby Fuller; they did shows with emerging psychedelic bands like the Seeds and the Strawberry Alarm Clock. "It's so confining [to] be put into the Latin bag," exclaims Espinoza. "I love our roots and I appreciate that, but that's *not* who we were. I almost know that all the guys are screaming inside, because historically, we were always a crossover band. It's weird when history tries to pigeonhole you."

It's especially weird since the group's final dozen or so singles in 1966-69—containing numerous tracks never on LP—were such a zigzag of genres that it's difficult to imagine any pigeonhole big enough to hold them. There was the haunting soul ballad "It'll Never Be Over for Me," with Dominguez's mandolin-like guitar effects, organ, and Righteous Brothers-type reverb combining to remarkably ethereal effect. On "Thee Walking Song," they did a fair impression of the Impressions. On "The Big Ranch" (sung in Spanish), they went into madcap comedy, Garcia impersonating a Mexican bandleader who loses control of his group midway through a mariachi number, as the musicians suddenly break into defiant garage guitar and organ licks despite the singer's protests. On "Breakfast on the Grass," there was psychedelic pop a la the Strawberry Alarm Clock. "Tu Despedida" was an earnest romantic Spanish-sung bolero with mandolin and violin, proving that despite "The Big Ranch" Thee Midniters had a genuine affection for traditional Mexican music when it was done right.

"Jump, Jive and Harmonize" was their best hard rock number, its shrill unison guitar and bass lines leading into boastful garage rock, then to the trademark Thee Midniters instrumental break where all instruments dropped out save the rhythm, brought back to full intensity by a brief duel of harmonica and organ riffs. (Espinoza: "I think we were thinking, subconsciously, of Stevie Wonder when he did 'Fingertips.' It has that echoey hall effect.") The instrumental "Thee Midnite Feeling," buried on a B-side, had smoking interplay between big-band horns, searing lead blues-rock-garage guitar, and turnarounds of almost cinematic grandeur where the beat dramatically slowed and accelerated in tandem with anthemic horn lines. Then there were the quasi-Chicano Power statements of "The Ballad of Cesar Chavez" and a Latin-soul instrumental actually titled "Chicano Power." They were being all things to all people, but it was also an anti-Marketing 101 course if there ever was one. According to Marquez, "I remember a review we got. They said, 'We can't understand. How can these guys be such great musicians, such a tight group, and yet, they don't have direction?'"

Far from regretting their reluctance to stick in any groove for more than a song or two at a time, the group members delight in remembering these one-off excursions, known for the most part only to a handful of record collectors. With instrumentals such as "Thee Midnite Feeling," says Espinoza, "We were showing off our chops, and trying to be a little psychedelic, rocky, into a movie area…sort of doing a goulash or potpourri of all different kind of instrument elements. We also did something called 'Dragon-Fly' [another rare-as-get-out B-side], which was cosmic space rock surf. We didn't mind trying it. We'd say, 'I don't know who's going to like this, but, oh well.'"

"Breakfast on the Grass," he goes on, "was kind of our answer to Sky Saxon. 'Cause we were doing a lot of those gigs [with bands like the Seeds] and Roy actually said, 'We can do that shit. We can do this psychedelic rock stuff.' That was our statement to the white community that we could cover anything. A lot of these groups were psychedelic in that they were in the emotional terrain, but they didn't have the musical chops we had. If you listen to the ending, we go into three-quarter time. We ended really unorthodox to show that we had musical chops. The background singing is going against the beat, and we were saying, 'If you want psychedelic, *this* is psychedelic.' Because we're bending time: 'If I was on acid, this is how we'd bend the time signature.' We had so much fun doing that. The organ solo is a triad backwards; I said, 'Let's play it backwards, 'cause that's what we're kind of doing anyway.' But it's still against the 4/4 time." Marquez's outlook on the song is not as rosy: "'Breakfast on the Grass' was just a stupidity thing. Eddie Torres came in with some screwed-up lyrics."

Adds Espinoza, "'Tu Despedida' had to be around the time [of] 'The Ballad of Cesar Chavez' and 'The Big Ranch.' We were already fishing into the Mexican thing. But 'Tu Despedida' was probably our most serious attempt at showing our roots, saying, 'If you really want to go there, this is us.' It's a beautiful song. We were fishing in the stream; that was from the heart."

Although 'The Ballad of Cesar Chavez' might be viewed as an indication that the band members were growing with the times by developing a social consciousness, they make it pretty clear that the song was *not* where their hearts lay. "We just did it as a favor," says Garcia, in a tone that makes it clear he's reluctant to discuss the song at all. "The song was ghostwritten by Bruce Morgan's mom. It was Eddie Torres' idea to release it, capitalizing on Cesar Chavez's notoriety at the time. He was fasting, and [there] was a lot of things going on with the farm workers' union. It was real folk, they wanted a troubadour-sounding song. It wasn't even really a good recording, to be honest with you." Espinoza is blunter: "This woman [Torres] knew came to a recording session to say, 'You guys gotta do something about Cesar Chavez. It's the latest thing, he's a farm worker, organizing,' told us the whole story. And the band actually couldn't give a rat's ass about that. We weren't political. We were a band. We weren't trying to make any statements about Chicano, black, or white. We were just, 'Man, leave us alone for Christ's sake. This is so corny.'"

The very appearance on a single of a song the band wanted nothing to do with, and that seemed design to exploit a political cause in the hope of getting some attention (and perhaps even seemed designed to exploit the musicians themselves), was a symptom of a band (or management) beginning to take desperate measures by 1968. After its release, they suffered more damage to their reputation and career than any misbegotten single could have caused when Willie Garcia left the band. "For me, it was devastating," says Prado. "Who could replace Willie, for crying out loud? We were uncertain of our future as a band without Willie."

For Espinoza, it was especially vexing as he felt the group was reaching a new peak of symbiotic interaction. This is best heard on the instrumental cover of "Walk on By" on the *Giants* album, where Thee Midniters sound as much like an improvising rock-influenced jazz band as they do a jazz-influenced rock one. "The drum-bass player relationship, we integrate where I play a lot of his same rhythm patterns, or he plays my rhythm patterns in and out, we mate, and then we leave, and then we mate. It was so much fun recording that. Our level of creativity was really getting hot. We were really free and confident. The band was even more honest than it had been in the beginning. 'Cause in the beginning we were just having fun, but now there was a maturity about it and we were reaching deeper. If you listen to 'Walk On By,' and you listen to 'Goin' Out of My Head' [also on *Giants*, although Garcia is not on vocals], you'll sense that in the music and approach."

There was one last blast of glory for Thee Midniters, even without Garcia on hand, for the 1969 single "Chicano Power." Essentially an instrumental with periodic "Chicano power" and "sock it to me" chants, whoops, and whistling, this was written by Prado while he was in the Army, and recorded after he left the service to rejoin the band full-time. Even more than his previous "Chile Con Soul," it was their best fusion of Latin jazz with soul and rock music, with irresistibly snaky riffs and grooves. When they reached the song's turnaround, these bore a passing similarity to (and predated) those heard on Traffic's own 1970 jazz-rock instrumental, "Glad." Eddie Torres put out the 45 on La Raza ("The Race"), a new sister label to Whittier; there was even a peace sign on the label, to further link Thee Midniters with late 1960s political action. The band members sounded like they were having a hell of a party on the finished track, but as with "The Ballad of Cesar Chavez," their memories of its genesis reveal some disgruntlement.

"Eddie was into the Brown Beret movement at the time," notes Prado. "That's why we recorded 'Chicano Power.' He's the one that added the lyrics. It was an instrumental, but I wanted it named something else. I don't even *like* the word Chicano. I'm a Mexican-American; I'm not a Chicano. I'm offended at that word. But he wanted to call it that, so we all went with it." Agrees Espinoza, "It was Eddie's attempt to get us into a movement. I had a real aversion to being dragged into other people's political peccadilloes. We really didn't belong in that. That was Eddie Torres' fabrication. 'Cesar Chavez' and 'Chicano Power,' those were Eddie's agendas. They weren't the band's agendas."

"In my estimation, when they came out with it, I just saw the band trying to keep an audience," observes Garcia, who by this time had gone solo. "Not that we weren't politically conscious, but it was quite a departure from anything we had ever done. I said, 'I think they're clutching at a straw right now.'"

Torres was in fact fired by the band around the time of "Chicano Power," with Espinoza taking over as manager. Thee Midniters continued for a while without Garcia, taking a long residency at the Mardi Gras club in L.A., and putting out a single on Uni. Other members began to drift in and out — Benny Lopez even came back in for a while — before Thee Midniters' original incarnation, if such a thing existed of a band that had been through so many different lineups, petered out in the early 1970s.

Would the band members' ethnicity have been a factor in denying them the chance for national exposure they deserved? It should be mentioned that there were a few 1960s bands, from both within and beyond California, with Mexican-Americans that had big national hits, including the Sir Douglas Quintet (who somehow nonetheless tried to pass themselves off as British initially) and Sunny & the

Sunglows from Texas, and ? & the Mysterians (who made number one in 1966 with "96 Tears") from Michigan. Santana, under the leadership of Mexican-American guitarist Carlos Santana at the tail end of the decade, took the combination of rock, blues, soul, jazz, and Latin music characteristic of Thee Midniters and some other Latino bands in the United States to a huge international mass audience. Santana, of course, had a consistency of sound—from track to track and album to album—that Thee Midniters didn't, and may have not wanted, but which certainly made the music more readily accessible to a broad listenership. As it happened, a popular act Thee Midniters might have influenced, Chicago, had few evident Mexican-American influences, although as Espinoza relates, "I was told they took some influences from what we were doing, to further help develop their horn sound."

Thee Midniters' influence on subsequent generations is, like their sound as a whole, elusive to pin down. A somewhat bemused Espinoza sees how their garage-punk tracks—which comprised well under half of the band's total output—were adopted by bands such as new wave popsters Plimsouls, who Espinoza says played "Jump, Jive and Harmonize" at their live shows. "We have a lot of Hollywood underground bands that love 'Love Special Delivery,' 'Breakfast on the Grass.' [About] 'Never Knew I Had It So Bad' and 'Jump, Jive and Harmonize,' they would really say, 'God, you guys really sound punk.' And we said, 'What's that?' Punk wasn't even defined then [in the 1960s], but they give us this pre-punk kind of a thing, which is...that's nice. You know, you want to be loved by everybody, right?"

Cesar Rosas and Conrad Luzano of Los Lobos used to watch Thee Midniters years before Los Lobos came into being. David Hidalgo of Los Lobos just produced a new Willie Garcia solo album. Luzano and Espinoza recently spent three weeks transferring vintage Midniters material to DAT, with Rosas' equipment. And Los Lobos are currently the biggest Mexican-American band in the world. Thus it's also easy for some onlookers to code Thee Midniters as an ancestor to the Mexican-American Los Angeles rock tradition, a link in the chain currently leading to Los Lobos and similar bands. Yet Espinoza is adamant that Thee Midniters don't belong there. He feels Thee Midniters have been thrown into a "brown bag, and that was totally historically inaccurate. The band was a wonderful rock and roll-, R&B-, Latin jazz-flavored group of musicians. That's it."

Most of the musicians involved in Thee Midniters' 1964-1969 recordings continue to play and record, to small and large degrees, in the year 2000. Willie Garcia has gone through several life cycles, starting to play solo acoustic guitar gigs at the Ash Grove and the Troubadour even back when he was still in Thee Midniters in 1968: "It was sort of folkish, but I did some Curtis Mayfield stuff as well, and Antonio Carlos Jobim." In 1969 he put out a fine Chicano-conscious-tinged soul tune, "Brown Baby" (now available on *The West Coast East Side Sound Vol. 1* compilation), under the name Willie G. After playing with fellow East L.A. soul-rock vocal legend Lil' Ray in God's Children, he became lead singer of Malo, featuring Carlos Santana's brother Jorge on guitar, in the mid-1970s. For the last half of the 1970s Garcia struggled with heroin and cocaine habits, turning his life around after embracing Christianity in the early 1980s. Today he is a full-time evangelist at the Victory Outreach International Church in La Puente, California, although he takes his work on the road for "about 200 dates of the year."

Garcia has always sung gospel since devoting his life to religion, but has also mixed it with secular pop and R&B. Los Lobos' David Hidalgo brought his family to one of Garcia's concerts at the Victory Outreach church, approaching Willie afterwards to express his interest in working with the singer. Garcia's Hidalgo-produced album, *Make Up for the Lost Time*, was released by HighTone in early 2000. "I'm still doing horn-drenched R&B, with a pop flavor on the smoother stuff," says Garcia of the album. "And then the ballads. I can't get away from those ballads." Some of the tracks had horn arrangements by none other than Romeo Prado, who—along with Rendon, Espinoza, and others—continues to play in a present-day version of Thee Midniters. Roy Marquez and Benny Lopez are starting to make music together on a more informal basis, planning a "part two" or "takeoff" sequel to "Whittier Boulevard."

Jimmy Espinoza's post-Midniters resume is, like the Thee Midniters' discography, ridiculously wide-ranging. He played with "almost every single Latin group in town, black groups, Perez Prado, a Satanic cult group." He played with noted jazz musician Gerald Wilson, was bassist in the Cal State Symphony Orchestra, and served as conductor and arranger for Morton Downey Jr. As leader of the current version of Thee Midniters, he is the band member most responsible for keeping their legacy alive, although he is frustrated that the audience at many of his gigs primarily wants to hear the old soul ballads, and is less receptive to their hard rockers and other stylistic detours. At his company Blue Nova Entertainment, he is currently the administrator of all Thee Midniters products, and hopes to organize comprehensive reissues of 1960s material by the band, including, possibly, some unreleased tracks. The restoration of their catalog to wide availability would certainly do listeners—whether collectors who remember the band, or ones who never got the chance to hear them in the 1960s—a service. The original 45s and LPs are extremely hard to find, and Thee Midniters' only reasonably well-distributed best-of compilation, on the Rhino/Zyanya label, is currently only available on cassette. Many of their better or most idiosyncratic tracks—"Evil Love," "Heat Wave," "Tu Despedida," "Thee Midnite Feeling," even a soul cover of Tom Jones' "It's Not Unusual"—never made it to album at all.

What remains, when talking with the band members today, is both enormous pride in what music they made, and enormous regrets at what they *didn't* get to accomplish. Prado says that had the group's peak lineup been able to stay together longer, "I think the band would have been more artistic. Willie would have really embellished his art. He's got a lot of tunes. I mean, the guy can write songs almost on a daily basis, so I think he would have been a major star had that RCA deal transpired. Roy Marquez is an awfully talented writer also; he's not the best skilled as a musician, but great writer." Benny Lopez thinks the band might have gone into similar territory as Santana. Roy Marquez thinks Thee Midniters might have eventually sounded like Malo did when Garcia sang with the group on the album *Ascencion*— "you can hear Willie on top of what we could have done, maybe even better."

"You listen to 'Dreaming Casually,' the maturity of Willie's lyrics and the band's backing," advises Espinoza. "Those things are strong indicators of what we would have done, had we the support to do four or five albums, not have to worry about our careers anymore, and just make records as artists. I think it would have been one of the biggest groups, certainly competitive biggest groups, with all the other ones that were happening at the time. I know we would have been in the running, because of the talent, happiness, and love that was involved. Once that started getting frayed you lose heart. As life wore upon us, because of a lack of success, the adversity does make you dig deeper. I'm proud that we did come up with what we did, through the adversity. But if we would have had the support of a heart fully beating, boy, that is an extremely exciting idea."

Marquez is more succinct: "We all have personal tastes, but we put it in together. Sometimes that's the way a good marriage is." A troubled marriage, perhaps, given the parade of incoming and outgoing members throughout the 1960s, the conflicts over songwriting credits, and the lingering regret over the big record deal that never happened. A volatile marriage that was mirrored by the impossibly scattered musical forms and feelings they put to vinyl. A marriage, nonetheless, that took not just two but ten to make it work for as long as it did.

Recommended Recordings:

Best of Thee Midniters (1983, Zyanya/Rhino). The only reasonably comprehensive and, for a time, widely available Thee Midniters greatest hits compilation is now in print only on cassette, but still has a better chance of turning up used than any other LP by the band does. Numerous good songs are absent, and a truly representative best-of would double the length of this fourteen-song album. The selection is good, though, including their biggest singles ("Whittier Boulevard," "Land of a Thousand Dances" in the superior studio album version, "Love Special Delivery"); the ballads "That's All," "Dreaming Casually," and "The Town I Live In"; and key singles that never got on LP in the 1960s, like "It'll Never Be Over for Me," "Jump, Jive and Harmonize," and "Chicano Power."

Thee Midniters (1965, Chattahoochee). Their good, and not great, debut album is (like all their original releases) hard to find. If you do manage to get it, it's dominated by rock and soul covers that are for the most part very good, though sometimes ordinary.

Unlimited (1967, Whittier). The only Thee Midniters album comprised largely of original material has the standout jazz-soul ballads "Dreaming Casually" and "Making Ends Meet"; the Latin-jazz-soul instrumental "Chile Con Soul"; the overlooked "Cheatin' Woman," with its two-and-a-half-minute fusion of jazz, pop, rock, and soul; and good covers of "The Town I Live In" and "Everybody Needs Somebody." It's not without its dull spots, but it's the best representation, though a tentative one, of the band's music as it started to mature.

The Rationals

Detroit, and its satellite town Ann Arbor, were crucibles for some of the toughest white rock groups of the mid- to late 1960s. For a year or two, Mitch Ryder & the Detroit Wheels invaded the AM airwaves with white-hot medleys of 1950s rock classics and 1960s soul covers. A few years later and about forty miles west, Ann Arbor's MC5 and the Stooges brought pre-punk rage and furious metallic guitars to the underground. Ted Nugent (as part of the Amboy Dukes) and Bob Seger got their first national hits in the late 1960s with the psychedelic "Journey to the Center of the Mind" and the gritty "Ramblin' Gamblin' Man" respectively, although both would develop into highly commercial arena rock stars by the mid-1970s.

The consensus among those who were there is that there was one band that never did break out of Michigan that was at least as good as the ones that became nationally known. Like other Detroit and Ann Arbor groups, the Rationals were adept at blending soul, R&B, and blues influences into hard rock guitar arrangements. At their best, they were not just as good as Mitch Ryder at mixing soul and rock. They were as good as any blue-eyed soul-rock band, lead singer Scott Morgan rating as one of the finest blue-eyed soul singers ever. And if you weren't growing up in Michigan in the 1960s, you've probably never heard of them, despite several excellent singles that gave them the jump, temporarily, on friends like Iggy Pop and Bob Seger.

There are no riveting hooks to the Rationals' career. No mad geniuses, enigmatic brooding singer-songwriters, or tragedies that cut off their career just as the big enchilada seemed within reach. They weren't especially lucky, but they weren't especially unlucky either. There were a bunch of fine singles that could have been hits, perhaps, but didn't necessarily fail to break out nationally because of bad timing, a competing cover version, or some such calamity. There wasn't much internal dissension, the quartet's lineup remaining the same throughout its 1965-70 lifetime. There's just the high quality of those singles, some of them hits in Detroit and Ann Arbor. If there's any tragedy to their career, it's that the rights to those recordings are tied up in legal red tape that makes them almost wholly unavailable on any current legitimate reissue. The belated acclaim bestowed upon many other obscure artists from the era who have gotten their catalogs onto CD has eluded the Rationals.

The Rationals were still in ninth grade when guitarist/singer Scott Morgan formed the band in Ann Arbor around 1963 with bassist Terry Trabandt, guitarist Steve Correll, and drummer Bill Figg. The British Invasion changed the band's orientation from Chuck Berry, Ray Charles, and Jimmy Reed to the Beatles, Kinks, Animals, Rolling Stones, and even the Pretty Things, whose first album the band managed to find although the Pretties were virtually unknown in the States. In mid-1965 the Rationals' debut single, "Gave My Love"/"Look What You're Doing to Me," topped the Ann Arbor chart for four weeks. This was a time when it wasn't unusual for garage bands to have local hits on tiny labels that were barely or never distributed beyond a fifty-mile radius. The 45 was a decent British Invasion-style garage effort, the influence of the Kinks being especially noticeable on the B-side. If they had done nothing else, the Rationals would probably be just one of the hundreds of names strewn across *Pebbles*-type compilations of '60s garage rarities. But they had

The Rationals, in the spotlight. Left to right: Steve Correll, Scott Morgan, Bill Figg, Terry Trabandt. Credit: Courtesy Scott Morgan.

several assets in their favor that would enable them to cover more stylistic ground, and indeed last far longer, than the typical garage band.

One was their manager, Jeep Holland, who in time could be considered a hindrance as well as an asset. A legendary figure in Ann Arbor, Holland is primarily remembered today for running the A² label, which in turn is primarily remembered for issuing the first few MC5 singles. Only five years or so older than the Rationals, Holland was less the typically exploitative manager than a fan who loved and collected music as much as the musicians he represented did. An all-around entrepreneur, Holland had dropped out of the University of Michigan in Ann Arbor to work in town at Discount Records, and as a DJ for dances at the local YMCA. Ann Arbor was a liberal place with an artistic/intellectual bent, but it was small, overshadowed by nearby Detroit, and largely overlooked by talent scouts for the city-based music industry. By forming a label, managing a stable of local bands, and even producing A2 sessions, Holland would help change that and foster the scene from which the MC5, Stooges, and Bob Seger sprang, although Holland himself would reap little reward.

It was their second single, "Feelin' Lost"/"Little Girls Cry," that lifted the Rationals several echelons above the usual garage band, although Morgan and Correll (who would write most of the Rationals' original material) were still in high school. "Feelin' Lost" (actually sung by Correll, not Morgan) was simply a great number that wouldn't have seemed too out of place on one of the Beatles' 1965 releases, with its mix of charging country-influenced acoustic and electric guitars, rich vocal harmonies, constant stop-on-a-dime chord changes, and folk-influenced lyrics about a search for…something. The B-side, "Little Girls Cry," was more conventional teen rock, but with a garage charge to the guitars (the ragged solo is nothing if not punk Keith Richards), maturing soulful vocals, and more Beatlesque harmonies. The Rationals and Holland were canny enough to enlist help from some talented friends: Bob Seger coproduced (although he is not credited on the label), Iggy Pop (then known as Jim Osterberg) played bass drum on "Feelin' Lost," and soul singer Deon Jackson, who would have a national hit in 1966 with "Love Makes the World Go Round," wrote "Little Girls Cry." All to no avail, save art. "Feelin' Lost" was not even a local hit; Morgan remembers that it didn't get on Detroit radio because "they said, 'too much like the Beatles.'"

That accusation could not be leveled at the singles that followed in 1966 and 1967. "I don't know if Jeep came up with it first or we did," says Morgan today. "We just decided that we were gonna do more R&B music. I think that was kind of a conscious decision. Jeep had a great R&B collection; we tapped it and started doing R&B exclusively. That's when we had our biggest success." The Rationals were already more attuned to soul music than the usual American teen band due to their proximity to Detroit and Motown. As Morgan puts it, "It's a little bit of a symbiotic relationship, like we're this little moon circling Detroit, but it seems to be very influential. Any time that we hear rock music that doesn't have a black music influence in it, we're usually not as enthusiastic about it as if it's got more soul to it." It was already an unusual coup to have a black soul musician write a made-to-order song for a white rock band, as Deon Jackson had done on the Rationals' second single with "Little Girls Cry." With the "Respect"/"Leavin' Here" single, the Rationals took the soul-rock hybrid to more serious intensity (and Jackson, actually, was still present on organ and additional percussion).

"Respect" is now famous as a number one hit single for Aretha Franklin in 1967, but in 1966 it wasn't well known to rock listeners. Otis Redding had nudged the song inside the Top Forty in late 1965, but it had sold mostly to the R&B audience. The Rationals gave the tune a more rock-slanted reading, and their version was less notable for the playing than for Scott Morgan's singing, on which he first achieved full bloom as a *soul* singer, not just a rock one. The flip side, "Leavin' Here," was arguably better, covering a fairly obscure Motown single by Eddie Holland (no relation to Jeep, and part of Motown's hugely successful Holland-Dozier-Holland songwriting team). This number had already been recorded in Britain by the Birds (Ron Wood's first band) and the Who (whose 1965 version would not be released until the 1980s), though the Rationals had not heard these British covers and it seems unlikely that Jeep Holland would have.

"Jeep was convinced that 'Leavin' Here' was gonna be the hit," recalls Morgan with some amusement. "And the radio stations in Detroit turned it over and started playing 'Respect,' and that became the hit. Another person who was convinced that 'Leavin' Here' was a hit was Iggy Pop, James Osterberg. He worked in the same record store that Jeep worked in. And he bought all the copies of 'Leavin' Here' out of the record store, so that nobody else could hear the song. *He* was gonna have the big hit with it." Iggy, who in his pre-Stooges days was drumming for local bands like the Iguanas and the Prime Movers, never did record "Leavin' Here" before the Stooges formed. However, "1969," the first track on the first Stooges album, begins with riffs pretty similar to ones heard on the Rationals' arrangement of "Leaving Here."

"Respect" did break the Rationals in Detroit, where it was a big hit—number one, in fact on WPAG on September 12, 1966, right on top of the Four Tops' "Reach Out, I'll Be There." It also did well in some parts of the Midwest and got picked up for national distribution by Cameo-Parkway, which did the same thing with another local Michigan recording that year, ? & the Mysterians' "96 Tears," and got a number one national hit. "Respect" could go no further than number ninety-two in *Billboard's* national listings, however, and although Long Island's Vagrants (with a young Leslie West on guitar) would also try to get a hit with a rock cover of "Respect" in 1967, it would be Aretha Franklin who made the strategy pay off.

"We put out 'Respect' in '66, about a year after Otis Redding," recounts Morgan. "But because we didn't have a horn section, we had Steve and Terry sing the horn parts as backup vocal parts. At the time, [our version of] 'Respect' was just a huge hit; you couldn't live in Detroit and not hear that song on the radio. And Aretha Franklin—her sisters Carolyn and Erma were her backup singers, and Carolyn, I think, did a lot of the arranging of the backup vocals. Aretha said in an interview or two—I think that Carolyn listened to our version and said, 'We could do what they're doing, do the horn parts with our vocals. But we could do it a lot better.' And they did. About six or eight months after our version, their version came out, and it was just obviously much, much more professional, much better, much more soulful, much looser. The stuff they did with the backup vocals made the record."

Franklin's "Respect" came out on Atlantic Records, and Atlantic executive Jerry Wexler expressed some interest in producing the Rationals on his label. This might have been just what the Rationals needed to step up to a different league, but Jeep Holland turned it down. "He was a real smart guy," says Morgan of Holland, "so he applied some pretty smart tactics to his projects. He also was kind of a megalomaniac, so he wanted to do everything. He wanted to be the manager, producer, booking agent, take us to all the gigs, write the sets, do it all. He had a little trouble giving any of that up to anybody else."

So it was that the Rationals' recording career, while maintaining pretty consistent musical quality, would take some turns and bumps that in retrospect seem downright zany. There was, for instance, an ultra-rare Rationals album in Christmas 1966 that was intended for distribution only to the band's fan club, though only two acetates got pressed. While it was a mishmash of material including strange instrumentals ("Wayfaring Stranger" goes into a cool surf jam after starting out as a moody ballad), derivative British Invasion soundalikes, and a cover of the Kinks' "I Need You" (issued as an A^2 single a couple of years later, and now available on Rhino's *Nuggets* box set of 1960s garage rock), there were some excellent tracks, particularly a medley of "Smokestack Lightning" and the Animals' "Inside Looking Out" that was as imaginatively forceful and bluesy as the Yardbirds or Animals themselves. A blistering soul original with James Brown-style guitar by Correll and vocals by Morgan, "Turn On," was similarly thrown away as a promo-only disc that was also used as a radio commercial for a men's clothing shop. The Rationals should have been starting to do albums that would fully explore their diversifying cover interpretations and original tunes. However, as Morgan points out, "At the time, singles were driving everything, in our world, anyway. Albums were, like, for the Beatles. So we didn't feel the need to make an album."

During the time of "Respect," the Rationals, according to Morgan, "had gone strictly to rhythm and blues. We weren't doing any originals, we were doing covers of R&B. A lot of Memphis stuff, a lot of Stax—Eddie Floyd, 'Knock on Wood,' that sort of stuff. We were like sixteen-year-old white kids from Ann Arbor, and when we tried to cover Otis Redding, it didn't sound anything like Otis Redding. We were trying to sound like Otis Redding, or trying to sound like Aretha Franklin, but we didn't have the capability of doing it, at least not at the time. But it had its own energy and some sort of charm, I guess, because people bought it."

It was in a sense a regressive strategy on Holland and the band's part to concentrate on soul covers, at a time when white rock was hurtling at light-speed towards emphasis on original compositions. What made it work was Morgan's deft and convincing singing, sounding a good decade or so older than his teenage years, which could both sweat furiously and caress tender phrases. Correll and Trabandt's soul harmony backup vocals were in a far tighter and higher class than almost any white group could boast, and Correll was a multifaceted guitarist, capable of raw distorted blues-fuzz, funky chording, and subtle decorative R&B licks. The total impact was that of a band more urgent, yet also more inventive at varying moods, than almost any other blue-eyed soul act of the 1960s.

It also helped that they had a knack for ferreting out obscure, quality soul songs to cover, much in the manner that British groups of the mid-1960s dug up blues, R&B, and soul treasures that were virtually unknown to white rock listeners. Morgan: "We were recording songs by some of the top songwriting teams in the country. Holland-Dozier-Holland, Barry-Greenwich, Goffin and King. Not to try and fake people into thinking they were our songs, but just 'cause we thought it was a cool thing to do. I could give you a litany of obscure R&B covers [we did]. 'Temptation 'Bout to Get Me' [originally by the Knight Brothers], 'Hijacking Love' [Johnnie Taylor]. 'Leavin' Here,' I don't think it was a hit outside of Detroit. We did 'Misery' and 'I'm the Man' by the Dynamics, a big back-to-back R&B hit in Detroit when we were in high school, but I don't think it was a hit anywhere else."

The Rationals' second single for Cameo-Parkway, "Hold on Baby," fit their criteria exactly: a little-heard song by Jeff Barry and Ellie Greenwich, originally recorded by Sam "The Man" Hawkins. Again Bob Seger was drafted in to help, this time for high harmony vocals, while organ was donated by Robert Sheff, from Iggy Pop's pre-Stooges blues band the Prime Movers (and now a noted avant-garde keyboardist/composer going by the name "Blue" Gene Tyranny). "Hold on Baby" was a hit on some Detroit stations, but also banned on some for the innocuous-sounding line "gonna get up and do the thing with you, baby."

Although, as Morgan states, the Rationals were now almost exclusively a soul cover band, they were in fact continuing to write some original material at the urging of Holland, who wanted to get group compositions on the B-sides. So it turned out that "Hold on Baby" was outshone by its flip, "Sing!" which was soul-rock at its best: hair-on-end high "woo" harmonies and another commanding vocal from Morgan, as well as dabs of harmonica and a tremendous forward thrust that gave what was essentially a soul song a rock arrangement.

Morgan picks up the story: "So now we're up to the last Cameo-Parkway record, and that's 'Leavin' Here.' Jeep's convinced that it's gonna be a hit; he couldn't get it out of his head that it wasn't a hit. But we did it again [a rerecording that is different from the version that first appeared on the flip side of "Respect"], and that's when Cameo-Parkway folded. I'm not sure whether it just wasn't a hit, or whether the label went out of business [in] the middle of it." Again, the B-side, a gloomy cover of bluesman Albert King's "Not Like It Is," was arguably superior, with its catchy minor-key chorus.

If there was one single where you could say the Rationals finally got it right and put their best foot forward, it would be their cover of "I Need You," a wrenching soul ballad written by Carole King and Gerry Goffin, and originally performed by Chuck Jackson. This was one case in which a white soul cover clearly outdistanced the original, with a pleading vocal from Morgan, sympathetic light funk chords from Correll, and tremendous backup vocals by Correll and Trabandt. "They basically made 'I Need You,'" claims Morgan, "because their harmonies are just beautiful. It sounds like a gospel choir behind me or something, [but] it's just the two of them." It also sounds like a big 1960s hit, even to those who have no idea who the Rationals are, and it *was* a big hit in Detroit.

Yet despite getting placed on Capitol Records, it again failed to make it elsewhere, and in retrospect sparked the first major sign of disenchantment within the group. By this time they had released an album's worth of top-notch material on singles. There was well over an album of good music, actually, if you count items like the fan club-only album, the "Turn On" promo, and hot unreleased cuts like the haunting, chunky midtempo soul chugger "Listen to Me" and a cover of Little Johnny Taylor's "Part Time Love" with burning slow blues guitar. But there was little to show for it in terms of national progress, although some singles saw action in isolated markets like Florida and Hawaii. They had a big following in Detroit and Ann Arbor and got some TV spots in Cleveland, Chicago, and Philadelphia, but the shift between different labels wasn't helping them build vinyl sales. They didn't even have an actual album, at a point when the rock market was beginning to shift from singles to LPs. And the Rationals were no longer the high schoolers that Jeep Holland began to manage in the mid-1960s.

"The rest of the band wanted to get another manager, convinced that the reason we hadn't become bigger was because of Jeep," relates Morgan. "We were starting to head in a different direction musically. We were all out of high school now, living on our own. We didn't feel like we needed that babysitter kind of manager. I thought

Jeep had done a lot for us, and still could have done a lot for us. But he was reluctant to let us grow up, let us go, in any way. I wanted to keep the band together, so I felt like I had no choice. I think it kind of broke his heart, just really knocked the wind out of his sails when we left, 'cause we were his first band. It had happened before, when SRC [another popular local group, which would record three albums for Capitol] had left, so now he'd lost two of his main bands. He didn't really do too much after that."

Michigan rock in general was taking a harder and more metallic turn in 1968, with the MC5's first album hitting the stores and the Stooges waiting in the wings. The Rationals were cognizant of the changes pushing rock to psychedelia and beyond, and were undergoing changes themselves. On a mediocre-fidelity live recording from November 1968, released in 1995 as *Temptation 'Bout to Get Me*, the band had become unrecognizably different in style, playing extended hard rock covers of blues and soul tunes, and improv-heavy jams of their own making. Morgan, who had abandoned the guitar onstage and in the studio for a couple of years around the time of "Respect" to concentrate solely on vocals, returned to guitar and even dabbled in flute. "We were starting to bring in jazz, country and western, blues, soul, hard rock, psychedelic rock," explains Morgan. "It was becoming a melting pot kind of a situation. We would go up in the woods and play, take some acoustic guitars, conga drums, flutes, tripping out, having a good time. Then we decided we would take that to the stage. It became almost like a noodle band thing."

A single from around this time, "Guitar Army" (first issued on the small local Genesis label), exhibited not only the influence of the kind of hard rock played by the early MC5, but also the radical politics in the air in Ann Arbor in the late 1960s. The Rationals were close enough to the MC5 that when each was doing two of the same R&B covers, they arranged by mutual consent to drop a different one from the set (the Rationals took Screamin' Jay Hawkins' "I Put a Spell on You," and the MC5 took Ted Taylor's "Ramblin' Rose," putting the number on their first album). John Sinclair, manager of the MC5, was also founder of the White Panther Party, which advocated free love and revolution. Indeed, he would adopt "Guitar Army" as the title of one of his books, although Morgan made it clear in the song that he was advocating revolution through music, not violence.

"It was written as a response to everything that was going on at the time," remarks Morgan. "We were in the middle of getting deeper and deeper into the Vietnam War, the MC5 were starting the White Panthers, and there was a whole concept of, 'we have to fight fire with fire.' My idea was that true revolutionaries used revolutionary means. I had this vision: guitar players walking down the street, like in a squad, with these amps strapped to their backs. The lyrics kind of [were] an answer to the White Panther Party ten-point program. It was an answer song in general to what was going on around me at the time.

"But it was too much of a departure. Just a few months earlier, we had done 'I Need You.' It was such a left turn that people couldn't pick it up. They're going, 'What?' If you listen to *Temptation 'Bout to Get Me*, you can tell we're not playing the hits. We're not doing 'Respect,' we're not doing 'I Need You,' we're not even doing 'Guitar Army.' We're just doing what we want to do, experimenting, doing some R&B stuff we like, jamming and stretching out, letting things happen.

"You realize early on, when you have a hit like 'Respect,' that people expect you to play it over and over again, every night, and you get tired of it really fast. You want to do something else. But you're expected to keep doing it. After a while, it's like you want to get rid of the band uniforms, the structure, and the chaperone. You just kind of want to move on. And we did the same thing in the music."

As the Rationals languished without a national recording contract, Morgan turned down a left-field offer to audition for Blood, Sweat & Tears, who had just kicked out founding member Al Kooper and were searching for a lead singer. "They had their manager call me and say, 'Will you fly out for an audition in New York?' I'm going, 'No,'" Morgan laughs. "'No way! I got a band, we're putting out our first album, and if you kicked out Al Kooper, where would *I* stand?' I would be just like a sideman or something. It seemed all wrong. I said, 'No, I'd just be taking the money.' They're going, 'Come on, we'll just fly you out, we can just talk'; I'm going, 'It's you wasting your money.' I never regretted that. Having hit records and being in a band that I couldn't stand—I don't think the payback would be enough."

The Rationals did, somewhat surprisingly, manage to record a self-titled album at the tail end of the 1960s, issued on Crewe Records in early 1970. A case of too little too late, it had competent-to-decent soul covers and original material that betrayed the effects of progressive rock, particularly in the segues linking the tracks, heavier guitar sound, and Traffic-like flute. It lacked the fire of the band's 1965-68 singles, and Morgan admits that Crewe Records, run by producer Bob Crewe (who had produced hits by the Four Seasons and Mitch Ryder), "didn't have anything to do with what we were doing. We had recorded this record, and they couldn't find anybody to put it out. They were just gonna take the first legitimate offer they got, and that was it." The album did little, and "eventually our manager just kind of walked out, didn't even tell us he was leaving." The band broke up in August 1970.

It could be on this album that Holland's absence was most felt. For all Jeep's faults, Morgan acknowledges that he was a fine producer, not only in the studio but in an overall conceptual sense, as when Holland "sat me down in his office in his apartment and said, 'I want you to write a song about why you want to sing.'" That was how a tune originally named "Out in the Street" became "Sing!," one of the Rationals' best singles.

Morgan was the only one of the Rationals to record to any notable degree after 1970, most notably as a member of Sonic's Rendezvous Band, an early punkish group from the late 1970s that also featured Fred Smith of the MC5. There have also been low-profile releases by the Scott Morgan Band, and the Rationals actually reformed for a while in the early 1990s before tensions resurfaced and broke them up again. The Rationals' back catalog, lamentably, remains tangled in difficulties that have prevented it from being licensed for a comprehensive career retrospective CD compilation. Their early recordings for A² were controlled by Jeep Holland, and although some progress toward allowing their reissue was made in the late 1990s, Holland's death in 1998 has slowed down the process. Rights to the group's Cameo-Parkway singles will also be difficult if not impossible to obtain, as that label is notorious for being unwilling to license its catalog even for top sellers like Chubby Checker, Bobby Rydell, and ? & the Mysterians, let alone a non-hit regional sensation like the Rationals. In a weird happenstance, the Rationals track called "I Need

You" that appears on *Nuggets*, Rhino's four-CD box set of 1960s garage rock, is not the great soul smoocher that might be their best moment, but their cover of a Kinks song of the same name; while well done, it hardly rates as their best cut or even one of their better cuts. To find the prime early singles, collectors have usually had to resort to unauthorized bootleg compilations.

"We were too young," summarizes Morgan, unembittered but still at something of a loss to explain why the Rationals did not get the recognition they deserved. "Aside from all the business aspects—moving from one label to another and never getting on one major label and staying there, never graduating from the A^2 school of running everything out of Jeep's apartment kind of deal—we didn't have very much experience. We were kind of learning as we went along, and we didn't really know how it was done—how you get bigger, famous, or better. We were like seventeen when 'Respect' came out; we were still in high school. We couldn't tour. We just had to proceed at our own pace. In retrospect, it may be good that it didn't happen, because we could have been one of those child star prodigy things that makes it too soon, and later on you end up like Frankie Lymon [who died of a heroin overdose in his mid-twenties] or something. There was a lot of factors involved; I think that's one of them. We were too young."

Recommended Recordings:

The Rationals (1970, Crewe). The group's only official album is a fair but unremarkable set that is not representative of the Rationals at their best. It does include the noteworthy single "Guitar Army," and some respectable soul-rock matings, like "Handbags & Gladrags" and "Temptation 'Bout to Get Me." An unauthorized CD reissue on the Flash label adds a dozen tracks from non-LP 1965-68 recordings, including the electrifying singles "Feelin' Lost," "Little Girls Cry," "Leavin' Here," "I Need You," and "Sing!" However, this CD has been mastered from vinyl copies, not the original tapes, and is still missing key items like "Hold On Baby" and "Not Like It Is." A proper and comprehensive reissue from the original master tapes, adding their numerous rarities and unreleased recordings, is what's really needed to establish their legacy, though legal obstacles may prevent this from happening in our lifetimes.

Temptation 'Bout to Get Me (1995, Total Energy). Live at the Grande Ballroom in Detroit on November 27, 1968. Like *The Rationals*, this isn't the group at its peak, but does document the period in which they were transforming from blue-eyed soulsters into a heavy rock band, with extended covers of the staples "Temptation 'Bout to Get Me" and "I Put a Spell on You."

Folk-Rock Innovators

The fusion of folk and rock in the mid-1960s rates with the British Invasion as a key transformative movement of 1960s rock. The British Invasion, of course, had been crucial to begin with in motivating many acoustic folkies to turn electric and play rock 'n' roll. When the Beatles arrived in the U.S., Bob Dylan and others had only recently popularized the practice among folk singers of writing songs that addressed contemporary issues and personal feelings, rather than interpreting folk standards from the past. On top of that, within eighteen months or so of the Byrds' number one "Mr. Tambourine Man" single and Bob Dylan's first electric (half-electric, anyway) album, virtually every young folk singer-songwriter of note had "gone electric." It was truly the best of both worlds, bringing social consciousness and new levels of lyricism into rock 'n' roll, and—just as importantly—putting the best attributes of folk music to a rock beat.

We all know about the Byrds, Dylan, Donovan, the Mamas & the Papas, and Simon & Garfunkel. There simply wasn't enough room on the airwaves or the charts, however, to accommodate all of the talented folk-rockers of the last half of the 1960s, particularly as the adult-oriented album market—and the FM radio stations that would make such music its staple—had yet to fully develop. As a consequence many fine folk-rock troubadours, including some covered in the *Unknown Legends of Rock 'n' Roll* book (such as Nick Drake, Judy Henske, and the Bluethings) and some not covered in that volume or this chapter (Tim Hardin, the Leaves), remain relatively neglected. Certainly there are also some cult artists covered elsewhere in these pages that played folk-rock much or part of the time, particularly Kaleidoscope, the Beau Brummels, and the Fugs.

As it happens, the folk-rockers selected for this chapter have a sadder and more tragic history than most. Dino Valenti's contrary, bullish personality limited his solo recording opportunities to just one ill-distributed album; Richard & Mimi Fariña's partnership ended with Richard's death in a 1966 motorcycle accident; Tim Buckley died of a heroin overdose before the age of thirty, although he managed to make a wealth of great music in the prior decade; and Fred Neil voluntarily retired from the record industry after the 1960s, becoming a recluse of mythical proportions. Each did a great deal to advance the folk-rock form, however, and in some cases evolve beyond the style into other fields. Valenti and Neil both authored a folk-rock classic, only to see a cover version become the famous hit; both were crucial, underappreciated midwives between the acoustic and electric guises of folk music. In their brief career, Richard & Mimi Fariña incorporated both Appalachian and Celtic influences into folk-rock, with a breathlessly diverse repertoire that wove dulcimer-dominated instrumentals, sociopolitical comentary, literary lyrics, and tender love songs into one cloth. Tim Buckley, originally a folk-rocker, moved into jazz, the avant-garde, and blue-eyed soul to such an extent that he ultimately eluded categorization. None of the performers had easy rows to hoe, yet their music conveys as much celebration as it does pain.

"He was like my brother. I loved him very dearly, and I still do. But most of the time, I didn't like him."
>—Gary Duncan, Dino Valenti's band mate in Quicksilver Messenger Service, and best friend in the late 1960s and 1970s

"He is known as a rowdy, violent, noisy, kick-ass egotist. But he really was a fascinating man, and a great poet. All of that gift gets overlooked in the drama."
>—Cyrus Faryar, folk-rock musician and close friend of Valenti in the 1960s

"I get E-mail from either guys who couldn't stand Valenti or women who loved him (and still do). No in-between."
>—Brett Freedman, operator of Quicksilver Messenger Service fan page on the Internet

"He had a great innate understanding of music, lyrics, and euphonics. Just the beauty of certain words and their conjunction to another. I know he planned a lot of it, but I think a lot of it just came naturally to him."
>—Paul Kantner of the Jefferson Airplane/Starship

"He was an ugly person. Less than a no-talent, another good example of someone who should have never been in the music business. If he was still alive, I'd say the same things."
>—Carol Kaye, top Los Angeles 1960s session bass player, and backup musician on aborted session for Valenti's one solo album

"He was a little genius. Go to the moon, go to Mars, if they've got a Victrola and nine billion artists up there, you'll recognize Dino Valenti. That's what great artists are always built on."
>—Bob Johnston, producer of Valenti's 1968 solo album; also producer of 1960s hits by Bob Dylan, Johnny Cash, and Simon & Garfunkel

Dino Valenti

Dino Valenti was a mass—or, perhaps more accurately, a mess—of contradictions that could fill a book. A folksinger who was instrumental in starting the folk-rock revolution, yet who proved singularly unable to adapt to the electric guitar and a rock band situation himself. A cult singer-songwriter who wrote one of the 1960s' hippie anthems, "Get Together," yet could not practice the love and peace ethos of that song with any consistency. An artist who wanted desperately to be a star, but alienated major label record company executives with such speed that the one album he did manage to release as a solo artist was buried in an avalanche of nonpromotion. A man who attracted droves of female admirers and immense respect from fellow musicians, but also a man that, as even close friends and lovers readily admit, could be impossible to be around. A would-be star who had tantalizing brushes with the Byrds, Quicksilver Messenger Service, and Grace Slick in the mid-1960s, but never got into a big rock group when folk-rock and psychedelia exploded, spending most of those years in jail or threatened by imprisonment.

Nobody has a neutral opinion about Dino Valenti. Like the gangster Dinsdale brothers lionized by a fictional documentary in a Monty Python sketch, he seems to have inspired roughly equal measures of love and loathing, sometimes simultaneously. It is amazing how many folk and rock luminaries Valenti crossed paths with in the 1960s, and they all remember him well, whether they knew him for a night or a decade. But for all his talent, charisma, and influence, Valenti's output was surprisingly scant. There was just one poor-selling 1968 cult album that was impossible to find prior to its reissue on CD thirty years later, an even rarer proto-folk-rock single for Elektra in 1964, and a few albums as a member of Quicksilver Messenger Service in the early 1970s that did not adequately represent his talents. Valenti could not make himself a star because he was often his own worst enemy. Or, as Gary Duncan puts it less delicately, "He stepped on his own dick."

If it seems like Valenti was a gypsy wreaking havoc on the counterculture with his mind games, that might in large part be because for many years, life *was* a carnival for Dino—literally. Born October 7, 1937, as Chester Powers to a carnival manager-comedian father and singer mother, as a child he did "Punch and Judy" acts with his sister, learning to hustle from an early age. "He was born and raised on a fucking carnival," notes Gary Duncan, who would become Valenti's best buddy in the late 1960s and play guitar with Dino in Quicksilver Messenger Service. "That's his whole approach to the way he dealt with people. You were either with it, or you weren't. If you were with it, that meant you were with the carnival, and everybody else was a mark. He was on the outside of society looking in, like a gypsy."

After spending some time in the Air Force and on the road in the 1950s, Powers entered the folk scene, first in Boston and then in New York. By the time he got to Greenwich Village in the early 1960s, Chester Powers had become Dino Valenti. Slightly older than the generation of folk-rockers that would be led by Bob Dylan and the Byrds, he was also slightly younger than the old guard of traditional folkies, and with hindsight can be seen to have bridged the two. Although his repertoire was largely traditional, he played twelve-string guitar with a force that was more in line with rock 'n' roll, strumming hard and rapidly with an energy reminiscent of flamenco music, building to intense climaxes to emphasize particularly vital lyrics. His nasal voice, always a bone of contention among critics and listeners, was serious and intense, bringing the songs to life with a more dramatic flair than did most of his peers, who usually espoused a tamer and more reverent approach.

Valenti's coffeehouse act was noted and, at times, mimicked by competitors in the Village. "In all due respect to Richie [Havens], who is quite talented in his own right, 70 percent of his act is lifted from Dino," says Elaine Forzano, a girlfriend of Valenti in his New York years who would remain a good friend of Dino's throughout his life. "His guitar tuning, his strum, the way he holds his guitar, the way he closes his set by lifting the guitar up in the air and strumming it wildly, the way he taps his foot to the rhythm—that is all Dino's."

A seven-song 1961 demo acetate of Valenti survives, performed solo on acoustic guitar and comprised of traditional material such as "Wayfaring Stranger." It testifies to his knack for combining chunky guitar strumming, effective somber vocal phrasing, and haunting minor chords to build a tense atmosphere, and is not far from his 1968 solo album in mood, although by that time Valenti would have a

Dino Valenti in full voice.
Credit: Michael Ochs Archives.com.

wealth of original compositions and a more psychedelic attitude. Had an album of traditional folk material in this vein been recorded by Valenti in the early 1960s, he surely would have made an impact, alongside other Greenwich Village innovators like Bob Dylan and Fred Neil who brought contemporary energy and imagination to the folk community.

Valenti's music was admired and influential, but Dino himself was not universally liked. Offers Peter Stampfel, on the Village scene as a founder-member of the irreverent old-time-cum-satirical folk-rock act the Holy Modal Rounders: "Valenti looked like a motorcycle hood. Bob Dylan and Dino Valenti had both gone to see Woody Guthrie in the hospital [where Guthrie was dying of Huntington's chorea in the early 1960s]. They used to go and play for Woody. He was in his last days, and they both felt—Valenti more clumsily—that Woody would hear them play and say, 'Yes, you have learned your lessons well and you will carry on my glorious life when I am dead and gone.' Bob Dylan once did this tirade about, 'How dare Dino Valenti say that and feel that about Woody Guthrie.' I basically agreed with him."

"Dino loved to write and make music, but was extremely turned off by the recording process just as much as he hated publicity," wrote Richie Havens in his autobiography, *They Can't Hide Us Anymore.* "In fact, he strongly resisted the idea of recording so much that he just went through the motions with the two solo albums he made in the early sixties, neither of which was released." Valenti never did get to release a record during his New York days, following his girlfriend Judy Brunk to Los Angeles in 1962. Over the next few years he would flit between L.A. and San Francisco, influencing several young folkies who would shortly become pillars of the folk-rock scene. He shared a houseboat in the San Francisco area with a young David Crosby, and helped popularize a song that would become a folk-rock standard, "Hey Joe" (which Crosby would take the lead vocals on when the Byrds recorded it in 1966). Valenti sometimes took credit for writing "Hey Joe" as well, although it had actually been penned by Billy Roberts.

There have been rumors and mysteries about "Hey Joe"'s authorship for decades, and different versions have circulated as to how and why Valenti claimed to be the composer. According to Johnny Rogan's exhaustive Byrds biography *Timeless Flight Revisited*, Roberts sold the copyright to Valenti. However, Michael Hicks reports in his book *Sixties Rock* that Valenti sold the tune to Third Story Music, who copyrighted it in his name in October 1965, adding that when royalties started coming in for the song as it started to get covered by rock bands in 1966, the credit and royalties were transferred to Roberts. This transpired, according to Hicks, only after "a friend of Roberts confronted Third Story, who in turn confronted Valenti. Valenti admitted he had not written the song but simply 'picked it up.'"

However, there were undoubtedly some original compositions in Valenti's set, most notably "Get Together," which he would record as a solo acoustic demo for the San Francisco-based Autumn label in January 1964. The only original on a tape that also included the Gershwins' standard "It Ain't Necessarily So" and the emerging folk favorite "High Flying Bird" (which would be covered by the early Jefferson Airplane), it was one of the first—if not *the* first—songs to capture the love, peace, and brother-sisterhood vibe of the hippie generation. This version (now included on the compilation *Someone to Love: The Birth of the San Francisco Sound*) is on the dry side, its full potential not realized until it was picked up by electric folk-rock groups a year or two later.

It's certain that "Get Together" and other Valenti material was starting to get attention from fellow folk acts before that. A Valenti tune, the traditional folk-sounding "Pennies," was covered by the Modern Folk Quartet on the group's self-titled 1963 album. They also did Dino's "This Little House," which would be retitled "Birdses" when Valenti himself did it on an Elektra single, on their "Changes" LP (although it was for some reason credited to "Klonaris-Berger"). Modern Folk Quartet member

Jerry Yester also remembers that they were interested in doing "Get Together," "but never got around to it."

In 1964, Valenti recorded a rare single for Elektra, "Birdses"/"Don't Let It Down," that anticipated the folk-rock movement by almost a year in its marriage of folky tunes with full electric band backup. The tracks were tentative and, in places, awkward, the mix on "Birdses" emphasizing the nasal qualities of Valenti's vocal and decorated by an odd harpsichord. "Don't Let It Down," by contrast, was a bluesy up-tempo number that perhaps harkened back to his pre-folk gigs as a lounge singer back in the 1950s. An Elektra outtake from this time, "Black Betty," sounds remark-ably similar to the blues-folk-rock arrangements Bob Dylan would begin to employ in 1965 ("Black Betty" and another Valenti outtake, "Life Is Like That," surfaced on the rare compilation LP *Early L.A.*). The single was a stiff, but "Birdses" did find at least one important listener: when the Byrds were deciding upon a name in late 1964, Gene Clark, the group's principal songwriter at the outset, was taken enough by the song to suggest the band call themselves the Birdses, which was quickly amended to the Byrds. (Furthering the Byrds connection, the Elektra single had been produced by Jim Dickson, the Byrds' comanager.)

Was Valenti working towards a folk-rock fusion? Cyrus Faryar, a good friend of Valenti in the early 1960s who would move into folk-rock himself with the Modern Folk Quartet and as a session guitarist with Fred Neil, speculates: "I would be willing to bet that he played electric guitar before he played acoustic guitar, and that he just grabbed the acoustic guitar because it served his purpose. He was never just a folksinger. Before he was a folksinger, he was a lounge act. He would have loved the heavy artillery in a rock 'n' roll band to help project his persona and music. Because sometimes the guitar was not enough. Dino could have put a cannon onstage as an accompaniment to some of his tunes; he would have happily fired it off."

Guitarist John Forsha, who also saw Valenti play acoustic folk in California in the 1960s and would play on recordings by Fred Neil and Tim Buckley, isn't so sure. Valenti, in his view, had "a right-hand rhythm thing that was syncopated on acoustic guitar. It had a locomotive feel to it. It was almost like a Mexican guitar. It was like a full band accompaniment sound. This lick wouldn't have worked on an electric in-strument. 'Cause it was too fat, the sound would have jammed somewhere in the amplifier. It's too busy."

In addition, those who saw him are in agreement that some of Valenti's charisma proved elusive when it came time to roll the tape. "What you heard when you were in the room, watching him play and sing, never got to vinyl," emphasizes Faryar. "A hint of it got to vinyl, but not the whole thing. He was a major challenge for a record producer or A&R man to capture." Adds Paul Kantner of the Jefferson Airplane, "Nobody every captured Dino acoustically. He was an acoustic solo act that you had to go see, 'cause he was very engaging in his sort of arrogant gypsy way. Nothing ever stood out with Dino on tape, 'cause he really connected visually and verbally. Over and above the music, there was a certain thing to him that was not re-ally capturable, ever, really."

It seems likely that Valenti was at least considering joining a flat-out electric rock band by 1965. Valenti knew several of the Byrds, whose drummer Michael Clarke had briefly played with Dino. In early 1965, impatient for the Byrds to take off as "Mr. Tambourine Man" was about to be released, Byrds leader and guitarist Roger McGuinn contemplated the idea of forming a band with Valenti. "He had this great idea for a group," McGuinn told author Johnny Rogan in the Byrds biography *Timeless Flight Revisited*. "He had designed costumes with radio transmitters built into the jackets, a place in your belt buckle to plug in your guitar, and it was a workable idea…The delay between the recording and release of 'Mr. Tambourine Man' seemed like forever. Columbia Records weren't too excited about us, Dino was anxious to do something and it sounded like fun. He said he was getting spacesuits and wireless microphones. He hit me on the technological area which I was really keen on." In the end, however, "Mr. Tambourine Man" was not only released but went to number one, and Valenti's influence on McGuinn was largely limited to giving him the leather jacket that McGuinn wears on the cover of the first Byrds album.

Tom Donahue, a powerful San Francisco radio announcer who was also a co-partner in Autumn Records, tried to hook Valenti up with one of Autumn's bands, the Great Society, in late 1965. Featuring a pre-Jefferson Airplane Grace Slick on vocals, the Great Society was one of the first and most underrated psychedelic bands, and on paper the match-up sounded intriguing. But, as Great Society guitarist Darby Slick told Alec Palao in *Cream Puff War* magazine, Donahue "introduced Dino Valenti to us and wanted him to join, but he seemed too commercial. I liked him as a person, but I didn't want to be in a band with him; he was too L.A."

Around this time Valenti had ideas of getting an electric band together in San Francisco with guitarist John Cipollina, singer/harmonica player Jim Murray, and bassist David Freiberg. Confusion still reigns as to whether Valenti should be considered a founder-member of this group, which evolved into Quicksilver Messenger Service. He was busted for drugs, however, before he even rehearsed with these musicians once.

Accounts vary as to how often Valenti got busted in the mid-1960s and how much jail time he served, but it seems certain he served almost a year in prison. During that time the copyright to "Get Together" was sold to SFO Music; again accounts of this transaction vary, but it was reported in *Rolling Stone* in 1969 that it was sold to raise money for bail and subsequent court appearances. By the time he was out of jail for good, San Francisco's psychedelic scene was well under way. "Get Together," covered as early as April 1964 in a lame campfire sing-along version by the Kingston Trio (although this would not be released until the 1990s), was on its way to becoming a folk-rock standard after covers by pop-folk-rock act the We Five (famous for "You Were on My Mind") and, more crucially, the Jefferson Airplane, who did it on their debut album. Judy Collins sang it live at the Newport Folk Festival, as heard on her *Live at Newport* compilation, and Joni Mitchell included the song in her early concerts (as can be heard on several bootlegs), although she didn't record it for official release. Then the Youngbloods had a minor hit single with it; by the time a reissue of the Youngbloods' 45 made number five in 1969, the sale of Valenti's copyright had probably cost him a fortune.

A couple of years before "Get Together" made the Top Ten, however, Valenti's stock was still high in the industry. It's sometimes been speculated that the members of Quicksilver Messenger Service were waiting for Valenti to get out of jail so he could rejoin them, but according to Quicksilver guitarist Gary Duncan (who did not even meet Dino until after Quicksilver was gigging), there was no plan to get Valenti into Quicksilver in the late 1960s. Valenti, he says, was set on becoming a solo act, and Quicksilver in any case had moved beyond folk-rock to become one of the Bay Area's premier psychedelic groups. "In those days, Tom Donahue was his manager, and they were romancing him," recalls Duncan, still playing with an altered Quicksilver lineup in 1999, as he paces around his rehearsal studio in Marin County. "They got Dino a pad with a swimming pool, got him a nice car to drive, bought him some new clothes, and got him some new guitars. And he enjoyed it."

Valenti, as Ben Fong-Torres wrote in his 1969 profile on the singer in *Rolling Stone*, had a reputation as "the 'underground Dylan,'" and Columbia Records was going to try to capitalize on it. "When Dino first signed with Epic, for [Columbia executive] Clive Davis, that was a big feather in his cap," claims Duncan. "Because Dino was notoriously hard to deal with. In the business, he had a reputation of being a total fucking prick. When Clive got him to sign, everybody sort of went, 'Clive, all right, you got him.'" Ensuing events, however, would probably make everyone involved wish the Columbia-Valenti deal had never happened.

According to Duncan, Valenti first cut an album with producer Jack Nitzsche, who was vital to Phil Spector's "Wall of Sound" as an arranger, and had worked with other top acts like the Rolling Stones. "It was like a pop record," remembers Duncan, who played on some of the sessions. "It was well-produced little nuggets of radio stuff. He'd have been the new Bob Dylan. Nitzsche took Dino's songs, wrote arrangements, they had a certain length. He made 'em into a palatable, salable product. Dino's stuff lent itself so well to that format. He wrote songs like Beatles songs — they had bridges, they were magnificently written.

"They had the final mixes on it, and he didn't like it. It was too homogenized, it was too clean for him, and I could understand that from an artistic standpoint. From a *business* standpoint, it was a great record. It would have made him a fucking millionaire. But he didn't like it."

So an entirely different album was recorded, says Duncan, using some but not all of the original compositions on the Nitzsche-produced effort, and adding some other songs of Dino's. The result, *Dino Valente* [sic], was probably the best representation of Valenti's unique writing, singing, and guitar playing to get captured in the studio. Oddly, "Get Together" was missing. "I never heard Dino sing that song," states a bemused Duncan. "In all the years that I knew him — and I was with him all the time — he'd never sing it. I asked him to sing it a few times, and he wouldn't. I think he was pissed off, because somebody else did it and had a hit. [Losing the copyright] wasn't the only reason."

The ten songs that did make it onto the record, however, were effective and sympathetically produced, if not terribly commercial. The album's most arresting quality was the guitar playing, the twelve-string guitar layered in shimmering reverb as it strummed the sad but pretty melodies Valenti was so skilled in summoning. His vocals, too, were bathed in echo, creating a hushed, one-man-alone-in-a-barely-lit-room atmosphere. That ambience would also be the trademark of another low-selling cult acid folk album on Columbia in the late 1960s, Skip Spence's *Oar* (Spence, coincidentally, had also been considered for membership in the embryonic Quicksilver Messenger Service before getting spirited away to the early Jefferson Airplane).

While Spence invoked half-mad, ghostly echoes of country, blues, and folk that alternated between the angelic and the demonic, Valenti favored a sunnier if equally inscrutable vibe. Valenti was a notorious ladies' man, and many of the album's lyrics were trippy stream-of-consciousness one-sided conversations, seemingly directed toward a never-ending parade of beautiful but confused young hippie women. He and only he, Valenti seemed to be intimating, could understand the pain and changes they were going through, and only through his help could they, together, transcend them with beatific love.

There were other moods floating around the record too, such as the jazzy horns and phrasing of "My Friend," the troubadour folk of "Me and My Uncle" (written by John Phillips of the Mamas & the Papas), the symphonic pop of "Tomorrow" (the only cut that sounded like it could have fit into the lost Nitzsche-produced LP), and the unearthly flutes and echo spinning around Valenti's disembodied vocals on the most psychedelic cut, "Test." The melody for "Children of the Sun," reveals Duncan, was inspired by the pop-jazz standard "My Funny Valentine," whose chords Gary had taught to Dino. With valuable help from producer Bob Johnston, Valenti's twelve-string guitar and voice were sometimes embellished with subtle but tasteful additional horns, strings, harpsichords, background vocals, drums, and guitars, changing what could have been a solo acoustic album into a record that sat on the margins of psychedelic rock.

When Ben Fong-Torres asked Valenti about the album for his *Rolling Stone* profile, his reply was as elusive to grasp as the tunes themselves were. "Every song is different, like every day; a completely different thing, man. You sit down and something turns you on and you hear a timbre, a vibration because you're right this instant turned on about something. And it's in your mind that you hear it. It may be soft, it may be fine, it may be heavy, it's just a certain set of tonalities, or sometimes it's just a set of chords that start going around your head....

"Well, you sit down and start to play it on your guitar and as you play the music, sometimes you hear the music has words in it. And so then you find out what the song says. Other times you're down and may be pissed about something so you write the words without bothering with the music; then you listen to the words over and over again and you hear the music. When a song starts you don't think about anything but getting next to it without breaking it. It's like getting next to a wild horse."

The record was an artistic if enigmatic triumph, and as Tom Donahue (as quoted in Lillian Roxon's *Rock Encyclopedia*) proclaimed, "If every chick Dino's ever known buys the record, it will be number one." That didn't happen; in fact, hardly anyone even saw or heard a copy, and the album was nearly impossible to find before it was reissued on CD (with two previously unreleased bonus tracks) in 1997. Its poor sales performance was not solely due to the adventurous nature of the music. It was, perhaps, due more to Valenti's inimitable talent for alienating people.

According to Duncan, when Valenti wanted to scrap the Nitzsche-produced album, "Instead of trying to discuss this with Clive [Davis] in a sane manner, Dino did what he usually did. He got pissed off, called Clive in the middle of the night, woke him up, and insulted the fuck out of him. If he hollered long enough, he usually got what he wanted. Bob Johnston was hired by Clive Davis to get a record out of Dino that they could bury, and fulfill their contractual obligation with him. They didn't promote it. They misspelled his name." (Interestingly, the label *did* nonetheless place a full-page ad for the album in the September 14, 1968 issue of *Rolling Stone*.)

For good measure, Johnston—producer of classic and huge-selling albums and singles by Bob Dylan, Simon & Garfunkel, and Johnny Cash in the 1960s—says that Valenti pulled much the same tantrum on Columbia executive David Kapralik. "I was told that Kapralik came to him and said, 'I want all your publishing, I want your management, and if you give me that I'll make you a star.' Dino told me he called about five o'clock in the morning and woke Kapralik up. He said, 'I just wanted to tell you that in California, the sky is so blue. There's not a cloud in the sky, it's the most beautiful day I've ever seen in my life.' Kapralik says, 'You woke me up to tell me that?' And Dino said, 'Wait a minute. Something's happening. Oh my god, there's a big, dark, horrible-looking cloud that's blotting the sun out, and it's coming right over me. Oh Jesus, it started pouring. That cloud is *you*, David.' And that was pretty well the end of Dino."

That didn't mean, however, that Valenti and his pals couldn't party hardy on the way to commercial oblivion. "Bob at that time, from what I understand, was sort of like Epic Records' troubleshooter," says Duncan, who played on *Dino Valente*. "He was the producer they sent in for acts they couldn't really deal with. Bob Dylan. Johnny Cash. Dino Valenti. Guys that were temperamental. His job was to go in and make the artist feel comfortable, and get a performance out of him that they could sell. And that's what he did with Dino. He made Dino happy. He let him do what he wanted.

"There was a couple of days straight that we didn't do anything in the studio but fly paper airplanes. 'Cause Dino was in a bad mood. So Johnston came in with this international paper airplane book. It had all these paper airplanes that you could put together and fly. We spent two days in the studio—I don't know what it cost, but it wasn't cheap—to sit around and just fly airplanes. We didn't do any music at all. But that's the way Johnston did things. He made him feel like he was a king. And they got a record out of him that made Dino happy. He loved it.

"Dino had to have bagpipes on something, so they got these two pipers in. These guys were serious Scots, boy, I mean, you could barely understand what they said. They came in with their kilts on and their pipes, a father-and-son piper team. They never used these tracks. There's time that was spent in the studio, and money that got pissed away."

Johnston, while not oblivious to the goings-on in Valenti's entourage—"he carried a harem with him wherever he went, when he was in the studio, there was like anywhere from ten to thirty little girls popping up and out"—maintains his admiration for Dino's musical talents thirty years later. "I just went along for the ride, 'cause he was really special. He's a brilliant, brilliant guitar player.

"You had to bring him back into check because he'd start a song, and twenty-five minutes later he'd be playing the same song. When we first started, I told him that we had to pick songs for the album. He said, 'Well, let me do these two.' Two of them were about an hour, and I said 'OK, need to cut one of them off, Dino.' He said, 'What do you mean? I've only got two songs.'" Johnston pauses to laugh at the benign lunacy of the enterprise. "I said, 'I don't care. If you want to make an hour record, that's fine. But otherwise, you'll have one song.' He said, 'Oh man, you can't do that. What can I do?' I said, 'You don't have to ask me. Chop 'em up. I don't want to chop your songs up.'"

Another highly respected industry professional was most unimpressed with Valenti's unconventional methodology. Carol Kaye, who played on numerous Hollywood-recorded classics in the 1960s (including hits by Phil Spector and the Beach Boys), was the most highly regarded session bassist in Los Angeles, and remembers her session with Valenti as "really a chore, the worst record date. He put us all through hell that night. I had to write out the chord charts from his terrible unmusical tape. Mind you, I've worked with a great deal of nontalented people. It was our job to get everybody a hit, didn't matter if they could or couldn't sing, or how bad their songs were. That wasn't the problem. His demeanor, use of a lot of drugs, putting us in a dangerous situation, and his attitude and smart-ass ways were the problem. I don't mind a person being dramatic, but put it on stage where it belongs. I do mind open uses of drugs—it was a LOT of drugs there, turning the lights totally off, lighting candles and putting them on the teetering baffles that could be blown over easily by sound waves.

"After struggling with his awful nonmusical track for about one-and-a-half hours—now we were the best in the business—Dino decided to 'demonstrate' by throwing his long locks of hair around in the studio stage-style, putting on quite a big show while singing. I looked over at [guitarist] Dennis Budimer who was in stitches, grinning from ear to ear. He was trying to contain himself from busting out laughing, Dino was downright hysterical. I must have let out a half-smile as Dino stopped playing and said, 'What are you smiling at?'

"I replied, 'I wasn't smiling. I was looking at Dennis.'

"It went downhill from there. He said, 'What is wrong that you all can't play with my guitar track?' I said, still being very nice about the whole mess, 'Well...because of the situation, please let us cut you a basic good track so that we can all play together, as we just can't play along with your track.' He answered, 'Why can't you?' I finally said, 'because you have really BAD TIME' (like telling someone they have bad breath). At that, he said, 'Well, my bass player can play along with me just fine.' At that, I started packing up my instrument. 'Well, get your bass player then, as I have an early morning film call and we're never going to get this even if it takes ALL NIGHT with the way you want to overdub on YOUR track.' At that point, the producer from the booth said something like, 'I don't like the attitude here, you're all fired.' We all walked out in silence."

Counters Cyrus Faryar, "She was fit to be tied, and said something about what he was doing was funky—bad. And I remember him saying, 'It's not bad, or not wrong, it's just different.' He was hard to follow, for session people. Because he was very loose. He would not stick to a format when he got into the body of a song. He would just go where the song took him. And if it speeds up and down that's OK, because that's the drama of the story being told. That is very difficult for session players, who are used to playing very tight, which is a fabulous talent too. But following Dino was a chore. Or bridling him down was a chore."

After the album was released, Duncan reports, there was a failure which stung far more than its poor sales tally. "He did a show at Winterland [in San Francisco] between Jimi Hendrix and Buddy Miles. Dino was in the middle with his twelve-string guitar, and just as strong as either one of those bands by himself. That's how good he was. But that didn't make him happy.

"He went to New York to play Cafe Au Go Go. He was pissed at the folk scene in New York, because in his mind, they had spurned him, cast him aside, and treated him like shit. He was back to show them that he had gone to California and become a star. Nobody came to see him. Three, four people came. [Quicksilver manager] Ron Polte went to see him, and he said it was awful; the people who were there didn't even clap.

"It really fucked with his mind. That was the one incident I remember that totally changed his attitude. Prior to that, he had been a lot nicer. He got really bitter after that event.

"And then he got mad at *everybody*. He got mad at us [Quicksilver Messenger Service], because we were doing well, and he wasn't. He didn't want to be a solo artist anymore. He wanted to be in a band. And he wanted to be in Quicksilver, 'cause we were doing OK, 'cause he was pissed off at us, 'cause we had done one of his tunes." That tune was "Dino's Song," a gentle folk-rocker that was one of the highlights of Quicksilver's 1968 self-titled debut album; Valenti's old pals the Byrds had done a still-unreleased version in 1965 under the title "I Don't Ever Want to Spoil Your Party." (Quicksilver did another of Dino's compositions, "Stand By Me," on a non-LP 1968 single.)

Duncan had left Quicksilver at the end of 1968, frustrated with the band's static stage set and lack of interest in writing new material. He palled around with Valenti for a year, "just raising hell, riding motorcycles mostly, and getting laid." They tried to put a band together on several occasions in both New York and California without success, and were lured into Quicksilver for a show at the end of 1969. Duncan was reluctant to rejoin permanently, but was convinced by Valenti: "He said, 'We need to do it, because we need the money.' And he was right."

There were those who doubted whether Valenti's skills and temperament were suited for a band situation. As Paul Kantner puts it, "To me, Dino was always best solo. He was untouchable solo. He got swept up in wanting to be an electric rock star." Amplifies Duncan, "He didn't grow up as a band guy, he grew up as a solo player. I grew up playing in a band, so I learned to play with other musicians. I knew how to make a band work. Dino couldn't interact with other musicians like that.

"It was very hard to teach him anything. There were songs we did that he'd play the wrong chords in. I would tell him, 'Dino, you don't play the minor third in here. This is a major blues.' He refused to play the right chord, because I told him to. He would swear to god that the B-3 [organ] was out of tune; B-3's do not go out of tune. He would swear that the piano was out of tune, and you'd go 'the piano ain't out of tune, man.' He'd go, 'The fucking piano is out of tune. *I* ain't out of tune.'" Duncan also agrees that the hard-strumming twelve-string style characteristic of Valenti's solo material "was untranslatable to an electric instrument. They have electric guitars now that you can play that'll do that, but in those days they didn't. It would just distort. There was a way he could have changed his style a little bit, and been able to make that transition. But he was so stubborn about it that he wouldn't."

Nevertheless, Valenti became Quicksilver's principal singer and songwriter in the early 1970s. It's undeniable that Quicksilver's best work had been done without Valenti on its first two albums in the late 1960s, in which the band mixed melodic folk-rock with blues, extended psychedelic jamming, and even some Spanish guitar and jazz licks, spearheaded by guitarist John Cipollina's quivering sustain. Their major weaknesses were the lack of a first-rate lead vocalist and consistent quality songwriting, so the arrival of Valenti on the surface seemed like it might have been made to order, particularly as he had come close to playing in Quicksilver back in 1965. Yet his stint with the band is viewed with mixed feelings by Quicksilver fans and indeed all lovers of San Francisco psychedelia, some of whom felt that Valenti had essentially hijacked the group and made them his backup unit. The guitar-heavy, incandescent psychedelic music of Quicksilver's early incarnation was subsumed by Valenti's laid-back folk-rock and acquired-taste singing (often described as a whine by less charitable critics). The sound was so different that the band became nearly unrecognizable, particularly when Cipollina left after the second album with Valenti, *What About Me*.

Although Valenti did eventually recover the rights to "Get Together" with the help of Quicksilver manager Ron Polte, due to publishing complications he wrote many of his Quicksilver songs under pseudonyms, particularly Jesse Oris Farrow. Whether it was trouble adapting to playing in a band or a lack of inspiration, however, most of the compositions lacked the magic and mystery of those he had sung on his solo album, or the forthright melodic message of "Get Together." Instead they usually just meandered. Occasional tunes like "Gone Again" had the drifting, spacey feel Valenti had explored on his solo outing, and "All in My Mind" (written with Duncan) had an attractive Latin-influenced lilt. "Hope" and "Don't Cry My Lady Love" showed the most reflective and compassionate side of his personality, but when Valenti tried to write harder-rocking, boogying numbers, he fell flat.

Quicksilver actually rang up some of its strongest sales and airplay with the albums *Just for Love* and *What About Me*, the former featuring the small hit "Fresh Air" (which anticipated the sound of the Doobie Brothers somewhat). The jazzy title track of *What About Me*, an extended self-portrait of sorts in which the protagonist laments his eternal outsider status from the straight world, is the most familiar Quicksilver track from the Valenti era, and probably his most famous composition other than "Get Together."

Valenti and Duncan would keep Quicksilver going with various musicians for much of the 1970s, but their commercial prospects were often scotched by Valenti's mulishness, which was clearly by this point a trait that would not be erased or even alleviated. Duncan feels that Capitol did not promote the group as much as it should have due to Valenti's refusal to sign a contract with the label, as a solo artist or as a member of the band—"'I wouldn't sign a piece of shit paper with any record company.' That was his standard line." He says an opportunity to tour as the Rolling Stones' opening act throughout the United States was scotched when Valenti got wind of Ron Polte accepting the offer without asking Dino first: "His reasoning was, 'Don't you ever book a fucking tour and say I'll do it without asking me.'"

A chance to record another solo album for Warner Brothers in the early 1970s was thrown away in circumstances reminiscent of Valenti's ill-fated tenure with Columbia, the difference being that this time around there wasn't even a poorly distrib-uted finished album to show for it. Warners executive Mo Ostin, remembers Dun-can, gave Valenti an advance of about $45,000. "So Dino went to Hawaii and spent all the money in about six weeks, just blew it all. Had a vacation, had a good time. Came back. I had been talking to Mo, and Mo said, 'Why don't you go in the studio with Dino and just put down about ten or twelve tunes, just rough, and send 'em down to me, and we'll start working on the record.' We went into this little studio in [San Francisco], me and Dino, and two acoustic guitars. Mo calls up and tells me, 'There's about five tunes in there that I really think are good. The rest are kind of, well, I don't know. But I'd like to work on those five tunes.' He named these session musicians that he wanted to use, very good players; he wanted me to play guitar. He says, 'I got a guy in mind to produce it, I want to sit down with Dino, we'll take these four or five tunes, and I'd like to hear some more stuff, and maybe suggest to him a couple of cover tunes that he could do.'

"I told Dino this, and he flipped out. He said, 'Fuck Mo Ostin. He don't like my songs?' I said, 'He didn't say he didn't like your songs. He just said there was five that he liked.' He goes, 'Well, *fuck* him! He ain't getting shit out of me!' And eventually Mo just said, 'Tell him the deal's off, and as far as the money's concerned, we'll call it a wash.' That was the second chance he had to do something good, that he just pissed away."

Valenti had about fifteen years to live after the Duncan-Valenti-helmed Quick-silver disbanded around the late 1970s. There would be no more recordings and lit-tle public attention, although Valenti continued to write songs. According to Elaine Forzano, for a time he lived in a camper and worked on the Renaissance Faire (a craft fair in which workers dress in Elizabethan costume), living on the fairgrounds, selling "all his old rock 'n' roll threads and objets d'art at the flea market on week-ends." He kept in touch with Duncan and would play new songs for Gary once or twice a year, "and it was never anything I thought was outstanding. *He* thought it was outstanding. He loved every bit of it. But I didn't really hear anything that had that spark he had earlier." When Valenti asked Duncan to mix some tapes for him, it was the same old story, butting heads against Dino's counter-productive obstinacy. Valenti wanted Duncan to do a mix, but had to be convinced not to be there while the mix was done. Valenti gave him a track with a saxophone on it, but insisted he hadn't recorded sax when he later heard it on the mix. Valenti insisted that a certain vocal couldn't be used, but declared after Gary played a mix to him that used that vocal, "This vocal sounds great." And so forth.

Valenti developed an anterior venous malformation in his final years, and while surgery on it was successful and enabled him to live a little longer, his behavior be-came even more erratic. "He tells me that he lost part of his memory," says Duncan sadly, "but he conveniently only forgot the stuff he did that nobody liked. And I says, 'You motherfucker. You're bullshitting everybody, man. You didn't forget anything.'" He died on November 16, 1994, in Santa Rosa, California. The rights to "Get To-gether," the one guaranteed money-earner in Valenti's catalog, have still been hotly contested in recent years among relatives and lovers, now resting with one of his sons, Joli.

Gary Duncan is now fifty-four, a musician who has survived stardom, label-less drifting, and several points in between since making records with the garage band the Brogues in the mid-1960s before joining Quicksilver. He knows that Valenti ultimately wasn't worth the hassle he was causing the bigwigs. "In this business, you can be as weird as you want to be. As long as your talent balances out, it's OK. But when it gets to the point where your talent doesn't outweigh your temperament, they just get off you like a hot potato. That's what happened to Dino. He wasn't talented enough to overcome his own personality. Unfortunately, he never had anybody in the world that he'd listen to. I mean, he would listen to me probably before anybody else. And he wouldn't listen to *me*.

"But the guy was *alive*. The motherfucker was alive in a world of people that ain't really that alive."

Recommended Recording:

Dino Valente (1968, Koch). After all the controversy over Valenti's bluster, charisma, and pendulum-like personality has faded away, this is the *music* that will stand as his epitaph. In whispery, inquisitive psychedelic folk ballads like "Time," "My Friend," and "Children of the Sun," he was able to project a compassion and love that, from most accounts, he was unable to regularly muster in real life. The unearthly echo and sublimely gorgeous, moody guitar strums make the tracks glisten like morning sun on sea-soaked rocky beaches, with a fragility suggesting that the clouds could burst into a downpour at any moment. For variety there's the Hollywood pop-with-strings of "Tomorrow," the dark coffeehouse folk of "Me and My Uncle," and the psychedelic weirdness of "Test." The CD reissue adds two previously unissued bonus tracks which fit the mood of the album well.

Richard & Mimi Fariña, partners in marriage and music.
Credit: Alice Ochs/Michael Ochs Archives.com.

Richard & Mimi Fariña

Great duos are more than the sum of their parts, each partner spurring the other to heights that could not be scaled solo. The music of Richard and Mimi Fariña was an illustration par excellence. Mimi's high, clear vocals counterpointed her husband Richard's grainier, earthier tones. Her guitar and his dulcimer—an instrumental combination rarely attempted in rock music—blended and dovetailed around each other with deft, at times entrancing, grace. In their too-short recording career, their idiosyncratic albums were as diverse as any early folk-rock fusions. Political commentary was balanced with literary allegory, cynical blues with tender love songs, and sorrowful ballads with upbeat, celebratory anthems. There was tentative electric rock, but also dulcimer-dominated instrumentals that owed much to Appalachian and Celtic folk music, simultaneously twisting those traditional forms in new directions.

The tragedy of Richard and Mimi Fariña's story is that it ended almost as soon as it began, with Richard dying in a motorcycle accident shortly after their second album. The irony of their story is that as fine as their music was, neither of them are principally known for the music they made together. Richard is known to the public almost solely as a literary figure, primarily for the novel published just before his death, *Been Down So Long It Looks Like Up to Me*, whose prose and tone bridged the beat and psychedelic eras. If you've never read that book, you may well have heard of him as a friend and inspiration of Thomas Pynchon, one of the most prominent American writers of the latter part of the twentieth century. For the last quarter-century, Mimi has been known as the founder and driving force behind Bread and Roses, the San Francisco Bay-based organization that stages several hundred annual musical performances at prisons, old-age homes, homeless shelters, children's hospitals, and AIDS hospices. While their Vanguard recordings remain in print, it has often been forgotten that the Fariñas were among the first and most interesting of the folk-rock originators, and most likely only beginning to tap their potential at the time of Richard's death in April 1966.

When Richard and Mimi Fariña met each other in the early 1960s, they were known—in the folk music community, at any rate—not so much for who they were, but for other folk stars with whom they were associated. Mimi Fariña was then known as Mimi Baez, the younger sister of Joan Baez, by then one of the hottest concert and recording artists of the 1960s folk revival. Richard Fariña was the soon-to-be-divorced husband of noted folksinger Carolyn Hester, another (if less acknowledged) important figure in the folk boom. Richard was then, as now, known more for his writing than for his music, though at this point the debut novel that would be his key to a wide audience was still unfinished.

Richard's background is still a matter of some mystery, even to his wives and close friends. Born in 1937 to a Cuban father and Irish mother, both of whom came to the United States in the 1930s, he spent time in Brooklyn, Cuba, and Northern Ireland while growing up, attending Cornell University (where he met Pynchon) in the late 1950s. Even at that time, he was a maverick spirit, ending up as one of four upperclassmen suspended (though soon reinstated) during demonstrations against antiquated curfews for undergraduate women. (Incidentally, although his *Been Down So Long It Looks Like Up to Me* is thought of as a quintessential 1960s document, it is in fact based on his experience at Cornell in the late 1950s.) Apparently he'd also gone to Ireland as a teenager to work with the Irish Republican Army, and visited Cuba as that country was in the throes of Fidel Castro's revolution. In early 1960, however, he'd left Cornell and was working in New York as a copywriter for the J. Walter Thompson ad agency. It was the kind of establishment gig that was bound to be short-lived with someone of such multifaceted talents and restless countercultural leanings.

It was also early 1960 when he met Carolyn Hester, whom he married after a two-week whirlwind courtship. "So he quit J. Walter Thompson," remembers Hester, still active on the folk circuit forty years later. "When we married, he really decided to lay down the gauntlet and be an artist. And then he never did any other kind of thing, no other activity."

Under her influence, Fariña became interested in playing music as well as in writing prose. Hester introduced him to the dulcimer and taught him what she knew on the instrument. While Hester was performing at Club 47 in Cambridge, Massachusetts, in the summer of 1961, she and Fariña met a then-unsigned Bob Dylan. Dylan ended up making his second-ever appearance on a record (as harmonica player) on a session for Hester's self-titled Columbia album later that year. That session brought him to the attention of Columbia executive John Hammond, who signed Dylan himself to the label. And over the next five years Dylan would, as friend and songwriter, most likely influence Fariña's own music and attitude.

When Hester and Fariña first met, she muses, "I don't know that he'd entertained any ideas of having a musical career. I think he was really concentrating on writing, and had done a lot of short stories. And he told me his ideas about a book. Going along with his wanting to remain an artist, he decided that maybe he and I should do some singing together, and we could get some bookings, and get maybe paid as individual artists too. So in England"—where she and Richard lived for a while in the early 1960s—"we did some singing. We didn't sing too much together in America, really. It ended up that I was there when he really started in on the book in London. I remember I typed the first ninety pages of it. But we were in the process of really dissolving our marriage, and I left at that time to come back to the States, to start the divorce process."

Fariña did take advantage of his time in Europe to make modest advances in his musical career. He was one of two Americans officially invited to perform folk music at the Edinburgh International Festival in 1962, appeared on the BBC, and worked as a street singer in France. According to the liner notes of the LP he did with Eric Von Schmidt, he feigned blindness while busking to bring in more francs; he himself is quoted (in the bio accompanying *Been Down So Long It Looks Like Up to Me*) as remembering getting by on "music, street-singing, script-writing, acting, a little smuggling, anything to hang on."

Also, in January 1963, he made his recording debut in the basement of Dobell's Jazz Record Shop in London, for the aforementioned collaboration with Boston folksinger Eric Von Schmidt. Not released until 1967, the obscure *Dick Fariña & Eric Von Schmidt* LP was a typical and none-too-exceptional folk revival relic, the performers running through competent but rather dry renderings of blues, jug band, Appalachian, and traditional tunes. Fariña did offer a hint of things to come with the instrumental "Old Joe's Dulcimer," which anticipated the flavor of the dulcimer-coated instrumentals found on the Richard & Mimi Fariña albums. The record is highly valued by collectors, not so much for the music as for the presence of one Blind Boy Grunt—aka Bob Dylan, then visiting England as well—on harmonica and background vocals.

Asked what might have set Fariña aside from the overcrowded stable of aspiring folkies—such as the soon to be superstar Dylan and the far less celebrated Von Schmidt— Hester responds, "I believe that he had maybe more of a British-leaning influence in what he did, possibly because of all the time he'd spent in Ireland. Whereas a lot of people, say Von Schmidt and Bob [Dylan], were interested in that, but they—maybe Von Schmidt especially—leaned toward the blues. Maybe the British ethic appealed more to Richard's literary sense; he could get more words in there, or something."

Yet the most important event of Fariña's stay in Europe was meeting Mimi Baez, then living in Paris with her parents. When Richard Fariña sailed back to the

United States in 1963, he brought with him Mimi, whom he had already married in a secret ceremony (a more official one would follow in California that year). Mimi had just finished high school, and the Baez family did not give her unsteadily-employed groom the warmest of welcomes. As Hester reiterates, even back when he had started his first marriage, he'd "decided he was going to devote himself to his artistic side no matter what. And I'm afraid the 'no matter what' part is what got him in a lot of hot water with a lot of people, including the Baez family, probably." In their isolation in a one-room cabin in Carmel, California, the Fariñas began to craft the style that would color their musical duets, centered around the interplay between their voices, and between Richard's dulcimer and Mimi's guitar.

"The writing started when we started singing," reminisces Mimi. "I think he was inspired, probably, by the two instruments. We liked it, for sure, the Appalachian sound. And it sometimes crosses over with an Irish sound, because of fifths. The instruments being tuned in fifths made it easy to sing and write with harmonies and fifths.

"We would sit down after dinner in the evenings and sing, or play around in front of the fire. And, I guess, occasionally we would sing for neighbors, and that got us motivated to write lyrics and melodies. 'Pack Up Your Sorrows'"—probably the song for which the duo is remembered most—"came pretty early. My sister Pauline [Pauline Marden] had written the chorus, and stopped by the house and said, 'If you want to add any verses to this, go ahead.' So little by little, songs were being inspired, lyrics and music."

In Eric Von Schmidt and Jim Rooney's *Baby, Let Me Follow You Down: The Illustrated Story of the Cambridge Folk Years*, Mimi elaborated upon the good and bad times of their early Carmel days: "He was writing on a daily basis. He was up at six every morning. My own opinion is that he was taking quite a bit of speed. That's my opinion now—I had no idea then. He wrote hard all day long, worked and worked and worked...During that year, he shot a deer, which we ate. We had no money. After the wedding, the whole family wasn't getting along. Joan couldn't stand Dick. My father couldn't stand him to begin with. Nobody liked each other and I was in the middle, not knowing what to do."

The couple moved back to Cambridge for a while, continuing to forge ahead with their personal and creative partnership despite less-than-unanimous approval. One of their Cambridge friends was Debbie Green, a fixture of the 1960s folk scene in both Cambridge and Berkeley as a guitarist and cofounder of the Berkeley folk club the Cabale. "There was a folk music scene at the Club 47," she explains. "Joan [Baez] has a real sharp tongue to say the very least, and so do a lot of other people: Dylan, [folksinger and Dylan buddy Bobby] Neuwirth, [powerful Dylan/folk music manager] Albert Grossman. It was a very cliquish scene, and Dick was very much frowned upon. He was a wonderful child, alive, bright. I *loved* him. But he didn't quite play it by their rules, and Joan put him down. So therefore he got put down by this group. He was ostracized, and so was Mimi. So was Eric Andersen [Green's future husband and another singer-songwriter, whom Debbie accompanied on recordings as a guitarist, pianist, and vocalist]. And therefore, so was I. I was furious. I can't stand a group of people deciding to be mean to other people. We were all kind of outside the scene, so we hung out together."

"So we had a great time." Her tone changes abruptly as she breaks into a laugh. "And it was a wonderful time. I'd go over to their apartment, and they'd be writing, and Dick would be playing, and we'd just pick up guitars. They were very childlike and creative, laughing. They had a wonderful relationship." In comparison with the many other folksingers starting to write their own material in Dylan's shadow, she adds, Richard "was much more sophisticated. He'd lived around the world. He was a reader *and* a writer; he had read much more than anybody else who was writing in that genre at the time. So his lyrics were slightly different."

Fariña may have come to music somewhat later in the game than many of his peers, and indeed continued to keep his feet in both the literary and musical worlds. He kept plugging away at his novel and was still, to most of the public, known primarily as a writer. His short stories, poems, and articles appeared in *The Atlantic*, *Mademoiselle*, the *Village Voice*, and other publications. But he was also stockpiling original songs at a rapid rate, and Richard and Mimi Fariña's debut album, *Celebrations for a Grey Day*, consisted entirely of Richard's compositions (with Pauline Marden getting a cocredit for the aforementioned "Pack Up Your Sorrows"). Released in early 1965 on Vanguard—the label of Mimi's sister Joan Baez—it found the duo pulling contemporary folk in novel directions, while they themselves were being pulled into the just-emerging musical sea change known as folk-rock.

The most striking quality of *Celebrations for a Grey Day* (and indeed of all the Fariñas' albums)—and the one that most sets it apart from most other folk or folk-rock acts of the period—was its diversity. About half of the thirteen songs were instrumentals spotlighting the guitar-dulcimer mixture, sometimes in a relatively traditional folk mode bringing to mind bubbling brooks on a clear spring day, at others getting into more daring drones and counterrhythms that mixed Appalachian, Celtic, and even hints of Latin and Indian music. (One such Indian-flavored instrumental, "V.," was named after the then-recent novel by Richard's friend, Thomas Pynchon.) Arguably the instrumentals were over-emphasized on this particular LP, but they did unveil the pair's knack for creating unusual textures from instruments associated with traditional folk; "V.," for instance, sped up into a quasi-rave-up with slight dissonances and percussive rattles and taps that both recalled Indian styles and anticipated raga-rock. Mimi also varied the mix somewhat by occasionally playing autoharp instead of guitar. (Oddly, although the title track was virtually identical to the title of a poem, printed as "Celebration for a Gray Day," that Richard had written long before the album came out—and although Carolyn Hester remembers him converting poems to music when he first started writing songs—"Celebrations for a Grey Day" is presented as an instrumental.)

It was on the numbers with lyrics that the act really shined, though, both due to Richard Fariña's eclectic songwriting and the beautiful vocal harmonies. Richard was a man of many moods, in song at least, moving from the jaunty sing-along of "Pack Up Your Sorrows" and the rollicking blues of "One-Way Ticket" to sad, pretty ballads that sounded much like sea chanteys set to new words. Yet these were not likely to be sung by sailors: "Michael, Andrew & James" was a sad lament for Michael Schwerner, Andrew Goodman, and James Chaney, young civil rights activists murdered by Ku Klux Klansmen in Mississippi during 1964.

Richard's skills as a poet gave his lyrics a depth and multidimensionality missing from the lyrics of many of the songwriters then emerging in Bob Dylan's wake, lending themselves to multiple listenings that unveiled new layers of meaning. "The Falcon," for instance, sounds at first hearing like an ageless, doleful folk ballad. It gains new poignancy, however, when—as Richard explains in his always-elaborate liner notes (themselves indicative of his energetic stream-of-consciousness prose style)—it's realized that the falcon symbolizes the birds in Point Lobos, California, whose habitual calm vanished when members of the John Birch Society practiced armed maneuvers underneath on weekends. Heard in this light, "The Falcon" becomes a possible allegory for how otherwise rational, peaceful people can become riled into senseless violence.

Richard Fariña was always fond of mixing the personal and the social in song. "One-Way Ticket," as another example, sounds on the surface like a good-time traveling road tune, the twist being that the singers are merrily *escaping* the California sunshine for the snow and rain of the East, its satirical jibes at Californian culture hidden in the lines about oceans where swimming is nearly obsolete and you wake up to find your hair's turned blond overnight. There was a dark side to the composer's frequent good-humored, compassionate outlook as well, best heard in the compelling "Reno Nevada," its lyrics using the gambling town as a setting for a life in which there's little left to lose. The grinding guitar riffs and Mimi's winding, wordless backup vocal added to the majestically foreboding air of a song that might be Richard Fariña's best. Mimi reveals, surprisingly, that beloved jazz hipster Mose Allison "was gonna record that. I'm a Mose Allison fan, and so was Dick, but he never recorded it. I was so hopeful he would."

The couple's affection for Mose Allison was one indication that their musical interests and influences were not limited to acoustic folk. So, too, were several songs on the album that verged, however tentatively, on rock 'n' roll arrangements. Although no drums were used, Bruce Langhorne—who had accompanied Carolyn Hester in the studio, and also played on Bob Dylan's first album to feature electric folk-rock, *Bringing It All Back Home*, in early 1965—added electric guitar to several cuts. Langhorne, pianist Charles Small, and bassist Russ Savakus backed the Fariñas on "Reno Nevada" and "One-Way Ticket"; only the absence of drums held the music back from full-tilt folk-rock.

Langhorne had first met Richard at a Carolyn Hester studio session, becoming good friends with him and later Mimi before recording with them. As a guitarist on records by the Fariñas, Hester, Dylan, Gordon Lightfoot, Fred Neil, Richie Havens, Odetta, Joan Baez, Buffy St. Marie, Tom Rush, and others, he was one of the crucial (and more overlooked) figures of the 1960s folk and folk-rock scene. "A lot of people think that since I was so prominent in the music world, and in that particular part of the music business at that point, that I had a huge hand in everything I touched," he says now of his role in the Fariñas' albums. "But in this particular case, that really *wasn't* the case. Dick was the real mastermind.

"I think that certain musicians are capable of generating threads. A thread is something that other musicians can really hang on to, and build the whole thing. Bob Dylan is like that. And Dick was like that. He really came with a concept of what a song should be.

"The principal driving structure in all of the arrangements was what Dick was playing on the dulcimer. It was such an unusual instrument, and playing it the way he played it…because at that time, in that folk circle that included the people who played at [New York folk club] Gerdes, Club 47, and places like that, the premier dulcimer player was Jean Ritchie. [Still active today, Ritchie sang and played a repertoire oriented toward traditional Appalachian folk music.] She played traditional dulcimer, and she was really horrified by the way Dick played. Because Dick played these rhythmic phrases; he played the dulcimer like much more of a percussion instrument, and he played nontraditional stuff. He was quite an innovator on that instrument. That was definitely the thread and heart of the arrangements. My contribution was just to listen and see where I could help."

In addition to adding guitar, Langhorne also played "this giant Turkish tambourine that appears as percussion on some of their albums. The tambourine was really cool, because it had a bass tone, an edge tone, and jingle tones. So it could pretty much do what a drum set with a bass drum, a snare drum, and a hi-hat would do, because it would have something to say in all of those registers. I think Dick was interested in working with me on that, because it was a unique sound, and it complemented the unique sound of his dulcimer."

When the album was released in April 1965, Dylan's *Bringing It All Back Home* was barely on the shelves, and the Byrds' "Mr. Tambourine Man" had yet to climb the charts and make folk-rock a household term. Numerous folk musicians were already experimenting with fuller instrumentation by early 1965. But in the context of its era, *Celebrations for a Grey Day* stood out as a bold artistic move, at a time when the very notion of folk artists using electric instruments and bands was about to explode into a raging debate in the folk community. Mimi remains uncertain of how exactly those full-band arrangements came about, but acknowledges, "I think Richard had a desire to move into the rock arena. The very first album we made, I think those musicians may have been chosen by Vanguard. There was Russ Savakus; he was someone who just came in and picked up the music easily and was a nice guy, a pro, and sat in and backed us. That was sort of Vanguard-promoted.

"I was not used to that kind of professionalism. I'll never forget, when we finished our first session, and Russ Savakus wrapped up his bass, said goodnight, and left. And I thought, 'Well! Where is he going? Aren't we all gonna go hang out somewhere? Aren't we gonna party now?' But that's how professional musicians behaved. He was a studio musician, he was probably on to another gig; I learned about that later. The other musicians, some kind of came with the company, were supplied for us, and others were friends that we had made along the way. Bruce was definitely a friend."

Although the use of electric instruments and bands miffed folk purists, Langhorne counters, "Folk music is the music of the people. If you look at folk music in any country in the world from any era, the instruments that are used are the instruments available to the indigenous people. For us in America at that time, it happened to be the electric guitar. It was like everyone had electric guitars; there were electric guitars everywhere, and all the records you heard featured electric guitar. It was a perfectly natural evolution, and young, forward-thinking people like Dick and Mimi, and like Bob Dylan, had no choice but to move forward, because it was right there in their face, and they were contemporary artists. They were not traditional artists. It was sort of inevitable, and of course the resistance was also inevitable, because people don't like their icons to change."

Paul Williams, founder of *Crawdaddy!* (the first American magazine to cover rock music with serious critical appreciation), saw and heard the Fariñas as a teenager in the mid-1960s Cambridge folk crowd. As he sees it, the rock sensibility of Richard & Mimi Fariña came through even when they weren't backed by a full electric ensemble. "The two of them playing together, live, was as exciting and fulfilling as a rock 'n' roll band," he declares. "Unless, of course, you were addicted to the Chicago blues setup, and you were like, 'Oh, I can't enjoy this if I don't see an electric bass and drums.' The wonderful way that the melodies and rhythms interplayed, and the two voices worked together, created an excitement and tension. We—meaning a few hip people in Cambridge—knew that this was fully as advanced and sophisticated, and in the same direction, as the exciting new discoveries of the best rock 'n' roll bands at the time. The other singer-songwriters, not taking anything away from them, were not very far from Woody Guthrie and so forth, musically. But Dick and Mimi were exploring musical ideas in a way that's not unrelated to the explorations of the Beatles, the Grateful Dead, Buffalo Springfield, and other groups. They were very much in that spirit, although, obviously, they were not a rock 'n' roll group, and not trying to be."

Unlikely testimony to the Fariñas' ability to whip up a rock-like fervor was offered by Pete Seeger when the Fariñas were guests on an episode, broadcast some months after the 1965 Newport Folk Festival, of his short-lived educational TV show *Rainbow Quest*. That festival, of course, is remembered primarily for Bob Dylan's first performance with an electric band and the enormous controversy that greeted his new, loud rock sound. It is not as well remembered that several other performers at the event were heralding the dawn of a new rock era as well, including the Paul Butterfield Blues Band and the Chambers Brothers. While the Fariñas did not use an electric band at Newport, they did bring along Langhorne and washtub bassist Fritz Richmond. Seeger is remembered for his vehemently negative reaction to Dylan's electric show, attempting to cut the power cable with an axe, according to some accounts. Yet he could have hardly offered a more glowing, open-minded appraisal of the Fariñas' performance, which from his summary seems rather like a mini-preview of 1969's Woodstock festival:

"Last summer I'll never forget hearing them sing at the Newport Folk Festival. Dick Fariña had a dulcimer on his knee, and Mimi, his wife, playing the guitar, and they had some other instruments playing with them. And they were going at it hot and heavy. It was the middle of the afternoon, and 7,000 people had been sitting out there in the hot sun, getting hotter and hotter, perspiration dripping down. And all of a sudden, the sky gets dark and one of these sudden summer thundershowers comes along. Rain just poured down. And Dick and Mimi, having just gotten on the stage, decided to keep on playing. Someone put an umbrella up over them to keep the instruments dry. And 7,000 people up front, they'd been waiting to hear them. They weren't gonna leave.

"Well, I was standing backstage, and I peeked through the curtain there. And I saw a sight I'll never forget in all my life. Seven thousand people were getting soaking wet, and they said, 'What the heck, let's get wet.' They started stripping off their clothing and dancing to the music. It was a real rocking number with wonderful rhythm going. And there were people waving their shirts in the air and dancing all kinds of dances, women had stripped off their shirts, dancing in their bras. It was pandemonium. Seven thousand people dancing in the thundering rain, and Dick and Mimi pounding on. It was wonderful." (Two songs from that performance can be heard on the posthumous Richard & Mimi Fariña compilation *Memories*.)

For most mid-1960s cult artists, we have to take the word of those who were there as to the performers' live magnetism, and leave it at that. Fortunately, a remarkable, if rarely seen, testament to the Fariñas' live musicianship survives on that episode of *Rainbow Quest*, almost certainly filmed in late 1965 or early 1966. On a bare-bones set that couldn't seem to make up its mind whether it was emulating an indoor kitchen or outdoor picnic area, genial host Pete Seeger was joined by a quiet Mimi Fariña—wearing a long dark dress, with white trimming on top, of almost Amish severity—and the more ebullient Richard Fariña, wearing the expected dark sweater. Mimi both tapped her feet on the floor and her hand against the body of the guitar to set the beat of an exhilarating six-minute instrumental combining elements of "V." and "Celebrations for a Grey Day," inciting Seeger to join in on maracas and deliver a high-pitched whoop at its hectic conclusion. "I was waiting for you to start singing," said Seeger, almost apologetically, "and then I realized the whole point of it was the rhythm, and I couldn't keep still. I hope you don't mind my joining in. It would take a dead man not to move on that."

The Fariñas proceeded to uncork a highly charged "Bold Marauder," "Pack Up Your Sorrows" (joined by Seeger on guitar), and the then-unreleased "Joy 'Round My Brain," Richard infectiously scatting between letting out bursts of harmonica and harmonizing uplifting choruses with his wife. Richard took advantage of some chat time to speak at some length about Joan Baez's newly founded institute for the study of nonviolence, at which both he and Mimi worked and studied—not the usual dialogue broadcast on television in 1965-66, even on educational TV (not that Seeger was at all unhappy to discuss the topic). When the conversation turned to music, Seeger astutely pointed out, "This traditional instrument, you're playing it in a new way, combining two or three old traditions, aren't you. You're playing a Kentucky mountain dulcimer. It was only supposed to be played traditionally, traditionally, traditionally. Now I see you're playing counterrhythms to Mimi. She'll be playing in 6/8 time, she'll be playing in 3/4 time. And then you start accelerating the tempo as though you were playing an Indian sitar. And it puts me in mind of the fact that this is gonna happen all around the world, for good or bad."

The rock feeling that had been implicit in the Fariñas' early work became more explicit on their second album, *Reflections in a Crystal Wind*, recorded later in 1965. Richard and Mimi were accompanied by additional musicians on almost every track. Langhorne, Savakus, and Small were still in the fold, joined at times by friend John Hammond Jr. on harmonica, and Felix Pappalardi (later to produce Cream) on bass. On four cuts only, Alvin Rogers played drums, finally pushing the Fariñas into recordings that could only be called rock 'n' roll, and not be labeled as folk music. Langhorne's distinctive wavering, reverberant tremolo tone was an especially vital enhancement, adding electric power but retaining suitable delicacy, particularly on

"Raven Girl" and "Reflections in a Crystal Wind." The guitarist devised the tremolo by borrowing a twin reverb Fender amp from another Vanguard artist, Sandy Bull, who was fusing all kinds of instrumental world and folk music on acoustic and electric guitars, banjo, and oud on his own imaginative mid-1960s albums.

Furthermore, adds Langhorne, "I tried to find the tremolo that was compatible with the time of the tune. I was very influenced by Roebuck Staples [of the Staple Singers, who were using tremolo guitar on their own overlooked folk-leaning early-to-mid-1960s recordings]. Roebuck Staples used to play this Fender, and set up a tremolo that was in time to the song. The tremolo would be going wuh-wuh-wuh, wuh-wuh-wuh-wuh [Langhorne mimics the echoing sound] and the song would be going [he switches gears to mimic the rhythm] ch-ch-tm, t-t-ch-ch-ch-ch-ch. Wuh-wuh-wuh-wuh-wuh-wuh…it was just so excellent!" he ends with a hearty laugh.

Richard's songwriting was equally far-ranging this time around, perhaps acquiring a harder edge. *Been Down So Long It Looks Like Up to Me* was a few months away from publication when the album was released, but certainly the bluesiest tunes on the record were much like that novel's prose set to music: a steady march of impatient images, delivered with a cynical humor that embraced the absurdity of modern society as much as it railed against it. "Sell-Out Agitation Waltz" was certainly the most successful of these, with sterling Langhorne guitar work, barely audible Hammond harmonica trills, a propulsive jazz rhythm, and seductively moody unison vocals by Richard and Mimi. "House Un-American Blues Activity Dream" was a surrealistic fantasy worthy of Bob Dylan's oddest mid-1960s lyrics, following its unfortunate protagonist through haunted dreams of female Marines and jeans-wearing presidential candidates, a vacation to Cuba, and a Kafkaesque indictment and prison sentence upon return to the States. The House Un-American Activities Committee's witch hunt and the Cuban revolution were still fresh in the minds of the public in 1965. Satirizing blind American patriotism and single-minded zealots who attacked those who thought about things differently, even on a record, took some courage.

"Hard-Loving Loser," perhaps something of a self-portrait on Richard's part, is the most famous of the album's songs, due in part to the fabulous cover version that Judy Collins would put on her *In My Life* album about a year later. In fact, Collins did a much better job with the tune than the Fariñas did, adding an urgent ascending harpsichord riff, stop-start rhythms, and raucous barrelhouse piano to create what sounded like a surefire hit single. It wasn't, although she did put it on a single; Collins would have to wait until her cover of Joni Mitchell's "Both Sides Now" to break into the pop-rock market.

In fact, however, blues-rock was never the Fariñas' forte. Certainly "Mainline Prosperity Blues" was a pedestrian workout in that mold, falling perhaps a little too close—as do some of the other blues-rock songs on the album—to Bob Dylan's territory. Fariña, like other songwriter friends of Dylan such as Phil Ochs and Eric Andersen, had a complex relationship with Dylan, envious of his success and talent, and also subject to scathing face-to-face putdowns during Dylan's famous cutting sessions. For all that, there's no doubt that Fariña admired Dylan, and he wrote a piece on the singer for *Mademoiselle* magazine. "Dylan read it when we were all sitting out by the pool," reflected Mimi in her notes to *Long Time Coming and a Long*

Time Gone, an anthology of short written works by Richard, "and he said in private to Joanie [Baez]: 'Dick is one of the only people who knows what I'm all about,' or something to that effect. Which Joanie in private told me and I in private told Dick. That was really nice and it may well have been true. Dick was a little jealous: Dylan was much younger and getting a lot of attention; he was spinning miles around Dick in success. It got to Dick—that this younger person was able to do it in a bigger way."

As an aside, there was an amusing moment on the Pete Seeger show when the host pronounced, "I think you can gather that Dick here is a poet, basically. And you'd have to hear these songs several times over to start hearing all the meanings in his words. Of course, it's true of Bob Dylan too, isn't it?"

"Oh, absolutely," mumbled the usually voluble Richard, offering no further elaboration.

On *Reflections in a Crystal Wind*, Fariña ventured into his most original areas— territory that had little or nothing to do with Bob Dylan—on the songs that had little or nothing to do with blues or agitation. The sweetest, most optimistic side of Richard's persona came to light on the love song "Children of Darkness," with Charles Small's celesta adding another new color to the duo's arrangements. The title track was a cheerful folk-rocker in the cast of "Pack Up Your Sorrows," yet with elusive abstract wordplay. "A Swallow Song," like the similar "The Falcon," was a superb minor-key sad ballad; "Raven Girl" and "Bold Marauder" were like seafaring folk narratives that had been passed down through generations, but with freshly penned lyrics and a rock fullness to the guitar parts. And while "Bold Marauder" might have sounded like an anthem for pirates of several centuries past, it was in fact an allegory for the pirates, in suits and ties and government buildings, plundering foreign lands in the twentieth century. As Richard commented when introducing the song to Pete Seeger's TV cameras, "I'm fond of dedicating it to the memory of Barry Goldwater, sometimes to the memory of Ronald Reagan [then fifteen years away from entering the White House, pronounced by Richard as REE-gin]. It's really meant for anybody who feels that because they have the various gods and presidents on their side, they can send their armies marauding over the earth."

Although there were, again, dulcimer-guitar instrumentals throughout the LP, these were less in number (four), acting more as interludes than as core components of the set. And even those were delving into more adventurous fields than their counterparts on the debut album, with "Dopico" and "Allen's Interlude" getting into quasi-modal, world-fusion vibes; another, "Miles," was the one song recorded by the duo written by Mimi.

While "Hard-Loving Loser" and "House Un American Blues Activity Dream" were the songs that brought the Fariñas the most notoriety, they were not the ones dearest to Mimi's heart. "I always enjoyed Richard's love songs. The more political stuff got too angry for me. Sometimes it pushed the corny button, and you can get an audience riled up easily. It's much easier to make people cry than it is to make them laugh, and you can press certain buttons to get their attention. I felt, sometimes with the political material, that that's what he was going for. Certainly not all of it. I *loved* 'Michael, Andrew and James,' and the one about the girls who were killed. [She's referring to "Birmingham Sunday," an elegy for four schoolchildren bombed and killed at an Alabama Sunday school, recorded in 1964 by Joan Baez, and by Richard as a solo artist on the Elektra compilation *Singer Songwriter Project*; the Fariñas themselves did not release a version.] Sometimes it just didn't fit my particular taste.

"But they were all good songs. Dick was able to write love songs and political songs, mix those two metaphors together in a song. And I always appreciated that. He could deal with things that were very current and relevant to people in the moment, that also had long life and depth." And he was prolific, able to write anywhere, even dictating songs like "Hard-Loving Loser" to Mimi in the car. "He was sort of a non-stop person, so if he'd be thinking of lines and driving, then I would write down the lyrics." She adds with a chuckle, "and sometimes add things, I have to say." If the political aspect of Richard's songs was missed, he would sometimes direct attention to it in the track-by-track commentary of his own liner notes, as when he notes in his paragraph about "The Falcon," "Goldwater was about to win California primary and the skies were somewhat uneasy."

The critical attention upon Richard's songwriting has overshadowed Mimi's own underestimated contributions to their music. In addition to providing those angelic high harmonies, she was also a very good guitarist, supplying much of the rhythmic drive—sometimes by making percussive sounds with her feet and the guitar itself—that made the sound so much more galvanizing than most acoustic music of the period. Debbie Green played guitar with both of the Baez sisters when they were entering music, and points out, "Joan took a kind of easy road. In the beginning, she just learned what I was doing. She would learn every note I played, and that'd be it. Her guitar just supported the voice; the songs that did that, she was happy. But Mimi was, I don't think, more musical, but much more creative. She would find things." There is no better way to appreciate how much Mimi added than by hearing Richard's three solo contributions ("House Un-American Blues Activity Dream," "Bold Marauder," and "Birmingham Sunday") to Elektra's rare 1965 *Singer Songwriter Project* LP. Two of the three songs would also be done on *Reflections in a Crystal Wind*. Each was far superior when sung and played by both Richard and Mimi; while the solo versions were hardly poor, hearing them is akin to listening to one of the Everly Brothers without the other.

At the time of their release, the Fariñas' two albums made little impact on the pop or rock audience, despite boasting a mindset that could and should have made inroads beyond the folk scene. Not all of the blame for this can be laid on Vanguard, which was far more geared to the LP market than the singles one, and not able to gain commercial airplay for LP-oriented, literate rock artists in the days before the advent of FM radio. In this it was not alone: Its chief folk and folk-rock competitor, Elektra Records, also had yet to score even a moderate hit single when 1966 began. Vanguard did try, theoretically, to get the Fariñas into the singles market, putting out a 45 of the most likely contenders from their first album, "Reno Nevada"/"One-Way Ticket." It's doubtful that these got any AM airplay: When Paul Williams showed a DJ promo copy to Richard at a Philadelphia area performance in early 1966, "I got Dick to autograph it, and it was like he almost had barely seen the thing before."

Still, things could have hardly looked anything less than optimistic for the Fariñas in early 1966. Richard's long-awaited novel was on the verge of publication. *Cel-*

ebrations for a Grey Day may not have sold tons, but it had its important admirers, such as the *New York Times*, which named it one of the ten best folk records of 1965. Richard's songs were starting to get covered by artists with a higher commercial profile: Judy Collins, who had a peerless eye for material by emerging songwriters, did "Pack Up Your Sorrows" on her 1965 *Fifth Album*, while Joan Baez did "Birmingham Sunday" on *her* fifth album, *5*. Joan by this time was fully on Richard's good side; as she would write in *Esquire* in 1966, "He'd won me full over by the end, from a hostile, critical in-law of Dick the intruder, to a fond friend."

So much so, in fact, that as Mimi confirms, Joan "was making an album at one point with a producer who wasn't working out, and she called us—I think we were in California—and said, 'Come help me.' I know Dick had some ideas. So that was the starting point of them talking about his help. I think after that, there was talk about him [producing] an actual album, which never happened." Two Joan Baez tracks that Richard produced did later appear on *Memories*. One of these—the lovely "All the World Has Gone By," with music by Joan, words by Kim Chappell and Richard Fariña, and a haunting, baroque arrangement—was as good as anything Baez ever committed to record, and certainly one of her most overlooked tracks.

Richard and Joan never would collaborate on a full album, and—even more sadly—Richard and Mimi never would collaborate on another album. On April 30, 1966, in Carmel, California—where the couple was now living again—Richard was killed in a motorcycle accident, just a few hours after a publication party for *Been Down So Long It Looks Like Up to Me*. Police estimated that the motorcycle, driven by William Hind, was traveling at ninety miles per hour when it skidded off a road, over a five-foot bank, and through two fences. In a cruel coincidence, it was Mimi's twenty-first birthday.

While Richard's death devastated friends and fans, to some it was not wholly unexpected. With his boundless energy also came an appetite for risk, dating back to his days with the IRA as a teenager, which led to him being deported from Ireland at the age of eighteen. "He was flirting with danger a lot, and wild in that way," says Debbie Green. "So when he was killed, it all fit right in. It was sad, but it made a lot of sense, because he took a lot of chances."

Exactly how many chances Richard took will probably never be known for sure, given that even his wives were uncertain of what might have happened in the past, before he became a folksinger. Confessed Mimi in her notes to *Long Time Coming and a Long Time Gone*, "I never really knew exactly what he did when he went down there [to Cuba] (from college) to fight in the hills, or whatever it was he was supposedly going to do. Sometimes I didn't know the difference between his fantasy and his reality—he would tell me something he had done and I kind of had to nod and wonder or pick up what I could from other conversations, because he couldn't help exaggerating so."

"Anything was possible with Richard," laughs Carolyn Hester when asked if he might have embellished his past to some extent. "Yes, that very much could be. For me, I'm satisfied that those things did happen, and that he was a very moral person, basically. Like a Sinead O'Connor type of a person, a purist. That is something I don't think has really come out about Richard."

Hester also offers a chilling revelation as to an early incident that might have done much to shape Richard's character as an adult. "I went with him to Ireland [in the early 1960s] and stayed with his mother's family. Her brothers were also living in that household, and they were fishermen on Lough Neagh. They all talked about their IRA interests quite openly, so that led me to believe the story Richard told me, and probably told Mimi and maybe quite a few other people…that he had been involved [in the 1950s] in a bombing effort, where they swam with explosives in Lough Neagh and put them on a British patrol boat. And that it blew up. And then he found out later that there had been people on the boat. He hadn't been told that anyone was gonna be around there. It had been the opposite—he had been led to believe, 'there'll be an empty boat, we'll do this and this,' and so on.

"I think that was one of the shocks of his life, and maybe is really at the heart of his whole life after that. Going for broke, and 'I don't have anything to lose. I've already lost,' as it were. I honestly feel that's a key to his life. I'm sorry to say that, but looking back, I feel that that really affected him. He was a con man and he had a lot of problems, and left quite a trail behind him. But some of it was because of that shock, I think."

Nevertheless, Richard's death "was a huge event and a shock for the Cambridge folk music scene, really," says Paul Williams. "It was the first loss like that, of somebody who was so beloved and so dear, and so obviously bound for greater things." His abundant songwriting gift was confirmed even more by the appearance of a posthumous compilation of outtakes, live songs, and odds and ends, *Memories*, in 1968. Although Mimi says the album was assembled "just to fulfill a contract," in fact it was almost as good as their two proper Vanguard LPs. "Joy 'Round My Brain," with its images of hummingbirds flying upside down and congressmen tearing off their clothes, was as playful and whimsical as folk-rock ever got; "Almond Joy" was funky good-time blues that would have made a better choice for *Reflections in a Crystal Wind* than several of the blues-rockers that did make it onto that album; "Blood Red Roses" was stirring a cappella British-styled folk; and "The Quiet Joys of Brotherhood," sung by Mimi alone, was an eerie and dramatic Celtic-flavored tune with an epic sweep. "Morgan the Pirate," also sung by Mimi alone, was—according to the liner notes, which were not necessarily gospel—Richard's "farewell to Bob Dylan."

If these were leftovers, one wonders what was in store for the Fariñas if they'd continued to record, and as the times became more conducive to their open-minded alchemies of folk, rock, poetry, and world music. Would they have moved, as some of their folk-rock colleagues did, to full rock arrangements and even psychedelic rock? Would they have drawn out the Indian drones of their instrumentals even more to enter raga-rock, as Country Joe & the Fish—also on Vanguard, and also founded by folk musicians—would do by the end of 1966? Would Bob Dylan's absence from the music and recording scene from mid-1966 to the end of 1967—precipitated, ironically, by a serious motorcycle accident, albeit one that was not fatal—have left a commercial gap for the similarly complex folk-rock of the Fariñas to fill? Would Richard Fariña have focused on music at all, given the successful reception of his novel, which he didn't live to see?

As with all premature rock deaths from Buddy Holly on, it's impossible to say. "I know that Dick was very interested in heading towards the rock scene, and I probably would have toddled along," speculates Mimi. "I probably would have wanted to be a little more of a puritan, but"—she laughs softly—"would have seen the light after a while. I think Vanguard was beginning to feel that Dick was the leader of the two of us, and putting him up more in the forefront. I'm sure we would have explored more instrumentation." The Fariñas never did play live with a full rock band, although they sometimes had accompanists such as Langhorne, and "I don't know if someday we would have traveled with a band. That might have become a goal at some point."

Would he have concentrated upon music, writing, or both? "I don't know. But I do know that he said at some point, 'If people want to label me, I would prefer to be called an artist.' Maybe because that was all-inclusive." In any case, she agrees that his literary background "had to have influenced every creative aspect of his output, just because it was him. It was what he had to offer, and it was what he knew."

Speculates Langhorne, "I think that it probably would have continued to evolve and stay contemporary. Dick was of Irish and Cuban background; I think if Dick were alive today, he would be doing just really super-cool salsa. I believe that if Dick had lived, he would have turned out to be one of the top writers in the country. He was a genius writer. They would have been cultural icons: they were young, they were contemporary, they were hip, they were beautiful. There was no reason why they should not have gone to the top."

"Dick and Mimi as a team, and Dick as a writer, had certainly the talent and the creative potential of the best of the rock artists of that time," believes Paul Williams, still at the helm of *Crawdaddy!*, and now the author of several books of rock criticism, including a few on Bob Dylan alone. "When you're looking at, say Buffalo Springfield and Neil Young—if Neil had died after that first album came out, and you were trying to speculate about where he would have gone, absolutely you wouldn't know, although you would still say, 'Wow, these two or three things he did were great.' He also wanted to write, so he could just as well have buried himself in the next novel."

That's particularly true since *Been Down So Long It Looks Like Up to Me*, detailing the live-for-the-moment metaphysical, sexual, and intellectual adventures of Gnossos Pappadopoulis, was a success. It remains in print thirty-five years later, and eventually became part of Penguin's twentieth-century classics series. "When I first read the book, I was comparing it with my own experience of the same place, time, and people," wrote Thomas Pynchon, the best man at the Fariñas' wedding, in his introduction to a 1983 edition of the book. "It seemed then that Gnossos and Fariña were one and the same. It was also great fun recognizing the real-life counterparts of the other characters, being tickled by what he'd done with and to them. Now, nearly twenty years later, seeing a little further into his method, I think maybe it wasn't so simple. He didn't just take things that had happened and change names. He really worked his ass off, but the result is so graceful that the first time around I was fooled completely."

The book is remembered and read, but the music has had surprisingly little influence, perhaps because it's difficult to replicate, more likely because it isn't that widely known, particularly to listeners born after 1960. Certainly Richard and Mimi were among the first duos to blend male and female voices so effectively on contemporary folk compositions; prior to 1965, only Ian & Sylvia (who also used Russ

Savakus and Felix Pappalardi on bass) were matching the Fariñas in this regard. Richard Fariña's songs have been covered surprisingly infrequently, although Fairport Convention—another folk-rock act to employ male-female harmonies—did an excellent version of "Reno Nevada" with Richard Thompson on guitar. Recorded for the BBC in 1968, this was not issued until the 1980s; Mimi Fariña, unaware of this cover version when I spoke to her in the summer of 2000, was both surprised and pleased to hear of its existence. She *has* heard Fairport's cover of "The Quiet Joys of Brotherhood"—"that was lovely"—with Sandy Denny on vocals. Indeed, members of Fairport must have been avid fans, since Denny reprised "The Quiet Joys of Brotherhood" on her first solo album, and fellow early Fairporter Ian Matthews covered a few of the Fariñas' songs on his post-Fairport projects.

The Fariñas were certainly an influence on Judy Collins, who writes of Richard in her 1998 autobiography *Singing Lessons*, "I adored Dick. He was the buddy I had never had before, a pal I could tell anything. I needed his friendship." Her friendship with Mimi remained strong after Richard's death, and Collins recorded "Bread and Roses," a melody of Mimi's set to a poem by James Oppenheim, in the mid-1970s. Bread and Roses, of course, was also the name of the organization that Mimi founded, to bring music to those who weren't free or mobile enough to travel to where it's customarily performed.

Her career as half of Richard and Mimi Fariña, in fact, is viewed by many as a footnote or prelude to what turned out to be her true life's work. Although Mimi did continue to perform for a few years after Richard's death, joining the San Francisco satirical theater troupe the Committee, and doing an album with singer-songwriter Tom Jans in the early 1970s, she left the music business—the commercial one, anyway—to focus her efforts on Bread and Roses from the mid-1970s onward. It has not been easy to keep the nonprofit afloat, although it's been the model for more than a dozen similar groups across the country.

She weathered a bout with serious illness, hepatitis C, a few years ago, but is now facing an even greater challenge. While immersed in organizing Bread and Roses' 25th anniversary concert at the end of 1999, Mimi Fariña was diagnosed with cancer. The anniversary concert came off as planned, but she continues to battle for recovery. Our phone interview is limited to twenty minutes, her illness and medical treatments necessitating conservation of her strength.

"I can do about two more questions," she reminds me gently, after the allotted fifteen minutes have passed. I have just enough time to ask her if she finds it surprising that the Richard & Mimi Fariña albums remain in print, still managing to attract new listeners, albeit not in droves.

"I am surprised," she replies. "But I can only say it's because they have some depth to them, some long-term life to the lyrics. And I also think the sound is interesting. It's an interesting, unique sound. And pretty."

Recommended Recordings:

Celebrations for a Grey Day (1965, Vanguard). Evenly split between instrumentals and vocal numbers, this is a tentative but important step toward folk-rock. While the instrumentals, particularly "V." and the title cut, boast nifty guitar-dulcimer duets, it's the songs with words that really make an impact. Foremost among those are the jubilant "Pack Up Your Sorrows," the mournful "The Falcon," and the brooding "Reno Nevada."

Reflections in a Crystal Wind (1965, Vanguard). If only by a thin margin, this is their best album, with an added depth to the arrangements and some of Richard Fariña's finest compositions. The speed-rapped, jagged "Sell-Out Agitation Waltz" is their most effective use of a full rock band; "Bold Marauder" and "Raven Girl" have the sound of ancient odysseys; "Children of Darkness" is their most melodic, fragile love song; and instrumentals such as "Dopico" push their guitar-dulcimer duets into ground that's both exotic and rhythmic.

Memories (1968, Vanguard). Although this was pasted together from leftover studio cuts, two live songs from their 1965 Newport Folk Festival slot, and two Joan Baez tracks (on which the Fariñas don't sing) produced by Richard Fariña, it's hardly inconsequential. "The Quiet Joys of Brotherhood" and "Joy 'Round My Brain" are among their best songs, and "Almond Joy," "Morgan the Pirate," and "Blood Red Roses" aren't too far below that level. It also includes a different, though not necessarily better, version of "Pack Up Your Sorrows" with full rock backing, and Joan Baez's "All the World Has Gone By" is a tantalizing taste of what her Richard Fariña-produced album might have sounded like.

Pack Up Your Sorrows: Best of the Vanguard Years (1999, Vanguard). This is a good, lengthy (seventy-five-minute) "best of," including most of their two 1965 albums. Still, it's not perfect, missing "V." and "One-Way Ticket," and only drawing a couple of tracks from *Memories*. The one previously unreleased song is merely an alternate version of the instrumental "Tuileries."

Fred Neil

It is the lot of some musicians to enjoy greater renown among their peers than among the public. If respect from fellow musicians was the benchmark for fame, Fred Neil should have been a superstar. You've heard his songs, probably via the 1969 Top Ten cover of "Everybody's Talkin'" by Nilsson (also used as the theme for the classic movie *Midnight Cowboy*), or maybe when the Jefferson Airplane did "Other Side of This Life," which was a staple of the band's late 1960s concerts. John Sebastian, David Crosby, and Paul Kantner all speak of Neil's work in reverent tones. He also made his mark upon talented 1960s cult icons such as Tim Buckley, who covered Neil's "Dolphins" and had a similar vocal tone in his lower register.

Yet you probably haven't actually *heard* Fred Neil. Near-classic mid-1960s albums for Elektra and Capitol were not huge sellers, only in part because they were slightly in advance of the singer-songwriter boom and the shift of the popular market from singles to albums. Neil was not simply unsuited to stardom; he seemed indifferent to its very possibility. He shied away from arduous self-promotion and touring, and at the very moment at which the times seemed ripest for his breakout, he virtually stopped recording altogether. Probably he did not stop writing, but—almost uniquely among surviving 1960s musicians of any repute—he has had no interest in recording or performing since the early 1970s, or in talking about his legacy, although he apparently remains alive and in good health. Today there are only elusive rumors and sightings, usually conjuring the image of an itinerant troubadour wandering anonymously, probably in a warm Southern climate, and probably as likely to be spotted watching dolphins as playing guitar. It's as if he has decided to *live* the easygoing indifference to worldly cares and concerns espoused in so many of his compositions, rather than simply sing about it.

Of all the major figures who bridged the coffeehouse folk era and electric rock 'n' roll to pioneer the folk-rock explosion, Neil is the most idiosyncratic. In his acoustic days, he was never a typical folkie, playing his twelve-string guitar with a bluesy force that could echo rock; in his folk-rock period, he was never wholly immersed in electric music, blending acoustic and electric instruments into a seamless whole. Gospel, country, rhythm and blues, and even bits of jazz, pop, and Indian music were all part of his persona as well, but he never sounded like an ill-fitting jumble of puzzle pieces, as so many who try to mix and match styles do. He always sounded like himself. And the crucial asset that made him sound like his own man was that voice, which crooned with such an unhurried ease, especially when it hit the low notes. No white folk-blues singer in the 1960s—no singer period, really—was as skilled at massaging the lower reaches of the vocal register, summoning rich and soulful blue notes from not just the bottom of the soul, but from the bottom of the soles of his feet, so deep within himself did he reach.

The first twenty-five years of Neil's life were as mysterious as the last twenty-five years of his life have been. Even good friends and close professional associates, such as singer-songwriter John Sebastian, know only sketchy details of his early life. As with another cult mainstay of the early 1960s New York folk scene covered in this book, Dino Valenti, Neil seems to have gone through an entirely different musical lifecycle before emerging as a folksinger. Born in 1937, he spent much of his early

The pre-retirement Fred Neil.
Credit: Courtesy Gordon Anderson.

life in the South. Often he traveled with his father, who stocked jukeboxes with discs, probably exposing his son to a remarkably wide breadth of music at an early age.

By the late 1950s he was in New York, working as a songwriter and perhaps as a session musician (he plays the sole electric guitar on a Bobby Darin demo of the hit

"Dream Lover"). There were modest songwriting successes. He placed a tune, "Come Back Baby," with Buddy Holly (cowritten with Holly producer Norman Petty). He cowrote "Candy Man" with Beverly Ross, and the tune became the B-side of Roy Orbison's huge single "Crying," entering the Top Thirty in its own right. The song's easygoing yet cocky, bluesy strut was a sure indicator of Neil's own direction, and Fred would record his own version on a 1965 album.

Between 1957 and 1963, Neil also put out about a half-dozen scarce singles for a variety of major and minor labels, sometimes even attempting to ride the teen idol bandwagon. There was also a corny version of "Long Black Veil," recorded with the Nashville Street Singers, on Capitol in 1963 (which, with its B-side, is the only widely available relic of Neil's pre-mid-1960s work, now appearing on the reissue *The Many Sides of Fred Neil*). On the surface, Neil was nothing more than one of the numerous hopefuls scuffling on the edges of the Brill Building crowd—which included future folk-rock stars like Roger McGuinn of the Byrds, and Paul Simon—with that one fluke hit, "Candy Man," to his credit.

However, there was another Fred Neil that began to make himself known on the Greenwich Village folk circuit in the early 1960s. This Fred Neil was not entirely distanced from the pop and rock scene, but very much in the earthy, acoustic folk-blues bag ascending with the emergence of Bob Dylan, Dino Valenti, and many others. Dylan even once recalled in liner notes for a reissue how, when a virtually unknown Dylan first arrived in New York, Neil "would play mostly the sort of things Josh White would sing. I would play the harmonica for him, and once in a while get to sing for myself."

Neil's own folk recording career, however, was slower than Dylan's in getting off the ground, though he had three tracks on the rare folk compilation *Hootenanny Live at the Bitter End* (on the FM label). Recorded circa 1963 with an unidentified standup bassist accompanying Fred's acoustic guitar, these prove that Neil's rich blues-folk fusion was fully realized well in advance of his first folk recordings for Elektra Records. "That's the Bag I'm In," to be rerecorded in 1966 for his *Fred Neil* album, is introduced (almost certainly incorrectly) as a song learned from Dylan. The other two cuts, "Linin' Track" (with unidentified backup vocalist) and "The Sky Is Falling," were never redone by Neil, and like "That's the Bag I'm In," they blow the tame coffeehouse folk of the other artists on the LP—Len Chandler, Jo Mapes, and Bob Carey—out of the water.

"Fred was a natural linkup of various musical styles," observes John Sebastian, soon to play an important role in Neil's shows as an accompanist on harmonica, and soon after that to became a major folk-rock star as the principal singer-songwriter in the Lovin' Spoonful. "The thing that was so different about Fred was that he had not only a Southern background, but was one of the first guys that was crossing racial boundaries in his style in a sense. This gospel music that he had inherited was very much the gospel music of the black church. Some of his friends, like [black folksingers] Odetta and Len Chandler and some of the black musicians that were our first real close friends, had an affinity with Fred that they didn't have with the New York musicians. 'Cause we had very much of an Eastern background, and it simply didn't include as much of that rich musical heritage."

When Neil finally made his debut album, it was not as a solo artist, but as part of a duo with Vince Martin, another folk veteran who had sung on the Tarriers' pop hit "Cindy Oh Cindy" back in 1956. The rare *Tear Down the Walls* album, issued by Elektra in either 1964 or 1965, was a transitional effort, caught between the hootenanny folk era and the dawn of folk-rock. Including roughly equal measures of folk covers and Neil originals (and one Martin composition), it perhaps inadvertently emphasized that Neil was best as a solo performer, not as a partner or band member. On the vocal duets, Martin's more conventionally bright and higher timbres tended to mask the sensual and earthy qualities of Neil's much lower and bluesier voice. Neil's true character—that of the ambling, good-natured existentialist, best enjoyed in a late-night coffee-and-cigarette frame of mind—surfaced on blues-folk tracks like "Weary Blues" and especially "Wild Child in a World of Trouble," which he sang alone. "Baby," another standout, hinted at the Indian raga tinges that would more strongly inform some of his best later work.

Tear Down the Walls, in hindsight, was most noteworthy for the arrangements. The folk revival dwelled on spartan acoustic presentation, often played by only one performer. Here Neil and Martin were augmented by John Sebastian on harmonica, and multi-instrumentalist Felix Pappalardi (soon to become famous for producing Cream) on guitarron, a Mexican bass. The quasi-band sound was sometimes only a step or two from folk-rock. "Our instruments went well together," remembers Sebastian with pride of his association with Pappalardi. "The harmonica and the guitar could kind of sandwich a folk performer in a very flattering way. [Elektra producer] Paul Rothchild also heard this, and we began to get work as a kind of team that would rock a little harder on something that was basically a folk arrangement."

Neil took a big leap toward folk-rock—and a big leap forward in the quality of his material—with his proper Elektra solo debut, *Bleecker and MacDougal* (1965). Joining Sebastian and Pappalardi in the backup unit were Sebastian's one-time roommate Pete Childs (second guitar and Dobro) and Douglas Hatelid (bass). Only drums, and a greater electric guitar presence, would have been necessary to launch this into bona fide rock territory. In any case, the additional musicians supplied the oomph that Neil's progressively more sophisticated and gutsier compositions demanded.

"The Vince and Fred music was more related to commercial folk music, just by virtue of what you have when you put two singers and two guitarists together," feels Sebastian. "Once Fred was sort of on his own on a record, what would naturally come out would be more of the Southern musical hybrid. Whether he was doing it consciously or not, I can't say.

"He was a 'oh, we'll just feel it and it'll work out' kind of a guy. It was Felix's and my particular lot for those [Elektra] years to get Fred in the studio and nail it down a little bit, actually plan where a solo would be so that the guy would be ready when the solo happened. Peter Childs became another member of this 'keep Fred in line' team. Felix and I were in some degree or another baby-sitting these recordings a little bit to help Paul [Rothchild], who we could see had an enormous job to produce these projects."

The undoubted star of *Bleecker and MacDougal*, however, was Neil, now hitting his stride as a singer and writer. Arguably, no other white folk performer was as skilled at singing the blues—the real blues, not the second-hand stuff—as Fred Neil was. Instead of just aping old recordings or resurrected blues legends working the coffeehouse circuit in the 1960s, he worked out his own blues-rooted style, stretching out phrases with a serene confidence, caressing the low notes as if he was actually making love to them.

It was fortunate that Neil's compositions were often ideal for the languorous, sweet drowsiness of his deep, rich voice. Neil was not the troubadour bent on changing the world or exorcising his personal demons, as many of his competitors in Greenwich Village were. He was more the observer, content to go with the flow and roll with the punches. Sometimes he painted himself as the country boy come to the city and bemused, occasionally overwhelmed, by big-town temptations and confusions, wanting nothing more than to escape to the country, the sea, or the more peaceful recesses of his own mind. Not for Neil the conventional verse-bridge-chorus-laden structures of most popular tunes, despite his experiences at the edges of the New York music industry. The songs were laid out and delivered more as looping, ruminating states-of-consciousness, the mood and the *way* it was played and sung taking precedence over clear or instructive messages.

For a guy who came across as a lazy sod in many of his own lyrics, he certainly seemed to have entered a remarkably prolific and consistent period in 1965. All but one of the tracks on *Bleecker and MacDougal* were written by Neil, and all were at the least good; at the best, they were classic. There was "Blues on the Ceiling," one of his greatest worn-to-the-ground statements of fatalism. When he sang "up to my neck in misery, I'll never get out of these blues alive," it didn't seem to be a pose, even though he sounded more resigned than angry about the situation. "Little Bit of Rain" (covered by Linda Ronstadt on her 1967 debut album, as a member of the Stone Poneys, and also recorded in an unreleased version by top British folk-rock singer Sandy Denny) was a gorgeously drawn-out and tuneful ballad, enhanced by its lovely tremoloed guitar. The title song and "Country Boy" reinforced Neil's image as a man out of his depth in the Big Apple; on "Handful of Gimme," his nonchalance toward everyday responsibilities reached almost comical extremes, with its narrator torn between spending his last cents on a ferry ride or a bag of candy. Other numbers show his facility for swaggering blues, as in the remake of "Candy Man" and "Mississippi Train," which had the hardest electric guitar licks on what is still a largely acoustic album. There was also the soaringly melodic, blissfully unfettered "Other Side of This Life," bound to become his best-known and most-covered composition besides "Everybody's Talkin'."

Although folk-rock had made the jump from idea to reality by 1965, *Bleecker and MacDougal* stopped just short of being an actual folk-rock album, with no drums and spare dabs of electricity. "Whatever we were calling it, it definitely had the qualities of rock 'n' roll," muses Sebastian thirty-five years later. "But the styles were always just this side of rock 'n' roll. He was a great rhythm guitarist, but he had very little inclination to use an electric. I think that was a wise choice, because that twelve-string [had] a certain kind of a propulsion you probably couldn't get out of an electric instrument. He had no objection to anybody playing an electric guitar accompanying him, but there are certainly *both* acoustic and electric guitarists accompanying him in the various recordings, including the [post-Elektra] Capitol stuff."

Although Neil's Elektra records did not sell in huge quantities, his impact on folk and folk-rock performers of the mid-1960s was becoming quite substantial. In the liner notes to the reissue *The Many Sides of Fred Neil*, David Crosby—founder-member of the Byrds, the first (and best) popular folk-rock group—wrote, "I remember thinking how much I wished I had that beautiful deep river of sound coming out of my chest instead of the plaintive little thing I was stuck with...he taught me a sizable chunk of what music was about, and even more about the whys and wherefores of being a musician. He was a hero to me." In those same liner notes, Sebastian cited Stephen Stills and Richie Havens (who covered "That's the Bag I'm In" on his first LP) as others who "learned and borrowed" from Neil.

On a more immediate level, in 1965 Sebastian would become one of the leading folk-rockers as the leader of the Lovin' Spoonful, writing and singing the band's biggest hits. Several of the Lovin' Spoonful's big singles—"Daydream," "Rain on the Roof," and "Did You Ever Have to Make Up Your Mind"—had a lazy, good-natured swing that was certainly similar in mood to some of Neil's writing, without being explicitly derivative of it. Sebastian's also proud to note that one of the Lovin' Spoonful's better album tracks, "Coconut Grove," "was definitely Fred-inspired. My wife and I were staying at his house at the time."

Sebastian's songwriting, he adds, was influenced by "the natural way [Fred] could combine these various styles just by being who he was. It wasn't any kind of an alchemy thing of 'we're gonna pour a little of this, and a little of that.' That was very inspiring. It also was a real lesson in how to let a lyric sound like it just fell out of your mouth, like you hadn't really labored over it. Fred always had that quality about his songs. As a songwriter, at that time [when Sebastian and Neil were playing together], I maybe had written two songs. But I certainly was taking note of how effortless these songs sounded.

"As a matter of fact, in later years, I began to get a little critical about them. And say, 'Jesus Christ, you had this genius two verses, why didn't you write the third verse, for god's sake?' That was the only place that I could actually say I had any influence on Fred. Occasionally I did get up the nerve to say, 'Gee, we're kind of going back to this first verse faster than I really feel like doing it. Couldn't we have another verse, Fred?' That was part of the pincer movement that Felix and I were helping to apply, sort of on Paul Rothchild's behalf."

The Lovin' Spoonful also covered Neil's "The Other Side of This Life," which became a standard of sorts without actually becoming a hit for anyone, as it was covered by star folk-rock/psychedelic groups the Jefferson Airplane and the Youngbloods, as well as Peter, Paul & Mary. In the hands of the musicians in the Airplane—who were doing it in concert as early as 1966—it became a psychedelic improvisation that was a highlight of their concerts, as preserved on their late '60s hit live album *Bless Its Pointed Little Head*. "We explore it all over the place," enthuses Paul Kantner, one of the Airplane's singer-songwriters. "You can go any number of places with it as a basis. It's a beautiful chord lift that goes into the chorus, very unique." Neil also partially inspired Kantner to write the Airplane's "The Ballad of You and Me and Pooneil," which in his words "referred to Freddie and Winnie the Pooh sort of thrown into a Mixmaster on the psychedelic era."

Adds Kantner, "David Crosby actually turned me on to Fred Neil. Freddie was very evocative of a certain soulfulness that was generally lacking in the folk movement. His was deeper than most, came from an unexplained source, and therefore was sort of semimystical to us sort of white-bread middle-class children. Freddie just led us to places that normal folksingers didn't go. His albums became as important to me as the Weavers' albums, who were also part of my prime influence. Between the two of them it set me off on a really good path."

Judy Henske, who like Neil would traverse the folk, jazz, blues, pop, and rock idioms in the 1960s, was one of the first established artists to cover Neil's songs, putting "Little Bit of Rain" and "The Other Side of This Life" on her mid-1960s LP *Little Bit of Sunshine...Little Bit of Rain.* "The thing about Fred Neil's songs is that, remember, these are the old folk days," she says. "People are running around singing things like 'Green Broom'—'I went to the woods to cut broom, green broom.' Now how interesting is that? It was the longest folk song ever written; it, like, lasted twenty minutes. And it was the most *boring* song that was ever written. I used to sing it to punish audiences.

"But if you had a Fred Neil song to sing, you weren't punishing the audience. You were rewarding them for sitting there, because it was an inevitably really great song. When he wrote 'The Other Side of This Life,' it was a very well-considered and musically well-written piece of philosophy. He wrote slow music that was very thoughtful."

The husky-voiced Henske continues, "A big reason why I recorded his stuff is because he is what would pass for, if he was a woman, an alto, which means he was like a very low baritone. So the way his songs were written were for a voice that was very much like mine. Everybody else is always going for a high note, but Fred Neil was always going down. His melodies descended in a very delicate way." Chimes in Cyrus Faryar, who would play guitar on Neil's two studio albums for Capitol, "When you're singing in the lower register, it really is sort of effortless. There's not a lot of apparent physical effort to get between you and what it is you're trying to say. With Freddie, it's like whatever's on his mind, or however he's feeling at the time, is going to come easily out of his body." Along those lines, a little-noted song whose vocal delivery certainly seems Neil-inspired—though the tune was not Neil-composed—was "Never Say No," sung by Elvin Bishop in a lazy, super-low voice on the Butterfield Blues Band's 1966 *East-West* album.

In spite of the high esteem in which he was held by the in-crowd, Neil's idiosyncrasies could make him difficult to work with, and perhaps accounted for his short stint at Elektra. As Paul Rothchild complained in *Follow the Music,* the autobiography/oral history of Elektra Records and its president Jac Holzman, "For my sins I had to produce him. He was a brilliant songwriter and a total scumbag. The forerunner of the unreliable performer, the original rock flake. We'd book recording sessions and he'd show up or not show up. I mean, here's a guy who wrote 'Candy Man,' which Roy Orbison had a hit with, and the day he finished writing it he went to the Brill Building and sold it to about twenty different publishers for fifty bucks each. This is not a nice man. Here's a guy who would go to Izzy Young [who ran the Folk Center in Greenwich Village] and say, 'Izzy, I've got a gig tonight and I don't have a guitar.' Izzy would say, 'Freddie, you owe me for about twenty guitars, but I love you, here's another twelve-string.' And Freddie would go to the club fucked up, he was always fucked up—I've watched this on about ten occasions—couldn't get the guitar in tune, pick it up and smash it to smithereens on the stage. A guitar he didn't own."

On the same page of *Follow the Music*, Arthur Gorson, onetime manager of folksinger Phil Ochs, describes Neil as a "junkie." Holzman, in *MOJO*, volunteered, "Listening to him sing 'Blues on the Ceiling,' you could almost forgive him his irresponsibility as a human being. You don't borrow guitars from people then smash them up or sell them for dope."

Joe Marra, who booked Neil often at his Night Owl club in the Village, puts Neil's peculiarities in a less negative light, noting Fred's perfectionism. "He was very uptight as a performer; he wasn't cut out to be a performer. He could get very critical of himself. If he played a note, and the note was bad, he *knew*. Other musicians, it wouldn't upset so much. I remember once on stage, he said, 'Who's playing the radio?' And I'm looking around the place—where's this guy hearing a goddamn radio? [It was] on the corner, about twenty-five feet away, this guy on the street with a radio."

Cyrus Faryar also remembers Neil's fussiness with twelve-string guitars, which with their two sets of strings are infamous for being difficult to tune. "He would be tuning the guitar to the guitar, but also he would be tuning the guitar to other things. Once he was sitting in a club near Coconut Grove [in Southern Florida], and while he was tuning, an airliner came overhead that was going to land in some major airport some miles away. With his ears, he picked up the sound of this plane, and kind of tuned the plane all the way to the ground."

There is probably a phase of Neil's journey from folk to folk-rock that is lost to us now. In the mid-1960s, he performed live for a while at the Night Owl with the Seven Sons, who included Buzzy Linhart (later a singer-songwriter of some note himself) on vibes. Unfortunately there are no recordings of that lineup, and indeed only one of the Seven Sons on their own, a rare ESP album that is more experimental raga-folk-jazz than rock. Neil's first albums with a full, largely electric band would be recorded in Los Angeles for Capitol, with producer Nik Venet.

On the face of it, Venet was an odd choice for a cult singer-songwriter, as he was best known for his work on early Beach Boys records, as well as for mainstream pop singers like Glen Campbell, the Lettermen, the Four Preps, and Bobby Darin. By the end of the 1960s, however, Venet was getting into some more adventurous sounds, such as the weird Bay Area psychedelic band Mad River, the Stone Poneys (Linda Ronstadt's first group), early country-rockers Hearts & Flowers, and Neil's friend Karen Dalton, a grainy-toned folksinger who made Neil sound slick. Faryar points out that Venet "was a record producer, but his private life was another whole thing. I messed around and did weird things with Nik. Nik said, 'Hey, let's make a gong album.' So we hired all of these five or seven foot gongs, brought them into the studio at Capitol, and spent several hours just whacking the crap out of all these various gongs, recording them for some later magical use." Faryar also says the late Venet would travel to Civil War battle sites and be able to hear, in "clear audio," events like the Battle of Gettysburg.

Venet would not have to reenact the Battle of Gettysburg with Fred Neil. It would be enough to let the singer be himself, and surround him with topflight musicians—including Pete Childs from the Elektra days, Faryar, Jimmy Bond on standup bass, and drummer Billy Mundi (who also played with Tim Buckley, Bob Dylan, and Frank Zappa)—to aid his transition into full-flung electric folk-rock. And with his first album for Capitol, *Fred Neil* (released at the beginning of 1967), Neil nailed it, unleashing one of the greatest folk-rock albums of the 1960s.

"The Dolphins," the album's first track, could have hardly been a better introduction to Neil's newly electric sound, its waves of guitar reverb perfectly matching the shimmering melody and vocals. Drums finally made their first appearance on a Fred Neil record, and the bouzouki runs at the end of the song recalled Indian music, closing the classic with an appropriately exotic touch. The lyrics, too, were among Neil's very best, interspersing musings on the life of dolphins (his enthusiasm for dolphin study is well known) with regrets over ill-fated love, though as with many of his songs, the particulars of the situation are never quite clear.

Fred Neil is best remembered, however, for the original version of "Everybody's Talkin'." Much slower and more simply arranged than the famous cover by Nilsson, it clearly laid out his wishes to escape the madness of contemporary life—the city, perhaps, or the music business?—into a hermetic paradise. (That destination is most likely Southern Florida, where Neil would spend much of his post-1970 life, given the line about going to a place where the sun always shines through rain.) In *Goldmine*, Venet claimed that he was asked to ask Neil to rerecord the song in a faster tempo for *Midnight Cowboy*, but refused to do so.

Much of *Fred Neil* was nearly as strong as its most famous two numbers, however, and extended his lazy, nonplused man-in-the-hammock cheerfulness into some of its most hummable regions. "Ba-De-Da" was another irresistibly catchy statement of dissatisfaction with city life, topped off with some tasty harmonica licks by Canned Heat's Al Wilson. It and "Faretheewell" were showcases for Neil's knack for insinuating moan-hummed vocals. "That's the Bag I'm In" was fatalistic even by Neil's own tough standards, with a narrator who can't even be bothered to make his own breakfast over again after fouling it up. "He wrote that song to get an advance," claims Joe Marra. "He was going up to his publisher uptown in a cab, and he wrote that, just like that. Handed it in, got an advance of I think a couple hundred dollars."

The relaxed, even intoxicated atmosphere of the record, thinks Faryar, grew out of a similar ambience in the studio. "The sessions were very low-key, not heavily produced. Nik's ability was to make a comfortable situation and not interject a whole 'hey, we're paying for studio time' kind of thing. It was a matter of getting people together who would have an affinity for each other musically, who would have no personal or professional hang-ups in the way, to have a good time. Freddie would run a song down, people would find a place to sit in the music, and it was very relaxed. It was a situation of everybody getting musically comfortable, finding a nice groove, and then playing the song. And the song was in complete support of Freddie and his voice."

"The amplified instruments were mixed right in with the acoustic wash," adds John Forsha, another guitarist on the sessions. "Even when we got 'funky,' there was never a feeling in the studio of heavy electricity. Our amp volumes were way down. There was no heavy edge to anything in the room. You had a feeling, often, that there was a little too much guitar, when you get me and Cyrus and Pete and Freddie going all at once. Nik never really stepped in and said, 'Don't do that.' He got what he wanted. The results were quite tidy, and we hadn't a clue how he was going to arrive at that." Forsha also singles out Al Wilson's harmonica on "Ba-De-Da" for special praise: "He underplayed it beautifully."

Fred Neil was another album destined more for the rock elite than for the general public. Larry Beckett, close friend and frequent songwriting collaborator with singer-songwriter Tim Buckley, remembers visiting the sessions and watching "a huge room in darkness. Way off there, with just a tiny light, was Fred, Cyrus Faryar, and the rest of the guys doing a version of 'The Dolphins' completely unlike what wound up on the album. Then he would stop and change it and do something again, reconceive it. The sense of Fred's magnificent voice and total authenticity and commitment to creativity…you know, if Tim didn't have it already, he got it that afternoon." Buckley would record excellent live and studio versions of "The Dolphins," and also paraphrase a few of its lyrics on his composition "Once I Was," on Buckley's 1967 album *Goodbye and Hello*.

Adds Beckett, "The album *Fred Neil*, [Buckley] and I and all of our friends think of as one of the four or five albums of the '60s. I don't care what-all lists or sales charts anybody wants to throw up. To me, it's like the *Kind of Blue* of the '60s. [Miles Davis' classic jazz album] *Kind of Blue* is a disc you can listen to over and over, you never get tired of it, it's eternally fresh. And so is that *Fred Neil* album."

The final song on *Fred Neil*, "Cynicrustpetefredjohnraga," was a total departure from the rest of the record, offering raga-folk-rock from multiple guitars and chugging harmonica that rambled for eight minutes before finally exhausting itself. It was also a signpost to the kind of music that would dominate his next LP, *Sessions*, recorded in October 1967. Even if many of Neil's songs were vague and hazy, to this point they had also been concisely structured, executed, and recorded. Yet *Sessions*, as the title implies, consisted mostly of songs that sounded like live-in-the-studio jams. Indeed all seven tunes were marked by a take number, not just a song title, and the impression was that of musicians feeling their way around tunes in rehearsal, rather than running through finely honed arrangements. Despite some impressive passages, it was a puzzling move given Neil's strongest assets—melodic, hummable songs—and a disappointment on the heels of *Fred Neil*.

There were a couple of relatively succinct cuts on *Sessions*: "Felicity," which Sebastian has said (in *Goldmine*) was inspired by English folksinger Felicity Johnson, was among Neil's most attractive melancholy tunes, and his cover of Percy Mayfield's "Please Send Me Someone to Love" has such deep singing that you suspect your turntable of running at the wrong speed. The other five tracks, however, were drawn-out five-minute-plus exercises that often descended into heavily reverbed guitar and raga doodling. Certainly there were a lot of first class guitarists pitching in, as Faryar, Peter Childs, Eric Hord, and Bruce Langhorne (who had played on some of Bob Dylan's first folk-rock recordings) all contributed to the record. Neil's buoyant nature seemed to have taken a more lethargic and sometimes downcast tone, most pungently on "Look Over Yonder," where he asks his mother if she isn't sorry to have him as his son.

One suspects *Sessions* could have benefited mightily from some editing, as the singing was consistently fine and interesting melodic and lyrical ideas did bob up and down in the mix, like submarines coming up for air. On the other hand, it's just possible that what we hear on *Sessions* is actually more organized than much of what went down during these half-jams. Some Capitol outtakes from the period make *Sessions* sound positively disciplined in comparison, as Neil and his buddies endlessly attempted to get to grips with standards like "Brother Can You Spare a Dime," "Trouble in Mind," "It Ain't Necessarily So," "Riot in Cell Block #9," and "Will the Circle Be Unbroken."

"In the first album," speculates Faryar, "Freddie was an established artist for a long time, and had a lot of songs that were well-worn, well-received, and waiting to be captured and recorded. And that was what took place. In the second series of sessions, they were kind of like, 'We've got an album to make, we need to come up with material.' Having already used established material that was well known and well developed, there was a need to kind of fill up the time with looser, more like…'let's see if we can invent it as it happens.'"

Venet defended the album passionately in *Goldmine*, rationalizing that "in this case it was keeping everything out of the way of the music. I kept two machines running so I would never run out of tape, they would overlap each other…everything you hear on the album is as it happened in the studio. A couple of days after recording the album, I started handing out acetates. I ran into David Crosby at the Troubadour and he just reamed me. He thought it was embarrassing what I'd done, doing things in one take, and he was just so pissed off about the way the album turned out. I drove home that night and I was really starting to doubt my ability with what the hell I was doing.

"About a month later, I ran into David again and he apologized and he said that it was probably the most honest thing that he'd ever heard in his entire life. He didn't know how to handle it initially because he was in a group doing tracking and overdubbing and all that shit. I think he was still with the Byrds at the time and I think that after that David started getting absolutely honest with everything he did."

Counters Sebastian, "I hate to be the only naysayer here, but I've always felt like the Capitol recordings were a real letdown, a real 'oh, let's just give up and let Fred have his head and underachieve.' That Capitol material really didn't have that tautness created by having Pappalardi and I bugging the hell out of him about these arrangements and things. I think it was inferior to the Elektra body of work, simply because it did not have the effort. Venet, when he writes about Fred and those sessions, makes it sound like this was a real accomplishment to kind of let Fred have his way. But in fact, I thought it was a lazy man's approach."

The late 1960s should have been a time when Neil found his market, as album-oriented singer-songwriters such as Leonard Cohen, Laura Nyro, and Joni Mitchell really began to take off. Instead, *Sessions*—recorded when he was only thirty—turned out to be his last complete studio album. His third and final Capitol release, *Other Side of This Life*, was a contractual obligation throwaway, the first side of the LP comprising a live acoustic set in a Woodstock club with Monte Dunn on second guitar, the flip side devoted to a ragtag batch of outtakes. It was fairly enjoyable on its own merits, including as it did live versions of several of his best songs, and studio leftovers featuring appearances by jazz pianist Les McCann on "Come Back Baby" and Gram Parsons (on vocals and piano) on the cover of William Bell's country-soul classic "Ya Don't Miss Your Water." Venet had wanted to make a live album assembled from concerts throughout the United States, using several different musicians; he was disappointed by the aborted concept. He also claimed in *Goldmine* that subpar takes were used for some of the studio cuts on the LP, and that a vocal duet with Johnny Cash went unused.

Since *Other Side of This Life*, not a peep has been heard from Neil on record. Onetime Neil manager Howard Solomon (whom the irascible singer can be heard telling to shut up during the live part of *Other Side of This Life*) told *Goldmine* that Fred did sessions for a Columbia album in 1973. These were unfinished, although according to Solomon, they contain "some of the greatest songs I've ever heard, with Fred playing twelve-string, an acoustic piano player and [bassist] Harvey Brooks."

Michael Lang, a veteran manager most famous for coproducing the Woodstock festival in 1969, clarifies: "I made a deal for Freddie with CBS, and he hadn't really written in a long time. Fred was gonna write, and didn't really ever get around to writing. So we put a little group together, Harvey Brooks and a bunch of other people, and got a few tunes from some other people. But Fred never really wrote for the album, which is why the album never really got recorded. There were some tracks started in the studio, only sort of minimally and very few, and nothing was ever finished.

"We did take this troupe to Montreaux, and recorded a live tape there. Some of the classics were on that tape. It wasn't a set of new material; we didn't have enough for a set. We had maybe three or four songs that he had worked up with the band, which were nice, but nothing extraordinary. It was great to get Fred out and performing a little bit, and the trip was great. But Fred just never really had the motivation or the focus, at that point in his life, to sit down and spur himself to write. It's a shame, because I think there's still a lot of poetry in him."

Neil was simply uninterested in performing and recording from the 1970s onward, apparently hiding away in Coconut Grove in Southern Florida. And there, or somewhere, he's stayed, emerging only for some benefit concerts for his beloved dolphins and whales in 1976 and 1977, and some rare unannounced, low-key public gigs. (In fact Neil cofounded the Dolphin Project, an organization dedicated to stopping the capture, exploitation, and trafficking of dolphins around the globe.) Although noted indie rock musician Ben Vaughn attempted to contact Neil and offer him an opportunity to make an album in the early 1990s for the Nonesuch Explorer series, Neil politely declined. He was moved by Vaughn's letter, he told him, but didn't want to record, and recommended that Karen Dalton (who died shortly afterward) be recorded instead. The royalties continue to get generated by cover versions of "Other Side of This Life" and especially "Everybody's Talkin'," the Nilsson version of which is still in heavy oldies radio rotation, and which has also been covered by Neil Diamond and Willie Nelson.

Even close musical associates of Neil's in the 1960s, such as Sebastian and Faryar, have little idea of what exactly he is up to now. Paul Kantner speculates, "As I understand it, he was pretty abused by the harshness of the music business. I think he's a pretty gentle soul, and the music business just walks right over you. If you're not in the mood to take it, the thing to do is just to retreat to Coconut Grove and lay back. I think he's still in that mode." Surprisingly, Neil did make a public statement of sorts in the April 2000 issue of *MOJO*, writing a letter to the editor explaining the Dolphin Project, confirming that he had traveled to Havana, Cuba, with that organization to establish a Dolphin Watch.

"He's a very mysterious guy," says Joe Marra. "Once in a while I get a letter from him. But he doesn't want people to know where he's living. He wants to be tranquil and do what he wants. He really don't want to be bothered by a lot of people.

"He's not extravagant. I picture him with his guitar, the twelve-speed bicycle in a corner of a room somewhere, maybe some motel, somewhere where it's warm. He doesn't need a fancy car, fancy house, or a servant. He's content." The music may have continued to flow, in private, but it seems likely that the public at large has heard the last of Fred Neil, the most peculiar of the folk-rock forefathers.

Recommended Recordings:

Tear Down the Walls (1964 or 1965, Elektra). Recorded by the duo of Neil and Vince Martin, this wouldn't be the set you'd play as a sampling of, or introduction to, Fred's music. It's more something to pick up if you've developed a substantial interest in Neil, and want insight into the roots of his style. Much of this is in far more of a standard folk revival setup than Neil's solo recordings, and his world-weary blues-folk persona only peeks out occasionally, particularly on his solo vocal "Wild Child in a World of Trouble." Still, some of the folk covers are given decent readings by the pair ("Morning Dew," "I Know You Rider," "Dade County Jail"), and "Baby" hints at the slight Indian influence that would flower on some of his Capitol tracks. It's been long out of print in the U.S., but reissued on CD in Japan.

Bleecker and MacDougal (1965, Elektra). Backed by John Sebastian, Felix Pappalardi, and others on his debut solo album, Neil delivers a fine set of almost-folk-rock, steeped in folk, pop, and the blues. "Other Side of This Life" and "Little Bit of Rain" would have to be at the top of any list of Neil classics, and "Candy Man," "Blues on the Ceiling," and the title song aren't far behind. Like *Tear Down the Walls*, this is only available as a Japanese CD.

The Many Sides of Fred Neil (1998, Collectors' Choice Music). The ultimate document of his Capitol years, this two-CD set includes all three of his Capitol albums— *Fred Neil*, *Sessions*, and *Other Side of This Life*—as well as half a dozen previously unreleased outtakes (highlighted by his cover of John Braheny's "December's Dream") and his 1963 single with the Nashville Street Singers. The liner notes are by the author of this book.

Tim Buckley in the 1960s.
Credit: Courtesy of the Frank Driggs Collection/Chansley Entertainment Archives.

Tim Buckley

Between 1966 and 1970, Tim Buckley did not just devour as much stylistic ground as any cult rock artist of his time. He arguably ventured into as many areas, with as much success, as any rock musician of any era did within such a short period of years, and at such a young age. Depending on which album—or even song— brought Buckley to your ears first, you could be excused for pegging him as a folk-rocker, a psychedelic singer-songwriter, a languid jazz singer, a blue-eyed soul man, or an avant-garde interpreter of inaccessible art songs, hell-bent on both challenging and alienating his audience.

Such eclecticism could not have been pulled off without the pipes to back it up, and Buckley was blessed with the most versatile voice of his generation. His was not so much a voice as an instrument, its four-octave range encompassing low, bluesy growls, honey-toned jazz tenor crooning, and twisting upper-register shrieks that could inspire both fright and delight. He was also a composer of melodies both gorgeous and ambitious, and frequently supported by a lyricist, also his best friend, whose words matched Buckley's melodies in both class and adventurousness. He had movie star looks, and some of the best and most sympathetic backup musicians available live and in the studio. He recorded for a couple of the most musically progressive labels of the era—labels which were among those most willing to grant their acts artistic freedom.

Yet only one of his albums even made the lower reaches of the Top 100. By the early 1970s Buckley was unable to keep pushing his music over new boundaries, having exhausted the support of his label, management, and to some degree listeners with his experiments. There would be a few more albums and tours in a more standard Los Angeles rock and funk slipstream, but much of his fire seemed to have been doused. His death from a heroin overdose in 1975, at the age of twenty-eight, was nonetheless a tragedy, as a healthy Buckley no doubt had much left to give.

In the ensuing quarter century, much has been made of the demons and psychological confusion that probably spurred much of his best work, and probably also contributed to his premature death. His failure to reach a mass audience, however, was not solely due to erratic behavior, mistimed record releases, and demise by misadventure. Buckley's music was of the sort that takes a while to be digested, and decades, perhaps, to be fully comprehended and appreciated, even by listeners who heard the records the first time around. Buckley could not build a constituency, at least in part, because of the very restlessness that fascinates us today, abandoning one mindset for another just as he was on the verge of establishing himself as a master of a certain bag.

Buckley is most often categorized as a folk-rock singer-songwriter, and while he excelled at that style, to pigeonhole him into any genre is to deny the extraordinary breadth of idioms and artists he embraced before he even started recording. As a teenager growing up in Orange County, he played folk music and country, and, with the Bohemians, rock. His early repertoire encompassed folkie favorites by way of Leadbelly, Pete Seeger, Odetta, and Joan Baez, but also Frank Sinatra's "One for My Baby," Johnny Cash's "Big River," Ray Charles' "Drifting Blues," and contemporary compositions by emerging folk-rock singer-songwriters such as Fred Neil, Donovan, Tim Hardin, and Bob Dylan (whose unreleased "Quit Your Low Down Ways" Buckley probably learned from a printed version in *Sing Out!* magazine). "He was totally eclectic, totally accepting of every kind of music," says Larry Beckett, Buckley's close friend and frequent songwriting partner. "He had no aesthetic devotion or fixation on rock 'n' roll, folk music, folk-rock, or anything like that."

Beckett would play drums in the Bohemians, formed in the mid-1960s, which also included bassist Jim Fielder (later to join several other groups, most notably Blood, Sweat & Tears) and guitarist Brian Hartzler. Neither Buckley nor Beckett were composing songs at the outset, although Beckett was already writing poetry. However, with the Beatles and Dylan as inspiration, notes Larry, "We were growing really, really fast together as songwriters and went from these kind of cheapish pop ballads to rather poetic expression." As Beckett readily admits, it was Tim's beautiful, supple tenor voice that was the attraction at this point, not the material. "We would be writing our weak pop songs, he would stand up and start singing them, and everybody would go 'oh my god!' The same thing they said when he was singing folk songs by himself, solo acoustic. It was the sound of his voice. It certainly, at that stage, wasn't my lyrics at all."

It was also, most likely, Tim's voice that got the attention of Mothers of Invention drummer Jimmy Carl Black, who put them in touch with the Mothers' manager, Herbie Cohen. As manager of Fred Neil, Judy Henske, and the Modern Folk Quartet, Cohen was well aware of the excitement stirring as singer-songwriters made the unexpected transition to electric music in the mid-1960s, taking the air out of the acoustic hootenanny folk scene and funneling it into folk-rock within a matter of months. A Bohemians demo—often reported as six songs, though Beckett remembers there being only four—caught the ear of Elektra Records president Jac Holzman. Although according to Beckett only one of those demos ("She Is") was rerecorded for Buckley's first album, Holzman, in an Elektra press release, purported to be immediately enamored with the singer:

"Herb called to tell me that he had a new artist, that he thought we were the best label for that artist, and that he was sending us, and no one else, a demo disc with about six songs on it. I didn't have to play the demo more than once, but I think I must have listened to it at least twice a day for a week…whenever anything was bringing me down, I'd run for the Buckley; it was restorative. I asked Herb to arrange a meeting, but I had my mind made up already. We spent a late afternoon together, and my belief in Tim was more than confirmed. I explained to Tim that Elektra was growing in a creative direction at that time, and that he was exactly the kind of artist with whom we wanted to grow—young and in the process of developing, extraordinarily and uniquely gifted, and so 'untyped' that there existed no formula or pattern to which anyone would be committed. Tim understood that we understood, and he knew we wanted him for the right reasons."

Elektra had the soundest judgment and most progressive vision of any rock and folk independent label in the U.S. in 1966, with a roster including Love, Paul Butterfield, Judy Collins, Phil Ochs, and (by the end of the year) the Doors. It and Buckley were a good match. Before recording began, however, some changes had to be made, most crucially the dissolution of the Bohemians and the launch of Buckley as a solo artist. "[Herbie Cohen] put it to us that, in that year, bands were not the coming thing, but that single artists were," recalls Beckett without remorse. "But I think this was just something he said to let us off easy. Tim was clearly about ten times more talented at what he did than what any of us were at what we did, so it wasn't unfair." Fielder did play bass on the first two albums (Hartzler also played some guitar on these), and Beckett continued to write with Buckley and provide input at the sessions. Buckley would in any case regularly vary his accompanists onstage and in the studio throughout his career.

Tim Buckley, released in late 1966, has sometimes been undervalued by critics as an underdeveloped, twee period folk-rock piece. While there was a tentative feel to the proceedings that suggested untapped potential—Buckley was, after all, still only nineteen years old—it was nevertheless a beautiful record, overflowing with enchanting melodies that transcended the usual folk and blues progressions into a more baroque realm. That baroque quality was enhanced by the crystalline, multitextured production typical of 1960s Elektra rock albums, overseen by Paul Rothchild, who took the production reins on several of Elektra's finest releases (including most of the Doors' records), and Jac Holzman himself. Jack Nitzsche, famous for his arrangements on Phil Spector sessions, did the string arrangements; cult singer-songwriter Van Dyke Parks added harpsichord, piano, and celeste; and Lee Underwood, probably the most sympathetic of all the backup musicians Buckley would employ over the next few years, contributed glistening, liquid lead guitar lines. Both the structures and settings echoed jazz and classical music, even as folk and rock formed most of the foundation. The spookily reverbed guitars of "Song of the Magician" and "Song Slowly Song" hinted at a quasi-psychedelic mystery; the varispeed tempos of "Strange Street Affair Under Blue" at a carnivalesque atmosphere; and more standard compositions like "Song for Jainie" were almost mainstream tuneful folk-rock.

Buckley's voice did not explore as many timbres, or utilize the lower register as much, as it would within a few years. Yet his tenor exuded tenderness, intensity, and emotional fragility, achieving its greatest beauty at its highest arc, as in the closing notes to "Aren't You the Girl." The five tracks that Buckley wrote alone were delicate, occasionally precious romantic songs. Those in which Beckett supplied the lyrics were more obtuse and poetic, suggestive more of impressionistic and, yes, psychedelic states of mind, without entirely losing the romance. Only the routine bluesrocker "Understand Your Man"—improvised in the studio, according to Beckett, when one more track was needed to wrap the recording up—sounded like a concession to standard rock sounds of the era. Beckett, still a poet, writer, and lyricist today in Portland, Oregon, observes that his lyrics "are more literary, and use more literary devices. [Tim's] persisted in being personal sort of surrealistic statements of his own love life. It forms a nice balance, actually, when we have albums with both of our things on it."

Although *Tim Buckley* did not make the charts, it garnered good word-of-mouth and reviews among the burgeoning underground. For his second album, Buckley would work with producer Jerry Yester, and it may be that Elektra had more commercial designs for Buckley's product than the LP could fulfill. "Elektra was kind of auditioning me as a producer, and wanting to see where Tim was going after his [first] album," remembers Yester. "So we did two singles, and they were a lot more rock and roll; they were gonna go for a hit single kind of thing. There was a song called 'Once Upon a Time,' and one called 'Lady Give Me Your Key.' I always had kind of a fondness for both of those, and [Buckley and Beckett's] attitude about that was, 'Well, OK, we're consciously going to sell out and make a hit record.' Then Elektra heard those and said, 'OK, we believe you, let's just go out and do the album, forget those two songs. We want you to go on and do the more serious material.' We got into the album in earnest after that."

Although Beckett thinks the single was recorded after the second album, he does remember how Elektra "wanted a single" around this time. "The A-side was 'Once Upon a Time,' the B-side was 'Lady Give Me Your Key'; 'key' was slang for a certain amount of marijuana in those days. They said, 'Can you guys write a single?' As always, we said yeah. Then Tim and I went to my apartment in Venice, and listened to rock 'n' roll FM radio for like twenty-four hours straight. We decided that most pop songs were like little fairytales, really. So if we wanted to write a good single, it should be a fairytale.

"Then I wrote the words; I think he actually helped a little bit with the lyrics [with] 'Once Upon a Time.' We thought, 'OK, now that's your Top Forty stuff. But what about the stuff that everybody actually listens to, the hip people? Well, what they really like are songs that use images that could refer to sex, or drugs, but actually can't be banned because they're metaphorical. So couldn't we write a song that was along those lines? As the B-side, sort of the FM side of the single?' That resulted in 'Lady Give Me Your Key.' Both of 'em are sort of parodies, almost, of mid-'60s procedures in songwriting. 'Once Upon a Time' includ[ed] a Beatlesque freak-out section in the instrumental part with all kinds of weird overdubs. It sounded stupid when it was all done.

"On the other hand, 'Lady Give Me Your Key,' although it started out as this exercise in mimicking '60s songwriting maneuvers, turned—both in my writing and Tim's writing and singing—into this really beautiful, incredibly haunting poetic piece. One of the best things we ever did, as a matter of fact. It had this sort of damned beginning, but a glorious end. And of course, Elektra listened to both of them and said, 'Nah! Never mind. Not going to put out a single.'"

The tracks remained unreleased, and may not have been appropriate for the second album, *Goodbye and Hello*. As was the case with most of Buckley's albums, it would be much different in tone and style than the one that came before it. Beckett and Buckley were taking more risks as composers. The words could address the day's burning social issues or be structured almost as highbrow romantic poems. The melodies were shorn of much of the folk-rock that lingered on the debut album, delving deeper into jazz-classical forms and sometimes approaching the art song territory in their construction.

As for the production, notes Yester, "I was interested in working around what Tim was doing with his guitar, and not fitting him to a band, but fitting whatever else was on the record to *him*. The variety of the songs that he and Larry had was so great that it just called for a variety of accompaniment. Each song had a different thing going for it." The arrangements were thus considerably more elaborate and, to a degree, psychedelic than those on *Tim Buckley*, with several guitarists and a wider scope of percussion with the addition of Carter C. C. Collins' congas and former Kingston Trio member Dave Guard's kalimba. Don Randi and Yester himself played various keyboards, including harpsichord, harmonium, and organ.

Buckley must have been satisfied with the results, as he told *ZigZag* magazine several years later, "He did what a producer is supposed to do—not get in the way of the song, and the artist's feeling for it." John Forsha, one of the guitarists on *Goodbye and Hello*, adds that "Tim would ask you to stretch, and that was fun. On 'Pleasant Street,' I play electric rhythm chicks, acoustic rhythm, and electric lead at various moments. Tim would have ideas, and we had time to play with them, too. If you've done a lot of studio work, most of the time the clock is king, and you're looking over your shoulder. These dates were not like that. Whether they went horribly over budget, I don't really know. I imagine it was higher than it could have been, but I think the products are certainly worth the time."

Goodbye and Hello's more serious mood was evident from the very first bar of the first track: the atomic bomb explosion that opened "No Man Can Stop the War," sung with mournful sadness by Buckley (and concluding with another atomic blast, this time backwards). Explains Beckett, "The whole country was obsessed [with Vietnam], especially our idealistic generation, that was really honestly against war, and then [had] it thrust on us. The imagery has a kind of quick-cut quality, like you would see on network TV portrayals of the war. My idea behind it was that everybody always thinks, when they're in a war—even now!—are we going to beat Belgrade down or not? But that's not the *real* war. The real war is, where does this stuff come from? Where do these people come from that can treat other people so? That's the real war, inside, that nobody even *addresses*. They never talk about it on the network news. All they talk about is how many people were killed on each side, and those numbers are usually falsified anyway. It was part of my frustration that now, and back then, people are 'end the war and cure the symptom,' and the disease flourishes."

On "Hallucinations," there was an almost Eastern-African fusion quality with the eerily echoing percussion and doleful tune, amplified by the melancholy lyric of a girl, and a love, vanishing as inexplicably as a dream recedes from memory. "Every single song that we ever wrote together, I wrote the words first, except for 'Hallucinations,'" says Beckett. "[Tim] had the world's weirdest, shittiest record collection. He would pick things up, listen to them, and just give them to somebody else. It was always astonishing to me that somebody that was in music could be so little an archivist. One record I saw him with at some party was, like, this Moroccan street music. He was saying, 'Oh yeah, it's really fantastic.' He went away, listened to this album, and then came back like three days later and played me the melody of 'Hallucinations.' I could not believe my *ears*! I wrote words to that about a real-life love affair that I had had for the last two years. If you listen to 'Political World' on Dylan's *Oh Mercy*, listen to the first thirty seconds of that, and then listen to the first thirty seconds of 'Hallucinations.' And tell me if *Bob* doesn't listen to Tim. It's the same thing!"

Few of the tracks were love songs (and indeed even the love songs weren't too straightforward), and the lyrics were filled with both specific images and elusive poetry that were far more evocative, if sometimes overreaching, than even most psychedelic rock of 1967. There were the distraught singer and juggling clown of the hurdy-gurdy "Carnival Song"; the extended romantic opus "I Never Asked to Be Your Mountain" (which simultaneously seems to be lamenting a failed affair and declaring a need for independence); and the elegiac "Morning Glory," with its dialogue between the narrator and a hobo who cannot seem to measure up to the singer's expectations. (Under the title "Hobo," Linda Ronstadt recorded this twice, first in the late 1960s as a member of the Stone Poneys, and then in the mid-1970s as a solo artist.) "Once I Was," which would be used for the soundtrack in the closing scenes of the popular Vietnam vet movie *Coming Home* in the late 1970s, illustrates Buckley's growing use of the bluesy lower register. It also reveals his debt to folk-rock songwriter Fred Neil, with a chorus that almost quotes a couple of lines from Neil's

"Dolphins" verbatim. Overall there is a kaleidoscopic vibe to the songs and arrangements that reflects both the best and most nightmarish qualities of dreams.

Nowhere were more chances taken than on the eight-minute title cut, with its cowed dungeon dwellers, vaudeville generals, king, queen, and magician tromping, sometimes violently, through a contemporary jumble of highways, billboards, and broken marriages. This seeming indictment of the madness of the straight world is alternated with more optimistic, placid lyrics, mirroring the struggle between the Establishment and the counterculture in the late 1960s. Although envisioned by Beckett as a piece in which two voices would sing different lyrics (parts of which are even laid out in different columns on the album cover) and counterpoint melodies, Buckley ended up just alternating lines from the two sets of prose. In tandem with the track's ornate orchestration, it had more in common with the European art-theatrical creations of composers such as Jacques Brel than it did with rock.

It, and the album as a whole, might not have been what Elektra had in mind at the outset, but as Beckett points out, "Elektra was really good about that. All aesthetic control was handed over to the artist, which was kind of rare in those days." Not that their enthusiasm was unflagging. As Yester recalls, as the track "Goodbye and Hello" was being prepared, "Jac Holzman called up as I was going over the score with the orchestra and said, 'So, I hear you have an orchestra. If there's any way I can cancel that session, I would.' I went, 'Jesus, Jac.' He says, 'Why didn't you call me?' I said, 'Well, it just happened kind of fast, I didn't think I needed to call you.' 'Well…if I could cancel it, I would.' Then he slammed the phone down. The next time I saw him was when we were mixing it, and he said, 'This is the greatest piece I've ever heard,' just giving me all kinds of praise."

There would be great Buckley music in years to come, but *Goodbye and Hello* is his most fully realized and effective album. It also strikes the best balance between the melodic folk-rock that was the bedrock of his finest work, and his hunger for experimentation with genre-blending, songwriting, and production. It also fit fairly well into the psychedelic climate of 1967, and while it wasn't a big hit, reaching number 171 in *Billboard*, it sold better than its predecessor and seemed a good stepping-stone to a bigger audience. It did not, however, represent a groove he wanted to stick to or repeat with some variation.

There are indications that between his second or third album he was searching, and perhaps struggling, for new sounds and ideas. A *Hit Parader* article reported that two weeks of sessions in New York went unused in early 1968. Four songs from these, featuring just Buckley, Underwood, and an unknown acoustic bassist (probably Jimmy Bond), did surface on the 1999 release *Works in Progress*, including the lovely "Danang" and a sparse version of "Song to the Siren" (which would be rerecorded for the 1970 album *Starsailor*). *Works in Progress* also has tracks from the summer of '68, including alternate versions of some songs that would end up on the third LP and the subsequent *Blue Afternoon*, as well as covers of outside material like the folk standard "Wayfaring Stranger" and "Hi Lily, Hi Lo."

Beckett adds that these were not the only unreleased tapes from the early years that show Buckley playing around with different formats. Shortly after Buckley was signed to Elektra, Herb Cohen arranged for Buckley to record a wealth of tunes, with just Tim's own acoustic guitar and Jim Fielder's acoustic bass as backup. "Herb's instructions were, 'Sing every single song you guys have written.' [Tim] did magnificent performances. Much of that material is as good as anything that he or I ever did since, and easily as good as anything on the first two albums. Also, it has a more timeless quality in that it's just acoustic guitar and bass, so it doesn't have that sort of antiquated arrangement sound that things get."

Happy Sad was in a sense scaling back toward a more basic sound, using only four other musicians and less painstaking multiple takes and overdubs, but there were other momentous changes as well. First there was the suspension (temporarily, as it turned out) of the Beckett-Buckley songwriting partnership. Beckett was about to be drafted into the army anyway (and discharged a year later as unsuitable). He thinks his absence might have cost him and Tim an opportunity to write the theme song for *Midnight Cowboy*, which Herbie Cohen was pushing for (Nilsson ended up singing Fred Neil's "Everybody Talkin'" for the film, landing a huge hit).

Larry postulates that Tim thought that the "rather startling success of *Goodbye and Hello*, and in fact maybe his entire career, was perhaps due to my lyrics. Which was something that he never expressed to me, and is in retrospect ludicrous. But knowing Tim and the depth of the self-doubt into which he could fall, totally believable. He decided that he would try to do an album all on his own, just to see if it was his magic." Just as crucially, Buckley swung his sound from folk-rock to small combo folk-jazz. While Lee Underwood's guitar was present on *Happy Sad*, and Carter C. C. Collins remained on the congas, the quintet was filled out by Juilliard graduate David Friedman on vibes, and standup bassist John Miller.

Although *Happy Sad* was a substantial departure from *Goodbye and Hello*, it was accessible enough that it did not alienate the fans Buckley had picked up via his initial two LPs. Buckley was now favoring elastic jazzy grooves—all but one of the six tracks were longer than five minutes, and a couple passed the ten-minute mark. While there was still a dreamlike quality to the songs, it was more like the dreams one has while dozing in and out of sleep on a quiet beach, rather than the hurly-burly march of imagery on *Goodbye and Hello*. The shift toward lower register crooning hinted at on "Once I Was" was in full gear for much of the set, although he could still uncork piercing high notes (in fact male rock vocalists rarely get above the notes he reaches on parts of "Gypsy Woman"). "Strange Feelin'," built around a 3/4 blues riff altered from "All Blues" on Miles Davis' classic *Kind of Blue*, was evidence of an interest in Davis' aesthetic that would expand as the decade wound to a close.

The album did raise itself out of its languor on the exhilarating "Gypsy Woman," with its nervous funky guitar strums and Carter C. C. Collins' propulsive congas building into a frenzy. The beautiful concluding number, "Sing a Song for You," was the only song that could have possibly fit onto his previous recordings, with its simple acoustic guitar-dominated arrangement. On "Dream Letter," Underwood devised an approach to the guitar in which he used fingers from both hands on the fretboard to play chords and melodies at the same time; he would continue to use it on the subsequent Buckley albums *Lorca* and *Starsailor*.

Despite the pleasant buzz of the music, *Happy Sad* is not a pleasant memory for Jerry Yester, who produced it with Zal Yanovsky (whom Yester had replaced in the Lovin' Spoonful). "I got along fine with Tim, but his band was really hard to get along with. We just didn't really have that much to do, except supervise the recording. They had this 'we're better than you guys' kind of attitude, they just kind of pissed me off right from the beginning. If the session ended a minute after the clock …it was like, 'we gotta get double-scale,' and I was kind of looking out for Tim and saying, 'Do you think that's right?'" Yester also was not in sync with the band's feeling that the song should get captured on the first take. "That was fine with me if we got it on the first one. Sometimes, when you're working with a five-piece band in a room with a live singer, there can sometimes be problems, especially on the first take, and especially if they don't want to run it down very much first."

One bit of production trickery was necessary to rescue a take, and actually ended up enhancing the mood of "Love from Room 109 at the Islander (On Pacific Coast Highway)," with its underlying bed of ocean waves crashing onto the beach. It was accidentally recorded with Dolbys in "play" (instead of the proper "record") position, which generated a lot of hiss. Yester: "I said, 'We had a problem on that one, can you guys do it again?' The band is like shitting all over themselves. Tim came in"—he can't stop himself from laughing—"and he had a flying temper tantrum. His voice went up like three octaves or something, almost out of the range of human hearing. I didn't laugh, but it was all I could do not to laugh. But he was so upset by it. We listened to it again and it was absolutely a really good take, no two ways about it. They were adamant they weren't going to do it again.

"I said, 'Listen. It's about a house out on the coast highway. How 'bout we record some stereo surf and put it under there? The surf is right around that same frequency as the hiss, and it will probably mask it pretty well.' He had a house right down on the water, and the surf would wash under his house. He had his road manager string two mikes under his house. Put one mike on one side of the house, and one mike on the other, and got this hour of stereo surf. Brought it into the studio, we laid it behind there, and it sounded just fine."

Happy Sad would not be released until April 1969, itself an indicator of how much effort Buckley was putting into redefining his sound. It was also his highest-charting album, reaching number eighty-one and remaining in the Top 200 for twelve weeks. On the surface, the defiantly inaccessible left turns his records would take in the next eighteen months—and, not coincidentally, his concurrent commercial downward spiral—seem inexplicable. To understand them, it is necessary to look at a wider picture, to which the vast majority of listeners at the time were not privy.

First, it must be realized that not all of the music Buckley was making or writing in the late 1960s made it onto the three official albums that appeared. It is a measure of his abilities and prolific diversity that two live albums that did not appear until the 1990s were not so much souvenirs, or documents, as works unveiling wholly new facets of his style and repertoire. The double CD *Dream Letter*, taken from an October 1968 London concert, was Buckley unplugged (long before that term was popularized by MTV), with no drums: just guitars, vibes, and Danny Thompson of Pentangle on acoustic bass. Similar to the *Happy Sad* setup instrumentally, it is starker, jazzier, and more minimal, including a number of sensual blues-jazz-folk tunes (originals and covers) that he did not include on studio albums. Although the link with Thompson was brief, it has been reported how the pair improvised on one of Buckley's songs for over an hour at a television rehearsal, with only three listeners in attendance; Clive Selwood of Elektra U.K., one of those three, described it to MOJO as "the most exhaustingly magical performance I have ever witnessed."

More difficult than *Dream Letter*, but more rewarding and adventurous, is *Live at the Troubadour 1969*. On that recording Buckley can be heard shifting from mellow jazz-folk to free-form jazz, his voice not so much a vehicle for lyrics as one of the instruments, meaning conveyed by phrase and pitch rather than words, and loose improvisation welcomed. There was also an unreleased soundtrack he recorded for the obscure movie *Changes*, with both vocal and instrumental fragments that recalled *Happy Sad*, using guitar, vibes, and conga.

It must also be emphasized that Buckley's musical interests were remarkably eclectic. In interviews, he name-checked an astonishing roll call of artists as influences, to the extent that one might have suspected a put-on if the wide scope was not corroborated by associates like Beckett. Soul singers Marvin Gaye, Curtis Mayfield, Ray Charles; jazz greats Miles Davis, John Coltrane, Cecil Taylor, Charles Mingus, Roland Kirk, and Eric Dolphy; avant-garde opera singer Cathy Berberian; contemporary classical composers Penderecki, Boulez, Satie, and Messiaen; jazz and pop singers Nat King Cole, Peggy Lee, and Cleo Laine; Hank Williams; composers Rodgers and Hart; Dr. John. Chuck Berry, Little Richard, Hoagy Carmichael, Leadbelly, and Louis Armstrong. Least mentioned were his rock 'n' roll and folk-rock peers, although even then he did single out the Kinks, Eric Clapton, and Tim Hardin for praise. And then there was his enigmatic quote (in *Melody Maker*), "The Beatles songs are really great for playing at half-time during football matches. The Beatles wrote a lot of great marching songs and so did Burt Bacharach."

"Tim was ready at any point to put out a five-album set," claims Beckett. "He loved so many kinds of music, and was so good at it, that limiting him to the two sides of an LP was almost ridiculous. Even in public, like you see on the live stuff as it starts to [get released], he would start to diverge. In private, he would diverge even farther, and play and sing all kinds of stuff, either covers or originals, that had nothing to do with anything. I mean, they're just out from left field."

There are few albums that are further left field than *Lorca*, Buckley's final Elektra release. That was apparent from the ten-minute opening track, its dissonant tones and pipe organ more reminiscent of contemporary composers such as Olivier Messiaen or Arnold Schoenberg than of rock, folk, or even jazz. Buckley proceeded to moan with a shaking vibrato, often wordless, sometimes rumbling and sometimes gliding into pealing shrieks, that conveyed not so much anguish as it did sheer agony. It was art, but to unschooled rock listeners, it sounded like the atonal soundtrack to an acid-fueled monster movie. The free-jazzish track occupying the remainder of side one, "Anonymous Proposition," was only slightly more approachable, impressive as it was in Buckley's almost athletic journey across several octaves and vocal shadings. Never mind that the second side of *Lorca* had material far more in the jazz-folk-blues mode of *Happy Sad*, albeit looser and funkier. With *Lorca*, Buckley was beginning to lose his audience. As even Buckley admitted to interviewer Michael Davis in 1975, "To this day, you can't put it on at a party without stopping things; it doesn't fit it."

Lorca would not be released until early 1970, as several projects and business interests began to collide in a fashion that remains confusing today, and would help deep-six Buckley's commercial viability. The exact sequence of events has been reported differently, but at around the same time as Buckley cut *Lorca*, he also recorded *Blue Afternoon*, a far more conventional set. Buckley himself told *Melody Maker* that *Blue Afternoon* was done right after *Lorca*, describing the former LP as "half-finished." *Blue Afternoon* went back to the jazzy mood of *Happy Sad*, but even more jazz-soaked and somnambulant, as if the sweet daze of *Happy Sad* was on the verge of torpor. Although the record is extremely pleasant and Buckley's vocals excellent as usual, one suspects that the record was a bit of a throwaway, done to satisfy someone or something as he prepared to get even further out.

Somehow, *Blue Afternoon* was released first, at the beginning of 1970, with *Lorca* appearing just one month later. Not only that, they appeared on different labels, *Lorca* on Elektra, and *Blue Afternoon* on Herbie Cohen's Warner-distributed Straight imprint. Two virtually simultaneous albums, for different companies and of radically different styles, by an artist who wasn't a big seller to begin with. They couldn't help but cancel each other out, although *Blue Afternoon* did peep into the charts briefly at number 192 as the final Buckley record to make the Top 200. Even by the oft-loony standards of record scheduling and promotion circa 1970, this was madness. It also seems that each album was matched to the wrong label. Straight was notorious for uncommercial weirdness like Captain Beefheart's *Trout Mask Replica* and the unmusical groupies the GTO's; Elektra was progressive, but more mindful of selling units. Yet it was Elektra that got the weird disc, and Straight that got the, well, straighter one. Said Jac Holzman about the *Lorca* era in *Musician*, "He was really making music for himself at that point. Which is fine, except to find enough people to listen to it."

Buckley was, by some accounts, reaching the point at which he not only didn't really care about pleasing his audience, but was sometimes contemptuous of it. A 1969 *New York Times* article described him taking a red carnation from a fan at the Philharmonic Hall, chewing the petals, and spitting them out. A 1970 *Rolling Stone* concert review, titled "Buckley's Yodeling Baffles Audience," had him responding "How about horseshit?" to a request for "Buzzin' Fly," and launching into "a tasteless monologue which consisted of snatches from various Ken Nordine riffs in the 'Word Jazz' series…. Backed by the free improvisations of his new band, Buckley exhibited little respect for or understanding of Nordine by butchering the man's work terribly, misplacing inflections, leaving out key lines and crushing its subtleties." At the same concert, Buckley mixed older material with a twenty-minute-plus "Gypsy Woman" with, according to reporter Michael Cuscuna, "disjointed tempo changes, improvised choruses, extensive use of gong, wooden flutes, bells and other little percussive instruments, and all the while Buckley shouting and purring, yodeling and screaming."

"This is why he could not live beyond the age of twenty-eight," says a resigned Beckett today. "In the old days, he would do, like at the Troubadour [club], a totally haunting, charismatic set, get off the stage. Somebody'd come up and say, 'God! Magnificent, Tim!' And he'd say, 'Ah, it sucked.' Insulting the person who had complimented him, misreading his own performance. 'Cause he was wrong—it *didn't* suck. It was good. But a lot of times he couldn't feel it. He castigated himself.

"That was the early manifestation. The later manifestation was where he thought of the audience as a bunch of idiots. They were nicknamed Lobo, for Lobotomy. Meaning 'these people, who have paid to see me, who are applauding, have no idea about anything about music, can't follow me, never heard of the name Kristof Penderecki, and couldn't conceive of a 15/17 time signature. So what's the point?' He actually conceived this kind of hostility."

In performance, Beckett continues, "He was almost too unprofessional to care about reproducing the sound on the album. He was just born to recreate whatever material he was singing in the moment. Now we've come to respect that kind of thing, and think that it's rare. We think it's a big deal if Dylan does something with a reggae beat. Tim, it just made no sense for him to even bother to try to do something the same way twice. He wasn't really an entertainer who cultivates the audience, the kind that becomes beloved in that way. He put all his effort into being authentic, continuing to grow, and then performing with all of his heart when the time came. He would hope that the performance of a challenging piece that no one had ever heard would be enough to sway them."

Rolling Stone noted that according to a Straight press release, Buckley's second album for the label was going to be "an Afro-Cuban-jazz-Motown extended suite." *Starsailor*, issued in late 1970, wasn't exactly that, but it was just as strange and ambitious. With a band that now included Lee Underwood, bassist John Balkin, and one-time Mothers of Invention horn players Buzz Gardner and Bunk Gardner, Buckley was taking the free jazz and contemporary classical improvisations from the first side of *Lorca* into more disciplined and rhythmic ground. Influenced by the jazz vocals of Leon Thomas—famed for lengthy scats that could sound like a yodeling seal, particularly on saxophonist Pharoah Sanders' famous track "The Creator Has a Master Plan"—Buckley was using his voice like a serious male counterpart to Yma Sumac (the exotica singer famous for her astonishing, ear-roasting operatic range).

On some of the more difficult compositions, such as the whirling title track—which had no less than sixteen vocal overdubs, creating a ghostly musique concrete maelstrom—he did not sound so much like a rock singer as someone having his liver slowly extracted. Said Buckley of this composition to writer Susan Ahrens: "Larry Beckett and I wrote the whole thing as a view of the universe through the eye of a bee." The troubadour of 1966 and 1967 had all but vanished. "He was getting inspired by John Balkin's interest in contemporary classical music," comments Beckett, who was back from the army and writing with Tim on half of the tracks, after being absent from the previous three albums. "*Starsailor* is more like [Central European composer] Ligeti than anything else."

Yet at the same time, Buckley would also intersperse a lovely song with relatively tangible words and messages, like "Song to the Siren," which he had first sung years before while sitting in a car in a Monkees television episode, of all places. Buckley's arrangement of the song on *Starsailor* was quite different, and the story behind its transformation yields some insight into his insecurities. When Buckley sang it on *The Monkees*, believes Jerry Yester, "It was just beautiful, he and his twelve-string. But the version he recorded was hideous." The original version also had a line, "I'm as puzzled as the oyster," that Buckley changed after being teased about it by singer Judy Henske, Yester's wife at the time. "I love that line myself," maintains Yester. "He changed it to 'a newborn baby,' I think. I thought that was kind of a yawn. But I like the idea of sticking up for lines like that. And if somebody doesn't like it, screw 'em, you know." Yester, indeed, produced a cover version of the tune on an album by Pat Boone, of all people.

Starsailor was largely characterized by dissonant, jazzy pieces with some word-less vocals, occasionally suggestive of not entirely pleasant free-falls off mountainous precipices. Still, in the midst of this demanding listen was a jaunty French tune, "Moulin Rouge," that would have been at home in the song list of European chanteuses. The song, relates Beckett, was Buckley's "idea completely, doing some chanteuse-like song, and he wanted me to write in French. He did not know French at all, and actually I coached him. I wrote it out so that he could just read what I had written, and sound it out. And he *still* screwed it up royally. Although I was there for most of the sessions of *Starsailor*, I wasn't there for that one, so it got in the can screwed up. But musically, it's very strange. All it really is, is him saying, once again, 'You don't know me. I love all kinds of music you never even thought about.'"

In some respects, Buckley was by now emulating the career path of Miles Davis, an innovator who would jump into new and unexpected styles quickly, before listen-ers even had a chance to fully absorb his latest albums and manifestations. Beckett agrees with the parallel: "In the late '60s, we were really inspired by *Bitches Brew* and Miles Davis. And Miles' entire career: his complete integrity to himself and his vi-sion. I think Tim really wanted to model himself after that in some way. Just write austere, forbidding music that he heard, not really care about his accessibility, and even confront people with that."

A key difference between Buckley and Davis, however, is that Miles had already developed a large audience before he leaped into electric jazz-rock fusion with *Bitches Brew*. Even if he alienated many of his old listeners, many would stay with him, and combined with the new ones he picked up, he managed to come out ahead of the game and have enough support and sales to continue his experiments. Nor was Buckley someone like Jackson Browne, who also began playing folk-rock as a teenager in Orange County in the mid-1960s, and who steadily built a large con-stituency by laying out and refining a consistent style. Buckley only had a cult audi-ence to begin with, and by the time of *Starsailor*, even much of that cult had left (despite its five-star review in the jazz magazine *Downbeat*), uninterested in negotiat-ing Buckley's musical maze. Nor, evidently, were his manager or record label, which in Buckley's case was pretty much one and the same thing.

Beckett's view "is that the record company eventually said, '*Starsailor*, whatever else its value is, it's just not something we can afford to produce. Either you come up with a completely different, more accessible sound, or you can't even record at all.' Tim had always told me that if that ever happened, he was going to walk away and drive a bread truck. My dream for the past is that he had done so, and all these years later, you could be talking to him first, and me second. That's what *should* have hap-pened. But that's not what *happened*."

For a while, Buckley kept a low musical profile. He played live sometimes with a group that included Emmett Chapman, inventor of the Chapman stick (a guitar-like instrument played with two hands instead of the customary one, and ten strings instead of the customary six). He wrote an inscrutable piece on Beethoven for the *New York Times* (whose byline, rather inaccurately, read "Tim Buckley, rock star"), part of which read, "Of course Beethoven would have been the perfect pop star. His entourage would be a bit too expensive to take on the road, of course. But if he were around today, Rex Reed would be his road manager, Broadway his toilet, and he wouldn't jam the Blues." He worked on a peculiar film script which had him playing a struggling musician blowing up a theater of fans requesting old songs, and included a role for a vulture friend played by an animated cartoon. Back in 1969 he had told the *New York Times* of his intention to play an American Indian named Fender Guitar in a film called *Wild Orange*, and he got his chance to act with O. J. Simpson in the unreleased 1971 film *Why?* Another *Why?* costar, Linda Gillen, told *MOJO* the movie had "no sex, violence or car crashes. No nudity. Just this bunch of weirdoes sitting on a bench talking about their *prahblems*! And no solutions!"

When Buckley did go back into the studio, he emerged with an album that, characteristically, was another turnabout in direction. For the first time, however, it could be considered a swing to the right, not to the left. Much of 1972's *Greetings from L.A.* was funky, sweaty rock with a Los Angeles studio sheen. Buckley was still exploiting his range as few other rock and pop singers could, and sometimes getting into the type of vocal improvisations that were found on his 1969-70 albums. He claimed to have started singing in Swahili in a Warner Brothers bio, and told Michael Davis that he used the "technique of talking in tongues" for the record; whether or not he ever did sing in Swahili, he certainly seems to be speaking in tongues in *Greetings from L.A.*'s weirdest passages, especially in "Devil Eyes."

The arrangements, however, were far more ordinary than those employed on *Starsailor* or indeed anything he had recorded up to that time. Lyrically, the impenetrable mysticism of years past was replaced by open-hearted carnal lust, as in the visit to the meat rack tavern that opens "Move With Me," and the exhortations for his lover to "Get On Top," although the lowdown acoustic blues-funk of "Hong Kong Bar" struck a more musically satisfying mood. Critical opinions diverge sharply on *Greetings from L.A.*'s merits, some seeing it as yet another example of Buckley's facility for mastering unexpected idioms. Yet it sounds, to these ears, less a product of the heart than a concession to the marketplace. Buckley himself acknowledged in *ZigZag* that "I listened to the radio a lot before writing the songs for this album. There's a lot of radio music in it. It's full-out blues-type barrelhouse rock." It didn't get Buckley *on* the radio much, though, failing to chart.

Deterioration really began to set in on *Sefronia* (1973), which for the most part consisted of slick, pedestrian blue-eyed funk. Glimpses of the old Buckley were apparent on his beautiful rendition of Fred Neil's "Dolphins," which he finally got to cover in the studio after doing it in concert for years, and the two-part title song, the last ambitious Buckley-Beckett collaboration to be preserved on record, enhanced by Buckley's tasteful operatic delivery. Beckett's contributions to Tim's material were by this time becoming infrequent, and he summarizes Buckley's final few albums as follows: "I don't think it was at all comparable [to his other recordings], singing that kind of stuff, or playing with those people. It was against his will; it was not his natural direction."

John Forsha, tour manager for Buckley for a time in the 1970s, adds, "Personally, he was fine. Artistically, I think he was kind of cranking it out. I think something was slipping in his life. He was living for the performance. He wasn't writing, and there was a little bitterness to him. His performances were good. When he was doing the rock 'n' roll, it was [like] James Brown performancewise, physical, squealing, shrieking, alternately whispering and screaming, and a lot of sweat. I was not real happy with the music he was doing at the time. His band was adequate, and it could have been better. It was, 'OK, that'll get it,' but *just* got it. It wasn't stunning." Sadly, Buckley's final album, *Look at the Fool* (1974), was worse than adequate, continuing the downward trajectory into lame soul-rock. Even more alarmingly, Buckley's voice, the one thing which had always excelled on his recordings, was beginning to sound thin and frayed, particularly on the high notes, which now seemed more ghoulish than virtuosic.

Contrary to what was heard in the grooves, Buckley's ambition remained intact. He discussed a possible double live LP consisting of rerecordings of his favorite material from previous albums, claiming in *Melody Maker*, "I intend to use every musician that I've ever worked with somewhere on the album." To Michael Davis in an interview printed in *Goldmine*, he spoke of getting a record deal that would allow him to record both commercial music and classical music involving "choirs and different stories."

Beckett confirms that "in the last month before his death, he and I were engaged in creating a new piece together, which was going to be a song cycle, something we'd kicked around since the beginning. An actual set of songs that tied together narratively, called 'The Outcast of the Islands,' based on Joseph Conrad's second novel. It was going to have the kind of sound you can't even really categorize. Not pop or jazz or classical or anything, but some kind of fusion of everything. That's the direction he was going, in some even more ambitious, even more inclusive kind of music. I felt that had the record company not intervened, that would have happened immediately, not been postponed by these rock-'em-sock-'em albums." To Michael Davis, Buckley revealed, "We wrote different songs for each of the eight characters and by the end of the eight songs, you understand the whole story."

"He called me shortly before he died," says Jerry Yester, "and said he wanted me to work with him again. I thought it was great, I really loved the idea. He sounded great, he sounded like his old self. And then a couple of months later I heard he was dead. It was a very big bringdown." On June 29, 1975, Buckley had overdosed on heroin that he picked up at a friend's house. The *New York Times'* obituary called him, again, a "rock star" in its headline. The *Rolling Stone* obit mentioned that he was working on a screenplay and novel, and was being "seriously considered" for the role of Woody Guthrie in Hal Ashby's *Bound for Glory* docudrama.

Buckley's life had always reflected the inner turmoil expressed in his music. Back in 1968, David Anderle, director of the West Coast office of Elektra, had told Jerry Hopkins, "He's a loner man. He was placed on this earth to suffer because he can't mingle. He's not here to turn on bunches of people, but as a chronicler." In retrospect this was perhaps not the kind of thing for your own label to advertise, and Buckley's insecurities were also reflected in some of his own interviews. Though loquacious, these need to be judged carefully owing to his tendency to embellish and even make up facts, as in his erroneous claim to have played Roger McGuinn's guitar parts on early Byrds records. "He kind of played pretty fast and loose with the truth," admits Beckett. "He had some kind of deep-down inadequacy that he was making up for with language."

He had been using heroin for some time in the last part of his life—on 1969's *Live at the Troubadour*, he can be heard, perhaps facetiously and perhaps not, jokingly advising the audience to "give smack a chance." Opinions differ as to whether his death was accidental or inevitable, but Beckett sadly offers: "Deep inside, if you'd ever known him, if you just walked in on him eating breakfast, you would think, my god, this guy's heart is broken. You sort of had this feeling, he's just not going to make it. In those days we didn't think it would end in death, because we were all so young. But sure enough it did."

The Buckley renaissance has been slow in coming, though it's been mounting since the 1980s. In the mid-1980s This Mortal Coil covered "Song of the Siren," with Elizabeth Fraser of the Cocteau Twins on vocals, and had a small British hit single. A Swiss band, Comebuckley, devoted its entire self-titled 1989 album to Buckley tunes. In 1990, *Dream Letter* was released, and while not among Buckley's best work (or even his best from the late 1960s), it reawakened appreciation of his catalog, paving the way for the release of more previously unissued live and radio material. A tribute concert to Buckley was organized by producer Hal Willner in 1991, featuring noted New York avant-rockers such as guitarists Robert Quine and Elliot Sharp. Chrissie Hynde, a fan of Buckley's since *Happy Sad* who had interviewed him in 1974 for the *New Musical Express* in her rock critic days, wrote an appreciation for *MOJO* in tandem with that magazine's Buckley feature. And, above all, Tim's singer-songwriter son Jeff—who had hardly known his father—was on the way to stardom with a similar voice, though not terribly similar material, when he too died young, drowning in the Mississippi River at the age of thirty in 1997.

One reason Buckley is not more widely known, however, is that his songs are not easily covered. Linda Ronstadt covered no fewer than three of his compositions in the late 1960s on her third album as a member of the Stone Poneys; Blood, Sweat & Tears covered "Morning Glory" on their first album; Pat Boone did that off-the-wall version of "Song of the Siren"; and This Mortal Coil did that same tune fifteen years later. Yet unlike Fred Neil and Dino Valenti—two other cult singer-songwriters covered in this book—there was no "Everybody's Talkin'" or "Get Together" to become a standard. Buckley was a rarity—a one-of-a-kind voice who also had one-of-a-kind songs. He is not easily imitated. And he was never outdone at his own game.

Recommended Recordings:

Tim Buckley (1966, Elektra). Although Buckley is sometimes termed a folk-rocker, his debut is his only album to fit that label comfortably. His voice and material had yet to fully mature, but it's enticingly fragile and beautifully sung, with the shimmering production that was par for the course on Elektra's 1960s rock recordings.

Goodbye and Hello (1967, Elektra). His best and best-known album. Poetic lyrics, ear-stretching vocals, unusual melodies, and ambitious arrangements came together here more effectively than they did on any other Buckley release. Almost every song is exceptional, with the somber "No Man Can Find the War," the trance-inducing "Hallucinations," the symphonic "Goodbye and Hello," and the placid parable "Morning Glory" ranking with his finest work.

Dream Letter: Live in London 1968 (1990, Manifesto). A double-CD of concerts featuring just guitars, acoustic bass, and vibes behind Buckley as he runs through songs from his late '60s albums, as well as a few originals and covers that never made it onto those releases. The atmosphere is actually a little too mellow, even sleepy, for its own good, but it does give us a chance to hear a different dimension to the singer than was usually captured in the studio.

Once I Was (1999, Strange Fruit, U.K.). Largely taken from a 1968 BBC broadcast of live versions of *Goodbye and Hello* tunes, this has drumless arrangements similar to those heard on *Dream Letter*, but the performances are a little peppier. Also includes a twelve-minute live 1968 version of "I Don't Need It to Rain" and a couple of BBC tracks from 1974.

Happy Sad (1969, Elektra). Buckley's best mixture of folk-rock and jazz is dominated by some of his longest and dreamiest compositions, such as "Strange Feelin'" and "Love from Room 109 at the Islander (On Pacific Coast Highway)." In contrast, the jazz-funk-folk of "Gypsy Woman" unfolds with more rhythmic intensity than anything else he did, and "Sing a Song for You" is one of his most affecting troubadour odes.

Works in Progress (1999, Rhino Handmade). Something of an alternate version of *Happy Sad*, with previously unreleased 1968 outtakes, including different takes of cuts on *Happy Sad*, some songs that would be redone on *Blue Afternoon* and *Starsailor*, some that would provide pieces of his "Love From Room 109 at the Islander" opus, and a sad number ("The Father Song") from the *Changes* soundtrack. This is not just extraneous odds and ends, for fanatics only. There's much fine music, particularly the lovely "Danang," and the different (usually less ornate) versions of songs that appear elsewhere are both pleasing to hear and a historically valuable insight into the material's evolution. Issued as a limited edition of 7,500 in October 1999, available only via the Internet at www.rhinohandmade.com.

Live at the Troubadour 1969 (1994, Manifesto). A missing link between his Elektra folk-rock and his subsequent nerve-wracking jazz improvisations, this seventy-eight-minute disc has live workouts on material from his late 1960s albums, and other numbers that he declined to put on LPs at the time. Although sometimes haphazard, it's also impressive evidence of Buckley's facility for live vocal gymnastics and extemporization, reaching its peak on the fourteen-minute "Gypsy Woman."

Blue Afternoon (1970, Straight). There's a bit of a son-of *Happy Sad* tinge to these drowsy jazz-blues meditations, but certainly the combination of Buckley's humming vocals and the easy-on-the-ear melodies is seductive. "Happy Time" and "Blue Melody" are among his more attractive songs, and the closing eight-minute "The Train" offers a glimpse of the gonzo vocal experiments that would bloom on *Starsailor*.

Lorca (1970, Elektra). The title track is one of Buckley's least accessible and most jarring pieces, admirable in its daring and, like the next cut "Anonymous Proposition," occasionally wearying to endure. For those who can't handle it, the remaining three songs are far more approachable, though still elongated, jazz-funk-folk-rock-blues ruminations.

Starsailor (1970, Straight). The culmination of Buckley's appetite for arty, difficult material, genre-mixing, and testing the limits of what was possible with the human voice. While at times this is more akin to contemporary classical music than to pop or rock, it's never less than interesting. And it's not entirely bereft of conventional songs, containing as it does "Song to the Siren," the where'd-that-come-from French chanteuse miniature "Moulin Rouge," and another steamy jazz-folk-blues potboiler in "Down By the Borderline."

Greetings from L.A. (1972, Straight). The funk-rock arrangements, mediocre material, and studly lyrical posturing on this album are often disappointing. Buckley's vocals do remain impressively dynamic, and "Hong Kong Bar" at least does shed the production gloss for some earthy acoustic folk-blues. For a live document of this period, Manifesto issued a November 1973 concert, *Honeyman*; while on the whole let down by a so-so band and some subpar songs, it's highlighted by a fine cover of Fred Neil's "Dolphins."

Index

The best way to listen to the music of the overlooked innovators portrayed in this book is to check out their full albums, as noted in the recommended recordings section of each chapter. It's unlikely that all of you have all of these recordings, and it's not likely you'll be able to find and buy all of them soon, or to buy all of them at once. And it's even less likely you'll hear many of them on the radio. The CD accompanying this volume contains a taste of these sounds, drawn from the catalogs of six of the artists covered in these pages, touching upon the British Invasion, folk rock, protest rock, psychedelia, garage, and good old rock 'n' roll.

1. Richard & Mimi Fariña, "Reno Nevada." The highlight of their 1965 debut album *Celebrations for a Grey Day*, "Reno Nevada" set a magnificently moody melody against Charles Small's doom-laden piano, Mimi Fariña's wind-blown scatting backup vocals, and Richard Fariña's foreboding lyrics. Wrote Richard of the tune in his characteristically enigmatic liner notes, "Existential Futility in the Guise of a One-Arm Bandit? Modern Man in Search of His Neon Destiny? La-la, pooh-pooh. More like here we are in the land of magenta ski-pants and congo ruby eyeshade; so pull the cord and hope for the best. Either up goes the ballroom, or you fall through a trap door into the alligator pit. Call it a song about chance." The Fariñas were hoping that jazz-bluesman Mose Allison would record a version; he didn't, but Fairport Convention did an excellent cover on the BBC in 1968, eventually released on that band's *Heyday* compilation of late-1960s BBC sessions. The Fariñas' original version is available on CD through Vanguard Records, 2700 Pennsylvania Avenue, Santa Monica, CA 90404, www.vanguardrecords.com. (Songwriter: Richard Fariña; publishing credit: © Warner/Chappell Music, Inc.; master credit: courtesy of Vanguard Music.)

2. The Fugs, "Kill for Peace." One of the wittiest and most vicious anti-war rock songs of the 1960s, Tuli Kupferberg's "Kill for Peace" was a highwater mark on 1966's *The Fugs Second Album*. As Kupferberg explains, "It was during the Vietnam War. The postal service, I don't know if they do it any more, but they had a little slogan they would put on with their cancellation. One of them was 'pray for peace.' This was at the time when they were killing people by the thousands, or tens of thousands, or a million, or maybe more. So I thought 'kill for peace' could be applied to their slogan. I thought that would have been more appropriate then." Available on CD through Fantasy Records, Tenth and Parker, Berkeley, CA 94710, www.fantasyjazz.com. (Songwriter: Tuli Kupferberg; publishing credit: © Heavy Metal Music, BMI; master credit: courtesy of Heavy Metal Music.)

3. The Electric Prunes, "I Had Too Much to Dream (Last Night)." As a studio single, "I Had Too Much to Dream (Last Night)" reached #11 in early 1967. It has been assumed that a track so laden with effects and sonic trickery must have been hard to replicate in concert. Recorded at a gig on December 14, 1967 in Stockholm, Sweden for broadcast on Swedish radio, this live version demonstrates that the band could do so more than capably, right down to the memorable jet-takeoff-intensity hum of the opening guitar riff. Prefacing the song was singer James Lowe's spoken apology, on behalf of the entire United States, for the Vietnam War. The entire show was released in

1997 on the CD *Stockholm 67*, available through Heartbeat Productions, 407 Fishponds Road, Bristol BS5 6RJ, England, www.heartbeat-productions.co.uk. (Songwriters: Annette Tucker and Nancie Mantz; master and publishing credit: © Swedish Broadcasting Corporation. Recorded by the Swedish Broadcasting Corporation at the Concert Hall in Stockholm, Sweden, December 14th, 1967. Produced by Klas Burling. Engineered by Göte Nilsson. Remixed by the Swedish Broadcasting Corporation, P3 LIVE, producer Maths Broburg and engineer Janne Waldenmark, at The Broadcasting House, Stockholm, in 1995.)

4. Thee Midniters, "Jump, Jive and Harmonize." The toughest and hardest-rocking side of this astonishingly versatile band erupted on this 1967 single, recorded on two-track at a theater in which the group rehearsed. Although Thee Midniters often used jazzy soul-rock horn arrangements, on this number they went for all-out punky blues-rock, reflecting their deep admiration for British bands such as the Rolling Stones. Built around a killer unison guitar-bass riff and Willie Garcia's coolly raunchy lead vocal, it climaxed with a frenzied harmonica-organ duel as the track wound itself up to maximum rave-up heat. (Songwriters: Espinoza, Garcia, Marquez; publishing credit: © Tormid Music, BMI, Jimmy Espinoza; master credit: courtesy of Jimmy Espinoza, Blue Nova.)

5. The Bobby Fuller Four, "Never to Be Forgotten." Co-written by Bobby and Randy Fuller, this 1965 single was a commercial bust, but nevertheless one of their group's finest moments. Kicking off with a twanging riff reminiscent of Western movie themes, it was quickly reinforced by Randy Fuller's fuzz bass and one of the group's most anthemic melodies. The reverb-heavy production, as well as the dense mass of backing harmonies and the manner in which Bobby Fuller's lead vocals drifted into space at the end of the verses, bore out producer Bob Keane's claim that "we had a little Wall of Sound going with Bobby." About a year later, Bobby Fuller was dead, the title of this song serving as an eerie epitaph of sorts. Available on CD through Del-Fi Records, PO Box 69188, Los Angeles, CA 90069, www.del-fi.com. (Songwriters: Bobby Fuller and Randy Fuller; publishing credit: © Bug Music obo Warcloud Music; master credit: courtesy of Del-Fi Records, Inc.)

6. The Poets, "Some Things I Can't Forget." From 1965, the B-side of the Poets' fourth single, written by lead singer George Gallacher and guitarist Hume Paton, was one of the most glorious efforts from Scotland's finest 1960s band. Reminiscent of the Zombies in its mastery of captivating minor-keyed melody, it was suffused in a layer of extra gloom by singer George Gallacher's habitual hurt, anguished vocals, the group's echoing, urgent guitar strums, and high, ghostly harmonies. Capping the performance was Andrew Loog Oldham's typically eerie production, setting the cavernous clang of the guitars against tambourine rattles mixed so high that they virtually became lead instruments. The song is on the six-CD box set compilation *Immediate: The Singles Collection*, available through Sequel Records, A29 Barwell Business Park, Leatherhead Road, Chessington, Surrey KT9 2NY, England, www.castlemusic.com. (Songwriters: George Gallacher and Hume Paton; producer: Andrew Loog Oldham for Andes Sound; publishing credit: © abkco Music; master credit: courtesy of (P)2000 Immediate Records.)

When it Comes to Music, We Wrote the Book.